Real Data Analysis

a volume in
Quantitative Methods in Education and the Behavioral Sciences:
Issues, Research, and Teaching

Series Editor:
Ronald C. Serlin, *University of Wisconsin, Madison*

Quantitative Methods in Education and the Behavioral Sciences: Issues, Research, and Teaching

Ronald C. Serlin, Series Editor

Structural Equation Modeling: A Second Course (2005)
edited by Gregory R. Hancock and Ralph O. Mueller

Real Data Analysis (2006)
edited by Shlomo Sawilowsky

Real Data Analysis

edited by

Shlomo S. Sawilowsky
Wayne State University

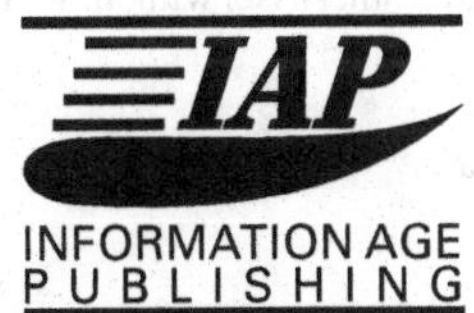

Charlotte, North Carolina • www.infoagepub.com

Library of Congress Cataloging-in-Publication Data

Real data analysis / edited by Shlomo S. Sawilowsky.
p. cm. — (Quantitative methods in education and the behavioral sciences)
Includes bibliographical references.
ISBN-13: 978-1-59311-564-7 (pbk.)
ISBN-13: 978-1-59311-565-4 (hardcover)
1. Social sciences—Statistics—Methodology. 2. Social sciences—Research—Methodology. I. Sawilowsky, Shlomo S.
HA29.R32 2007
300.72—dc22

2006033775

ISBN 13: 978-1-59311-564-7 (pbk.)
ISBN 13: 978-1-59311-565-4 (hardcover)
ISBN 10: 1-59311-564-4 (pbk.)
ISBN 10: 1-59311-565-2 (hardcover)

Credits: The back cover image is by Student (William Sealey Gosset), "Probable error of a correlation coefficient," *Biometrika,* 1908, *6*(1), p. 305, copyrighted by Oxford Unversity Press, and reprinted with permission.

Printed in the United States of America

CONTENTS

See Preface, p. x.

PREFACE

BS"D

After obtaining a PhD in educational statistics, measurement, evaluation, and research at the University of South Florida (USF) in 1985, I accepted a joint appointment as a visiting assistant professor and as an associate of the Institute for Instructional Research and Practice (IIRP). The task of the IIRP was to develop master teacher tests for the state of Florida's career ladder program.

The external evaluators of the project were Professors William Mehrens of Michigan State University, an expert in legal issues pertaining to standardized testing, and Frank B. Baker of the University of Wisconsin, who was the Chairman of their Laboratory of Experimental Design. I learned from them that in applied data analysis I should not conduct a statistical test just because I could.

In late 2003, I obtained a run of the *Journal of the American Statistical Association* for 1954 though 1970, which provided valuable back-issues. Having journals at home to read at one's leisure permits cover-to-cover reading; something that I have never been able to accomplish in the university or departmental library with physical copies, or with electronic copies.

I came across a review by Dr. Baker for a book by Paul F. Lazerfeld and Neil W. Henry titled, *Readings in Mathematical Social Sciences*. Dr. Baker commenced with the comment,

Real Data Analysis, pp. ix–xxii

> The casual peruser of this book of readings is likely to get the impression that it is the usual "hodge podge" of articles collected into a book of readings. Such an impression is given by the range of topics covered. [However] such an initial impression is dispelled by the introductory chapter in which the editors discuss ... the common thread which ties the articles of a given section together.
>
> Each of these ... articles [were] written by authors well known within the social sciences and most of the authors' names would also be recognized by statisticians. (Baker, 1968, p. 681)

I recalled these comments the following year when I was appointed to edit this volume, which is the second book to appear in the American Educational Research Association Educational Statisticians book series under the general editorship of Dr. Ronald Serlin of the University of Wisconsin.

The assigned topic is real data analysis. For convenience, I refer to it as RDA. I adopted the topic description for the title of this edited volume. I wanted to frame this book after the fashion of Dr. Baker's comments. Therefore, I tried to determine who, in my view, are leading authors in RDA, (2) invite those scholars to participate in whatever fashion they so desire, and (3) get out of their way. I trust the authors of this volume agree that I have done just that.

The invited authors have been prolific in the arena of RDA, collectively leaving a major footprint on the discipline. Combined, we have approximately 3,247 articles in refereed journals, published 127 books, obtained U.S.$45.3 million in extramural research funding, been the recipients of 34 teaching and 92 research awards, serve(d) as editor/assistant editor/editorial board member for 95 peer reviewed journals, and provide(d) ad hoc reviews for 362 journals. The invited scholar was encouraged to include participation with current or former students, or with colleagues, in their submission for this book. If not the first listed author, those who chose to do so are identified with an asterisk. The exception is the chapter by Professors Wilcox and Keselman, both of whom were invited.

This left me the task of making a cogent presentation of RDA for the reader. I must confess that this is not a simple undertaking. As an illustration, consider what happened when I invited one our generation's most prestigious statisticians to write a foreword. To my delight, the offer was readily accepted. All that was necessary was the task of e-mailing the draft chapters, and await glowing words of praise and adulation.

Alas and alack, the scholar recapitulated. The reason given was quite instructive. The material did not present an orderly "beginning, middle, and end." I accepted the dismissal without rebuttal, because RDA does not have a beginning, middle, or end. That is what makes it real data analysis.

The chapters are arranged in four parts: (1) Foundations, (2) Statistics, (3) Measurement, and (4) Data Analysis. My intention is not to summarize their contents here, but to explain to the reader the logical flow and natural order of the material, as I see it.

Part I: Foundations

This edited volume is launched with an observation on the relationship between the clock speed of computer central processing units (CPU) and the capabilities of statistical software. Every researcher must wrestle with issues pertaining to sample size and missing data, which is discussed next. I consider Monte Carlo studies to be responsible for much of what we know about the small samples properties of statistics used in real research environments, and therefore, the next topic pertains to methods for simulating data that actually model real data. Part 1 concludes with an entertaining view on working with messy data.

Part II: Statistics

This section begins with a practical example, which works, on increasing learning outcomes in the teaching of statistics. The balance of the section pertains to theoretical issues of applied data analysis, such as the use of computer-based randomization tests, advances on more traditional statistical techniques, and dealing with their underlying assumptions and the consequences in terms of robustness and power. The section concludes with observations on the general linear model—ANOVA and ANCOVA—from a sums of squares perspective.

Part III: Measurement

It has been decades since new research has appeared on classical measurement theory. Therefore, it should not be surprising that the major theorists in the field are working on measurement issues as they apply to item response and latent trait theory, which is the topic of this section. Strong statistics trump weak measurement, but the bottleneck of every research agenda is the quality of the data collection instrument.

Part IV: Data Analysis

The first five chapters pertain to data analysis applications directly relevant to education and psychology. Estimation problems are a classic; in this section the reader will read an application from a modern hierarchical linear models approach. Current issues are examined, such as grade inflation, gender differences, dropout rates, and the application of nonparametric techniques to program evaluation. The final three chapters touch on topics of interest in allied fields, such as the treatment of pain and neural activation. The book concludes with an examination of senate voting patterns, which may help explain why governors have been more successful in being elected president of the United States.

PERSONAL REFLECTIONS ON RDA

This preface concludes with a brief forum for my personal reflections on real data analysis. The serious reader will benefit by skipping directly to the first chapter.

Real Data Collection

A corollary of RDA is real data collection, which can be a comedy of errors. In the early 1980s when I was at USF, I was assigned the task of spearheading a survey for the Center for Excellence in Mathematics, Science, Computers, and Technology. An extant piece of stationery indicates I was a graduate assistant assigned to the project. This was a high-profile survey, with participation from the university's president, a few deans, and a department chairman. The survey contained sensitive questions regarding high school teachers' employment. I noted in the cover letter that the responses would be respected in terms of confidentiality and anonymity.

The response rate was dismal. I spent a considerable amount of time trying to detect where the process had gone awry. A nonrespondent revealed that despite my promises, there was a matching code handwritten on the outside of the envelope and on the return envelope. I was chided for promising anonymity when obviously I had no such true intention.

I was as bewildered by the presence of the handwritten codes as was the nonrespondent. Eventually, the case was solved when I asked the department secretary if she could shed any light on the handwritten codes. Because the survey was thrust so suddenly upon us, she did not have time to have envelopes made with the codes to indicate which department was to be charged for the outgoing and incoming postage. Therefore, in an effort to get the project out on time, she wrote mail codes on the outer and return envelopes. Apparently, many recipients assumed these codes served the purpose of identifying them, and thus, elected not to participate.

I instructed the secretary to prepare another mailing, with explicit instructions that no mail codes were to be used. I would instruct the workers at the university post office regarding which account to charge.

The response rate from the second mailing, however, was more appalling than the initial mailing. I contacted a teacher who had been sent the survey and asked why it had not been returned. The answer was several teachers had opened their envelopes while sitting together in the teacher's lounge, and despite claims of anonymity in the cover letter, each found their survey printed on different colored paper. They believed this was a technique being employed to identify them.

Immediately, I went to the department secretary to inquire what had happened. She once again expressed regret for inadvertently causing problems with the first mailing, and she was determined to make up for it. She took me to the copy machine room, where the surveys were produced, and opened a supply cabinet. There I saw, for the first time, copy paper in azure, chartreuse, fuchsia, goldenrod, ochre, and sepia, among others. The secretary proudly informed me of how she had painstaking assured that no one school's set of teachers were sent the same color surveys!

Statistics Versus Data Analysis

I presented a talk at the first International Conference on Multiple Comparison in Tel Aviv (Sawilowsky, 1996). I excerpted parts of it, and along with Patric Spence, have freshened it for inclusion in this book.

Admittedly, my material was a bit of a stretch with regard to the call for papers. Famous mathematical statisticians were presenting papers, including Drs. Pranab K. (P. K.) Sen, Charles W. Dunnett, Juliet P. Shaffer, Yosef Hochberg, Sture Holm, Ajit C. Tamhane, Yoav Benjamini, and Donald A. Berry. As the saying goes, the only presenter on the roster whose name I did not recognize was my own!

The week-long conference was replete with mathematical statistical papers of the highest order. The format provided for one presentation to be given at a time, with all other presenters and attendees present for each paper.

It became increasingly obvious that my presentation, based on Monte Carlo methods, was of a different genre than the others. Midweek came. My paper was to be presented as soon as the attendees returned from the luncheon break. While setting up the overhead projector, and to help settle the crowd in taking their seats, I made the following remarks.

> As I listened with awe to the previous papers that have already been presented, three thoughts came to my mind. First, what is this fixation on deriving expected values? Second, who in this room really has the proverbial asymptotic infinite number of subjects available for an experiment? And third, even if you did, why would you employ *all* of them to study an *infinitesimally* small treatment effect?

There was silence. I continued,

> Apparently, I am "the only statistician who is forced to work with very small samples" (Student, 1908, p. 302).

More silence.
So, I decided to shift gears, literally.

> Let me tell you how I feel about presenting before you at this conference. Over a dozen years ago I was attending USF, and being a bit impoverished, as are many graduate students, I could not afford the high price of a parking decal. I would park at a nearby apartment complex and walk the rest of the way. At the time, I was a graduate assistant assigned to tutor statistics.
>
> One day, while walking to school from the apartment complex in the hot Florida sun, someone driving a LP5000 S Countach Lamborghini stopped to give me a lift. The driver, dressed in a white sleeveless Florida sun suit, was a graduate student who I had recently tutored. She was a pretty young thing who had married a banker, a man twice her age. The Lamborghini had been his wedding gift to her.
>
> Not being the type of person who would pass on a free ride to campus in the hot Florida sun, I somehow managed to get into the vehicle. The difficulty on entry was that the Lamborghini didn't have traditional doors. The horizontally-hinged doors lifted up. A few quick taps on the accelerator resulted in our arrival at the campus. I began the process of extricating myself from her motorcar.
>
> As I was doing so, I looked up and saw another student in the parking lot. He was chaining his bicycle to a post. I recognized him as a member of *Chabad* House, which provided *Kosher* food. The student's eyes widened. He stared at me, glanced at her, looked at the Lamborghini, stared at me once more, and then said, "*Oy Vey*, are you in the wrong place!"

My colleagues at the conference sat there for a moment aghast. Suddenly, the entire auditorium erupted into laughter. The presentation of the Monte Carlo study went over fairly well after that, despite the preconceived notion that it would be invalid.

The following morning, I went to a restaurant where a handful of conference attendees were gathered. Despite the paper being fairly well received (P. K. gave it the "thumb's up"), barriers are hard to break, and I was given the "you c'aint sit here, Forrest" look.

As I glanced around the dining room, I saw the late Professor K. Ruben Gabriel. He was not a presenter at the conference, but he attended the speeches and some of the social activities. He was sitting at a table for two, but the second chair was empty. He motioned for me to join him for breakfast.

Sensing my predicament, he related the following story.

> I understand your feelings about the hierarchy in statistics. I concur with your sentiments. Long ago, I was applying for my first position after I received my degree. The interview was at an Ivy League university. The department chairman asked me what statistics I knew. I replied that I knew analysis of variance, regression, canonical correlation, and discriminate function analysis. He interrupted me and said that I would simply not be the right man for the job. "That's not statistics," he said with a frown. "That's data analysis!"

Monte Carlo Simulation

Much of what I've learned regarding RDA has come from a decade and a half and U.S.$3.5 million in extramural grant work on self determination for students with and without disabilities (Field & Hoffman, 1994; Field, Hoffman, & Sawilowsky, 1995, 2005). However, I have also greatly benefited from Monte Carlo studies and Monte Carlo simulations.

Carroll (1987) wrote, "I never experienced the real joy of programming until 1978 when I acquired a TRS-80 model I personal computer and no longer had to run hat in hand to ensconced computer-center bureaucrats to get computing time or disk space" (p. ix). I did not enjoy the same experience with my first personal computer. It was given to me by my uncle, Miles J. Ram of Aiken, South Carolina, a writer and thespian, who could not get his TRS-80 Model I to work as a word processor. Unfortunately, I could not find a use for it either.

In late 1981, I acquired my second computer, which was an 8 bit TRS-80 Model 3 with a 2.03 Mhz Zilog Z-80 CPU and 48 K RAM. I wrote my first Monte Carlo program on this machine, using the TRS-DOS operating system, TRS Model III Disk Basic, and its RND pseudo-random uniform number generator.

I coded the two independent samples t test, which was performed on two samples of $n_1 = n_2 = 30$, with nominal $\alpha = .05$. Messages were written to the screen indicating when each iteration of the experiment concluded. The obtained t value was displayed, along with the statistical decision to reject or fail to reject. If a reject decision was indicated, a counter in the appropriate tail (lower or upper) was incremented.

It took about 1.2 seconds for an iteration of the experiment to be written to the screen. The number of repetitions was set at 10,000. The program would complete in 3 hours. (In contrast, on current personal computers the program would take less than 1.2 seconds to complete.) I launched the program, and left my apartment for the evening's activities. I returned 3 hours latter to discover that someone had broken into my apartment through the window located above the desk where the TRS-80 was situated.

The thief forced the window open, stepped down onto the TRS-80 as if it were a stepstool, and proceeded to locate what few valuables a graduate student might have. Amazingly, the thief did not take the computer! Apparently, the thief did not see the TRS-80 as an object of value (a view shared by members of the Commodore Amiga and Texas Instruments personal computing community of that time period).

To complete the historical record on this matter, the Type I error rates were approximately 0.025 for both the lower and upper tail, demonstrating the t test's robustness in terms of Type I errors to the uniform distribution. I remember thinking at the time what a pity it is that real data in education and psychology are neither normally nor uniformly distributed.

A few years later, recollection of this incident prompted me to reconsider the design considerations of the classical Monte Carlo work on the robustness of common parametric tests. In these studies, smooth, mathematically convenient distributions were sampled, such as the normal and the uniform. In the epitome of silliness, it purportedly has been said about the t distribution with three degrees of freedom: "t_3 is a suitable example of what high-quality data can look like" (Huber, cited in Hampel, Ronchetti, Rousseeuw, & Stahel, 1986, p. 23).

In subsequent telephone conversations with my major professor, R. Clifford Blair, professor emeritus from USF, the idea surfaced to sample from real data sets. Thanks to Dr. Theodore Micceri, my office mate when we were graduate assistants, I had access to eight prototypical data sets from real educational and psychology research (Micceri, 1986, 1989; Sawilowsky, Blair, & Micceri, 1990). Although I was aware of previously voiced concerns with Monte Carlo sampling from real data sets (Stigler, 1977, p. 1057), I forged ahead anyway, culminating in Sawilowsky and Blair (1992). This began my work on Monte Carlo *simulations*. I was gratified to read that Maxwell and Cole (1995) subsequently promoted this approach as a useful tip for conducting worthwhile methodological research.

Zero Sum of Squares and Significance Ex Nihilo

In the late 1980s, I was hired to consult on a project comparing a traditional text-based curriculum with an innovative pictorial-based curriculum for automotive repair. A mesh of tiny, interwoven automobile parts were either described in words, or presented in photographs. The former required high reading comprehension, and thus the latter was touted to be a faster and more efficient method of acquiring the cognitive skills pertinent to the program. The setting was a training unit in the automobile industry.

The in-house researcher drew participants randomly from a nationwide accessible population, and randomly assigned them into pretest-posttest treatment (pictorial) versus comparison (text) groups. In addition to the pretest, a reading comprehension scale was used as a second covariate. The correct analysis, permitted due to the use of randomization, is ANCOVA on the posttest scores, with the pretest and reading comprehension scores serving as covariates.

The results, contained in Table P.1, are unequivocal. Despite the efficacy claim, the covariate corrected posttest results did not statistically significantly differ based on receiving the intervention ($p = .971$).

I was brought in for an opinion at this point. I was immediately interested in the sum of squares for the effect being tested. It did not seem possible, so I reran the analysis using three different statistical software packages. All three reported the sum of squares for the effect was *zero*! Either a picture is truly worth a thousand words which is confusing because a sentence will do, or pictures indeed do lie.

Table P.1. ANCOVA on Posttest Scores for Text and Picture Groups With Pretest and Reading Comprehension Scores as Covariates

Source of Variation	*Sum of Squares*	*DF*	*Mean Squares*	*F*	*Sig of F*
Covariates	24.47	2	12.24	7.03	.002
Pretest	4.75	1	4.75	2.73	.102
Reading comprehension	21.58	1	21.58	12.40	.001
Main Effect					
Posttest	**.00**	1	.00	.00	.971
Explained	24.75	3	8.25	4.74	.004
Residual	146.24	84	1.74		
Total	170.99	87	1.97		

A review of the instruments' psychometric properties was in order. The Spearman-Brown correction to Cronbach Alpha, a measure of internal consistency, was .87 for the pretest, .75 for the reading comprehension scale, and .94 for the posttest, all of which are acceptable. Levene's test for homoscedasticity was unremarkable. Although the Kolmogorov-Smirnov test for normality was statistically significant at the $\alpha = .05$ level, it was tempered somewhat by plots indicating the data were symmetric with light tails.

Subsequent analyses were indicated, but the question was what? I settled on (1) pretest to posttest gain scores, and (2) the time it took participants to successfully master the curriculum. Results indicated the pictorial-based group's gain scores were 29.3% larger than the text-based group. Furthermore, this increase in gain occurred in 21.7% less time. Both results were statistically significant at the $\alpha = .001$ level!

As might be expected in a business climate, the increased gain scores were appreciated, but the pictorial-based curriculum's time efficiency was cause for ecstasy. As I was walking out the door, I suggested that in a follow-up study, perhaps the curriculum writers could increase the intervention's effectiveness depicting the mesh of tiny, interwoven automotive parts by using pictures in color instead of nearly imperceptible shades of gray.

RDA in Court

In 1997, Dr. Patricia Lovie, senior lecturer at Keele University, United Kingdom, was the editor of the *British Journal of Mathematical and Statistical Psychology*. She invited me to join a group of colleagues to write a reaction to a position paper on the teaching and practical application of robust methods, written by Dr. Rand Wilcox, professor of psychology at the University of Southern California. I agreed, and marshalled various arguments in favor of using robust methods in real data analysis. Due to the journal's space limitations, the following anecdote was scrapped by the editor, but I revived it for this preface.

In 1992, I provided expert testimony for defendant in a civil trial in Detroit, Michigan. Plaintiff (the sole female employee) and 40 male coworkers were employed by the defendant, a private company servicing the automobile industry.

Plaintiff claimed she had been discriminated against in terms of salary inequity on the basis of gender. Logic and reason dictated this was an untenable complaint. She was earning close to the median salary, despite having the lowest education level, the least amount of training, and the least number of years of experience as compared with all male employees. However, courts operate by law, not logic and reason.

Defendant was in trouble, because prior to my arrival on the case, defendant's counsel stipulated plaintiff was earning less than the mean of her male coemployees. (This stipulation was apparently negotiated in return for plaintiff excluding data indicating that the top three employees earned threefold more than the next employee.) Defendant decided, near the end of the discovery period, that expert testimony was in order. Unfortunately, I was bound by a stipulation not to mention the mean salary in court. Plaintiff's counsel declined to depose me prior to trial, because it would have meant she would have had to curtail her vacation.

After taking the stand, I began to discuss modern methods of data analysis, where estimates of location, such as the arithmetic mean, were being replaced with robust measures such as the Tukey biweight. I noted these methods were especially pertinent for data sets that contained outliers.

Plaintiff's counsel objected that the witness had breached stipulations agreed to by both sides. At the request of defense's counsel, I responded that I had no intention of revealing the specific mean salary or outliers. Rather, my testimony would be based on statistics that are superior to the mean.

Plaintiff's counsel interrupted, finding this to be incredulous, if not ridiculous, and mistakenly asked a university professor to kindly explain how the well known arithmetic mean could possibly be replaced by a better statistic. A short demonstration of the biweight with defendant's salary database ensued. Jurors found for the defendant. I suppose this is what its proponents mean when they say robust methods are powerful.

Although I am a proponent of robust methods as descriptive statistics, its transition to inferential statistics is still in its infancy. Despite revisionist history and protestations to the contrary by its adherents, robust methods were developed assuming an underlying normal structure with perturbations.

Statisticians Versus Data Analysts

Colleagues have enquired why I use the self-appellation "careful data analyst" in the author's bio sketch when I publish occasionally in the journal that I founded and edit, the *Journal of Modern Applied Statistical Methods* (http://tbf.coe.wayne.edu/jmasm). The reason pertains to work I conducted on the rank transform, along with R. Clifford Blair and Professor James J. Higgins, who is professor of statistics at Kansas State University.

Gloria L. Thompson, a noted mathematical statistician who at that time was at Southern Methodist University, attributed the discovery of the failure of the rank transform in testing interactions in ANOVA, despite its promotion by a former president of the American Statistical Association, to the fact that I was a "careful data analyst" (1991, p. 410). I assumed this implied two things: (1) "careful," because I examined realistic ANOVA layouts, and (2) "data analyst," because my work was based on Monte Carlo methods (Sawilowsky, 1985; Blair, Sawilowsky, & Higgins, 1987; Sawilowsky, Blair, & Higgins, 1989), as opposed to asymptotic results subsequently published by many others researchers.

A mere 47 pages later in the same journal, Professor Michael G. Akritas, of Pennsylvania State University, decided the results were obtained because I was a "more careful data analyst" (1991, p. 457), although it remains unclear as compared with whom. Nevertheless, results published by a careful data analyst, even with the cognominal prefix "more," must not be compelling evidence. The controversy on the usefulness of the rank transform in experimental design raged on.

Eventually, Professor Joseph W. McKean, of Western Michigan University, and one of his former doctoral students, Thomas J. Vidmar, seemed to be responsible for finally putting the matter to rest (McKean & Vidmar, 1994). As part of a larger study, they replicated my Monte Carlo results. They buttressed it with sufficient squiggles to gain entry to the *American Statistician*, whose editor had previously rejected my offering on the same topic. Apparently, a careful data analyst is one who discovers, but does not squiggle.

Shlomo S. Sawilowsky,
More Careful Real Data Analyst
February, 2006, West Bloomfield, Michigan

ACKNOWLEDGMENT

I would like to take this opportunity to acknowledge the assistance of Dr. Patric Spence, who not only served as editorial assistant for five issues of the *Journal of Modern Applied Statistical Methods* while working on his doctoral dissertation in communications, but who also served in the same capacity in putting this edited volume together. I would also like to thank Dr. Ronald Serlin, and the AERA SIG/Educational Statisticians, for appointing me as editor of this book. Finally, I would like to thank the authors for their collaboration and communication on topics of mutual interest, and of course, for contributing their chapter.

REFERENCES

Akritas, M. G. (1991). Limitations of the rank transform procedure: A study of repeated measures designs, Part I. *Journal of the American Statistical Association, 86*, 457-460.

Baker, F. B. (1968). Book review. *Journal of the American Statistical Association, 64*, 681-683.

Blair, R. C., Sawilowsky, S. S., & Higgins, J. J. (1987). Limitations of the rank transform in factorial ANOVA. *Communications in Statistics: Computations and Simulations, B16*, 1133-1145.

Carroll, J. M. (1987). *Simulation using personal computers.* Englewood Cliffs, NJ: Prentice-Hall.

Field, S., & Hoffman, A. (1994). Development of a model for self-determination. *Career Development for Exceptional Individuals, 17*, 159-169.

Field, S., Hoffman, A., & Sawilowsky, S. (1995). *Self-Determination Knowledge Scale, Form A and Form B*. Austin, TX: Pro-Ed.

Field, S., Hoffman, A., & Sawilowsky, S. (2005). *Self-Determination Knowledge Scale, Form A and Form B* (Rev.) Austin, TX: Pro-Ed.

Hampel, F. R., Ronchetti, E. M., Rousseeuw, P. J., & Stahel, W. A. (1986). *Robust statistics: The approach based on influence functions*. New York: Wiley.

Maxwell, S., E., & Cole, D. A. (1995). Tips for writing (and reading) methodological articles. *Psychological Bulletin, 118*, 193-198.

McKean, J. W., & Vidmar, T. J. (1994). A comparison of two rank-based methods for the analysis of linear models. *Journal of the American Statistical Association, 48*, 220-229.

Micceri, T. (1986, November). *A futile search for that statistical chimera of normality.* Paper presented at the annual meeting of the Florida Educational Research Association, Tampa, FL.

Micceri, T. (1989). The unicorn, the normal curve, and other improbable creatures. *Psychological Bulletin, 105*(1), 156-166.

Sawilowsky, S. S. (1985). *Robust and power analysis of the 2×2×2 ANOVA, rank transformation, random normal scores, and expected normal scores transformation tests.* Unpublished doctoral dissertation, University of South Florida, Tampa, FL.

Sawilowsky, S. S. (1996, June). *Controlling experiment-wise type I error of meta-analysis in the Solomon four-group design.* International Conference on Multiple Comparison Procedures. Tel Aviv, Israel.

Sawilowsky, S. S., & Blair, R. C. (1992). A more realistic look at the robustness and type II error properties of the *t* test to departures from population normality. *Psychological Bulletin, 111*, 353-360.

Sawilowsky, S. S., Blair, R. C., & Higgins, J. J. (1989). An investigation of the type I error and power properties of the rank transform procedure in factorial ANOVA. *Journal of Educational Statistics, 14*, 255-267.

Sawilowsky, S. S., Blair, R. C., & Micceri, T. (1990). REALPOPS.LIB: a PC FORTRAN library of eight real distributions in psychology and education. *Psychometrika, 55*, 729.

Stigler, S. M. (1977). Do robust estimators work with real data? *The Annals of Statistics, 5*, 1055-1098

Student. (1908). Probable error of a correlation coefficient. *Biometrika*, *6*, 302-310.

Thompson, G. L. (1991). A unified approach to rank tests for multivariate and repeated measures designs. *Journal of the American Statistical Association*, *86*, 410-419.

PART I

FOUNDATIONS

CHAPTER 1

THE COEVOLUTION OF STATISTICS AND HZ

Joseph M. Hilbe

For the past 8 years I have served as the software reviews editor for *The American Statistician* (TAS), a publication of The American Statistical Association. For some 10 years prior to that I wrote a number of reviews related to statistical software for TAS, *PC Magazine*, *Stata Technical Bulletin*, and other publications. And during most of these years I was also involved in writing statistical software for several commercial packages. I even had a stint as chief executive officer (CEO) of a statistical software company in the mid-1980s. I thus have gained a certain perspective—and perhaps, attitude—regarding statistical software and how it has advanced during the past 20 years. This chapter will provide a brief overview of this advancement, with an underlying theme of how the statistics profession has itself advanced in concert.

Most statistical work during the first half of the twentieth century was accomplished using simple pencil and paper—and likely a good erasure. There were times, however, when calculating machines were used as well. For example, Ronald Fisher use a hand-cranked mechanical calculator during the early 1920s in his work at Rothamsted, an agricultural research facility north of London. The machine, called Millionaire,

Real Data Analysis, pp. 3–20

allowed the user to add, subtract, multiply, and divide. It was cumbersome and slow. To multiply, for instance, 256 times 36, the user would place the so-called platen on the unit's position, input the number 256, and crank the lever six times. Following this, the platen would be placed on the tens setting, with the number 256 again set, and the lever cranked three times. The correct answer of 9,216 would be displayed. For his first major publication in 1921 titled, "Studies in Crop Variation I," Fisher (1921) produced 15 tables and four rather sophisticated graphs. At a minute for each large multiplication or division problem, it has been estimated that Fisher spent some 185 hours using Millionaire to produce each table. This estimate relates only to calculation on Millionaire, not for the time required for collection of the data, study design, and graphic production. Today the calculations could be completed in a few seconds.

Hand-cranked calculators were a rare commodity, and available to statisticians at only the most well funded research or business institutions. Karl Pearson had one at his London based Galton Biometrical Laboratory. Called "Brunsviga," Pearson employed a number of women to manually perform the tedious task of turning the crank by hand, while many more sat at long tables writing results and making additional calculations that Brunsviga was unable to calculate. Men stood by to assist the women when various slots became inevitably jammed. This manner of analyzing large amounts of data lasted until World War II.

It is remarkable that many of the statistical routines commonly used today in research were developed during this period of pencil and paper and bulky expensive calculating machines. Pearson developed his fundamental Skew distributions in 1895. He believed that these identified Skew probability distributions underlie all statistical measurements and that they could be differentiated by four parameters, or moments: the mean, standard deviation, symmetry, and kurtosis. After he took over the biometric laboratory from Francis Galton in 1897, Pearson hired a host of young women to calculate (they were called "calculators") the parameters for the many skew distributions of human measurements earlier collected by Galton and his staff. Pearson, Galton, and Raphael Weldon formed the first statistical journal, called *Biometrika*, to disseminate the results they found to other statisticians, as well as to the general scientific community.

William Gossett, better known as "Student," a pseudonym he used to hide research in statistical algorithms and methodology he developed from his employer (Guinness Brewing Company), discovered the Student's *T*-test in 1908. Fisher discovered a distribution for the correlation coefficient in 1915. A year later Francesco Cantelli and Joseph Glivenko developed what was called the fundamental theorem of mathematical statistics, the Glivenko-Cantelli lemma—the rather intuitive insight that an empirical distribution function approaches the true distribution by increasing the number of observations. This Lemma later served as a theoretical background for bootstrap and other computer intensive methods. Maximum likelihood theory was conceived by Fisher in 1925, and was used successfully as the foundation for a variety of early statistical models.

Many other researchers contributed to the creation of basic statistical methodology during this early period. In fact, many commonly used procedures are named for their developers; for example, George Yule, Andrie Kolomogorov, Prasanta Malalanobis, and Samuel Wilks. These statisticians, together with a number of other lesser known names, shaped statistics into a separate discipline. They were able to develop nearly all of what we term today as descriptive statistics. They also derived many of the commonly used methods of hypothesis testing, ordinary least squares regression, basic quality control, sampling and survey statistics, and table chi-square analysis. For the most part, these techniques are the same as taught in contemporary introductory statistics classes nationwide. And they did so using only paper & paper, and if fortunate, a calculating machine.

Statistics may well have remained at the same level of sophistication as it was at the World War II if it were not for the creation of the computer. Computers changed the discipline, and the world.

The first freely programmable computer, named the Z1 computer, was developed by Konrad Zuse in 1936. It had extremely limited capability, and hence had little impact on the research community. In 1942 another computer, called the ABC, was fashioned, and also met with little success. The world was at war and nearly all matters of scientific, or of calculational, interest needed to be geared more to the war effort. The ABC was not. The situation changed, however, with the development and implementation of Harvard's Mark I computer. Codesigned by Howard Aiken and Grace Hopper, the Mark 1 was perhaps the first truly useful computer, and it was the first on which a viable statistical problem was solved.

Soon after the end of World War II, Wassily Leontief, a Columbia University economist, was working on a problem which would later be recognized with the Nobel Prize in Economics. He believed that the U.S. economy could be separated into various material and service sectors, each interrelated with the other. The model to be developed required data from each of these sectors as well as an understanding of how they may relate. Leontief sought the services of the Bureau of Labor Statistics for assistance. Jerome Cornfield, a young statistician with the bureau was assigned to assist Leontief with the project. They determined that the interrelationships between defined sectors could be understood by what is known as "input-output" analysis, which involved the constructing the sectors as a matrix and inverting. Since they identified 12 such sectors, they needed to invert a 12 × 12 matrix. Cornfield managed the task by hand in a week, but discovered that 12 sectors were insufficient—they needed 24 sectors, entailing the inversion of a 24 × 24 matrix. Cornfield informed Leontief that it would take over a hundred years of working 12 hours per day to invert such a matrix, not counting time to correct errors. The solution was to call upon Harvard's Mark 1, which had not been used since the war had ended. After some difficulty determining how the run at Mark 1 would be paid for, the matrix was successfully inverted—taking only several days rather than hundreds of years. Such an inversion takes only microseconds now—using a laptop computer. This was the first use of a computer for statistical purposes, albeit econometric statistics. It was the beginning of a new way of doing statistics.

The few computers in existence during the 1940s were large bulky monsters, consisting of numerous vacuum tubes lined up in rows like soldiers. The invention of the transistor by Bardeen, Brattain, and Shockley of Bell Laboratories in December 1947 would later revolutionize computing, as well as the new electronics industry in general. It was not until 1956 until the first transistorized computer was constructed. It was named by its MIT designers the TX-0.

The first commercial computer, one that could be used by business enterprises, was the UNIVAC (Universal Automatic Computer), invented in 1951. It was used to predict the U.S. presidential winner in the 1952 elections—Eisenhower over Stevenson. IBM (International Business Machines) came out with its first computer, the IBM 701 EDPM 2 years later, and started an industry that would forever change the business world.

John Backus of IBM wrote the first high level programming language for its new computer. He called it FORTRAN (Formula Translator). There are still some statisticians using FORTRAN code 50 years later. BASIC (Beginners All-Purpose Symbolic Instruction Code), did not appear until 1963. Developed at Dartmouth University, it would later be rewritten by Bill Gates and Paul Allen of Microsoft to serve as the first higher language for personal computers.

In 1955 the banking industry was changed by the construction of ERMA, the Electronic Recording Method of Accounting. I readily recall ERMA, since it directly impacted my life as a young teller at Bank of America in 1962-1963. I took a year off between high school and college, working at the Paradise branch, located in the mountains of northern California, some 100 miles north of Sacramento. When I began working as a teller, each deposit had to be recorded by hand on a card listing the deposits and withdrawals of the individual account. At the end of the day I would take the packet of deposit and withdrawal slips to the back of the room, pull each card as needed, and add or subtract totals as necessary. Mistakes were time consuming to track. In 1963 the branch went on

ERMA, completely revising the process. Errors certainly occurred, but tracking was easier to follow. But when ERMA, located in Sacramento and servicing the entire State of California, crashed, the bank was practically shut down.

The first hard drive was developed by IBM in 1956. It consisted of 50 two foot diameter platters. In 1958 the integrated circuit was developed, which was later to allow the development of the personal computer. It was first made of Germanium, but was changed to a Silicon Oxide surface the following year. This is essentially the same compound currently used for magnetic memory storage.

Minicomputers were developed for commercial use beginning with Digital's PDP-1 in 1960. It had the first keyboard and monitor combination, but the cost was a rather prohibitive $120,000. Universities failed to purchase any brand of microcomputer for many years.

Computing at the universities and research organizations in the 1960s was a matter of card punching and submitting a batch file to the computer for processing. Statistical analysis was performed, but one had to apply, and find funding for, computer time. Interaction with the computer was practically nonexistent. One would submit a batch, wait overnight, or sometimes for days, and then see the results on a long printout. If a change was perceived to be required, the user started again with a new request, batch file setup, funding request, and run. Sometimes a relatively simple initial request could take weeks to find an appropriate solution. Needless to say, such requests were forced to be parsimonious, thought out, and as error free as possible. I remember having to submit requests to our university computer in such a manner until the early 1980s. Even today, when a mainframe computer is requested for the solution of a mathematical/scientific problem, and not simply used for mass data storage and manipulation, batch files have to be established and submitted, and users typically have to wait at least overnight for results.

There were a number of statisticians whose careers overlapped the era of pencil and paper and mainframe digital computer. Some whose calculating world was solely by pencil & paper had careers lasting into the age of personal computers—but not many. Those making foremost contributions to the discipline during this time of overlap included Chester Bliss, whose primary publications ranged from 1935 until 1970, David Cox (1958-1987), and Francis Anscombe (1949-1981). Other well known statisticians of the period that come to mind include Joseph Berkson, head statistician at Mayo Clinic, Frank Yates, Hirotugu Akaike, Nathan Mantel, Frank Wilcoxon, Harold Hotelling, Samuel Wilks, Emil Gumbel, William Cochran, Walter Shewhart, George Box, and John Tukey. Each of these names calls to mind statistical procedures of considerable importance.

And each helped develop methods which would later find their full fruition when powerful PCs became available for statistical analysis.

Of particular interest to our overview is Tukey's 1962 long, yet engaging article, "The Future of Data Analysis" (pp. 1-67). He predicted sweeping advancements in statistical analysis due to the increasing computational power of digital computers. In fact, in 1965, Tukey developed together with IBM programmer John Cooley the Fast Fourier Transform algorithm enabling digital computers to solve problems that were, to that point, only solvable using the cumbersome analog computers we earlier described. Historians of statistics may recall that it was only in 1960 that Matthew Efroymsom had written a FORTRAN algorithm for the calculation of multiple regression in an edited book detailing computer algorithms and code for a number of mathematical functions, models, and theorems (Efroymsom, 1960).

A pivotal year in computing was 1969. Honeywell released H316, the world's first home computer, to the general public. Called the "Kitchen Computer," it was marketed as a kit to be constructed by the purchaser. This strategy had served electronic manufacturers for nearly 20 years. It was quite popular amongst electronically minded folk to purchase radio and TV kits which were soldered, screwed, and bent into working condition. My father spent many hours with these kits, resulting in a host of radios and TVs around the house. However, times had changed and the market was not good for Honeywell's new product. But it was likely the $10,600 price tag that stifled interest more than anything.

With the 70s came the possibility to finally have personal computing power. In 1970 Intel designed the first dynamic 4-bit RAM (Random-access Memory) chip. Called the Intel 1103, it was superseded the following year by Intel's 4004 microprocessor—the first of its kind. This same year IBM created the first floppy disk, an 8" floppy plastic disk.

In 1972 Texas Instruments designed the TSM 1000 with a 4-bit processor and 32 bytes of RAM. The following year the Scelbi Computer Consulting Company introduced their Scelbi-8H microcomputer kit. Employing the new Intel 8008 microprocessor, it had 1 KB (Kilobyte) of programmable memory and sold for U.S.$565. An optional 15 additional KB of memory could be purchased for $2,760. Memory was expensive. In 1974 Intel made a substantial leap by releasing its 2-MHz ((Megahertz) 8-bit 8080 chip. It accessed 64 KB of memory and incorporated some 6000 transistors. The chip found its way into a variety of kits in both the United States and in Europe.

The point at which computers could be purchased as a unit came in 1975. MITS, which manufactured the new Altair computer, released its 8800 computer kit for $397. It sold for $439 if already assembled. It had the new 2 MHz Intel 8080 processor with 256 bytes of RAM. The computer also incorporated the BASIC programming language which could be used to program instructions and solve problems. In early January Paul Allen and Bill Gates had written to MITS (Micro Instrumentation and Telemetry Systems) advising them that they had written a BASIC language for the 8080 processor. They offered to license it in turn for royalty payments. MITS agreed—which led to Paul and Bill actually writing the language within a month. They demonstrated it to MITS in February, loading it into the Altair and solving a simple 2 + 2 = 4 instruction flawlessly. Paul also wrote a "Lunar Lander" game entirely in BASIC the same month. It became the first software program ever run on a personal computer, and was licensed with the computer. In April, Allen and Gates formed Micro-Soft, and an industry began. By June MITS had made over 1 million dollars on Altair sales. The personal computer had come of age, and many statisticians saw the potential for its use.

Apple Computers, developed by Steven Jobs and Steven Wosniak, was incorporated on April 1, 1976. Wosnick had tried to license their circuit board to Hewlat Packard and Atari, but were turned down. Finally they sold it themselves as a kit in July, calling it the Apple 1. In April 1977, Apple released Apple II, with 6505 CPU, 4 KB of RAM, 16 KB ROM (Read-Only Memory), built-in BASIC, game paddles, and a color display. The system took off, becoming quickly the major personal computer on the market. There were a host of competitors, to be sure—such as the Commodore, Atari, TRS-80, TI99/4, ZX-80, Osborne-1, Epson HX-20, Compaq, and Coleco's Adam, but most failed after a few years of sales. Educators were one of the first to exploit the Apple for educational and analytic purposes. Word processors (Wordstar was first, then WordPerfect), spreadsheets (first VisiCalc, then Lotus), and databases (dBase) were quickly developed and adapted for Apple use. Businesses soon followed suit, but in general preferred to stick with mainframe and minicomputers.

In the meantime in 1976, IBM Japan manufactured and sold the IBM 5100 desktop computer to businesses in Japan. It had a 5" monochrome monitor and sold for $10,000. The first U.S. IBM PC was introduced in August 1981. Called the IBM 5150 PC, it had 4.77 MHz. 8088 processor, 16 KB of RAM, and a 5.25" floppy disk drive. It sold for $1,500, and allowed MS-DOS (Microsoft Disk Operating System), with built-in BASIC, as an option. Programs ran from the floppy—it did not have a hard drive.

In 1983 IBM released the PC/XT with a 10 MB (Megabyte) hard drive, 128 KB RAM and a monochrome monitor. It sold for $5,000—a tidy sum in the early 80s. The XT as it came to be known, became popular with educators, and most major university departments had a room with an XT and Apple II for faculty use. A host of statistical programs were developed for the XT. They could be found in the many books on scientific programming as well as programming in general that were starting to appear in Walden and Dalton bookstores, and also in university bookstores nationwide. I well recall writing a BASIC program for a *t*-test and an ANOVA in 1983 on the department XT. Many professors had their statistics students spend considerable time at the XT working on the development of statistical algorithms. The use of Apple II was also common, but not at my university.

Personal computer power saw a huge leap in 1984. Apple came out with the Macintosh, sporting a 9" 512 × 342 monochrome graphics monitor, 7.8 MHz Motorola 6800 processor, and 128 KB RAM all for only $2,000. Macintosh's became the PC of choice for most of the education and business world. But the same year saw IBM release the PC/AT, with a 6 MHz 80286 processor, MS-DOS 3.0, 256 KB RAM, a 1.2 MB floppy drive, and a huge 20 MB hard drive. A color monitor could be purchased as an option. By early 1985 IBM increased the AT's RAM to 512 KB, with the possibility of the user enhancing it to 640 KB. I remember flipping dip switches and installing the extra RAM to get that 640. The system cost me, at a substantial faculty discount, $4,200 in January 1985. But the computing power was worth it. I could write statistics programs in BASIC that were quite complicated, including a multiple regression module that allowed inversion of matrices of rather high dimensions.

In my opinion, the PC/AT helped sway statisticians and economists away from Apple to the IBM series. Most were not hesitant to get their hands dirty by enhancing their machines by hand—a task that was unavailable to the Apple user. With Apple, you had what you bought.

I might also mention here that Microsoft released a FORTRAN-80 complier in April 1977 for a sales price of $500. Statisticians had been using it since it was first written in 1954 with mainframes to solve complex statistical problems. Most individuals with a mathematical and scientific background had experience with FORTRAN, so when it became available for use in personal computers, much of the code could transfer as well with little effort. The tremendous advantage allowed by PCs, of course, is the interactive nature of submitting a program for analysis of data, obtaining the results immediately (in most cases) and resubmitting it directly afterwards if needed. For simple statistical tasks, the time between instruction and feedback is nearly instantaneous.

In late 1985 Intel developed the 80386 chip, a 32-bit processor consisting of 275,000 transistors. IBM and IBM clones, as they became known, using the 80386 chip, came sequentially with 16, 20, 25, and by 1989, 33 MHz versions. The 33 MHz system ran on what was named the 80386SZ chip, having 855.000 transistors. The jump in computing memory and speed from the XT in 1984 to the 80386SZ 5 years later was phenomenal.

From 1989 to 1993 IBM based PCs sold the 80486 chip. This was a 32-bit processor consisting of 1.2 million transistors. The chip increased speed by doubling; that is, 25 MHz technology became 50 MHz, 33 MHz became 66 MHz. A prime advance, one important to calculations, was the built-in floating point (FPU) capability of the new chip. One did not have to purchase a separate math coprocessor for floats, longs, and doubles.

In late 1993 Intel came out with the Pentium chip. This was the same as an 80586 processor, but legalities prohibited Intel's continued use of the traditional series numbering system. When it was released, the Pentium gave the user 60 MHz and a bit later 100 MHz of speed. It stayed as a 32-bit internal processor, but advanced to 3.21 million transistors and 64-bit external bus. Clock speeds increased during 1993-2004 from 60 MHz to a final 200 MHz.

The next major advance was the Pentium II chip in 1997. It was also a 32-bit internal processor, but ran at up to 300 MHz speed. The 1998 "Deschutes" version increased speed to 450 MHz. 1999 bought us the Pentium III chip. Released in February under the name "Katmai," it ran at 450 MHz, but with a 100 MHz bus. The 2000 release of "Coppermine" increased both to 1 GHz (Gigahertz) clock speed and 133 MHz bus.

Finally, the Pentium IV was introduced in November 2000. The so-called "Williamette" version hosted 400 MHz bus and a whopping 42 million transistors. The "Northwood" version of Pentium IV was released in 2002, and upped the ante to 55 million transistors, 2.0, then 2.2 GHz clock speed. The last Pentium IV upgrade to this point is 2.53 GHz speed using 533 MHz front side bus. Everything moves very quickly.

I am writing this in January 2005, using a Gateway laptop with 3.30 GHz clock speed, 1.85 GHz bus, 100 Gigabytes of hard disk storage, and 512 MB RAM. And this is a laptop costing approximately $1,700! How very far we have come in the past 23 years since IBM's release of its first personal computer.

Software for statistical analysis has advanced equally with the processing power and speed of computers. I believe that the very profession of statistics itself has changed as well. I shall review the progress of five statistical packages: SAS, SPSS, S, R, and Stata. Each is at least 20 years old and is still playing a major role in current day statistical analysis.

SAS

Recall that the first programming language, specifically designed for scientific and mathematical work, was FORTRAN, designed and first used at Dartmouth University in 1954. For the next quarter of a century the majority of statisticians used it to construct statistical algorithms for use on mainframe computers. Statistical software packages were a thing of the future. SAS Institute in 1976 was the first company to develop what can be called a statistical package—although they still prefer to call it a "data management and analysis environment." SAS had its first offices in Raleigh, NC and began operations with a partnership with IBM. The package, called SAS BASE, was designed to work with IBM mainframes. SAS moved to Cary in 1979, where is had remained ever since. In 1984 SAS designed a system to work with minicomputers, which many smaller companies used for business data management and analysis.

In 1985 SAS released SAS for PC DOS. It was an immediate success. They also set up site licenses with major universities to provide PC statistical resources for faculty. For nominal yearly fee, somewhere in the range of $100, a faculty member could install copied SAS diskettes (over 30) on their IBM AT computers. Of course, many professors preferred to use the department PC rather then purchase the computer for themselves. The expense was prohibitive to many. SAS also provided a facility to link PCs to mainframes allowing users to work with mainframe SAS but download results to their PCs. Users with SAS installed in their PC could also access data maintained on mainframes. Statisticians could interactively manipulate mainframe-stored data on their PCs—a major step in analysis.

In 1986 SAS partnered with Microsoft and added SAS/STAT and SAS.IML to the PC BASE software. Three years later the institute released JMP, a smaller more graphical version of SAS, for use on Apple Macintosh computers. To that point Apple users had limited statistical capability.

Windows and OS/2 became available platforms for PC-based SAS 6.08 in 1993. More data management and analysis components had been added each year to the product, so much so that piling each reference and technical support manual on top of each other resulted in a heap some four feet high.

I was a member of a team of reviewers hired by *PC Magazine* to rate the major statistical software packages then on the market (*PC Magazine*, Vol. 12, No. 9, May 11, 1993). I reviewed SAS and GENSTAT, a British statistical package. SAS sent me its entire collection of manuals and tech reports. I actually did measure the stack since I was so impressed with the amount of documentation sent.

The packages reviewed in the *PC Magazine* report included BMDP, Genstat, Minitab, NCSS, P-Stat, SPSS, Stata, Statgraphics, Statistica, SYSTAT, and SAS. Unfortunately SAS's new Windows product was only in Beta version at the time of the review, hence it could not actually be ranked. But it was clear that SAS took up more computer resources than the other packages. 8 MB of RAM was required—a huge amount at that time—and 100 MB of disk space. The new 486 DX2 33 Mhz computers being marketed then were capable of handling the entire SAS package, but most academics had computers that fell far short of those requirements. This situation was soon to change with the next iteration of lower cost, higher RAM computers.

SAS has continued to be the foremost statistical package used by the general research community. Each year finds a new SAS version with evermore added capability. Faster clock speed and higher RAM allows SAS to presently incorporate exact statistics, kernel density estimation, bootstrap and jackknife methods, and complex multilevel models. In 1993 many of these methods were prohibitive on the PC. SAS was not the only player in the early statistical market. Three very early products were SPSS, SYSTAT, and S. I shall look at SPSS first, then S.

SPSS

In 1968, Norman Nie, Tex Hull, and Dale Bent invented the Statistical Package for the Social Sciences, or SPSS. Development began at Stanford University in California where Nie was a doctoral candidate in operations research. Hull had graduated with a degree in business administration. Nie designed the internal file structure, and Hull programmed the first version, which was intended for local academic circles. However, social scientists and econometricians at other universities soon sought to use the package for their own analysis. Run on mainframes, Nie and Hull sent updated tapes of code to cohorts as enhancements were made.

In 1969 Nie obtained a position at the National Opinion Center at the University of Chicago. Hull joined him at Chicago, heading the universities Computation Center. Bent, a Canadian, decided to leave the project and took an academic position at the University of Alberta. He did, however, contribute to the writing of the first SPSS manual, published by McGraw Hill in 1970.

The University of Chicago encouraged Nie and Hull to continue work on SPSS, while also engaging in their primary duties. However, the university laid claim to any monies obtained from SPSS sales. Nie, Hull, and Brent received only royalties for manual sales.

Thanks to the IRS, SPSS became incorporated separately with Nie and Hull as company heads. It seems that in 1971 the IRS targeted SPSS as a software company, which violated the nonprofit status of the university. Incorporation was not finalize until 1975, after considerable discussion among the principals. Regardless, SPSS was marketed solely to academic institutions, and used code that was portable to all of the major academic computer systems. Government and businesses also began to use the package, which was highly modularized.

In the mid-1980s SPSS ported the mainframe package to the PC environment. I used one of the first releases on my AT in 1986. By 1987 one could install SPSS on an AT using some 30 plus 5¼" floppies. The task took hours.

The first SPSS for Windows package was released in 1992, prior to SAS's release a year later. SPSS sales boomed with the Windows release, so much so that by 1996 sales reached 84 million dollars. In 1994 SPSS purchased SYSTAT. From 1997 through 2002 SPSS acquired a number of ancillary products, ranging from market research software (Quantime), data mining software (ISL), business intelligence software (ShowCase), Web software (NetGenesis and netExs), and text mining software (LexiQuest). They also sold a variety of ancillary products.

SPSS now includes a wide variety of statistical methods, from basic statistics to mixed models and multiple response analysis. It also has taken methods used by other single purpose software and incorporated them into SPSS proper. Missing value analysis and exact statistics are two foremost examples. SPSS also includes add-on packages, such as AMOS, Answertree, Clementine, DecisionTime, Sample Power, Smart Viewer Web Serfver, SPSS Data Entry, SPSS Servfer, WebApp, Visualization Toolkit, and Text Analysis. It is by far the most complete analytic package, or perhaps group of packages, available to statisticians and researchers.

There are certain areas of analysis missing in the vast SPSS offerings. Some of these are important to areas such as biostatistics. For example, SPSS has no direct Poisson or negative binomial regression program, which is extremely useful for the analysis of count data. But I leave the reader to research the reviews found in *The American Statistician* for comparative capabilities between packages. The next software to be addressed is more of a programming environment than a package.

S and R

S version 1 was originally developed in 1976 at ATT&T Bell Laboratories under the direction of John Chambers and Trevor Hastie, although the former seems to get the majority of the credit. S was written in C as a higher programming language. Separate algorithms were developed for each statistical procedure, and a rather primitive data management facility allowed for the proper set up of data being submitted to the S program. The original version 1 could only work with Honeywell mainframes at Bell. Version 2 appeared in 1980 and was ported to the UNIX environment. In 1984 S was licensed for use outside of Bell. From 1984 to 1993 statisticians and users outside of Bell continued to add procedures and capabilities. Most importantly, Classes and generic functions were added to allow enhanced internal calling capability between procedures and S functions.

In 1993 S was licensed to Mathsoft, and later to Insightful. As a commercial product it became known as S-Plus. User conventions were held, and S classes were taught through North America. I was hired several times to teach the S Advanced Models course. The last time was at Laval University in Quebec. These courses brought the S language directly to faculty, and resulted in many departments subscribing to S-Plus software. Aside from the lower cost compared to SAS and SPSS, users could freely add to the procedures and post programs to the S-Plus Web site to share with others. This academic spirit made S-Plus extremely popular in academic circles, but its share of the business market has remained relatively low.

An S clone, called R, was developed by Robert Gentleman and Ross Ihaka in 1990 at the University of Auckland, New Zealand. They intended it to serve as a teaching tool, and decided to design it with S-like syntax due to the popularity of S-Plus. Unlike S-Plus, it was designed to be used on a Macintosh. Rather than use their work for commercial purposes, the designers placed R on the Statlib Internet site to be shared with the general academic community. Initially, few took advantage of it. But in June 1995 it was decided to be released as freeware. This spurred activity, and 2 years later an R core group of 10 members was formed to control the direction of R development—John Chambers was added to the core group in 2000. Now major upgrades are being released every 6 months and R is one of the hottest statistical packages—or rather programming environments—in use. Each issue of *The American Statistician* finds at least one article using R; other journals are having a similar experience. As of January 2005, due to user input and good product control, R has surpassed S-Plus in statistical capabilities. Students are now being taught to use R in the classroom and it is sure to advance in user numbers over the next several years, unless perhaps it takes the same eventual commercial route as S. The main feature of R is the ease of programming and its ability to use every bit of RAM and speed that the computer allows.

STATA

The final software I wish to discuss is Stata. Stata, manufactured by Stata Corp in College Station, Texas began as a two-person exercise in 1984 by Bill Gould and Bill Rogers in Santa Monica, California under the corporate name of CRC. Both Bill's were trained as economists. Stata began as a small executable written in C accompanied by a number higher language programs written in Stata's proprietary higher language. The idea underlying their project was to offer the user speed. Data and executable were together held in RAM, and Stata's well written code and sparse interface allowed statistical tasks to be run at optimal speed. Initially written for DOS, early marketing stressed both speed and graphics. By the later 1980s sales were few and the company was on the verge of failure. The two Bill's and one wife ran the entire company.

Gould decided to offer an academic price of $79 for the product in 1989. Hoping to entice academics by the cheap price, the nifty graphics, and speed, he saw sales rise rather dramatically. I bought in as well. But instead of speed and graphics, I was mostly impressed with the Stata language.

In 1990 Stata consisted of the standard descriptive statistics, logit and probit regression, Cox proportional hazards regression, a good suite of graphics, and a few other programs. Early in 1990 Larry Hamilton of the University of New Hampshire and I wrote Stata statistical procedures using what were called ado files. Ado stands for automatic do, or batch files. Hamilton authored a robust regression routine while I constructed a logistic regression program incorporating all of the new Hosmer-Lemeshow diagnostic statistics. These were published in the *Stata News*, a quarterly newsletter distributed free to all registered users of Stata. Other users soon followed suit and commenced submitting programs that were not yet in official Stata, but which would likely be of use to the majority of users. This same method of user support was the reason for the success of both S and R as well.

In late 1990 Stata was selected as the software of choice for the Medicare Infrastructure Project (MIP), a data management and analysis project sponsored by the Health Care Financing Administration (HCFA, the regulatory agency responsible for Medicare). Project principal investigator, Henry Krakauer of HCFA was impressed with the ease of learning as well as the capability of Stata's higher language facility. He hired Bill Rogers to write a Bailey-Makeham 4 parameter survival model which would be used to establish national parameters for average length of stay and confidence intervals for each DRG, or diagnostic related group, used by HCFA for reimbursement and quality of care analysis. Resultant parameters and statistics would guide the work of all peer review organizations (PRO) throughout the United States during the so-called 4th Scope of Work. PROs were private companies licensed to regulate all Medicare activity in their state, sometimes incorporating several states. All PROs were required to use Stata for health care analysis and tutorials were given throughout the nation to health analysts on how to use Stata for research. HCFA, and other governmental agencies, funded these workshops.

I was hired by HCFA to serve as the lead biostatistician for the project. While on sabbatical in 1988 I had designed algorithms to detect quality of care outliers for hospitals in the western United States. The algorithms were approved for use by the San Francisco Regional office, and evidently got the attention of HCFA headquarters in Baltimore. Anyhow, as I began to write programs in Stata for the project, I came to the belief that if the forum were provided, many Stata users would likely want to author additional statistical and data management routines in Stata—ones that would help them in their own projects, and ones that simply seemed to call out for inclusion into Stata. I called Bill Gould in February 1991 suggesting that Stata sponsor a technical journal in which users could add programs, discuss various statistical techniques, and in which Stata itself could update Stata by means of an update diskette. The journal, called the *Stata Technical Bulletin* was first issued in May 1991. This first issue included a complete life table analysis program authored by Krakauer, a likelihood ratio test procedure, a Poisson regression with rates program, a full fledged nonlinear regression package, a function to calculate exact and cumulative Poisson probabilities, additions to my logistic regression program, and an article on how to program Monte Carlo simulation using Stata. Other data management and graphical capabilities were added as well.

Subsequent issues included a complete generalized linear models package, a suite of time series analysis programs, kernel density estimation, quantile regression with bootstrapped standard errors, a sample size calculator, and many other similar programs—and a host of smaller program and utilities. All this was within the first 2 years of the STB. Initially, the major interest was the development of biostatistical and epidemiological tools due to Stata's widespread use in the health care community. But as the years progressed the STB found itself publishing comprehensive econometric, business statistics, and social/physical science oriented algorithms. After 10 years and three editors, the STB became the *Stata Journal* in the fourth quarter 2001. Although the majority of theoretical articles in the STB were refereed, all Stata journal manuscripts go through the standard two referee process.

Stata developed a Windows version as well as platforms for Macintosh, UNIX, SUN and others in the coming years. It also joined the Internet. Beginning around 1995 a Stata user LISTSERVER was started at Harvard, which continues through today. Complete copies of discussions are maintained at a Boston University site, which has proved valuable for research. None of this would be possible if it were not for the enhanced computing power and connectivity that the industry has enjoyed the past 15 years.

In 2001 Stata also incorporated a separate Stata press. Standard sized texts on maximum likelihood programming, generalized linear models, survival analysis, categorical response regression models, and graphics have been published through 2004. Five more are in preparation. Data sets and author-written programs can be downloaded from the Stata-Press

Web site. And for Stata—because users began to contribute a variety of elaborate, complex, and useful statistical programs and data management tools over the past 15 years, Stata has grown from a two person shop on the verge of extinction to perhaps the third most used statistical package worldwide behind SAS and SPSS.

I have elaborated a bit on SAS, SPSS, S-Plus/R, and Stata because of their longevity and impact on the worldwide statistical community. I could have discussed GLIM, one of the very first statistical packages dating from 1972 in Great Britain, but it ceased production and support with its version 4.0 in 1994. GENSTAT, also a NAG production in Great Britain, is still in existence, but sales are pretty much limited to British Empire nations, and sales have dropped considerably in recent years. Most previous users have switched to Stata, S-Plus, or R.

Standard statistical packages that base statistical models on asymptotics have grown to fruition. For instance, packages such as Stata and SAS have the capability to bootstrap and jackknife standard errors, employ a host of robust variance estimators, and have complex kernel density estimators. They can be used to model sophisticated GEE, random effects and mixed models. S-Plus, XploRe, Data Desk, JMP, and several other packages allow the user to perform nearly every diagnostic plot described in Chamber, Cleveland, Kleiner, and Tukey's, *Graphical Methods for Data Analysis*, which was published in 1983, but for which it took many years before a commercial package to implement.

Until recently, computers did not have the capability to engage in highly iterative techniques such as bootstrap and jackknife. Many of the major packages now incorporate such methods. But a new statistical technology is taking hold of the statistical community. It is a method which would have been literally impossible 10 years ago. I refer to exact statistics.

Several packages have implemented Fisher's chi-square exact statistic for a 2 × 2 table. Others such as Stata have the capability to employ an exact Chi2 test for 2 × k tables. However, Cyrus Mehta, and Nitin Patel designed efficient algorithms to use exact statistics; that is, calculate *p*-values based on exact permutation statistics for nearly every nonparametric method that has appeared in the literature. The algorithms are put together in a single package called, "StatXact," manufactured by Cytel. Moreover, Mehta and Patel have led a team of statisticians in developing methods to calculate exact parameter values and *p*-values for both binary and grouped logistic regression, and in the last year for Poisson regression. These capabilities are found in Cytel's "LogXact." In the newly released version 6.2 of StatXact and LogXact 6.0 (released January, 2005); exact and Monte Carlo methods are available for sample size determination and other tests. LogXact has also added parametric statistics to the program, including multivariate statistics. But exact methods are as yet unavailable for these methods. Other packages have attempted to follow Cytel's lead. Testimate in Germany has a nice group of nonparametric tests, and SAS and SPSS have used Mehta and Patel's published algorithms to develop exact statistics modules to sell as options with their Base packages. To date, XPro is the only package to utilize exact *p*-values for parametric routines, including linear regression, ANOVA, *T*-tests, and other hypothesis tests. Robert Oster and I have reviewed these packages extensively in recent issues of *The American Statistician*.

It is my opinion that procedures incorporating exact statistics for nearly every major statistical routine will be common in the next 10 years. At the present time computer memory, speed, and power relegate exact statistics to rather limited sizes. When computing power fails to perform the needed permutations required of a task, StatXact and LogXact simply revert to Monte Carlo methods. But this is a temporary interlude.

The result of exact statistical analysis, as well as more complex nested and multilevel modeling, will be a new statistics, fashioned by computer gigahertz speed. As computers ever enhance, even perhaps to the point of having DNA and atomic chips, new statistical methods will develop, and new requirements will be made for practitioners of the statistical profession. I have attempted to provide an overview of how the advancement in statistical capability has followed first of all computing power, and secondarily available statistical software—the toolbox of the statistician.

I have argued that the statistical routines employed for the analysis of data at any given point in time is a reflection of the available tools, whether it be pencil and paper, or sophisticated computers. In the current era, software is dependent on computing speed in terms of Hertz and available RAM. In the process we have looked at how the computer industry evolved, and how it impacted business, statistics, and society in general. Statisticians now rarely engage in paper and pencil analysis; the only time may be when teaching introductory level statistics courses. Many introductory books still discuss at length how to construct *T*-tests, ANOVAs, several nonparametric tests, and typically a one predictor linear regression. I suspect that this training is not really needed any longer, that it is preferable to teach students how to use the computer to manage data, run basic statistics, and check for the adequacy of the routine via goodness-of-fit tests and residual analyses. Numerical methods courses can address the algorithms involved. Regardless, statistics in the early twenty-first century is not at all the statistics of the early twentieth century, nor of even the mid-twentieth century.

For a simple example of how statistics has changed as a result of computing power, consider the once well used multivariate discriminant analysis. In the 1970s and 80s it was the prime method of classification and prediction. There were drawbacks, such as the assumption that each group be from a multivariately normal distribution, which rarely was the case. But there were typically no alternatives found in commercial software. The algorithm was straightforward, involved a matrix inversion, but no iterations. However, in the 1990s, with increased computer speed, discriminant analysis began to be pushed into the background, with logistic regression, ordered logit and probit, and multinomial regression taking the stage. When estimating a logistics regression program in 1990, which iteratively estimates parameters via maximum likelihood, it took a minute or more to run. Sometimes, for larger models, iteration would take a half hour or more. Now the results are near instantaneous, with iterations screaming down the output page. Logistic regression and other like models can be programmed to allow bootstrapped, jackknifed, and robust standard errors. There is little wait time; unlike only 5 years ago when computer speed provided bootstrapped results in terms of minutes and hours rather than seconds. Kernel density estimation with bootstrapped confidence intervals also takes seconds to determine—5 years ago few software programs would even offer it as a capability.

It is enjoyable to ponder what statistical analysis might be like in the early twenty-second century. It is quite likely that we would barely recognize it now. How computers will alter the statistics profession in the future is yet to be determined; we can be quite sure however that most analyses will take a form more like present day exact statistics than asymptotics, which will be regarded as primitive. 3-D graphics, or possibly holographic graphics displayed in seeming midair is a possibility. Consider for a moment how Galton would perceive current advanced statistical analysis and our contemporary calculating machines.

REFERENCES

Efroymsom, M. A. (1960). Multiple regression analysis'. In A. Ralson & H. S Wilf (Eds.), *Mathematical methods of digital computers* (Vol. 1, pp. 191-203). New York: J Wiley.

Fisher, R. A. (1921). Studies in crop variation, I. An examination of the yield of dressed grain from Broadbalk. *Journal of Agricultural Science, 11,* 107-135

Salsburg, D. (2002). *The lady tasting tea: How statistics revolutionized science in the twentieth century.* New York: Henry Holt.

Tukey, J. (1962). The future of data analysis. *Annals of Math Statistics, 33,* 1-67.

CHAPTER 2

EFFECTIVE SAMPLE SIZE

A Crucial Concept

Thomas R. Knapp

INTRODUCTION

A problem that has persistently plagued much research in the social sciences is the nonindependence of observations. The typical study has investigated a research question of the form "What is the relationship between *X* and *Y*?," where *X* and *Y* are measurements obtained on individual persons who are nested within clusters (families, schools, etc.), and the data are assembled across the clusters (sometimes called aggregates or groups). There is a vast literature concerned with how to (and how not to) analyze such data, starting with the cautions regarding the appropriate unit of analysis (UOA) expressed by Robinson (1950), Cronbach (1976), Knapp (1977, 1984), Burstein (1980), and others, and continuing through the work that is referred to as hierarchical linear modeling (HLM)—for example, Wu (1995), Osborne (2000), and Raudenbush and Bryk (2002). See also Kalish, Riester, and Pocock (2002) regarding adjustments for 2 × 2 contingency tables for which the observations are not independent.

Real Data Analysis, pp. 21–29

Concern regarding units of observation and units of analysis actually dates as far back as Karl Pearson (1896), who found that the correlation between length of skull and breadth of skull was .09 for males, –.14 for females, and .20 for the two sexes combined. And E. L. Thorndike (1939) created a hypothetical set of data for which the correlation between IQ (intelligence quotient) and number of rooms per person was 0 for individuals within each of 12 city districts, was .45 for individuals pooled across those districts, and the between-district correlation was .90. For additional references regarding the analysis of multilevel data see Knapp (1977, 1984), Goldstein (1986), and Liou and Peng (2006) elsewhere in this volume.]

More recently there has appeared in the biostatistical and epidemiological literature (see especially the articles by Burton, Gurrin, & Sly, 1998 and by Hanley, Negassa, Edwardes, & Forrester, 2003, and the books by Hardin & Hilbe, 2003 and by Small & Wang, 2003) a technique for handling nonindependence called generalized estimating equations (GEE), in which one can determine for nested designs the "effective sample size" (ESS), that is, an estimate of the number of observations associated with the nested study that would be approximately equal to the number of independent observations in a comparable study without the nesting.

The purpose of this chapter is to call to the attention of the social research community a procedure for determining effective sample size and to illustrate that procedure with both hypothetical and real examples. The formulas involved in the GEE calculations are not provided, but the reader who may be interested in such formulas is referred to Hanley et al. (2003) and to sources cited in their article.

A Simple Hypothetical Example

Hanley et al. (2003) used the following hypothetical data to illustrate the GEE calculations:

Table 2.1.

Cluster	*Observation*
1	15
1	13
2	10
2	9
2	8

Suppose you were interested in estimating the (individual level) mean in the population from which those observations were drawn, and in establishing a 95% confidence interval around that estimate. No matter whether the population standard deviation were known or unknown, you could not simply calculate the unweighted mean of 11.0 for those five observations and lay off /n or s/n a couple of times on the low side and a couple of times on the high side, because those five observations are not independent. (If they were, s would be equal to 2.92.) The appropriate approach is to use GEE to find the "best" weighted mean, taking into account the "correlatedness" of the observations within each of the clusters, accompanied by a standard error that is a function of the effective, not the actual, sample size. The calculations are iterative and rather complex, but Hanley et al. (2003) show them all, step-by-step, for this example in Figure 4 on page 369 of their article, and there are also computerized routines for carrying out such computations (see the appendix to the Hanley et al. article and the article by Horton & Lipsitz, 1999).

For this hypothetical example, the (irrelevant) unweighted mean is 11.0, the (also irrelevant) equally-weighted mean is 11.5, and the best weighted mean (after the GEE process has converged) is 11.47. The effective sample size is found to be 2.19, which together with an estimated standard deviation of 2.96 produces an estimated standard error of 1.80. Using the *t* sampling distribution, the 95% confidence interval would extend from 11.47 – 2.78 (1.80) to 11.47 + 2.78 (1.80), that is, from approximately 6.47 to 16.47. Compare that interval with the interval that would often be employed (but would be incorrect) from 11.0 – 2.78(2.92)/5 to 11.0 + 2.78(2.92)/5, that is, from 7.37 to 14.63 and you can see that the GEE approach produces a wider, yet more statistically defensible, interval.

Does the effective sample size of 2.19 make sense? Having two clusters, one with two observations and the other with three observations, is no better than having slightly more than two independent observations?! The answer to both questions is "yes"; the observations within a cluster are very similar to one another but very different from the observations in the other cluster, so those five particular observations have not "bought you" very much.

Perhaps an example of real data will be more convincing.

The Forrester Data

In their article, Hanley, Negassa, Edwards, and Forrester (2003) include the raw data obtained in a study carried out by Forrester, Scott,

Bundy, and Golden (1990) of the heights of 144 children in a sample of 54 randomly selected households in Mexico (household was the cluster). The number of children per household ranged from one to nine, and for each of the households the researchers had an indicator of socioeconomic status (there were six levels: 3, 4, 5, 6, 7, and 8). Their interest was in estimating the mean height in the population from which the families were drawn and the percentage of "short" children (where "short" was defined to be a z score of less than –1.00 with respect to U.S. norms) in that population.

On the basis of a GEE analysis of the data for the 90 children in the 34 households of lowest socioeconomic status (levels 3, 4, and 5), it was determined that the ESS was equal to 48.3. (The estimated mean was –1.02, with a standard error of .16; the estimated percentage of "short" children was 54.2, with a standard error of 7.0.)

Forty-eight point three is a far cry from 90. Why? Just as in the hypothetical example, the within-cluster variability was considerably less than the between-cluster variability (understandably so, since some families tend to have taller children while other families tend to have shorter children). Estimates derived from children nested within families (nonindependent observations) are less precise than estimates derived from children not thus nested (independent observations), all other things being equal.

Another Real-Data Example

Rosner and Milton (1988) found an effective sample size of 130 for a sample of 100 persons for whom they had data on both eyes (eye was nested within person; cluster size = 2 for all clusters); that is, the 200 observations (one for each eye) for their study were equivalent to 130 nonnested observations, given the GEE calculation of within-eye correlation for their data.

Survey Research, Design Effect, and Effective Sample Size

Although GEEs are fairly new (most authors attribute their first appearance to Liang & Zeger, 1986), the concept of effective sample size is not. It dates at least as far back as Kish's (1965) and Cochran's (1977) classic works on multistage cluster sampling. And in their very readable article, Killip, Mahfoud, and Pearce (2004) provide the following formulas for determining ESS for a sampling design as a function of the "design effect" (DE) for k clusters and m observations within each cluster:

$$DE = 1 + \rho(m - 1)$$
$$ESS = mk/DE$$

where ρ is the intracluster (intraclass) correlation coefficient.

An Artificial Example of Effective Sample Size Using Design Effect

In his article on within-cluster, across clusters, and between-cluster correlations, Knapp (1977) included a simple numerical example for two levels of aggregation in which the correlation between two variables varied from a within-cluster value of 0 to a between-cluster value of 1. There were seven observations within each of five classrooms within each of three schools. The data for School 1 in are presented in Table 2.2.

For these data, $k = 5$, $m = 7$, $= 1/3$, $DE = 1 + 1/3(6) = 3$, and $ESS = 7(5)/3 = 11\ 2/3$ or approximately 11.67 (call it 12). The total number of observations across classrooms within School 1 = 7(5) = 35. Therefore the effective sample size is considerably less than the actual total sample size; and a confidence interval for the population correlation should be based upon an "*n*" of 12, not 35. (See Andersen, 2003, for another simple one X, one Y example.)

Comparison With UOA and HLM Approaches

The reader who is familiar with some of the UOA literature and/or the HLM literature, but is not familiar with GEEs, is probably thinking about how the nonindependence problem would be handled in either of those traditions for the examples treated here. For the artificial example just described (5 clusters, 7 observations per cluster), a UOA approach would entail the estimation of the population correlation from each cluster separately (the estimated correlation is 0 within each of the clusters) and the combination of the two estimates into one if it were determined that the estimates should be combined (they are obviously "poolable" for these data). [Cronbach (1976) argued that a cluster-level analysis might also be defensible for such data (if the clusters themselves were of greater substantive interest than the individuals who comprise them) but an individual-level analysis ignoring cluster membership is of very little interest because of the confounding of within-cluster and between-cluster effects. The classroom-level correlation between X and Y for this artificial example is .50, using the five classroom *means* for X and Y of (3, 3), (4, 5), (5, 7), (6, 4), and (7, 6).]

Table 2.2.

	Pupil ID	*X*	*Y*
Classroom 1	11	0	3
	12	1	1
	13	2	2
	14	3	6
	15	4	5
	16	5	4
	17	6	0
Classroom 2	21	1	5
	22	2	3
	23	3	4
	24	4	8
	25	5	7
	26	6	6
	27	7	2
Classroom 3	31	2	7
	32	3	5
	33	4	6
	34	5	10
	35	6	9
	36	7	8
	37	8	4
Classroom 4	41	3	4
	42	4	2
	43	5	3
	44	6	7
	45	7	6
	46	8	5
	47	9	1
Classroom 5	51	4	6
	52	5	4
	53	6	5
	54	7	9
	55	8	8
	56	9	7
	57	10	3

HLM advocates would undoubtedly carry out all three types of analyses (for individuals within-classroom, for individuals across classrooms, and between-classrooms), with a different interpretation for each. Specifically, they would report the results for the individual-level within-cluster estimates pooled across clusters ($r = 0$); the individual-level estimate across clusters (r = 1/6 or approximately .17); and the cluster-level estimate (r = .50).

Neither the UOA approach nor the HLM approach would specifically involve the estimation of the effective sample size (of persons), whereas that is an essential element in the GEE approach. And as Hanley et al. (2003) point out near the end of their article, GEE explicitly models within-cluster similarity rather than between-cluster variation (the latter being the focus of UOA and HLM approaches) and in the process produces more accurate standard errors and confidence intervals with correct coverages.

Longitudinal Research

GEEs can be and have been used in longitudinal research (the original context for the Liang & Zeger, 1986 article), where the cluster is the individual person and the observations across time are nested within person. They are particularly helpful when there are missing data, resulting in varying numbers of observations per cluster.

A Caution

There is an excellent article by Russell Lenth titled "Some Practical Guidelines For Effective Sample-size Determination" (2001, pp. 187-193), but it has nothing to do with the concept of effective sample size as used in generalized estimating equations or in multistage cluster sampling.

Summary

Faced with nested data, the concerned researcher has essentially three choices:

1. Carry out a multilevel approach such as that described by Liou and Peng (2005);
2. Carry out a full-blown hierarchical linear modeling analysis; or
3. Use generalized estimating equations to produce a single estimate of the parameter of particular interest, accompanied by an estimate of the corresponding standard error.

No one of these approaches is "right" and the others "wrong." They're just different.

REFERENCES

Andersen, R. (2003, Summer). *Regression for dependent data.* [Lecture 10 of a course titled "Regression Analysis III: Advanced Methods" at the University of Michigan.] Retrieved June 1, 2005, from http:socserv.mcmaster.ca/andersen]

Burstein, L. (1980). The analysis of multilevel data in educational research and evaluation. In D. C. Berliner (Ed.), *Review of Research in Education,* (Vol. 8, pp. 158-233). Itasca, IL: Peacock.

Burton, P., Gurrin, L., & Sly, P. (1998). Extending the simple linear regression model to account for correlated responses: An introduction to generalized estimating equations and multi-level mixed modelling. *Statistics in Medicine, 17,* 1261-1291.

Cronbach, L. J. (1976, July). *Research on classrooms and schools: Formulation of questions, design, and analysis.* Paper presented at the Stanford Evaluation Consortium, Stanford University, California.

Cochran, W. G. (1977). *Sampling techniques* (3rd. ed.). New York: Wiley.

Forrester, J. E., Scott, M. E., Bundy, D. A. P., & Golden, M. H. N. (1990). Predisposition of individuals and families in Mexico to heavy infection with *Ascaris lumbricoides* and *Trichuris trichiura. Transactions of the Royal Society of Tropical Medical Hygiene, 84,* 272-276.

Goldstein, H. (1986). Multilevel mixed linear model analysis using iterative generalized least squares. *Biometrika, 73*(1), 43-56.

Hanley, J. A., Negassa, A., Edwardes, M. D. deB., & Forrester, J. E. (2003). Statistical analysis of correlated data using generalized estimating equations: An orientation. *American Journal of Epidemiology, 157*(4), 364-375. [See also the letters regarding this article by Godbold and by Zou, and Hanley's reply (*American Journal of Epidemiology, 158,* 289-290.]

Hardin, J. W., & Hilbe, J. M. (2003). *Generalized estimating equations.* Boca Raton, FL: Chapman & Hall/CRC .

Horton, N. J., & Lipsitz, S. R. (1999). Review of software to fit generalized estimating equation regression models. *American Statistician, 53,* 160-169.

Kalish, L. A., Riester, K. A., & Pocock, S. J. (2002). Accounting for non-independent observations in 2 × 2 tables, with application to correcting for family clustering in exposure-risk relationship studies. *Journal of Modern Applied Statistical Methods, 1*(2), 379-386.

Killip, S., Mahfoud, Z., & Pearce, K. (2004). What is an intracluster correlation coefficient? Crucial concepts for primary care researchers. *Annals of Family Medicine, 2,* 204-208.

Kish, L. *(1965). Survey sampling.* New York: Wiley.

Knapp, T. R. (1977). The unit-of-analysis problem in applications of simple correlation analysis to educational research. *Journal of Educational Statistics, 2,* 171-196.

Knapp, T. R. (1984). The unit of analysis and the independence of observations. *Undergraduate Mathematics and its Applications Project (UMAP) Journal, 5,* 363-388.

Lenth, R. (2001). Some practical guidelines for effective sample-size determination. *American Statistician, 55,* 187-193.

Liang, K. Y., & Zeger, S. L. (1986). Longitudinal data analysis using general linear models. *Biometrika, 73(1),* 13-22.

Liou, S-M., & Peng, C-. Y. J. (2006). The use of hierarchical ANCOVA in curriculum studies. *Journal of Modern Applied Statistical Methods, 5*(1), 230-247.

Osborne, J. W. (2000). Advantages of hierarchical linear modeling. Practical *Assessment, Research & Evaluation, 7(1).* Retrieved June 1, 2005, from www.pareonline.net

Pearson, K. (1896). Mathematical contributions to the theory of evolution, III. Regression, heredity and panmixia. *Philosophical Transactions of the Royal Society (Series A), 187,* 253-318.

Raudenbush, S. W., & Bryk, A. S. (2002). *Hierarchical linear models: Applications and data analysis methods* (2nd ed.). Newbury Park, CA: Sage.

Robinson, W. S. (1950). Ecological correlations and the behavior of individuals. *American Sociological Review, 15,* 351-357.

Rosner, B., & Milton, R.C. (1988). Significance testing for correlated binary outcome data. *Biometrics, 44,* 505-512.

Small, C. G., & Wang, J. (2003). *Numerical methods for nonlinear estimating equations.* Oxford, England: Oxford University Press.

Thorndike, E. L. (1939). On the fallacy of imputing the correlations found for groups to the individuals or smaller groups composing them. *American Journal of Psychology, 52,* 122-124.

Wu, Y. -W. B. (1995). Hierarchical linear models: A multilevel data analysis technique. *Nursing Research, 44,* 123-126.

CHAPTER 3

ADVANCES IN MISSING DATA METHODS AND IMPLICATIONS FOR EDUCATIONAL RESEARCH

Chao-Ying Joanne Peng, Michael Harwell, Show-Mann Liou, and Lee H. Ehman

Consider a scenario in which a freshly minted PhD showed off his bound dissertation to a fellow graduate student who was known among her peers to be a "number cruncher." As she leafed through the pages of the methods section, she quickly noticed that all missing data were coded zero, instead of being declared as missing. She also saw that all analyses in this dissertation, including factor analysis, multiple regression, discriminant function analyses, and so forth, were based on all data including the zeros. No one on the dissertation committee caught this mistake. In another scenario, a PhD candidate explaining the results of the data analyses to her dissertation committee noted that the choice of listwise deletion led to the removal of approximately one third of the data. Both the candidate and committee members failed to recognize the possibly devastating effects on inferences due to these missing data. Variations of these scenarios may occur more frequently in educational research than is commonly believed or acknowledged.

Real Data Analysis, pp. 31–78

Missing data in research studies are the rule rather than the exception. For example, various literatures indicate that a 20% attrition rate has been held as a benchmark for studies related to youth, school-based programs, and clinical research (Hall, 1993; Kellam, Rebok, Ialongo, & Mayer, 1994; Mason, 1999). Many reasons contribute to data missing from research projects: subject's attrition in pretest-posttest or longitudinal designs, equipment failure, unclear instructions or intrusive questions on a survey, and poor data entry and/or record keeping in archived data—the latter was shown to introduce hidden bias in the data (Dworkin, 1987). Whatever the reason(s) for missing data, the impact on quantitative research has been a great concern to methodologists.

In survey research, missing data problems are particularly acute, with substantial amounts of missing data frequently appearing (Little & Rubin, 1987). To combat these problems, investigators spend enormous time, funding, and energy to minimize incomplete data or nonresponse among respondents (Mason, 1999). Procedures have been devised by statisticians to mitigate inferential or descriptive problems caused by missing data (Dempster, Laird & Rubin, 1977; Glasser, 1964; Rubin, 1987; Schafer, 1997). The development of these principled procedures is a unique feature of the survey research literature. For the past 2 decades, the statistical properties of these procedures have been studied and disseminated, and many have been incorporated into widely accessible software since 1990 (Cool, 2000; Kim & Curry, 1977; Mason, 1999; Raymond & Roberts, 1987; Witta, 2000). Even so, an examination of articles published in 11 education journals for the past 7 years reveals that, in studies where missing data were reported and care was taken to treat missing data, an overwhelming majority used ad hoc methods, such as listwise and pairwise deletion, to handle missing data. Ad hoc methods are characterized by their failure to take into account the mechanism that led to missing data. Yet the recent APA Task Force on Statistical Inference explicitly warned against the use of these methods:

> Special issues arise in modeling when we have missing data. The two popular methods for dealing with missing data that are found in basic statistics packages—listwise and pairwise deletion of missing values—are among the worst methods available for practical applications. (Wilkinson & Task Force on Statistical Inference APA Board of Scientific Affairs, 1999, p. 598)

Newer and principled methods take into consideration conditions under which missing data occurred. In this chapter, we promote the use of three such methods, namely, two single-imputation methods and one based on multiple imputation. These methods are illustrated with a real-world data set, and the results are shown to differ from those obtained from listwise deletion. Key issues guiding the use of these methods are also discussed. Since these methods have been implemented into statistical software (e.g., SPSS® and SAS®) and should be widely available, their use by educational researchers is expected to substantially increase. Throughout our illustration and discussion, the focus is on handling cases in which partial information is missing rather than a complete lack of information.

The remainder of this chapter is divided into nine sections: (1) Problems Caused by Missing Data and Missing Data Treatments, (2) Missing Data Methods Reported in 11 Education Journals, (3) Missing Data Mechanisms, (4) Overview of Five Ad Hoc Missing Data Methods, (5) Principled Single Imputation—FIML, (6) Principled Single-Imputation—SPSS® EM, (7) Multiple Imputation—SAS® PROC MI, (8) Importance of Statistical Assumptions, and (9) Implications and Recommendations for Educational Research.

PROBLEMS CAUSED BY MISSING DATA AND MISSING DATA TREATMENTS

Why are missing data a problem? The most serious concern is that missing data can introduce bias into estimates derived from a statistical model (Becker & Powers, 2001; Becker & Walstad, 1990; Holt, 1997; Rubin, 1987). For example, it is possible that respondents with incomplete responses might have different response profiles compared to those who responded completely. Thus, the remaining sample is no longer representative of the population from which it was randomly drawn. If the researcher chose to draw conclusions based solely on those who responded, the conclusions could be biased.

Furthermore, missing data result in a loss of information and statistical power (Anderson, Basilevsky, & Hum, 1983; Kim & Curry, 1977). The elimination of subjects with missing information on one or more variables from the statistical analysis in listwise deletion decreases the error degrees of freedom (*df*) in statistical tests such as the *t*. This decrease in turn leads to reduced statistical power and larger standard errors compared to those obtained from complete random samples (Cohen & Cohen, 1983; Cool, 2000).

Similar loss of *df* and statistical power occurs with pairwise deletion, where standard deviations, correlations and covariances are calculated on the basis of available data on each variable or variable pair (Glasser, 1964; Raymond & Roberts, 1987). As a result, the sample composition differs from variable to variable, and the population to which the results are generalized is no longer clearly defined.

Another problem with missing data is that they make common statistical methods inappropriate or difficult to apply (Rubin, 1987). For example, when missing data are present in a factorial analysis of variance, the design is unbalanced. Consequently, the standard statistical analysis that is appropriate for balanced designs is no longer appropriate under this condition. Even if data are assumed to be missing in a completely random fashion, the proper analysis is complicated. Multivariate statistical methods, as they are programmed into commercial statistical software, are applicable to complete data sets by default.

Finally, valuable resources are wasted as a result of missing data. Time and funding spent on subjects who subsequently leave a study or produce missing data represents a loss (Buu, 1999; Holt, 1997). Such loss is a particular concern in longitudinal research, large-scale assessments, high-stake studies, and surveys that ask sensitive information or target respondents who are not accustomed to responding to opinions surveys (such as the first generation Hmong immigrants). Efforts to achieve higher response rates and complete profiles from respondents require researchers to allocate additional time and resources to trace cases who failed to respond or those whose responses were incomplete or unusable. These efforts may not always pay off.

MISSING DATA METHODS REPORTED IN 11 EDUCATION JOURNALS

In order to understand how educational researchers currently deal with missing data, we reviewed the quantitative studies published in 11 education journals from 1998 to 2004. The 11 journals were *American Educational Research Journal* (AERJ), *Educational Researcher* (ER), *Journal of Counseling Psychology* (JCP), *Journal of Educational Psychology* (JEP), *Journal of Research in Science Teaching* (JRST), *Journal of Special Education* (JSE), *Journal of School Psychology* (JSP), *The Modern Language Journal* (MLJ), *Research in Higher Education (RHE)*, *Journal for Research in Mathematics Education* (RME), and *Theory and Research in Social Education* (TRSE). These journals were selected because of their emphasis on research, broad coverage of research topics, relevance to subfields in education, and reputable editorial policies. We assumed that the research reported in these 11 journals reflected the mainstream topics and research methods used in educational research.

Within the review period, we identified 1,666 studies in 1,432 articles that met our criteria for quantitative research (Table 3.1). For each study, the methods, findings, and discussion sections (or their equivalents) and all summary tables reported were examined by two of the authors. Special

Table 3.1. Summary of Missing Data Methods Used in Research Published in Selected Education Journals

Journal[a]	Duration	# of Studies, N/Articles	Studies With or Without Missing Data[b]			Missing Data Method Used[c,d]							
			Complete	*Missing, n*	*Unknown*	*LD*	*PD*	*MS*	*HD*	*RE*	*EM*	*MI*	*Unknown*
AERJ	1998-1999	**29**/27	2 (7%)	**21** (72%)	6 (21%)	19 (90%)	1 (5%)	0	0	0	0	0	1 (5%)
	2000-2004	**73**/71	19 (26%)	**40** (55%)	14 (19%)	27 (67.5%)	6 (15%)	2 (5%)	0	0	1 (2.5%)	1 (2.5%)	3 (7.5%)
ER	1998-1999	**3**/3	0	**2** (67%)	1 (33%)	2 (100%)	0	0	0	0	0	0	0
	2000-2004	**3**/3	0	**2** (67%)	1 (33%)	1 (50%)	0	0	0	0	0	0	1 (50%)
JCP	1998-1999	**108**/73	40 (37%)	**41** (38%)	27 (25%)	35 (85%)	5 (12%)	0	0	0	0	0	1 (3%)
	2000-2004	**224**/186	101 (45%)	**107** (48%)	16 (7%)	83 (78%)	13 (12%)	3 (3%)	0	0	0	0	8 (7%)
JEP	1998-1999	**147**/111	47 (32%)	**71** (48%)	29 (20%)	64 (90%)	7 (10%)	0	0	0	0	0	0
	2000-2004	**409**/309	184 (45%)	**183** (45%)	42 (10%)	141 (77%)	37 (20%)	0	0	0	2 (1%)	0	3 (2%)
JRST	1998-1999	**34**/33	11 (32%)	**18** (53%)	5 (15%)	16 (89%)	0	0	0	0	0	0	2 (11%)
	2000-2004	**95**/93	37 (39%)	**47** (49%)	11 (12%)	22 (47%)	17 (36%)	0	0	0	1 (2%)	0	7 (15%)
JSE	1998-1999	**21**/21	3 (14%)	**15** (72%)	3 (14%)	13 (87%)	1 (7%)	1 (7%)	0	0	0	0	0
	2000-2004	**41**/41	11 (27%)	**26** (63%)	4 (10%)	15 (58%)	10 (38%)	0	0	0	0	0	1 (4%)
JSP	1998-1999	**29**/28	4 (14%)	**16** (55%)	9 (31%)	15 (94%)	0	0	0	0	0	0	1 (6%)
	2000-2004	**93**/89	27 (29%)	**53** (57%)	13 (14%)	39 (74%)	10 (19%)	0	0	1 (2%)	1 (2%)	0	2 (4%)
MLJ	1998-1999	**30**/30	13 (43%)	**13** (43%)	4 (13%)	12 (92%)	0	1 (8%)	0	0	0	0	0
	2000-2004	**57**/55	26 (46%)	**23** (40%)	8 (14%)	14 (61%)	4 (17%)	0	0	0	0	0	5 (22%)
RHE	1998-1999	**56**/54	7 (13%)	**28** (50%)	21 (37%)	24 (86%)	0	1 (4%)	0	1 (4%)	0	0	2 (7%)
	2000-2004	**146**/143	31 (21%)	**76** (52%)	39 (27%)	56 (74%)	13 (17%)	2 (3%)	0	2 (3%)	0	0	3 (4%)
RME	1998-1999	**23**/19	10 (44%)	**6** (26%)	7 (30%)	6 (100%)	0	0	0	0	0	0	0
	2000-2004	**29**/27	15 (52%)	**10** (34%)	4 (14%)	6 (60%)	4 (40%)	0	0	0	0	0	0
TRSE	1998-1999	**4**/4	1 (25%)	**2** (50%)	1 (25%)	2 (100%)	0	0	0	0	0	0	0
	2000-2004	**12**/12	3 (25%)	**6** (50%)	3 (25%)	5 (83%)	1 (17%)	0	0	0	0	0	0
Total		**1666**/1432	592 (36%)	**806** (48%)	268 (16%)	617 (77%)	129 (16%)	10 (1%)	0	4 (<1%)	5 (<1%)	1 (<1%)	40 (5%)

Notes: Percentages are listed in parentheses. Details about each journal articles may be obtained from the first author. [a]Journal abbreviations: AERJ: *American Educational Research Journal*; ER: *Educational Researcher*; JCP: *Journal of Counseling Psychology*; JEP: *Journal of Educational Psychology*; JRST: *Journal of Research in Science Teaching*; JSE: *Journal of Special Education*; JSP: *Journal of School Psychology*; MLJ: *The Modern Language Journal*; RHE: *Research in Higher Education*; RME: *Journal for Research in Mathematics Education*; TRSE: *Theory and Research in Social Education*. [b]Percentages in parenthesis are based on *N*. [c]Percentages in parenthesis are based on *n*. [d]Missing data method abbreviations: LD: Listwise deletion; PD: Pairwise deletion; MS: Mean substitution; HD: Hot deck; RE: Regression estimation; EM: Expectation-maximization; ML: Maximum-likelihood based; MI: Multiple imputation.

attention was given to the total sample size, the *df* of the test statistics reported, and information regarding authors' treatment of missing data. The unit of analysis was studies, not articles, as many articles presented two or more empirical studies.

Of the 1,666 studies, 592 (or 36%) did not report any missing data problem, 806 (48%) exhibited evidence of missing data, and the remaining 268 (16%) did not provide sufficient information (such as the total sample size, *df* of the statistics, means and percentages, etc.) to determine if missing data were present. Among the 806 studies that showed evidence of missing data (such as the mismatch between the sample size and error degrees of freedom), 766 (95%) explicitly or implicitly reported dealing with such a problem. Of these 766 studies, 617 (80.5%) used the listwise deletion (LD) method and 129 (16.8%) used the pairwise deletion (PD) method. The heavy reliance on listwise or pairwise deletion is probably attributable to the fact that several popular and accessible statistical software programs, such as SPSS® or SAS®, default to listwise or pairwise deletion for handling missing data

A small number of studies (20 or 2.6%) in the review used mean substitution (MS), regression estimation (RE), the EM method, or the MI method for handling missing data (Table 3.1). A breakdown of the statistics by 1999, when the APA Task Report was published, revealed that only five studies (all published in or after 2000) used the newer, more principled EM method; only one study employed the MI method. None used the other widely recommended full information maximum likelihood (FIML) method. These results suggest that educational researchers have not as yet actively applied principled missing data methods in empirical studies, and refereed journals have not yet encouraged authors to steer away from LD or PD methods.

MISSING DATA MECHANISMS

Missing data occur to varying degrees and in various patterns (Cohen & Cohen, 1983, pp. 275-299). The impact of missing data on the validity of research findings depends on the mechanisms that led to missing data, the pattern of missing data, and the proportion of data missing (Tabachnick & Fidell, 2001, p. 58). Each is discussed below.

It has been shown that the mechanism and the pattern of missing data have greater impact on research results than does the amount of data missing (Tabachnick & Fidell, 2001, p.58). However, both are critical issues a researcher must address before choosing an appropriate procedure to deal with missing data. According to Little and Rubin (1987), mechanisms that lead to missing data can be classified as: *missing completely at random, missing at random*, and *nonignorable missing*. As defined by Little and Rubin, "if the probability of a response depends on neither the observed nor the missing value that could have been collected or recorded, the missing data are *missing completely at random*" (p. 14, italics in orginal).

As an example, consider the hypothetical data comprising measurements of 10 subjects on three variables (Y, X_1, X_2) in Table 3.2A. For purposes of discussion, let us assume that Y represented posttest scores, X_1 pretest scores, and X_2 IQ scores. If the likelihood that Y is missing is unrelated to the missing value itself, nor with X_1 or X_2, either collected or missing, then Y is said to be *missing completely at random* (abbreviated as MCAR). Under the MCAR condition, missing data can be treated as a random subsample of the potentially complete data, and the missing data mechanism capturing the reasons for missing data can be ignored for sampling-based and likelihood-based inferences (Little & Rubin, 1987, p. 15).

More formally, let $\boldsymbol{Y}$ denote a data vector composed of two parts: those completely observed and those potentially missing. In other words, $\boldsymbol{Y} = (\boldsymbol{Y}_{observed}, \boldsymbol{Y}_{missing})$. If the probability of $\boldsymbol{Y}$ being missing does not depend on the missing value itself, but does depend on observed values of $\boldsymbol{Y}$ or other completely observed variables ($\boldsymbol{X}$'s), then missing data are said to be *missing at random*. The *missing at random* (abbreviated as MAR) assumption states that

$$\text{Probability } (\boldsymbol{Y}_{missing} \mid \boldsymbol{Y}, X_j, j = 1 \text{ to } k) =$$
$$\text{Probability } (\boldsymbol{Y}_{missing} \mid \boldsymbol{Y}_{observed}, X_j, j=1 \text{ to } k). \quad (1)$$

Equation 1 implies that the conditional probability of $\boldsymbol{Y}$ being missing, given both $\boldsymbol{Y}$ and X_j is the same as the conditional probability of missing

Table 3.2A. Hypothetical Data of 10 Subjects on Three Variables

Subject	Y *(Posttest)*	X_1 *(Pretest)*	X_2 *(IQ)*
31	22	17	107
32	24	20	100
33		22	110
34	25	11	104
35	24	15	99
36		18	118
37	31	27	122
38	26	25	115
39			90
10	23	19	112

Table 3.2B. Monotone Pattern of the Hypothetical Data of 10 Subjects on Three Variables

Subject	Y (*Posttest*)	X_1 (*Pretest*)	X_2 (*IQ*)
1	22	17	107
2	24	20	100
4	25	11	104
5	24	15	99
7	31	27	122
8	26	25	115
10	23	19	112
3		22	110
6		18	118
9			90

values on Y, given observed values of Y and completely observed variables X_j. Put another way, MAR means that the distributions of $\boldsymbol{Y}_{\text{missing}}$ and $\boldsymbol{Y}_{\text{observed}}$ are the same conditional on a set of predictors X_j. Using the hypothetical data in Table 3.2A, MAR means that any student's missing score on Y (the posttest) could be related to X_1 (pretest) or X_2 (IQ) but not to the missing Y score that could have been collected.

MAR is less restrictive than MCAR; thus, MCAR is said to be a special case of MAR. Under the condition of MAR, the missing mechanism is *ignorable* for likelihood-based inferences (Little & Rubin, 1987, p.15). According to Allison (2001, p. 5):

> The missing data mechanism is said to be ignorable if (a) the data are MAR and (b) the parameters that govern the missing data process are unrelated to the parameters to be estimated. Ignorability basically means that there is no need to model the missing data mechanism as part of the estimation process. However, special techniques certainly are needed to utilize the data in an efficient manner. Because it is hard to imagine real-world applications where condition (b) is not satisfied, I [i.e., Allison] treat MAR and ignorability as equivalent conditions in this book. Even in the rare situation where condition (b) is not satisfied, methods that assume ignorability work just fine, but you could do even better by modeling the missing data mechanism.

Based on this logic, MAR and ignorability will be treated as interchangeable in this paper. In contrast to missing at random, the missing data are nonignorable if the probability of missing data depends on the missing values themselves. Again, using the hypothetical data in Table 3.2A, suppose that students missed the posttest (Y) because they believed they were poorly prepared for the test and their scores were likely to be low. In this case, the missing data on *Y* would be said to be nonignorable. Unlike the ignorable case, the missing data mechanism must be specified by the researcher and incorporated into the data analysis in order to produce unbiased parameter estimates, a formidable task. Understandably, nonignorable missing data in educational research are particularly likely to occur in studies that seek to gather sensitive or personal information. Unfortunately, no statistical test exists at the present to examine if this condition is met. Pilot testing of the instrument or common sense can sometimes detect this type of missing mechanism. All missing data methods presented in this paper are applicable under either the MCAR or the MAR condition.

The condition of MCAR may be examined using Little's multivariate test, which tests whether the MCAR condition is tenable for the data (Little, Roderick, & Schenker, 1995). Whether the data are consistent with the MAR condition can be examined by a simple *t*-test of mean differences between the group with complete data and that with missing data (Diggle, Liang, & Zeger, 1994; Kim & Curry, 1977; Tabachnick & Fidell, 2001). Both approaches are illustrated with a data set at http://www.spss.com/SPSSBI/SPSS/mva/. Schafer and Graham (2002) criticized the practice of creating a dummy-coded variable that indicates whether a value is present or missing because it redefines the parameters of the population. We caution readers that the results of these tests cannot be interpreted as providing definitive evidence of either MCAR or MAR.

If the pattern of missing data is monotone, then the estimation of parameters in a multivariate distribution can be simplified. A monotone missing data pattern is illustrated in Table 3.2B in which missing data are progressively more prevalent between the pretest and the posttest. For such a monotone missing data pattern, the less restrictive MAR assumption allows for a simplification of the estimation of parameters in a joint, multivariate distribution. Let's illustrate this point with three variables in Table 3.2B. For the joint, multivariate distribution of Y, X_1, and X_2, the probability function $f(Y, X_1, X_2)$ can be expressed as a product of the marginal probability distribution of X_1 and X_2 multiplied with the conditional probability distribution of Y given X_1 and X_2, as in Equation 2:

$$f(Y, X_1, X_2) = f(X_1, X_2) f(Y \mid X_1, X_2). \tag{2}$$

By the same token, Equation 3 is also true:

$$f(X_1, X_2) = f(X_2) f(X_1 \mid X_2). \tag{3}$$

Parameters in $f(X_2)$ are estimated using the 10 subjects in Table 3.2B who had complete data on IQ (X_2). Parameters in the conditional distribution of the pretest (X_1) given IQ are estimated from 9 subjects for whom complete data are available. These results can be combined to estimate parameters in the joint distribution of X_1 and X_2 in Equation 3. By the same logic, parameters in the conditional distribution of posttest (Y) given the pretest (X_1) and IQ (X_2) are estimated from 7 subjects with complete information on all three variables. Results from this inference can be combined with results of Equation 3 to make inferences about parameters in the joint probability distribution of all variables, as in Equation 2. If the MAR assumption holds for missing data, the conditional distribution in both equations is often estimated using regression equations, such as regressing the pretest (X_1) on IQ (X_2) in Equation 3 or regressing the posttest (X_3) on both pretest and IQ, as in Equation 2. Thus, the problem of missing data is solved by replacing missing values with imputed scores derived from regression equations. More on this approach is presented in the next section, "Overview of Five Ad Hoc Missing Data Methods."

Regarding the question of how large a proportion of missing data can be tolerated by missing data methods, there are few general guidelines agreed on by statisticians at present. If the percentage of missing values in a random pattern from a large data set (i.e., the MCAR condition holds) is large, for example 20% or higher, there is fairly wide agreement that the problem can be very serious (Cohen & Cohen, 1983; Cool, 2000; Downey & King, 1998; Graham & Schafer, 1999; Tabachnick & Fidell, 2001). For smaller amounts of missing data, there is agreement that the problem is less serious and that different procedures for handling missing data will often produce similar findings; however, the precise cutoff of what constitutes a small amount of missing data varies across authors. For example, Downey and King (1998) used 20% as the cutoff, Brockmeier, Kromrey, and Hogarty (2002) focused on 10%, and Schafer (1997, p. 1) cited 5%. Whatever the precise cutoff, it is clear that smaller percentages of missing data are less likely to produce problems for researchers than larger percentages.

When the missing data are not MCAR, there is general agreement that some missing data methods are superior to others, but little agreement on what percentage of missing data is small enough that its effects can be ignored.

OVERVIEW OF FIVE AD HOC MISSING DATA METHODS

The history of the development of missing data methods can be divided into three periods (Schafer, 1997). In the first period, prior to 1980, most widely applied methods dealing with missing data were ad hoc. These include LD, PD, mean substitution, simple hot-deck method, and various regression-based methods. They are easy to use, yet typically produce biased results. In the second period, roughly beginning with the publication of Little and Rubin (1987), principled methods, such as the full information maximum likelihood (FIML) and the Expectation-Maximization (EM) algorithm, began to appear. These methods are generally superior to ad hoc methods in that they are statistically efficient and produce parameter estimates with acceptable standard errors. Even though these methods are model-specific and can be difficult to implement, they are viewed as breakthroughs in the history of missing data methods.

The third period in the development of missing data methods began in the late 1980s and early 1990s; it was characterized by the introduction of multiple imputation methods to overcome limitations of single imputation methods. Computer simulation studies have shown this method to be flexible and to yield smaller standard errors than those obtained by other procedures. Even though the multiple imputation method represents the latest effort by methodologists to deal with missing data, the results of the literature review presented in Table 3.1 reveal that it has not been widely adopted by educational researchers.

In this section, we review five ad hoc methods for handling missing data due to their prevalence in statistical software. These include two described earlier (i.e., listwise and pairwise deletion), along with mean substitution, simple hot-deck, and regression. The strengths and weaknesses of each method are discussed in terms of parameter estimation and hypothesis testing, along with evidence available on their performance under realistic data conditions. Most of the evidence comes from computer simulation studies in which data are simulated according to properties specified by researchers, for example, normally-distributed data for a regression model in which particular percentages of values are missing under MCAR or MAR. Different methods for handling missing data are subsequently applied to the simulated data and various statistical indices computed. The difference between these values and known parameter values is recorded and represents bias in estimating parameters. Typically, this process is repeated many times and the bias resulted from the missing data methods studied is averaged. A summary of the features, strengths, and weaknesses of all methods is given in Table 3.3.

Listwise Deletion (LD)

As noted earlier, LD removes subjects that have missing information on one or more variables from the statistical analysis. As Kim and Curry (1977) show, 59% of the data can be lost using LD if only 10% of the data

Table 3.3. Comparison of Eight Methods for Handling Missing Data

Method	*Ad Hoc Methods*					*Principled Methods*		
	LD (Listwise Deletion)	*PD (Pairwise Deletion)*	*MS (Mean Substitution)*	*HD (Simple Hot-Deck)*	*RE (Regression Estimation)*	*FIML (Full Information Maximum Likelihood)*	*SPSS' EM (EM = Expectation-Maximization)*	*MI (Multiple Imputation)*
Features	• Discards cases with a missing value • Uses the remaining data to compute results • A default option in most statistical packages • Valid only when data are missing completely at random	• Cases with nonmissing values are used to compute means and variances • Pairs of cases with nonmissing values are used to compute correlations and covariances • Valid only when data are missing completely at random	• Missing values are substituted by means or subgroup means • Statistical analyses are based on the entire data set • Valid when data are missing completely at random	• Missing values are replaced by randomly drawn data already collected in the data set • Complete data for statistical analyses • Valid when data are missing completely at random	• Missing values are replaced from predicted values in a regression equation • The regression equation is formed from observations with complete data • Regression model is specified by researchers • Valid when data are missing at random	• Available data for each subject used to compute a likelihood and to estimate parameters • Requires specification of an imputation model containing variables believed to be predictive of missingness • Subject likelihoods are summed and maximum likelihood is used to obtain parameter estimates for the summed likelihood	• Each iteration consists of two steps: an E-step followed by an M-step • Iteratively computes maximum likelihood estimates for parameters • Iterations continue until the observed log-likelihoods produced in two consecutive iterations are almost identical • Valid when data are missing at random	• Consists of three steps: imputation, analysis and pooling • Takes into account the uncertainty multiple imputations • Solves the missing data problem at the beginning of the analysis • Valid when data are missing at random

						• Valid when data are multivariate-normal and missing data are missing at random		
Strength	• Easy	• Easy	• Easy	• Easy • Does not distort the marginal distribution	• Easy	• In AMOS • Efficient • Makes use of all available data • Produces unbiased parameter estimates	• In SPSS MVA • Efficient	• Efficient • Flexible • Programs available from http://www.stat.psu.edu/~jls/ or • SAS version 9 or later
Weakness	• Loss of information • Biased • Inefficient	• Loss of information • Varied sample sizes • Inefficient	• Biased • Inefficient	• Distorts correlations and covariances • Inefficient	• Biased • Inefficient	• Model specific or dependent • Failure to specify a reasonable imputation model or to satisfy multivariate-normality can bias estimates	• Time-consuming • Model specific or dependent	• Need to specify an imputation model as well as an analysis model • The third stage—pooling is for parameter estimates and standard errors

were eliminated randomly from each variable in a data set with five variables.

LD is the easiest and most common method for handling missing data. It was used in 77% of the studies published in 11 education journals between 1998 and 2004. This popularity is in large part due to the use of LD as the default setting for multivariate and several univariate statistical procedures in popular statistical packages such as SPSS®, SYSTAT®, and SAS®.

As long as the MCAR assumption holds for missing data, Allison (2001, p. 84) asserted that

> among conventional methods for handling missing data, listwise deletion is the least problematic. Although listwise deletion may discard a substantial fraction of the data, there is no reason to expect bias unless the data are not missing completely at random. In addition, the standard errors also should be decent estimates of the true standard errors. Furthermore, if you are estimating a linear regression model, listwise deletion is quite robust to situations where there are missing data on an independent variable and the probability of missingness depends on the value of that variable. If you are estimating a logistic regression model, listwise deletion can tolerate either nonrandom missingness on the dependent variable or nonrandom missingness on the independent variables (but not both).

In other words, under MCAR, LD does not generally produce biased estimates and standard statistical procedures are applicable to the remaining data. This result is supported by several computer simulation studies (Brown, 1994; Buck, 1960; Enders, 2001; Raymond & Roberts, 1987; Roth & Switzer, 1995; Wothke, 2000). Still, the reduction in statistical power and precision of estimation typically associated with LD should not be overlooked, nor can they be compensated. An interesting but as yet unexplained finding in this literature is the evidence that LD can be safely used if the correlations among four or fewer variables are low to average and only a small proportion of missing values are present (Buck, 1960; Haitovsky, 1968; Timm, 1970).

If the missing data are MAR, the results of several computer simulation studies indicate that LD typically produces biased parameter estimates and potentially biased statistical tests because results are unrepresentative of the population sampled. Graham and Schafer (2002) reported bias results for a small study in which bivariate normally-distributed data for $n = 50$ cases were simulated. Using real data for guidance, these authors removed 73% of the cases in such a way so as to produce MAR, computed various statistics such as the sample mean, standard deviation, and correlation coefficient, and, in comparing these statistics to known values of the parameters, found substantial bias. Muthen, Kaplan, and Hollis

(1987) examined the impact of LD for data for a structural equation model and reported that, under normality, this missing data method produced biased parameter estimates when MCAR was violated.

Enders and Bandalos (2001) also reported biased parameter estimates using LD, when MCAR did not hold, and simulated data from normal distributions for a structural equation model. Furthermore, the bias increased as the percentage of missing data increased from 2% to 15%. Wothke (2000) reported similar results for growth models using normally-distributed data with large amounts of missing data (80%). Enders (2001) simulated nonnormal data for a structural equation model when MCAR did not hold and found substantial bias in parameter estimates under LD; the bias increased as the percentage of missing data increased from 5% to 25%. Little (1988) simulated normal and nonnormal data with 22% missing, and reported that LD produced biased estimates under MAR. Brockmeier et al. (2002) simulated normally-distributed nonignorable missing data, and reported that LD produced estimates whose bias tended to increase somewhat as the percentage of missing data increased from 10% to 60%.

These results reinforce the conclusion of Wilkinson and The APA Task Force on Statistical Inference (1999) that LD is in general not a satisfactory solution to the missing data problem.

Pairwise Deletion (PD)

PD retains all available data provided by a subject. If this approach is applied to data analysis, descriptive statistics and a few inferential statistics (*t*-, *z*-, and chi-square, etc.) are computed from nonmissing data on each variable (Glasser, 1964; Raymond & Robert, 1987). It is the default setting in SPSS®, SYSTAT®, and SAS® for descriptive, correlation, and regression analysis using either correlation or covariance matrices. Though PD is as easy as LD, it is not as widely used as LD. Approximately 16.8% of the studies we reviewed used PD. According to Kim and Curry (1977), PD is most attractive when there is a small number of missing cases on each variable relative to the total sample size, and a large number of variables are involved.

Compared with LD, the PD approach utilizes information obtained from partially complete observations. Its disadvantage is that the sample data change from variable to variable, creating practical problems such as the determination of sample size and degrees of freedom. It is especially problematic for multivariate statistical analyses where solutions and intermediate computations are often based on the entire raw data matrix (Rubin, 1987). Cool (2000, p.7) states "When correlations and other statistics are based on different but overlapping subsamples of a larger sample, the population to which generalization is sought is no longer clear. It is possible to compute correlation matrices with mutually inconsistent correlations." Because of this problem, sample correlation or covariance matrices may not be Gramian (or semipositive definite) (Malhotra, 1987), meaning that solutions obtained from factor analysis, structural equation modeling, or other correlation/covariance based modeling or maximum-likelihood based estimation methods are not valid (Little & Rubin, 1987).

Available evidence of the effects of PD on parameter estimation are more mixed than those for LD. Haitovsky (1968) performed a computer simulation study for a linear regression model for normally-distributed data under MCAR and reported that PD was an acceptable method for handling missing data even when the percentage of missing data was quite large (90%), as long as the correlations among variables were generally low. Arbuckle (1996), Enders (1999, 2001), Enders and Bandalos (2001), Marsh (1998), and Roth and Switzer (1995) reported that PD produced relatively little bias in estimating parameters under MCAR. However, Kaplan (1995) reported that PD produced positively biased chi-square goodness-of-fit tests for normally-distributed data under MCAR. Brown (1994) also reported that PD produced biased estimates under MCAR.

Computer simulation studies by Wothke (2000), Muthen et al. (1987), and Arbuckle (1996) in structural equation modeling reported biased parameter estimates under PD when MCAR did not hold. The results of Enders (2001) for a structural equation modeling problem showed that, when MCAR did not hold, some of the estimated path coefficients were biased under PD for nonormally-distributed data. Furthermore, the bias increased as the percentage of missing data increased. Switzer, Roth, and Switzer (1998) found similar patterns of bias for PD regardless of whether missing data were MCAR or MAR for a regression model with normally-distributed data and 10% or 20% missing data. Little (1988) reported that PD produced biased estimates under MAR. Brockmeier et al. (2002) reported that for nonignorable missing data, PD produced estimates whose bias tended to increase noticeably as the percentage of missing data increased from 10% to 60%.

These results indicated that PD cannot be counted on to produce unbiased estimates under MCAR. PD may produce biased parameter estimates, a problem that appears to worsen as the percentage of missing data increases. In conjunction with the effects of using different samples of data in the same analysis, PD is not a satisfactory solution to the missing data problem (Wilkinson & Task Force on Statistical Inference, 1999).

Mean Substitution (MS)

The MS approach "solves" the missing data problem by replacing the missing values with the mean of the variable (Wilks, 1932). This step is accomplished at the onset of data analysis. It therefore assumes that the mean of the variable is the best estimate for any observation that has missing information on that variable. In contrast to LD and PD, the MS method does not alter the sample mean of the variable and does not discard any information already collected. Although MS is available in some software programs (e.g., SPSS®), only 1.2% of the studies we surveyed used this method to treat the missing data problem.

A variation of MS is to impute the missing value with a subgroup mean. For example, if the observation with a missing value is a Republican, the mean for all Republicans is computed and inserted in place of the missing value. This procedure is not as conservative as inserting the overall mean of the variable (Tabachnick & Fidell, 2001).

Regardless of which version of MS is applied, this method has many statistical pitfalls. According to Little and Rubin (1987), the limitations include: (a) sample size is overestimated, (b) variance is underestimated, (c) correlations are negatively biased, and (d) the distribution of new values is an incorrect representation of the population values because the shape of the distribution is distorted by adding values equal to the mean. The bias introduced into the population variance, correlation, and variable distribution depends on the amount of missing data and on the actual values that are missing. Little and Rubin's recommendation is to never use the MS method.

The theoretically known effects of MS on bias have generally been reproduced in the computer simulation literature. Although Raymond and Roberts (1987) reported less bias for MS than LD when estimating correlations for normally-distributed data under MCAR, bias increased somewhat across the amounts of missing data studied (2%, 6%, 10%). The study by Downey and King (1998) investigated how two mean substitution methods (item mean versus person mean) for missing data collected from Likert scales impacted the recovery of the data and the reliability (Cronbach's alpha) of these scales. These authors used (1) a large sample of respondents (n = 834), (b) small numbers of items (15 and 20), and (c) well-established constructs measured by two Likert-scaled instruments. Their results suggested that both methods recovered data quite well as long as the number of respondents with missed items and the number of items with missing responses were less than 20%. As this percentage increased, the person mean substitution method tended to inflate the reliability of the Likert-scaled instrument. King, Fogg, and Downey (1998) reported similar findings for samples of less than 200.

Switzer et al. (1998) found that MS performed poorly for both MCAR and MAR for normally-distributed data, and that bias tended to increase as the percentage of missing data increased from 10% to 20%. This method, as expected, also reduced variation in the data. Timm (1970) and Kim and Curry (1977) reported that MS produced more bias in estimating covariances under MCAR than did LD, and Gleason and Staelin (1975) reported that it produced more bias than PD. Kromrey and Hines (1994) and Brockmeier et al. (2002), in studies of simlated nonignorable regression data, reported that MS produced more bias than LD or PD under MCAR for a wide range of percentages of missing data (10%–60%), and reduced the variances of variables whose missing values were imputed.

Collectively these results suggest that there are virually no circumstances in which MS should be recommended.

Simple Hot-Deck (HD)

The HD method replaces each missing value with a randomly drawn value from the set of data values already collected on the same variable (Reilly, 1993). None of the studies in our review used this method to impute missing data. Parameters estimated by this method have larger variances, compared to those estimated by MS, but smaller variances than those obtained from complete data. The most serious deficiency of this method is the lack of theoretical work establishing its properties under MCAR or MAR (Roth, 1994). An empirical drawback is the distortion of correlations and covariances, as demonstrated in the results of Switzer et al. (1998), who found that the HD method produced similar bias values for MCAR and non-MCAR conditions, and that the amount of bias was noticeably greater for the larger percentage of missing data (20% versus 10%).

There is little evidence that HD is an appropriate method to deal with missing data, and a conservative course of action would be to avoid this method, especially when correlations or covariances are to be computed for the imputed data (see statements earlier regarding the same problem associated with PD; Little & Rubin, 1987).

Regression Estimation (RE)

The RE method imputes missing values with predicted values derived from a regression equation based on variables in the data set that contain no missing values (Buck, 1960). Variables with missing data are treated as criterion variables and are predicted by all of the variables having complete data. Four studies reported using this method to handle missing data; they constituted less than 1% of the studies surveyed.

If the missing data exhibit a monotone pattern, as illustrated in Table 3.2B, and are assumed to be MAR—the weaker and more realistic assumption, the RE method can be used to simplify the estimation of population parameters (see earlier comments referring to this method under "Missing Data Mechanism"). Compared to other methods already discussed, the RE method is more informative because it utilizes information already existing in a data set. The AM procedure in BMDP® applies this method to estimate missing values as well as out-of-range data points (BMDP Statistical Software, 1992, pp. 959-976).

Similar to the MS and HD methods, RE has the advantage of preserving cases with missing data and, thus, maintaining the sample size. Disadvantages of RE include: (i) a regression model needs to be specified; (ii) imputed values are always perfectly predicted from the regression model, thus, correlations and covariances are inevitably inflated; (iii) it can be difficult to apply RE to multivariate data sets when more than one variable has missing values; (iv) predicted values may exceed the logical range of scores for the missing data; (v) may require large samples to produce stable estimates (Donner, 1982); (vi) can produce leptokurtic distributions (Rovine, 1994); and (vii) if good and relevant predictors of missing data are not available in the data set, predicted values are no better than the mean. In other words, RE and MS yield approximately the same results if an effective regression model cannot be identified.

To overcome limitation (ii) discussed above, statisticians have suggested a modified RE method in which imputed values have a random error added to them (Beale & Little, 1975). The random error is randomly generated from a normal distribution with a mean of 0 and a standard deviation equal to the square root of the mean square error of the regression model (Little & Rubin, 1987). The Missing Value Analysis module in SPSS® offers users this adjustment.

As stated above, the MS, HD, and RE ad hoc methods "solve" the missing data problem by imputing missing values once, thus they are referred to as single imputation methods. The single imputation approach unfortunately does not reflect the uncertainty in missing data estimates. That is, the error term in the estimation equation, of whatever form, used to impute missing values is set to zero. Furthermore, the sample size is overstated, confidence intervals for estimated parameters are too narrow, and Type I error rates are too high (Little & Rubin, 1987).

Available empirical evidence of the performance of RE indicates that it is usually, but not always, superior to LD, PD, or MS. Buck (1960) examined its performance by starting with a real dataset of 72 samples, randomly removing 40% of the samples, and using RE to impute missing values. The bias associated with parameter estimates, compared to the values produced by the original 72 samples, was generally less than that produced by LD. Buck's study is not a simulation study in the usual sense, but his results are consistent with those produced by stimulation studies in which computer algorithms simulated data.

Chan and Dunn (1972) performed a small simulation study in discriminant analysis with normally-distributed data, and reported that RE showed approximately the same bias as LD and PD under MCAR. Beale and Little (1974) reported that RE showed less bias than LD for normally-distributed data that were simulated for a regression analysis with the percentage of missing values of 5%, 10%, 20%, or 40% under MCAR. Timm (1970) also reported RE to show less bias than LD under MCAR. Raymond and Roberts (1987) reported that RE showed less bias than either LD or MS under MCAR. Similarly, Gleason and Staelin (1975)'s study found RE to produce less bias than MS under MCAR in a simulation study in which the percentage of missing data was fixed at 20%. Switzer et al. (1998) found that MS produced similar levels of bias under the MCAR and non-MCAR conditions, and that the amount of bias was noticeably greater for 20% missing versus 10%. Brockmeier et al. (2002) reported that RE produced noticeably less bias for nonignorable data than LD, PD, or MS.

Principled Single Imputation—FIML

FIML stands for Full Information Maximum Likelihood; it represents a principled method for estimating means and covariances based on incomplete data when the missing values are assumed to be MAR. In maximum likelihood (ML), parameter estimates are derived such that the likelihood of reproducing the data, given the parameter estimates, is maximized. The FIML method for estimating parameters in the presence of data missing at random makes extensive use of ML.

FIML has its roots in the work of Hartley and Hocking (1971). Given q groups, one for each pattern of missing data, FIML first calculates the likelihood for each of the q groups or patterns. If there are no missing data, then $q = 1$. The intent of FIML is to use the information in each missing data pattern to estimate parameters. Under the assumption of a multivariate normal population distribution, the q likelihoods are summed. The resulting summed likelihood serves as the basis for finding parameter estimates using ML. FIML is conceptually similar to the q-group method of Hartley and Hocking, except that the likelihood is calculated for each case, using whatever data are available for that observation.

To illustrate how FIML estimates parameters in the presence of missing data, let's suppose that data are collected for N cases on three variables Y, X_1, and X_2, and the researcher's interest is in estimating the population means, variances, and covariances, denoted below in the vector μ and the matrix Σ:

$$\mu = [\mu_1, \mu_2, \mu_3] \tag{4}$$

$$\Sigma = \begin{pmatrix} \sigma_{11} & \sigma_{12} & \sigma_{13} \\ \sigma_{21} & \sigma_{22} & \sigma_{23} \\ \sigma_{31} & \sigma_{32} & \sigma_{33} \end{pmatrix}$$

It is further assumed that X_2 is missing for some cases. FIML computes a likelihood function for each case using variables specified by the researcher, say, in a regression equation that were observed for that case. Under the assumption of multivariate normality, the case-wise likelihood functions are summed across the entire sample and the summed likelihood is maximized. If case #1 has no data for X_2, it contributes only to the estimation of μ_1, μ_3, σ_{11}, σ_{13}, σ_{31}, and σ_{33}. After N likelihoods have been computed, they are summed and ML is used to estimate the means, variances, and covariances based on the summed likelihood. These parameter estimates are unbiased and efficient in the presence of missing data under MAR and multivariate normality assumptions.

There is far less computer simulation evidence of the performance of FIML estimators than those already summarized. What is published on FIML estimators has generally suggested that this method produces unbiased estimators under more conditions than other ad hoc methods. Arbuckle (1996) examined the bias of FIML estimates for 30% missing data in a structural equation modeling problem under the multivariate normal condition. He reported that it produced less bias than both LD and PD under MCAR or MAR. Wothke (2000) reported that FIML estimates for a latent growth curve model were unbiased for both MCAR and MAR conditions, while LD and PD produced biased estimates under MAR. Enders (1999) also reported that FIML produced unbiased estimates under both MCAR and MAR for several missing data percentages (2%, 5%, 10%, 15%, 25%) in a structural equation modeling problem for normally-distributed data.

In sum, the missing data literature provides substantial guidance for choosing an appropriate method to handle missing data. In the unlikely case that the missing data are MCAR, the LD, RE, and FIML estimators generally produce unbiased estimates, although large amounts of missing data (e.g., 60%) may require large sample sizes for unbiased estimation, for example, 500 (Arbuckle, 1996). As always, the use of LD to produce unbiased estimates under MCAR must be weighed against the potentially negative consequences of reduced statistical power and precision. Under the MAR condition, RE appears to be superior to LD or PD, and research results published so far suggest that FIML is superior to RE. This conclusion appears to hold across varying amounts of missing data.

ILLUSTRATION OF FIML USING THE AMOS SOFTWARE

In this section, we illustrate how different methods of handling missing data, FIML versus LD, can yield different parameter estimates and, potentially, different inferences. To illustrate these effects, we used a data set from 1,302 U.S. colleges and universities for the 1993-1994 school year.

Data Set

The data set was provided by U.S. News & World Report and is available at http://portfolio.iu.edu/peng/articles/persist.sav. For this data set, hereafter referred to as the *Persist* data, we were interested in modeling variability in student persistence, as measured by graduation rates, as a function of college-related predictors, such as tuition and institutional quality. Because the cases were colleges and universities, each institution's graduation rate (*GRADRATE*), in percentages, was the unit of analysis and served as a proxy for student persistence.

Three latent variables, often described in the literature as predictors of student persistence, appeared in the path model: student's ability, quality of institutions, and costs. These were manifested in financial cost (room and board or *RMBRD*), additional student fees (*ADDFEES*), in-state tuition (*INSTATE*), cost of books (*BOOKCOST*), selectivity (or quality) of the institution (*SELECT*), percent of faculty with PhD's (*PCTPHD*), student to faculty ratio (*STUDFACT*), percent of full time students (*PCTFULL*), expenditure per student (*PERSPEND*), and student quality and preparedness, measured by the average SAT Math and Verbal scores (*AVESAT*). The amount of missing data for these variables ranged from 0.2% to 40.3%, with the percentage of missing data for graduation rate (*GRADRATE*) equal to 7.5%. All variables thought to contribute to the missingness were included in FIML, even if some of them were not included in subsequent analyses (Schafer, 1997).

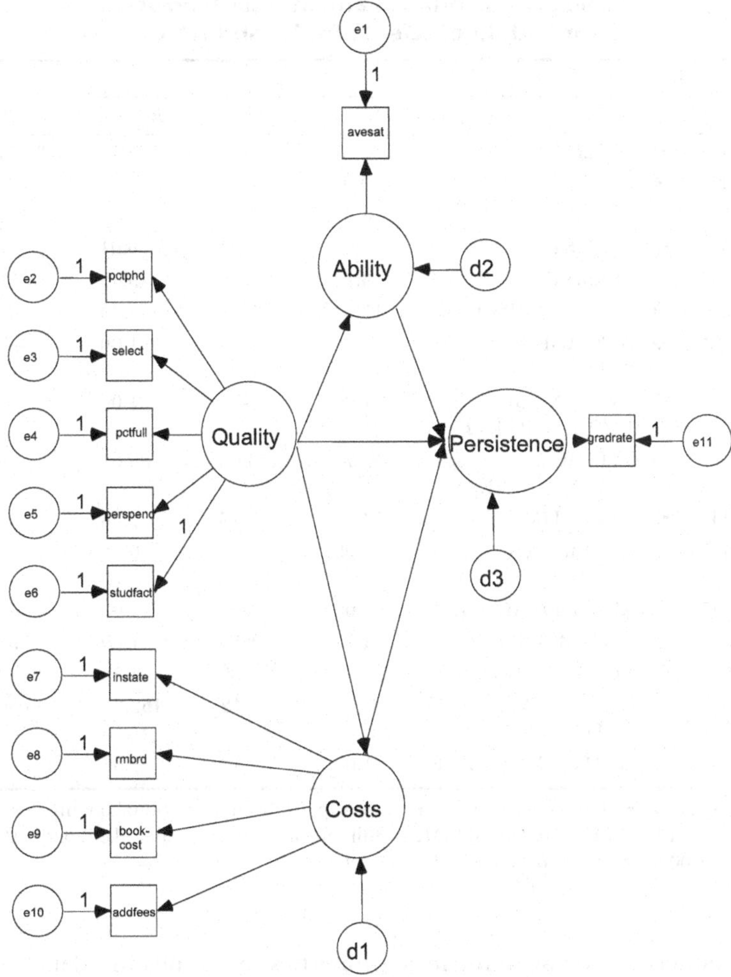

Figure 3.1. Path model fitted to graduation data.

Statistical Modeling

The AMOS software (Arbuckle, 1995) was used to fit the path model in Figure 3.1 to the Persist data. Both FIML and LD methods were used to handle missing data. For each method, we examined its effect on model conclusions based on estimated path coefficients and their standard errors. We did not attempt to find the best-fitting model under each method for two reasons: first, the best model might be different; second, different best models might be attributable to the vagaries of finding

Table 3.4. Estimates and Standard Errors for Path Coefficients for LD and FIML

Missing Data Method			*LD*		*FIML*	
		Paths	*Estimate*	*SE*	*Estimate*	*SE*
QUALITY	→	ABILITY	88.87	15.36	155.78	33.71
QUALITY	→	COSTS	10.05	8.20	14.99	8.97
COSTS	→	PERSIST	–1.44	1.39	–0.57	0.32
ABILITY	→	PERSIST	0.06	0.01	0.01	0.009
QUALITY	→	PERSIST	3.43	1.09	–3.48	1.23
QUALITY	→	%FACULTY PhD	15.94	3.26	18.43	3.49
ABILITY	→	AVERAGE TOTAL SAT	1.00	—	1.00	—
QUALITY	→	STUDENT to FACULTY RATIO	1.00	—	1.00	—
QUALITY	→	AVERAGE EXPENDITURE	13.71	23.68	83.61	33.29
QUALITY	→	%FULLTIME	13.97	3.18	22.38	4.27
QUALITY	→	No. Admitted /No. Applied	0.06	0.01	–0.14	0.04
QUALITY	→	ADDITIONAL FEES	1.00	—	1.00	—
COSTS	→	COST BOOKS	2.17	1.55	1.69	0.99
COSTS	→	ROOM and BOARD	96.34	42.66	44.52	25.22
COSTS	→	OUT of STATE TUITION	38.2	76.12	152.83	86.56
PERSIST	→	GRADUATION RATE	1.00	—	1.00	—

Notes: Quality → Ability reflects the direct effect (path) from institutional quality to student ability; LD = listwise deletion, FIML = full information maximum likelihood; estimates of 1.00 were specified as part of the model.

these models as well as to intrinsic properties of the missing data methods. Because of these reasons, the path model was fit once by each method to the data. Table 3.4 presents the estimates and standard errors of the path coefficients using both FIML and LD.

COMPARISON OF AMOS FIML RESULTS WITH THE LD RESULTS

The results in Table 3.4 show several differences in the estimated path coefficients and their standard errors as a function of the missing data method used. FIML produced larger estimated path coefficients for eight out of twelve paths. The size of the standard errors for the two methods was equally divided, with FIML standard errors larger than LD-based values in six out of twelve paths. In two paths, the signs were reversed between the FIML- and the LD-estimated coefficients. For example, the estimated path coefficient of QUALITY on student's graduation rate (*GRADRATE*) using FIML was –3.48, whereas the LD-based coefficient was 3.43. The FIML coefficient (–3.48) means that an increase in institutional quality was associated with a decrease in student graduation rates, with other effects (or paths) held constant. The LD coefficient (3.43) suggested that increasing institutional quality was associated with higher student graduation rates. These results provide empirical evidence that the choice of method for handling missing data can substantially affect inferences.

COMMENTS ON FIML

Though FIML has been implemented in the AMOS software (Arbuckle, 1999), the study of FIML, as suggested above, has been primarily in structural equation modeling. Results from these studies indicate that, as expected, parameters estimated using FIML are unbiased and efficient when the data are multivariate-normal and the MAR assumption holds. However, failure to satisfy the multivariate normality assumption can dramatically bias FIML estimates (Enders, 2001).

Another drawback of FIML is that tests of goodness-of-fit are not always available. For example, in regression modeling with missing data on the dependent variable *Y*, the estimates of regression coefficients are unbiased and efficient under the assumption of MAR and normality. However, a test of the overall model fit to data is not possible because there is no value of *N* applicable to the entire sample. Similar problems with FIML emerge in structural equation modeling in which the goodness-of-fit test and several commonly prescribed measures of fit are not available. Another potential problem is that the covariance matrix may be indefinite, which can lead to significant parameter estimation difficulties, although these problems are often modest (Wothke, 2000).

A practical issue with using FIML in the presence of missing data is that variables believed to be predictive of missingness must be in the regression or structural equation model, even when these variables are not of substantive interest. In some instances, the presence of such variables may have an important impact on variables of substantive interest in the model.

PRINCIPLED SINGLE IMPUTATION—SPSS® EM

EM stands for Expectation-Maximization; it is a principled method for handling missing data. Dempster, Laird, and Rubin in their seminal paper on this method coined the term EM (1977). According to Little and Rubin (1987),

> The EM algorithm formalizes a relatively old ad hoc idea for handling missing data: (1) replace missing values by estimated values, (2) estimate parameters, (3) re-estimate the missing values assuming the new parameter estimates are correct, (4) re-estimate parameters, and so forth, iterating until convergence. (p. 129)

Each iteration of the EM algorithm consists of two steps: an E (Expectation) step followed by an M (Maximization) step. In the E step, the expectation of the complete data log-likelihood is derived, given the observed data and the estimated parameters from a previous iteration. In the M step, the conditional expectation of the complete data log-likelihood is maximized. The observed data log-likelihood is increased until a stationary point is reached (Dempster et al., 1977). In other words, the algorithm continues until the observed likelihoods produced in two consecutive iterations are almost identical. Only five studies (less than 1%) we reviewed used the EM method to treat missing data problem.

The Missing Value Analysis (MVA) module available in SPSS® version 10 and beyond implements the EM algorithm indirectly as a single imputation method. First, it employs the EM algorithm to derive ML estimates of parameters based on a researcher's specification of a probability model for the data (e.g., multivariate-normal). Operationally, this involves using a series of regressions for each missing data pattern similar to Buck's RE method (Buck, 1960).

After the EM algorithm converges, MVA computes imputed values for missing data based on means and covariances estimated from the last iteration of the EM algorithm. The imputed values replace missing data to yield a complete data set, which is subsequently analyzed by the statistical method(s) of a researcher's choice. We consider the EM algorithm used in MVA to be a principled, single-imputation method for handling missing data.

Empirical evidence available thus far on the EM approach suggests that it performs well under a variety of conditions. Beale and Little (1975) reported that, for normally-distributed data, the EM approach showed bias similar to that produced by LD and RE; the bias was not affected by the amount of missing data (19%, 20%, 40%) under MCAR. Donner and Rosner (1982) simulated normally-distributed data for a regression model under MCAR. Their results revealed that parameter estimates obtained with EM showed less bias than those with LD, PD, or RE. Raymond and Roberts (1987) reported results similar to those of Donner and Rosner. Little (1988) showed that, under MAR, the EM approach yielded less bias in estimating means, correlations, and regression coefficients, but produced biased standard deviations. Brockmeier et al. (2002) reported that, for nonignorable data, the EM approach produced estimates with noticeably less bias than LD, PD, or MS, but about the same amount of bias as RE.

On the other hand, Basilevsky, Sabourin, Hum, and Anderson (1985) reported that the EM approach produced biased estimates similar in magnitude to those obtained with LD and PD. In general, though, the literature suggests that the EM approach is superior to ad hoc methods across different amounts of missing data.

ILLUSTRATION OF SPSS® EM METHOD

In this section, we describe how the SPSS® EM Method was applied to impute values for missing data for a multivariate data set. This was followed by fitting a logistic regression model to help predict adolescent's behavioral risk. Results are presented in terms of regression coefficient estimates and standard errors.

Data Set

Self-reported health behavior data were collected from 517 adolescents enrolled in two junior high schools (Grades 7 through 9) in the fall of 1988. On the day of data collection, two questionnaires were administered: the Health Behavior Questionnaire (HBQ) (Ingersoll & Orr, 1989; Resnick, Harris, & Blum, 1993) and Rosenberg's self-esteem inventory (Rosenberg, 1965). Among the 517 students, 85 did not complete all questions. Thus, the sample size with complete information was 432 (83.4% were Whites and the remaining Blacks or others), with a mean age of 13.9 years and nearly even numbers of girls (n = 208) and boys (n = 224).

The HBQ asked adolescents to indicate whether they engaged in specific risky health behaviors (Behavioral Risk Scale) or had experienced selected emotions (Emotional Risk Scale). The response scale ranged from 1 (*never*) to 4 (*about once a week*) for both scales. Cronbach's alpha reliability was 0.84 for the Behavioral Risk Scale and 0.81 for the Emotional Risk Scale (Peng & Nichols, 2003). Adolescents' self-esteem was assessed using Rosenberg's self-esteem inventory (Rosenberg, 1965). Self-esteem scores ranged from 9.79 to 73.87 with a mean of 49.97 and standard deviation of 10.09. Furthermore, among the 432 adolescents, 12.27% (or 53) indicated an intention to drop out of school; 44.68% (or 193) were from intact families, 22.69% (or 98) were from families with one step-parent, and 32.63% (or 141) were from families headed by a single parent. The data set is hereafter referred to as the *Adolescent* data [available from http://portfolio.iu.edu/peng/articles/logregdata(peng).sav as an SPSS® data file or from http://portfolio.iu.edu/peng/articles/logregdata.por as a portable data file].

Research Question and Statistical Modeling

For the Adolescent data, we were interested in identifying adolescents at the greatest behavioral risk from their gender, intention to drop out from school, family characteristics, emotional risks, and self-esteem scores. Given this objective, the research hypothesis was stated as follows: "The likelihood that an adolescent is at high behavioral risk is related to his/her gender, intention to drop out of school, family structure, emotional risk, and self-esteem." Scores on the Behavioral Risk Scale of the HBQ ranged from 40.44 to 95.21 with a mean of 47.23 and a standard deviation of 8.40, and it was decided that adolescents scoring 52 or above (i.e., more than a half of SD above the mean) were identified as being at high behavioral risk, and those with scores below 52 were not at high risk.

A logistic regression model was fit to the data using adolescents' risk level on the Behavioral Risk Scale of the HBQ as the dependent variable and gender, intention to drop out of school, type of family structure, emotional risk, and self-esteem score as covariates or the explanatory variables.

SPSS® EM Method for Imputing Missing Data

As stated earlier, out of the 517 students, 85 did not complete all questions. Most missing data occurred on Behavioral Risk Scale (77 cases) or Emotional Risk Scale (34 cases); only six adolescents did not indicate if they intended to drop out from school. To impute values for missing data, the entire data set was submitted to the MVA module in SPSS® version 11.01. The imputation model specified included gender, intention to drop from school, behavioral risk score, emotional risk score, self-esteem score, family configuration (intact family, step family, or single parent family), and living arrangement (living with both parents, father alone, mother alone, neither, father and step-mother, or mother and step-father). These variables were predictive of the missingness for the Adolescent data (Peng & Nichols, 2003).

Once the imputation model was defined in MVA and the EM estimation method was selected, we further specified a multivariate normal distribution for all variables selected and 50 iterations for the EM iteration. The result was a complete data set with missing data replaced by imputed values obtained from the last iteration of the EM algorithm. This complete data set was subsequently analyzed by the logistic regression procedure in SAS® version 8.2.

Analysis Results

Using the criterion of 52 points on the Behavioral Risk Scale of the HBQ, 102 adolescents were identified to be at high behavioral risk while 415 were not. To entertain the research hypothesis that "the likelihood that an adolescent is at high behavioral risk is related to his/her gender, intention to drop out of school, family structure, emotional risk, and self-esteem," a logistic regression model was fit to the data that yielded the following result:

$$\text{Predicted logit } (Y = \text{high behavioral RISK}) = -1.6120 + (1.1014) * \text{GENDER} + (2.5369) * \text{DROPOUT} + (0.4084) * \text{FAMILY} + (0.00809) * \text{EMOTION} + (-0.0443) * \text{ESTEEM}. \quad (5)$$

According to this model, the log of the odds of an adolescent being at high behavioral risk was positively related to gender ($p < .0001$, Table 3.5), intention to drop out of school ($p < .0001$), and family structure ($p < .01$); it was negatively related to self-esteem ($p < .01$), and insignificantly related to emotional risk ($p = 0.5405$). The effectiveness of Equation 5 in explaining the data was examined using (a) overall model evaluations, (b) statistical tests of each covariate, (c) goodness-of-fit statistics, and (d) measures of association. These indices were recommended in the literature for evaluating logistic regression results (Peng, Lee, & Ingersoll, 2002; Peng, So, Stage, & St. John, 2002); and they are presented in Table 3.5.

COMPARISON OF SPSS® EM RESULTS WITH THE LD RESULTS

The same logistic regression model was fitted to 432 cases with complete data. This approach was equivalent to treating the missing data with listwise deletion. Results are presented in Table 3.6. According to Table 3.6, the LD approach led to the following logistic model:

Table 3.5. Logistic Regression Analysis of Adolescent's Self-inflicting Behavior Risk by SAS® PROC LOGISTIC (version 8.2), n = 517

Predictor	β	*SE* β	*Wald's* χ^2 *(df=1)*	p	e^{β} *(Odds Ratio)*
CONSTANT	–1.6120	1.3165	1.4991	.2208	Not necessary
GENDER (boys = 1,girls = 0)	1.1014	0.2777	15.7291	<.0001	3.0083
DROPOUT (yes = 1, no = 0)	2.5369	0.3221	62.0297	<.0001	12.6404
FAMILY	0.4084	0.1505	7.3601	.0067	1.5044
EMOTION	0.0081	0.0143	0.3198	.5717	1.0081
ESTEEM	–0.044	0.0155	8.1678	.0vb043	0.9570

Overall Model Evaluation

Tests	χ^2	*df*	p
Likelihood Ratio Test	122.04	5	<.0001
Score Test	135.07	5	<.0001
Wald Test	88.03	5	<.0001
Hosmer & Lemeshow Goodness-of-fit Test	5.54	8	.6865

Notes: Cox and Snell R^2 = 0.2124. Nagelkerke R^2 (Max rescaled R^2) = 0.3361. Kendall's Tau-a = 0.200. Goodman-Kruskal's Gamma = 0.627.
Somers' D_{xy} = 0.625. c-statistic = 0.813.

Predicted logit (Y = high behavioral RISK) = –1.6341 + (1.0470)*GENDER + (2.0772) * DROPOUT + (0.4628) * FAMILY + (0.0065) * EMOTION + (–0.040) * ESTEEM. (6)

According to Equation 6, the log of the odds of an adolescent being at high behavioral risk was positively related to gender (p < .0002, Table 3.6), intention to drop out of school (p < .0001), and family structure (p < .003); it was negatively related to self-esteem (p < .02), and was not related to emotional risk (p = .6459). Essentially, Equation 6 uncovered the same relationship as Equation 5 did between the likelihood of high behavioral risk and the five covariates. The standard errors of the estimated regression coefficients in Tables 3.5 and 3.6 were virtually identical.

However, there were noticeable differences between these two results. First, the Wald's chi-square test of the *ESTEEM* coefficient was significant at an alpha level of 0.01 in Table 3.5 yet it was significant at an alpha level of 0.05 in Table 3.6. Second, the measures of association shown at the bot-

Table 3.6. Logistic Regression Analysis of Adolescent's Self-Inflicting Behavior Risk by SAS® PROC LOGISTIC (version 8.2), n = 432

Predictor	β	*SE* β	*Wald's* χ^2 *(df = 1)*	*p*	e^{β} *(Odds Ratio)*
CONSTANT	–1.6341	1.3001	1.5797	.2088	Not necessary
GENDER (boys = 1, girls = 0)	1.0470	0.2818	13.8058	.0002	2.8491
DROPOUT (yes=1, no=0)	2.0772	0.3368	38.0385	<.0001	7.9821
FAMILY	0.4628	0.1546	8.9597	.0028	1.0648
EMOTION	0.0065	0.0142	0.2111	.6459	1.0065
ESTEEM	–0.040	0.0155	6.5224	.0107	0.9608

Overall Model Evaluation

Tests	χ^2	*df*	*p*
Likelihood Ratio Test	80.89	5	<.0001
Score Test	86.24	5	<.0001
Wald Test	63.22	5	<.0001
Hosmer & Lemeshow Goodness-of-fit Test	5.23	8	.7322

Notes: Cox and Snell R^2 = 0.1708. Nagelkerke R^2 (Max rescaled R^2)=0.2675. Kendall's Tau-a = 0.189. Goodman-Kruskal's Gamma= 0.578. Somers' D_{xy}= 0.576. c-statistic = 0.788.

tom of Table 3.6 were smaller than those of Table 3.5. These differences speak to the consequences of decreasing sample size and lowering statistical power that resulted from applying the LD method.

COMMENTS ON EM AND SPSS® EM METHOD

Applications of EM-type algorithms have a long history (McLachlan & Krishnan, 1997, pp. 34-37). The popularity of the EM algorithm among statisticians is largely based on the fact that this approach allows many complex statistical problems to be reformulated as a missing data problem in a way that greatly simplifies parameter estimation (e.g., mixture models, random effects models, hierarchical linear models, unbalanced designs including repeated measures). In most applications, it is assumed that data follow a multivariate normal distribution.

In addition to taking the missing data mechanism into account, the primary advantages of the EM algorithm are simplicity and ease of computing (Dempster et al., 1977; Little & Rubin, 1987). Since fewer than 1% of the studies we reviewed reported using the EM method to handle missing data, we suspected that the low frequency of usage might be partly attributable to its drawbacks. First, the M-step of the algorithm does not produce sampling variances of the parameter estimates. Several extensions of the EM algorithm have appeared in the statistical literature that estimate standard errors (Meng & Rubin, 1992; McLachlan & Krishnan, 1997, pp. 28-29). But in general these methods have not been implemented in missing data programs such as the MVA module in SPSS®. Second, all likelihood-based methods including the EM method are iterative and model-specific (or model-dependent). Because of their dependency on specific models, these methods are not available in all statistical procedures in a general-purpose statistical package, such as the SPSS® regression or the SAS® PROC GLM. Third, the convergence rate during iterations is proportional to the percent of completely observed data in a data set (Little & Rubin, 1987, p.130). As a result, the rate of convergence can be painfully slow if the percentage of missing data is high (Buu, 1999; Little & Rubin, 1987).

Buu (1999) investigated the Type I error rate control and the precision of parameter estimation of three missing data methods: the SPSS® EM approach (i.e., MVA), the direct, one-step EM algorithm, and SAS® PROC MIXED. SAS® PROC MIXED uses either the Newton-Raphson algorithm (the default) or the Fisher scoring algorithm (when the Newton-Raphson algorithm fails to converge) to find the maximum likelihood estimates of parameters. While EM accomplishes this by iterating between the E (expectation) step and the M (maximization) step, the Newton-Raphson and the Fisher scoring algorithms do so by iteratively estimating the parameters via the computation of second derivatives of the observed data log-likelihood function (Jennrich & Schluchter, 1986; Littell, Milliken, Stroup, & Wolfinger, 1996). Buu's study was conducted in longitudinal studies using simulated and empirical data. Her results revealed that the SPSS® MVA approach rejected the null hypothesis more frequently than it should, resulting in inflated Type I error rates, though it estimated parameters accurately. These findings were obtained in repeated-measures ANOVA using both empirical data and data simulated from multivariate normal distributions. The direct, one-step EM and SAS® PROC MIXED yielded very similar and correct Type I error rates with SAS® PROC MIXED slightly outperforming the EM algorithm. Buu's study is unique in the literature as most missing data methods were evaluated in between-subjects designs rather than within-subjects or time-series studies (Roth, 1994).

MULTIPLE IMPUTATION—SAS® PROC MI

To overcome the limitations of methods that fail to take into account the uncertainty associated with imputed values, Rubin and his associates developed the multiple imputation (MI) method in the 1980s. MI is a valid method for handling missing data under the MAR condition. It is a general-purpose method, highly efficient even for small sample sizes (Graham & Schafer, 1999). Merely one study we reviewed used this method. For an introduction to MI, we recommend Schafer's 1999 paper (Schafer, 1999). MI generally consists of three steps: imputation, analysis, and pooling. In the first (imputation) step, each missing value is replaced by not one, but $m > 1$ simulated values. Imputed values are drawn from a distribution that is specified by the researcher. At the end of the imputation step, m complete data sets are created. In the second (analysis) step, each of the m complete data sets is analyzed by standard complete-data methods. Finally, results of the m analyses are integrated in the third (pooling) step to yield a final result such as an interval estimation of a population parameter, a p-value of null-hypothesis testing, or a likelihood-ratio test statistic. In the next section, we elaborate on each of these three steps applying PROC MI and PROC MIANALYZE in SAS® version 8.2 (SAS Institute, 1999) to the Adolescent data set described earlier.

Illustration of the MI Method

The research question posed to the Adolescent data set and the logistic modeling approach are described in the section titled, "Illustration of SPSS® EM Method."

Step 1—Imputation

In this step, each missing value is replaced by $m > 1$ imputed values. The model we adopted for imputation was the same logistic regression model that would be used subsequently to analyze the data, though these two models need not be identical (see the section, "Comments on the MI Method" and Schafer, 1997, pp. 139-143). The data matrix consisting of one dependent variable (the behavioral risk score) and five covariates was submitted to PROC MI in SAS® version 8.2 to impute missing data 5 times (the default). Since the missing rate for the current data was 16.44%, $m = 5$ imputations were considered sufficient (Graham & Schafer, 1999). The entire SAS® program is available from http://portfolio.iu.edu/peng/articles/lr-em.fit.sas. The syntax for PROC MI was as follows; the upper case commands are SAS® keywords and lower cases are user-specified variable names or SAS® data set names.

```
PROC MI DATA=risk SEED=37851 OUT=outmirisk ROUND=1 1 1 1 1 1;
        VAR behrisk gender dropout emotion esteem family;
```

The keyword, SEED, specifies a starting value for the random number generator whereas ROUND specifies units of rounding for imputed values. To revalidate the imputation results, a researcher can reset SEED to a different number that will result in a different set of initial estimates for parameters (i.e. regression coefficients for the Adolescent data set).

PROC MI assumes that missing data were missing at random (the MAR condition) and that the population data distribution is multivariate-normal. Both assumptions were deemed reasonable for the present data (see the section titled "Importance of Statistical Assumptions for Principled Method"son the importance of satisfying these two assumptions). At the end of the imputation, 5 data sets with $N = 517$ cases were created. Table 3.7 summarizes the increase in variability as a result of multiple imputations for the three variables that had missing data, i.e., dropout, behavioral risk, and emotional risk. The increase in variability reflected the uncertainty in the imputed values—an uncertainty not accounted for by single imputation methods. Thus, variables associated with larger amount of missing data (e.g., behavioral risk) tend to have greater uncertainty (or increase in variance) in estimated parameters than those associated with smaller amounts of missing data (e.g., dropout and emotion risk).

Step 2—Analysis

In the second (analysis) step, each of the *m* complete data sets is analyzed by a standard complete-data method, such as the logistic model prescribed for the Adolescent data. Consequently, each data set obtained from Step 1 was analyzed by PROC LOGISTIC in SAS® version 8.2 to determine if and how the likelihood that an adolescent was high at behavioral risk was related to his/her gender, intention to drop out of school, family structure, emotional risk, and self-esteem. The SAS® syntax for PROC LOGISTIC for these five data sets was as follows:

```
PROC LOGISTIC DATA=outmirisk;
    MODEL risk=gender dropout family emotion esteem/
            RSQUARE LACKFIT;
    FORMAT risk br.;
    BY _imputation_;
```

Again, the upper case commands are SAS® keywords and lower cases are user-specified variable names or SAS® data set names. The FORMAT statement applied labels (such as "high" and "low") to numerical codes (such as "1" and "2") of the dependent variable, *risk*. The BY statement applied the logistic regression modeling repeatedly to all imputed data

Table 3.7. Relative Increase in Variance and Fraction of Missing Information in the Adolescent Data Set

Variable	*Relative Increase in Variance*	*Fraction of Missing Information*
Dropout	0.0270	0.0267
Behavioral Risk	0.3195	0.2634
Emotional Risk	0.0435	0.0425

sets. The variable name, _imputation_, was created in the preceding PROC MI to denote each imputed (complete) data set. At the end of Step 2, five logistic regression results, similar to those presented in Tables 3.5 or 3.6, were obtained.

Step 3—Pooling

The last stage in MI is to pool results of the m analyses to yield a final result, using a formula available in Rubin (1987) and Schafer (1997). To accomplish this step, we invoked PROC MIANALYZE in SAS® 8.2 as follows: [the entire SAS® program is available from http://portfolio.iu.edu/peng/articles/mianalyze-lr.fit(5var).sas]

```
PROC MIANALYZE DATA=outest;
        VAR intercept sex drop famstruc emorisk selfest;
RUN;
```

In the program above, the keyword DATA= specifies a covariance matrix of parameter estimates (i.e., the intercept and logistic regression coefficients) obtained from PROC LOGISTIC in Step 2 above. From this covariance matrix, PROC MIANALYZE was able to yield a single (pooled) estimate of six logistic regression estimates (Table 3.8).

As shown in Table 3.8, the log of the odds of an adolescent being at high behavioral risk was linearly related to five covariates according to the following function:

$$\text{Predicted logit } (Y\text{=high behavioral RISK}) = -1.9398 + (1.1860)*\text{GENDER} + (2.0751) * \text{DROPOUT} + (0.4343) * \text{FAMILY} + (0.0090) * \text{EMOTION} + (-0.035) * \text{ESTEEM}. \quad (7)$$

The interpretation of the significance of the overall model and each covariate was similar to that of Equation 5. In other words, the predicted logit was positively related to gender ($p < .002$), intention to drop out of school ($p < .0001$), and family structure ($p < .003$); it was negatively related to self-esteem ($p < .02$), and not statistically significantly related to

Table 3.8. Pooled Logistic Regression Analysis Results of Adolescent's Self-Inflicting Behavioral Risk by SAS® PROC MI and PROC MIANALYZE (version 8.2), $n = 517$

Predictor	*b*	*SE β*	*t-test* $(df_m)^a$	*p*	*95% Confidence Lower Limit*	*95% Confidence Upper Limit*
CONSTANT	−1.9398	1.2052	−1.61 (12241)	.1075	−4.3021	0.4226
GENDER (boys = 1, girls = 0)	1.1860	0.3305	3.59 (26.025)	.0014	0.5068	1.8654
DROPOUT (yes = 1, no = 0)	2.0751	0.3215	6.45 (616.45)	<.0001	1.4436	2.7065
FAMILY	0.4343	0.1450	3.00 (463.71)	.0029	0.1495	0.7192
EMOTION	0.0090	0.0131	0.69 (37846)	.4884	−0.0165	0.0346
ESTEEM	−0.035	0.0142	−2.45 (4922.2)	.0142	−0.0627	−0.0070

[a]The definition of df_m is given in Equation (12).

emotional risk (p =.4884). The comparison of this model to Equation 6, based on the LD method, is presented in the next section.

The pooled estimates shown in Table 3.8 are computed using formulae from Rubin (1987). For an imputed data set i, let the regression coefficient estimate for a covariate be denoted as b_i and its variance as V_i, $i = 1$ ..., m (= 5 in the present illustration). The final, pooled point estimate for the regression coefficient is the average of all b_i's:

$$\bar{b} = \frac{1}{m}\sum_{i=1}^{m} b_i. \tag{8}$$

The within-imputation variance of these point estimates is given by

$$WV = \frac{1}{m}\sum_{i=1}^{m} V_i. \tag{9}$$

The between-imputation variance of these point estimates is given by

$$BV = \frac{1}{m-1} \sum_{i=1}^{m} (\bar{b}_i - b)^2 \tag{10}$$

Thus, the total variance associated with the pooled estimate $\bar{b}$ is

$$TV = WV + \left(1 + \frac{1}{m}\right) BV. \tag{11}$$

From the total variance, Rubin (1987) derived the sampling distribution (i.e., t) for the statistic $(b - \bar{b})/\sqrt{TV}$ with the df_m equal to

$$df_m = (m-1)\left[1 + \frac{WV}{(1 + m^{-1})BV}\right]^2. \tag{12}$$

The above df_m and its associated t-statistic were used by PROC MIANALYZE to compute the significance level (p) and 95% confidence intervals around estimated regression coefficients, as reported in Table 8. The level of confidence interval may be specified by researchers to a level other than 95%. Pooled estimates can also be computed by PROC MIANALYZE for a variety of statistical indices such as, means, variances, correlations, p-values, odds ratios, likelihood-ratio test statistic, and covariance matrices in both univariate and multivariate cases (Rubin, 1987; SAS Institute, 2000; Schafer, 1997).

Comparison of MI Results with the LD Result

Comparing results presented in Equation 7 and Table 3.8 to those expressed in Equation 6 and Table 3.6, one notices that both models uncovered the same relationship between the logit of the dependent variable and the five covariates. The standard errors in Tables 3.6 and 3.8 were also quite similar except for the GENDER predictor.

There was one key difference between these two results. The significance levels associated with the t-test in Table 3.8 were larger, i.e., less statistically significant, for variables GENDER, FAMILY, and ESTEEM than those associated with Wald's chi-square tests in Table 3.6. This difference illustrates how MI captures the uncertainty associated with missing values, and, consequently, leads to more valid statistical inferences in terms of both null hypothesis testing and interval estimation of the regression coefficients.

Comments on the MI Method and PROC MI in SAS®

Key to the successful implementation of the MI method is the specification of the imputation model. MI assumes that the imputation model is identical to the model that a researcher will use to analyze the data (i.e., the analysis model). In practice, though, these two models need not be identical. According to Schafer (1997), the imputation model should contain predictors that are important substantively, highly predictive of variables with missing data, and reflect special features of the sample design (e.g., probability surveys). The imputation model does not have to be conceptually meaningful. In practice, it typically contains the variables of substantive interest as well as predictors believed to reflect missingness. There is empirical evidence that the imputation model can be useful in reducing bias, even if it is mis-specified (Schafer). With the inclusion of auxiliary variables (the inclusive strategy) in an imputation model, estimation bias can be reduced and efficiency can be increased, at very minor costs (Collins, Schafer, & Kam, 2001). The inclusive strategy worked remarkably well even with liberal use of auxiliary variables and/or different missing data mechanisms (MCAR, MAR, or MNAR, i.e., missing not at random) (Collins et al.).

MI is a Bayesian approach; it is similar to the EM method in that maximum likelihood estimates of population parameters are calculated based on observed data only. Both approaches are iterative and must converge to a criterion established by the programmer or the researcher. Both methods summarize a likelihood function that has been integrated over a conditional distribution for the missing data, conditioned on the observed data and estimated parameters. The major difference between these two is that EM accomplishes this task by numerical algorithms whereas the MI method does so by Monte Carlo approaches. Specifically, PROC MI in SAS® and the NORM program written by Schafer use a data augmentation algorithm to create a Markov chain from which random draws of missing data are sampled from the conditional distribution of missing values, conditioned on the observed data and estimated parameters (SAS Institute, 2000; Schafer, 1997). These parameter estimates are themselves random draws from the posterior distribution finalized after the Markov chain becomes stationary.

The data augmentation algorithm used by PROC MI assumes multivariate normality for the complete data in order to impute values for missing data, or just enough missing values so that the imputed data sets have monotone missing patterns (SAS Institute, 2000). Violation of the multivariate normality assumption had little impact on inferences regarding the first and the second moments of the population distribution, i.e., the mean and the variance, as reported in Graham and Schafer (1999).

Table 3.9. Percent of Efficiency as a Function of Rate of Missing (γ) and the Number of Imputations (*m*)

	γ						
m	*.1*	*.2*	*.4*	*.5*	*.6*	*.8*	*.9*
3	97	94	88	86	83	79	77
5	98	96	95	91	89	86	85
10	99	98	96	95	89	93	92
20	100	99	98	98	97	96	96

The efficiency of a parameter estimate based on m imputations is $(1 + \gamma/m)^{-1}$, where γ is the rate of missing information (Rubin, 1987, p. 114). Table 3.9 relates the rate of missing (γ) with the number of imputations (m) for efficiency of recovery of the true parameter. It is clear from Table 3.9 that, for low rates of missing data (20% or less), no more than $m = 3$ imputations are needed to be at least 90% efficient. For higher rates of missing, $m = 5$ or 10 imputations are needed. In general, it is recommended to impute missing values 5 times before results are pooled (Schafer & Olsen, 1998). The MI procedure in SAS® defaults the number of imputations to 5.

The importance of correctly specifying the imputation model was discussed by Sinharay, Stern, and Russell (2001) based on a simulation study. In that simulation study, four aspects of data were manipulated: (1) missing data mechanism (MAR versus Missing not at random, or MNAR), (2) percent of missing data (10%, 40%, and 70%), (3) the true parameter values (the mean of a variable, say X_1, and the correlation between X_1 and X_2 with population values specified to be 0 0, 0.3, 0.6, or 0.8), and (4) the imputation model (a multivariate model with 2, 3, 10, or 20 variables to impute the missing values). For each combination of these conditions, 10,000 data sets were constructed and analyzed in order to yield estimates for the mean of a variable (e.g., *income* with missing values) and correlation between *income* and another variable (e.g., *education*). Results suggested that the efficiency of MI depend on the imputation model. If the imputation model is correctly capturing the underlying association between the variable (such as *income*) with missing values and other variables with complete data (such as *education*), MI yields good results even under the MNAR condition.

Despite its strengths, there are several concerns with MI that have been documented in the literature. The first concern is that each application of MI produces slightly different imputed values and associated statistics. Consequently, results cannot always be replicated if MI is used to handle missing data. Other things being equal, this issue becomes increasingly important as the amount of missing data increases. Second, Allison (2001) discusses difficulties with MI when the researcher's interest is in estimating interaction effects. A third concern is the limited availability of MI software in general-purpose statistical software. In addition to the two procedures (MI and MIANALYZE) implemented in SAS® version 8.2 and beyond, a free MI software NORM, written by Schafer (1997), can also be utilized to perform the multiple imputation under the multivariate normal assumption. This software is available from http://www.stat.psu.edu/~jls/misoftwa.html, along with three additional modules also written by Schafer: CAT, MIX, and PAN. CAT performs MI for categorical data under the loglinear distribution assumption, MIX performs MI for a mixture of continuous and categorical data under the general location distribution assumption, and PAN performs MI for panel data or clustered data under a multivariate linear mixed-effects distribution assumption. Although Schafer's software allows MI to be applied to a variety of missing data problems, some educational researchers may find these programs to be less than user-friendly.

IMPORTANCE OF STATISTICAL ASSUMPTIONS FOR PRINCIPLED METHODS

The FIML, EM, and MI methods described in the preceding sections rely on two key assumptions. One is that the missing data are missing at random. To maximize the likelihood of satisfying the MAR assumption, researchers need to plan for ignoralibility in the design of a study (Heyting & Tolboom, 1994). In other words, if a researcher anticipates the occurrence of missing data, he/she needs to plan on collecting information from variables believed to be related to, or predictive of, missingness as a routine part of the design of a study, even though these variables may be peripheral to the research question under pursuit.

According to Graham and Schafer (1999), data-analytic results are relatively insensitive to the misspecification of the missing data model because such a model does not distort the entire data distribution, only the portion that is missing. Similarly, Schafer (1997) argued that a missing data model that explains some, but not all, of the missingness reduces the bias accordingly, and is likely to produce parameter estimates superior to those based on LD. In a small simulation study investigating the consequences of failing to satisfy the MAR assumption, Schafer (1997) showed that treating the missing data as though they were missing at random produced less biased means and standard deviations than LD. Ezzati-Rice, Johnson, Khare, Little, Rubin, and Schafer (1995) and Heitjan and Basu (1996) reported similar findings. In sum, the best advice is for researchers to plan on collecting data so as to maximize the likelihood of satisfying the ignorability condition.

The FIML, EM, and MI methods (as implemented in SAS® PROC MI and the stand-alone NORM program) also assume that complete data follow a multivariate-normal distribution. Again, there is surprisingly little literature examining effects of nonnormality on parameter estimates. While it may seem reasonable to conclude that drastic departures from this assumption will seriously bias inferences derived under these methods, some authors disagree. Graham and Schafer (1999) claimed that nonnormality had little impact on inferences derived from MI because the imputed values would still resemble the observed data in their first and second moments (i.e., the mean and the variance). Since most data analyses of interest in educational research are based on the first and second moments, it can be argued that the damage inflicted by nonnormality is usually not severe enough to significantly bias inferences. Graham and Schafer went on to argue that nonnormality is more of a threat to inferences based on parameters other than the first or second moments, for example, a variable's 95th percentile. Despite the optimism of Graham and Schafer, it seems prudent to use missing data methods cautiously when there is evidence of substantial nonnormality. And there is some evidence that parameter estimates under FIML are not robust to departures from multivariate normality (Arbuckle, 1996; Enders, 2001).

IMPLICATIONS AND RECOMMENDATIONS FOR EDUCATIONAL RESEARCH

Just as qualitative researchers in education have struggled to keep up with rapidly emerging approaches during the past 20 years, so must quantitative researchers incorporate advances provided by methodologists in their realm of inquiry. The impact of missing data on quantitative research should be a concern to educational researchers. It has been addressed in the methodological literature (e.g. Afifi & Elashoff, 1966; Becker & Powers, 2001; Becker & Walstad, 1990; Cool, 2000; Coons, 1957; Kim & Curry, 1977; Rubin, 1987; Schafer, 1999; Tirri & Silander, 1998), and substantial progress has been made in the last 2 decades of the twentieth century (Little & Rubin, 1987; Schafer, 1997; special section of *Psychological Methods*, December 2001).

However, as shown in our review of quantitative studies published in 11 education journals between 1998 and 2004, this progress has not had an impact on the way educational researchers handled missing data. In studies where missing data were reported or detected, 92.6% treated the problem with either the LD or the PD method, 5% did nothing about this problem, and less than 1% used the principled EM or MI method. An APA task force (Wilkinson & Task Force, 1999) specifically warned against the use of LD and PD in empirical research.

Newer and more principled methods, such as the full information maximum likelihood and EM, take into account conditions under which missing data occur; hence, they should be preferred to the nonprincipled methods. The full information maximum likelihood and EM methods often produce little or no bias in parameter estimates. Nor do they artificially reduce variation in the sample across a range of missing data conditions and varying amounts of missing data. Simulation studies in general demonstrated the advantages of the principled methods extended to both the *missing completely at random* and the *missing at random* conditions. The inclusion of these methods in widely available statistical software (e.g., SPSS® and SAS®) increases their accessibility and attractiveness to educational researchers. In this chapter, we demonstrated the use of three of these principled methods for treating missing values, namely, the Full Information Maximum Likelihood (FIML) method, the SPSS® Expectation-Maximization (EM) method, and the Multiple Imputation (MI) method. Evidence of the performance of these methods, along with the ad hoc procedures, was documented.

To minimize, if not eliminate, potential bias in quantitative research findings and to ensure credible conclusions upon which we base much of our thinking, it is essential that educational researchers keep the following recommendations in mind.

First and the foremost, efforts should be exerted to collect data to the fullest extent and of the highest quality. By so doing, educational researchers keep missing data to a minimum and, therefore, reduce bias and distortion in estimating population parameters or testing pertinent hypotheses. Even though principled procedures for handling missing data have been devised, their validity depends on missing data mechanism and proper specifications of models for treating missing data. Everitt (1998, p. 9) asserted that "the percentage of missing data in a study can be considered as one indicator of the quality of the data and, therefore, the quality of the study. It is important not to be seduced into thinking that investigations that are carried out poorly can be rescued by sophisticated statistical analysis." Since no one procedure has proven to be uniformly superior to others, we concur with Anderson et al. (1983) that "the only real cure for missing data is to not have any" (p. 480).

Second, educational researchers should provide sufficient and consistent information in research reports so that readers may be able to evaluate the soundness of findings based on the methodology. Specifically, educational researchers should always report the actual sample size used in the analysis, the presence or absence of missing data, the cause(s) of missing data, and the treatment of missing data. If results are reported in percentages, it is necessary to also include the sample size on which the percentage is based. Summary statistics such as the sample size, the number of nonresponses, the response rate, and *df* of *t*, chi-square, or *F* statistics should be presented clearly and consistently in the text and/or summary tables throughout the report.

Third, if missing data are present, researchers must determine whether the cause and pattern of the missing data will seriously impair the quality of the inferences derived and which procedure, if any, is most appropriate for handling missing data. A careful examination of factors causing missing data and the missing data pattern allows researchers to decide if and how to best deal with missing data in a study. To this end, Table 3.3 may be a good place to start.

Last, it is our hope that these recommendations will move educational researchers as well as journal editors and reviewers toward formulating new standards in research practices and editorial policies for the treatment of missing data in quantitative research. These new standards may be worded similarly to those regarding the effect size reporting. If adopted by all journal editorials, they should enhance the quality of research results and publications in education. The improved quality of research findings should in turn help to construct a knowledge base that is supported by sound methodologies.

REFERENCES

Arbuckle, J. L. (1995) *Amos for Windows. Analysis of moment structures* (Version 3.6) [Computer Software]. Chicago: SmallWaters Corp.

Arbuckle, J. L. (1996). Full information estimation in the presence of incomplete data. In G. A. Marcoulides & R. E. Schumacker (Eds.), *Advanced structural equation modeling: Issues and techniques* (pp. 243-278). Mahwah, NJ: Lawrence Erlbaum.

Afifi, A. A., & Elashoff, R. M. (1966). Missing data in multivariate statistics: I. Review of the literature. *Journal of the American Statistical Association, 61*(315), 595-604.

Allison, P. D. (2001). *Missing data* (Sage University Papers Series on Quantitative Applications in the Social Sciences, 07-136). Thousand Oaks, CA: Sage.

Anderson, A. B., Basilevsky, A., & Hum, D. P. J. (1983). Missing data: A review of the literature. In P. H. Rossi, J. D. Wright, & A. B. Anderson (Eds.), *Handbook of survey research* (pp. 415-494). San Diego: Academic Press.

Arbuckle, J. L. (1996). Full information likelihood estimation in the presence of incomplete data. In G. A. Marcoulides & R.E. Schumaker (Eds.), *Advanced structural equation modeling* (pp. 243-277).Mahwah, NJ: Erlbaum.

Basilevsky, A., Sabourin, D., Hum, D., & Anderson, A. (1985). Missing data estimators in the general linear model: An evaluation of simulated data as an experimental design. *Communications in Statistics, 14,* 371-394.

Beale, E. M. L., & Little, R. J. A. (1975). Missing values in multivariate analysis. *Journal of the Royal Statistical Society, Series B, 37,* 129-146.

Becker, W. E., & Powers, J. (2001). Student performance, attrition, and class size given missing student data. *Economics of Education Review, 20,* 377-388.

Becker, W. E., & Walstad, W. B. (1990). Data loss from pretest to posttest as a sample selection problem. *The Review of Economics and Statistics, 72* (1), 184-188.

BMDP Statistical Software, Inc. (1992). *BMDP statistical software manual* (Vol. 2). Los Angeles, CA: Author.

Brockmeier, L. L., Kromrey, J. D., & Hogarty, K. Y. (2002, April). *Missing data in the multiple regression analysis: A comparison of ten missing data treatments.* Paper presented at the annual meeting of the American Educational Research Association, New Orleans.

Brown, R. L. (1994). Efficacy of the indirect approach for estimating structural equation models with missing data: A comparison of five methods. *Structural Equation Modeling, 1,* 287-316.

Buck, S. F. (1960). A method of estimation of missing values in multivariate data suitable for use with an electronic computer. *Journal of the Royal Statistical Society, Series B, 22,* 302-307.

Buu, A. (1999). *Analysis of longitudinal data with missing values: A methodological comparison.* Unpublished doctoral dissertation, Indiana University.

Chan, L. S., & Dunn, O. J. (1972). The treatment of missing values in discriminant analysis- I. The sampling experiment. *Journal of the American Statistical Association, 67,* 473-477.

Cohen, J., & Cohen, P. (1983). *Applied multiple regression/correlation analysis for the behavioral sciences* (2nd ed.). Hillsdale, NJ: Erlbaum.

Collins, L. M., Schafer, J. L., & Kam, C.- M. (2001). A comparison of inclusive and restrictive strategies in modern missing data procedures. *Psychological Methods, 6*(4), 330-351.

Cool, A. L. (2000). *A review of methods for dealing with missing data.* Paper presented at the annual meeting of the Southwest Educational Research Association, Dallas, TX. (ERIC Document Reproduction Service No. ED 438 311)

Coons, I. (1957, September). The analysis of covariance as a missing plot technique. *Biometrics,* 387-405.

Dempster, A. P., Laird, N. M., & Rubin, D. B. (1977). Maximum likelihood estimation from incomplete data via the EM algorithm (with discussion). *Journal of the Royal Statistical Society, Series B, 39,* 1-38.

Diggle, P. J., Liang, K., & Zeger, S. L. (1994). *Analysis of longitudinal data.* New York: Oxford University Press.

Donner, A. (1982). The relative effectiveness of procedures commonly used in multiple regression analysis for dealing with missing data. *The American Statistician, 36,* 378-381.

Donner, A., & Rosner, B. (1982). Missing value problems in multiple linear regression with two independent variables. *Communications in Statistics, 11,* 127-140.

Downey, R. G., & King, C. V. (1998). Missing data in Likert ratings: A comparison of replacement methods. *The Journal of General Psychology, 125*(2), 175-191.

Dworkin, R. J. (1987). Hidden bias in the use of archival data. *Evaluation & the Health Professions, 10*(2), 173-185.

Enders, C. K. (1999). *The relative performance of full information maximum likelihood estimation for missing data in structural equation models.* Unpublished doctoral dissertation, University of Nebraska, Lincoln, NE.

Enders, C. K. (2001). The impact of nonnormality on full information maximum-likelihood estimation for structural equation models with missing data. *Psychological Methods, 6*, 352-370.

Enders, C. K., & Bandalos, D. L. (2001). The relative performance of full information maximum likelihood estimation for missing data in structural equation models. *Structural Equation Modeling: A Multidisciplinary Journal, 8*, 430-457.

Everitt, B. S. (1998). Analysis of longitudinal data. *British Journal of Psychiatry, 172*, 7-10.

Ezzati-Rice, T. M., Johnson, W., Khare, M., Little, R. J. A., Rubin, D. B., & Schafer, J. L. (1995). A simulation study to evaluate the performance of model-based multiple imputations in NCHS health examination surveys. In *Proceedings of the annual research conference* (pp. 257-266). Washington, DC: Bureau of the Census.

Glasser, M. (1964). Linear regression with missing observations among the independent variables. *Journal of the American Statistical Association, 59*, 834-844.

Gleason, T. C., & Staelin, R. (1975). A proposal for handling missing data. *Psychometrika, 40*, 229-252.

Graham, J. W., & Schafer, J. L. (1999). On the performance of multiple imputation for multivariate data with small sample size. In R. Hoyle (Ed.), *Statistical strategies for small-sample research* (pp. 1-29). Thousand Oaks, CA: Sage.

Graham, J. W., & Schafer, J. L. (2002). Missing data: Our view of the state of the art. *Psychological Methods, 7*, 147-177.

Haitovsky, Y. (1968). Missing data in regression analysis. *Journal of the Royal Statistical Society, Series B, 30*, 67-82.

Hall, J. (1993). *Skills training for pregnant and parenting adolescents* (NIDA Monograph No. 156: NIH Publication No. 95-3908). Rockville, MD: National Institute on Drug Abuse.

Hartley, H. O., & Hocking, R. R. (1971). The analysis of incomplete data. *Biometrics, 27*, 783-823.

Heitjan, D. F., & Basu, S. (1996), Distinguishing between "missing at random" and "missing completely at random." *American Statistician, 50*, 207-213.

Heyting, A., & Tolboom, J. T. B. M. (1994). Discussion of the paper by P. Diggle and M.G. Kenward. *Applied Statistics, 43*, 49-93.

Holt, D. (1997). Missing data and nonresponse. In J. P. Keeve (Ed.) *Educational research, methodology, and measurement: An international handbook* (2nd ed., pp. 592-597). New York: Elsevier Science.

Ingersoll, G. M., & Orr, D. P. (1989). Behavioral and emotional risk in early adolescents. *Journal of Early Adolescence, 9*, 392-408.

Jennrich, R. I., & Schluchter, M. D. (1986). Unbalanced repeated-measures models with structured covariance matrices. *Biometrics, 42*, 805-820.

Kaplan, D. (1995). The impact of BIB spiraling-induced missing data patterns on goodness-of-fit tests in factor analysis. *Journal of Educational and Behavioral Statistics, 20,* 69-82.

Kellam, S., Rebok, G., Ialongo, N., & Mayer, L. (1994). The course and malleability of aggressive behavior from early first grade into middle school: Results of a developmental epidemiologically-based preventive trial. *Journal of Child Psychology and Psychiatry, 35,* 259-281.

Kim, J.- O., & Curry, J. (1977). The treatment of missing data in multivariate analysis. *Sociological Methods & Research, 6*(2), 215-240.

King, C. V., Fogg, R. J., & Downey, R. G. (1998, April). *Mean substitution for missing items: Sample size and the effectiveness of the technique.* Paper presented at the annual meeting of the Society of Industrial and Organizational Psychology, Dallas, TX.

Kromrey, J. D. & Hines, C. V. (1994). Nonrandomly missing data in multiple regression: An empirical comparison of common missing data treatments. *Educational and Psychological Measurement, 54,* 573-593.

Littell, R. C., Milliken, G. A., Stroup, W. W., & Wolfinger, R. D. (1996). *SAS system for mixed models.* Cary, NC: SAS Institute, Inc.

Littell, R. C., Roderick, J. A., & Schenker, N. (1995). Missing data. In G. Arminger, C. Clogg, & M. Sobel (Eds.), *Handbook of statistical modeling for the social and behavioral sciences* (pp. 39-75). New York: Plenum.

Little, R. J. A. (1988). Robust estimation off the mean and covariance matrix from data with missing values. *Applied Statistics, 37,* 23-38.

Little, R. J. A., & Rubin, D. B. (1987). *Statistical analysis with missing data.* New York: Wiley.

Malhotra, N. K. (1987). Analyzing marketing research with incomplete information on the dependent variable. *Journal of Marketing Research, 24,* 74-84.

Marsh, H. W. (1998). Pairwise deletion for missing data in structural equation models: Nonpositive definite matrices, parameter estimates, goodness of fit, and adjusted sample sizes. *Structural Equation Modeling, 5,* 22-36.

Mason, M. J. (1999, July). A review of procedural and statistical methods for handling attrition and missing data in clinical research. *Measurement and Evaluation in Counseling and Development, 32,* 111-118.

Meng, X. L. & Rubin, D. B. (1992). Performing likelihood ratio tests with multiply-imputed data sets. *Biometrika, 79,* 103-111.

McLachlan, G. J., & Krishnan, T. (1997). *The EM algorithm and extensions.* New York: Wiley.

Muthen, B., Kaplan, D., & Hollis, M. (1987). On structural equation modeling with data that are not missing completely at random. *Psychometrika, 52,* 431-462.

Peng, C.- Y. J., & Nichols, R. N. (2003). Using multinomial logistic regression models to predict adolescent behavioral risk. *Journal of Modern Applied Statistical Methods, 2*(1), 177-188.

Peng, C.- Y. J., Lee, K. L., & Ingersoll, G. M. (2002). An introduction to logistic regression analysis and reporting. *The Journal of Educational Research, 96*(1), 3-14.

Peng, C.- Y. J., So, T. S. H., Stage, F. K., & St. John, E. P. (2002). The use and interpretation of logistic regression in higher education journals: 1988-1999. *Research in Higher Education, 43(3)*, 259-293.

Raymond, M. R., & Roberts, D. M. (1987). A comparison of methods for treating incomplete data in selection research. *Educational and Psychological Measurement, 47*, 13-26.

Reilly, M. (1993). Data analysis with hot deck multiple imputation. *The Statistician, 42*, 307-313.

Resnick, M. D., Harris, L. J., & Blum R.B. (1993). The impact of caring and connectedness on adolescent health and well-being. *Journal of Pediatrics Child Health, 29*(1), 53-59.

Rosenberg, M. (1965). *Society and the adolescent self-image*. Princeton, NJ: Princeton.

Roth, P.L. (1994). Missing data: A conceptual review for applied psychologists. *Personnel Psychology, 47*, 537-560.

Roth, P. L., & Switzer, F.S., III. (1995). A Monte Carlo analysis of missing data techniques in an HRM setting. *Journal of Management, 21*, 1003-1023.

Rovine, M. J. (1994). Latent variable models and missing data analysis. In A. von Eye & C. C. Clogg (Eds.), *Latent variable analysis: Applications for developmental research* (pp. 181-225). Thousand Oaks, CA: Sage.

Rubin, D. B. (1987). *Multiple imputation for nonresponses in surveys*. New York: Wiley & Sons.

SAS Institute Inc. (1999). *SAS/STAT® user's guide, version 8, volume 2*. Cary, NC: Author.

SAS Institute Inc. (2000). *Proceedings of the twenty-fifth annual SAS® users group international conference*. Cary, NC: Author.

Schafer, J. L. (1997). *Analysis of incomplete multivariate data*. New York: Chapman & Hall.

Schafer, J. L. (1999). Multiple imputation: A primer. *Statistical Methods in Medical Research, 8*, 3-15.

Schafer, J. L., & Graham, J. W. (2002). Missing data: Our view of the state of the art. *Psychological Methods,* 7(2), 147-177.

Schafer, J. L., & Olsen, M. K. (1998) Multiple imputation for multivariate missing data problems: A data analyst's perspective. *Multivariate Behavior Research, 33*, 545-571.

Sinharay, S., Stern, H. S., & Russell, D. (2001). The use of multiple imputation for the analysis of missing data. *Psychological Methods*, *6*(4), 317-329.

Switzer, F. S., III, Roth, P. L., & Switzer, D. M. (1998). Systematic data loss in HRM settings: A Monte Carlo analysis. *Journal of Management, 24*, 763-779.

Tabachnick, B. G., & Fidell, L. S. (2001). *Using multivariate statistics* (4th ed.). Needham Heights, MA: Allyn & Bacon.

Timm, N. H. (1970). The estimation of variance-covariance and correlation matrices from incomplete data. *Psychometrika, 35*, 417-437.

Tirri, H., & Silander, T. (1998, April). *Stochastic complexity based estimation of missing elements in questionnaire data.* Paper presented at the annual meeting of the American Educational Research Association, San Diego, CA. (ERIC Document Reproduction Service No. ED 431 794)

Wilkinson, L., & Task Force on Statistical Inference APA Board of Scientific Affairs. (1999). Statistical methods in psychology journals: Guidelines and explanations. *American Psychologist, 54(*8), 594-604.

Wilks, S. S. (1932). Moments and distributions of estimates of population parameters from fragmentary samples. *Annals of Mathematics Statistics, 3*, 163-195.

Witta, E. L. (2000, April). *Effectiveness of four methods of handling missing data using samples from a national database*. Paper presented at the Annual Meeting of the American Educational Research Association, New Orleans, LA. (ERIC Document Reproduction Service No. ED 442 810)

Wothke, W. (2000). Longitudinal and multi-group modeling with missing data. In T. D. Little, K. U. Schnabel, & J. Baumert (Eds.), *Modeling longitudinal and multiple group data: Practical issues, applied approaches and specific examples* (pp. 219-240). Mahwah, NJ: Erlbaum.

CHAPTER 4

METHODS FOR SIMULATING REAL WORLD DATA FOR THE PSYCHO-EDUCATIONAL SCIENCES

Todd Christopher Headrick

INTRODUCTION

It has been documented that real world data sets in the educational and psychological sciences are often non-normal (e.g., Blair, 1981; Bradley, 1968, 1982; Micceri, 1989; Pearson & Please, 1975; Sawilowsky & Blair, 1992). The typical measures used to describe nonnormality are skew (γ_3) and kurtosis (γ_4). Scheffe (1959) noted that γ_3 and γ_4 are "the most important indicators of the extent to which nonnormality affects the usual inferences made in the analysis of variance" (p. 333). It is well known that when the assumption of normality is violated nonparametric tests can be substantially more powerful than the usual OLS parametric t or F tests. For example, the Mann-Whitney test, when juxtaposed to the two independent samples t test, has an asymptotic relative efficiency of 3 when the populations have exponential distributions (Lehmann, 1998, p. 80).

Real Data Analysis, pp. 79–97

A common practice used to investigate the effects of γ_3 and γ_4 on the properties of parametric or nonparametric statistics is Monte Carlo techniques. A method often used in Monte Carlo studies for simulating univariate or multivariate nonnormal distributions that allows for the systematic control of moments (or cumulants) and correlations is the power method transformation (Fleishman, 1978, Equation 1; Headrick, 2002, Equation 16; Headrick & Sawilowsky, 1999, Equation 7; Vale & Maurelli, 1983, Equation 11). The primary advantage of this method is that it provides computationally efficient algorithms for generating univariate or multivariate data with arbitrary correlation matrices.

The power method has been used in studies that have included such topics or techniques as: ANCOVA (Harwell & Serlin, 1988; Headrick & Sawilowsky, 2000a; Headrick & Vineyard, 2001; Klockers & Moses, 2002; Olejnik & Algina, 1987), computer adaptive testing (Zhu, Yu, & Liu, 2002), hierarchical linear models (Shieh, 2000), item response theory (Stone, 2003), logistic regression (Hess, Olejnik, & Huberty, 2001), regression (Harwell & Serlin, 1989; Headrick & Rotou, 2001), repeated measures (Beasley & Zumbo, 2003; Lix, Algina, & Keselman, 2003; Kowalchuk, Keselman, & Algina, 2003), structural equation modeling (Hipp & Bollen, 2003; Reinartz, Echambadi, & Chin, 2002), and other univariate or multivariate (non)parametric tests (Beasley, 2002; Habib & Harwell, 1989; Rasch & Guiard, 2004; Steyn, 1993).

THE POWER METHOD TRANSFORMATION

The analytical and empirical forms for the fifth-order power transformation are (Headrick, 2002, 2004a)

$$p(z) = \Sigma_{i=1}^{6} c_i z^{i-1} \tag{1}$$

$$p(Z) = \Sigma_{i=1}^{6} c_i Z^{i-1} \tag{2}$$

where Z is a continuous standard normal random variable with *pdf* and *cdf* of

$$f_z(z) = (2\pi)^{-\frac{1}{2}} \exp((-z^2)/2) \tag{3}$$

$$F_z(z) = \Phi(z) = \Pr(Z \leq z) = \int_{-\infty}^{z} (2\pi)^{-\frac{1}{2}} \exp(-w^2/2) dw\,. \tag{4}$$

Let the parametric forms of (3) and (4) be expressed as

$$f : z \rightarrow \Re^2 := f_Z(z) = f_Z(x, y) = f_Z(z, f_Z(z)) \tag{4}$$

$$F : z \rightarrow \Re^2 := F_Z(z) = F_Z(x, y) = F_Z(z, F_Z(z)) \ . \tag{5}$$

Using (4) and (5), Headrick (2004a) derived the parametric forms of the *pdf* and *cdf* associated with the polynomial in (2) as the compositions

$$\begin{aligned} f \circ p : p(z) \rightarrow \Re^2 &:= f_{p(Z)}(p(z)) = f_{p(Z)}(p(x, y)) \\ &= f_{p(Z)}(p(z), f_Z(z)/p'(z)) \end{aligned} \tag{6}$$

$$F \circ p : p(z) \rightarrow \Re^2 := F_{p(Z)}(p(z)) = F_{p(Z)}(p(x, y)) = F_{p(Z)}(p(z), F_Z(z)) \ . \tag{7}$$

The shape of the *pdf* in Equation 6 is contingent on the values of the constant coefficients c_i in Equation 1. These coefficients are determined by simultaneously solving Equations 11, 12, 13, 14, 15, and 16 in Appendix 1 for specified values of the first six standardized cumulants (γ_i) from a nonnormal distribution where the mean γ_1 and variance are set to zero and one, respectively. Provided in Figures 4.1 and 4.2 are examples of theoretical and empirical approximations to the standard exponential distribution. The c_i for this distribution are given in step 2 of Table 4.1.

The boundary of the class of distributions associated with the third-order transformation (Fleishman, 1978, Figure 1; Headrick & Sawilowsky, 2000b, Table 1) is subsumed under the broader class of distributions generated by the fifth-order transformation. That is, setting $c_5 = c_6 = 0$ in Equations 1, 2, and 11, 12, 13, and 14 in Appendix 1 would yield equivalent expressions given in Fleishman (1978, Equations 1, 5, 11, 17, 18) for solving for the first four standardized cumulants.

To ensure a nonnormal distribution generated by Equation 2 has a valid *pdf*, Headrick (2004a, Proposition 3.3) showed that $p(z)$ in Equation (1) must be a strictly increasing monotonic function. Thus, it is necessary that the correlation between $p(Z)$ and Z in (2) be bounded in the interval $0 < \rho_{p(Z),\,Z} = c_2 + 3c_4 + 15c_6 < 1$. Further, the coefficients c_i, for any given nonnormal *symmetric* distribution (where $c_1 = c_3 = c_5 = 0$), must yield nonzero imaginary parts to the solutions of z for the expressions

$$z = \pm\sqrt{\frac{\pm\sqrt{9c_4^2 - 20c_2c_6 - 3c_6} - 3c_4}{10c_6}} \text{ and}$$

$$z = \mp\sqrt{\frac{\pm\sqrt{9c_4^2 - 20c_2c_6 - 3c_6} - 3c_4}{10c_6}} \qquad (8)$$

or for an *asymmetric* distribution

$$z = \pm\frac{1}{2}\sqrt{S_4} \pm \frac{1}{2}\sqrt{S_6 \pm S_5} - \frac{c_5}{5c_6} \text{ and } z = \pm\frac{1}{2}\sqrt{S_4} + \mp\frac{1}{2}\sqrt{S_6 \pm S_5} - \frac{c_5}{5c_6}. \qquad (9)$$

The expressions for S_4, S_5, and S_6 are given in the Appendix 2. It should be pointed out that Headrick (2004a, Property 4.4) showed that the third-order power method transformation will not produce a valid *pdf* for distributions with cumulants associated with the chi-square family for $df \geq 2$ whereas the fifth-order transformation will. For example, see steps 1, 2, and 3 in Table 4.1.

Although any given power method transformation in Equation 2 will produce a distribution with a (marginal) mean of zero, there may be other measures of central tendency of concern when modeling real world data sets. The other three measures considered herein are the locations of the median, a trimmed mean, and mode(s) for any given power method distribution with a valid *pdf*. The median and the 100α percent symmetric trimmed mean associated with (6) are located at (Headrick, 2004a, Remark 3.7, Remark 3.8) $p(z = 0)\ c_1$ and

$$p(z) = (1 - 2\alpha)^{-1} \sum_{i=1}^{r=6} c_i \int_{F_Z^{-1}(\alpha)}^{F_Z^{-1}(1-\alpha)} z^{i-1} dF_Z(z)$$

where $\alpha \in (0, 0.50)$, respectively.

In terms of the mode(s), any valid power method *pdf* will have a major mode because (1) is a strictly increasing monotonic function and the standard normal *pdf* is unimodal. Thus, the major mode associated with (6) is located at (Headrick, 2004a, Remark 3.6) $f_{p(Z)}(p(\tilde{z}), f_Z(\tilde{z})/p'(\tilde{z}))$ where $\tilde{z}$ is the critical number that solves $dy/dz = d(f_Z(z)/p'(z))/dz = 0$ and globally maximizes $y = f_Z(\tilde{z})/p'(\tilde{z})$ at $x = p(\tilde{z})$. It is noted that, in general, there may exist other values of z that satisfy the first-order condition $dy/dz = 0$. These critical numbers can produce either local maxima or minima.

Local maxima are referred to as minor modes. Thus, having satisfied the first-order condition, the second-order condition d^2y/dz^2 is evaluated at the critical number(s) of z (e.g., $\tilde{z}$) where we must have $d^2y/dz^2 = 0$ to ensure that the critical numbers yield the mode(s).

NUMERICAL EXAMPLE USING A THEORETICAL DISTRIBUTION

To demonstrate the methodology, an analytical comparison is made between the standard exponential *pdf* and its fifth-order power method analog. Presented in Table 4.1 are the steps for determining if the power method will generate a valid *pdf* for this density and for computing the probabilities to make a comparison. The results in step 3 indicate that the power method will generate a valid *pdf* because all solutions of z associated with Equation 9 have nonzero imaginary parts.

Presented in Figure 4.1 is a graph of the power method's *pdf* (dashed lines) superimposed on the standard exponential density where $m_1 = m_2^{1/2} = 1$ in step 5 of Table 4.1. Inspection of Figure 4.1 indicates that the power method provides a good approximation of the upper 5% of the tail for this density. The measures of central tendency for the power method *pdf* are (a) mean: $m_2^{1/2}\gamma_1 + m_i = 1$, (b) median: $m_2^{1/2}c_1 + m_1 =$ 0.692260, (c) mode: located on the abissca at $m_2^{1/2}p(\tilde{z}) + m_1 = 0.052436$ with height $f_z(\tilde{z})/p'(\tilde{z})$ 1.09421 where $\tilde{z} = -1.73065$, and (d) a 20% symmetric trimmed mean of:

$$m_2^{1/2}[(1-2(.20))^{-1}\sum_{i=1}^{r=6} c_i \int_{-0.84162}^{+0.841213} z^{i-1}\, dF_z(z)] + m_1 = 0.760344.$$

Note that the power method's median and trimmed mean are close to that of the exact exponential *pdf* which has median: $-\ln(.5) = 0.693147$ and trimmed mean:

$$(1-2(.20))^{-1} \int_{.223114}^{1.609440} xe^{-x}\, dx = 0.761046.$$

PARAMETER ESTIMATION AND DISTRIBUTION FITTING USING DATA FROM PROJECT MATCH

Project MATCH (1993, 1997) was a multisite clinical trial of alcoholism treatments supported by a series of grants from the National Institute of

Alcohol Abuse and Alcoholism. For a detailed description of the methodology, participants, and the clinical research units involved in this study see Project MATCH Research Group (1993, 1997).

Briefly, the Project MATCH research group employed three individually delivered standardized alcoholism treatments over a 12-week period. Table 4.2 gives the sample moments m_i (see Appendix 3) and cumulants $\hat{\gamma}_i$ for the total number of drinks (TND) per 90-day period for $N = 311$ subjects receiving the 12-step facilitation (TSF) treatment intervention. Presented in Figure 4.3 is a frequency histogram of the TSF data and its associated fifth-order power method *pdf* parametric plot. The power method *pdf* was obtained by solving the system of equations in Appendix 1 for the $\hat{\gamma}_i$ and then imposing linear transformations on the polynomials using the location and scale parameter estimates of m_1 and $m_2^{1/2}$ listed in Table 4.2.

The fifth-order polynomial was able to preserve the estimates of $\hat{\gamma}_3$, $\hat{\gamma}_4$, and $\hat{\gamma}_5$ for these data. However, the estimate of $\hat{\gamma}_6 = -10.70020$ had to be increased to $\hat{\gamma}_6 = -0.28898$ to meet the restriction that Equation 9 must have nonzero imaginary parts for a valid power method *pdf* to exist. Table 4.3 gives a chi-square goodness of fit test with an associated asymptotic cumulative *p*-value of .394 which indicates that the power method *pdf* provides a good fit to the data. Note that the degrees of freedom (*df*) were computed as $df = 9$ (classes) -5 (estimates that fit the data) -1(sample size) $= 3$. The *p*-value is referred to as asymptotic because it is based on the method of moments rather than maximum likelihood.

The median (Mdn) and the 20% symmetric trimmed mean (Tm) for the TSF group are 633.600 (std. error = 42.880) and 680.752 ($N = 187$, std. error = 19.010), respectively. These estimates have associated 95% bootstrap confidence intervals of $566.300 \leq \text{Mdn} \leq 713.400$ and $643.098 \leq \text{Tm} \leq 717.640$. The intervals are based on 25,000 bootstrap replications drawn from the data of the TSF group. The median and trimmed mean for the power method *pdf* in Figure 4.3 are $m_2^{1/2}c_1 + m_i = 620.502$ and

$$m_2^{1/2}[(1-2(.20))^{-1}\sum_{i=1}^{r=6} c_i \int_{-0.84162}^{0.84162} z^{i-1}\, dF_z(z)] + m_1 = 664.096$$

which are both within the 95% bootstrap confidence intervals.

MULTIVARIATE DATA GENERATION

Multivariate (non)normal data generation begins by specifying k equations of the form in (2) as $p(Z_1)\ldots p(Z_k)$. Controlled intercorrelations between $p(Z_1)$ and $p(Z_j)$ is accomplished by solving the following equation (Headrick, 2002, Equation 26)

$$\begin{aligned}
\rho_{p(Z_i)p(Z_j)} &= 3c_{5(i)}c_{1(j)} + 3c_{5(i)}c_{3(j)} + 9c_{5(i)}c_{5(j)} \\
&+ c_{1(i)}(c_{1(j)} + c_{3(j)} + 3c_{5(j)}) + c_{2(i)}c_{2(j)}\rho_{Z_iZ_j} + 3c_{4(i)}c_{2(j)}\rho_{Z_iZ_j} \\
&+ 3c_{2(i)}c_{4(j)}\rho_{Z_iZ_j} + 9c_{4(i)}c_{4(j)}\rho_{Z_iZ_j} + 15c_{6(i)}c_{2(j)}\rho_{Z_iZ_j} \\
&+ 15c_{2(i)}c_{6(j)}\rho_{Z_iZ_j} + 45c_{6(i)}c_{4(j)}\rho_{Z_iZ_j} + 45c_{4(i)}c_{6(j)}\rho_{Z_iZ_j} \\
&+ 225c_{6(i)}c_{6(j)}\rho_{Z_iZ_j} + 12c_{5(i)}c_{3(j)}\rho^2_{Z_iZ_j} + 72c_{5(i)}c_{5(j)}\rho^2_{Z_iZ_j} \\
&+ 6c_{4(i)}c_{4(j)}\rho^3_{Z_iZ_j} + 60c_{6(i)}c_{4(j)}\rho^3_{Z_iZ_j} + 60c_{4(i)}c_{6(j)}\rho^3_{Z_iZ_j} \\
&+ 600c_{6(i)}c_{4(j)}\rho^3_{Z_iZ_j} + 24c_{5(i)}c_{5(j)}\rho^4_{Z_iZ_j} + 120c_{6(i)}c_{6(j)}\rho^5_{Z_iZ_j} \\
&+ c_{3(i)}(c_{1(j)} + c_{3(j)} + 3c_{5(j)} + 2c_{3(j)}\rho^2_{Z_iZ_j} + 12c_{5(j)}\rho^2_{Z_iZ_j})
\end{aligned} \tag{10}$$

where the left-hand side of (10) is set to a specified correlation between $p(Z_i)$ and $p(Z_j)$ and $\rho_{Z_iZ_j}$ is the (numerically solved) intermediate correlation between Z_i and Z_j. The intermediate correlation compensates for the nonnormalization effect of the coefficients such that $p(Z_i)$ and $p(Z_j)$ have their specified correlation $\rho_{p(Z_i)p(Z_j)}$.

Equation (10) is solved for all $k(k-1)/2$ intermediate correlations $\rho_{Z_iZ_j}$. These correlations are assembled into a $k \times k$ matrix, and this matrix can be factored (e.g., a Cholesky factorization) to generated standard normal random deviates correlated at the intermediate levels $\rho_{Z_iZ_j}$. The standard normal deviates are subsequently entered into the k equations of the form in (2) to produce the (non)normal distributions with the specified correlations $\rho_{p(Z_i)p(Z_j)}$. It should be noted that setting $c_5 = c_6 = 0$ in (10) will reduce this equation to what is associated with the third-order polynomial and is given in Vale and Maurelli (1983, Equation 11) or Headrick and Sawilowsky (1999, Equation 7).

MONTE CARLO SIMULATION

To demonstrate the methodology, three fifth-order power method distributions (sample sizes of N = 10, 10, 10) were simulated with the specified cumulants and intercorrelations listed in Tables 4.4 and 4.5 using an algorithm coded in Fortran 77. The algorithm employed the use of subroutines UNI1 and NORMB1 from RANGEN (Blair, 1987) to generate pseudo-random uniform and standard normal deviates. Table 4.6 gives the power method coefficients that were determined from solving the system of equations in Appendix 1 for the standardized cumulants associated with the chi-square distributions listed in Table 4.4.

Tables 4.7 gives the intermediate correlation matrix for the standard normal deviates which was determined by solving (10) for $\rho_{Z_i Z_j}$ given the specified coefficients and correlations listed in Tables 4.5 and 4.6. Tables 4.8 and 4.9 give the results from the Monte Carlo simulation. The entries in these tables were based on averaging procedures involving 25,000 repetitions and thus $N = 10 \times 25{,}000 = 250{,}000$ random deviates. The results from the simulation indicate that the power method distributions have standardized cumulants and correlations that are (on average) in close proximity to their associated population parameters.

The method described for multivariate data generation can also be extended for other purposes. For further details on methodology, extensions, and numerical examples see Headrick (2004a, 2004b), Headrick and Beasley (2004), and Headrick and Zumbo (2004) for simulating correlated (a) ranked data, (b) systems of linear statistical equations, and (c) intraclass correlations.

SOFTWARE

The coefficients for the fifth-order polynomials associated with the density in Figures 4.1 and 4.2 were obtained by solving the system of equations in Appendix 1 using the numerical equation solver FindRoot (Wolfram, 2003) and is available from the author. Solutions for these constant coefficients were accepted when the numerical error in the results was less than 10^{-24} and subsequently rounded to six digits. Further, *Mathematica* (Wolfram, 2003) source code associated with the power method is available from the author for (a) calculating percentage points (e.g., for determining a power method *pdf*'s tailweight as in Figure 4.1), (b) determining the location of a mode, median, or trimmed mean, (c) plotting parametric graphs of power method densities, and (d) determining intermediate correlations and Cholesky factorizations.

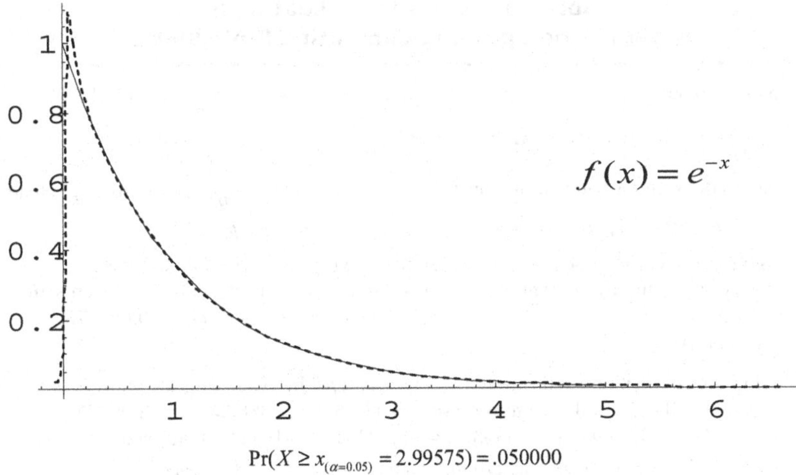

$$\Pr(X \geq x_{(\alpha=0.05)} = 2.99575) = .050000$$

$$\text{PM: } \Pr(m_2^{\frac{1}{2}} p(z) + m_1 \geq 2.99575) = .049992$$

Figure 4.1. A fifth-order polynomial power method (PM) *pdf* (dashed lines) approximation of the standard exponential density using Equation 6 where $m_1 = m_2^{1/2} = 1$ from step 5 in Table 4.1.

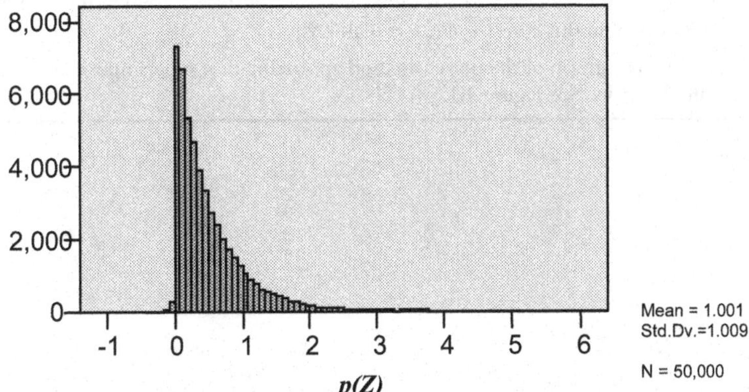

Figure 4.2. A frequency histogram of the fifth-order polynomial power method's approximation of the standard exponential density using Equation 2. Note that a constant of 1 was added to Equation 2.

Table 4.1. Steps for Validating a Power Method pdf and Computing Probabilities

An analytical comparison of the standard exponential density (or $\chi^2_{df=2}$) with the fifth-order power method transformation: $p(z) = c_1 + c_2z + c_3z_2 + c_4z_3 + c_5z_4 + c_6z^5$.

1. Obtain the standardized cumulants for the exponential (or $\chi^2_{df=2}$) density (e.g, Headrick, 2002, Table 1): $\gamma_1 = 0, \gamma_2 = 1, \gamma_3 = 2, \gamma_4 = 6, \gamma_5 = 24, \gamma_6 = 120$.
2. Using the cumulants, obtain the coefficients for $p(z)$ that approximate the exponential density by solving the system of equations given in Appendix 1. The coefficients are: $c_1 = -0.307740$, $c_2 = 0.800560$, $c_3 = 0.318764$, $c_4 = 0.033500$, $c_5 = -0.003675$, $c_6 = 0.000159$.
3. Using the coefficients, determine if $p(z)$ is a valid *pdf* by evaluating the expressions in Equation 9. The complex solutions are: $z = 11.3386 - 9.38863i$, $z = -2.09334 + 0.514451i$, $z = 11.3386 + 9.38863i$, $z = -2.09334 - 0.514451i$. Thus, $p(z)$ is a valid *pdf* because all solutions have nonzero imaginary parts and $p'(z) > 0$ because the transformation has a positive Pearson correlation of $c_2 + 3c_4 + 15c_6 = 0.903445$.
4. Select a critical value (cv) from the exponential density e.g., $Pr(X \geq x = cv = 2.99575) = 0.050000$.
5. Given the coefficients and cv from Steps 2 and 4, solve: $m_2^{1/2}p(z) + m_1 - cv = 0$ for $\tilde{z}$. The constants m_1 and m_2 are the first and second moments from a theoretical or empirical distribution (see Appendix 3 regarding empirical distributions). For this example $m_1 = m_2^{1/2} = 1$ because the standard exponential density has a mean and standard deviation equal to one. Numerically solving yields $\tilde{z} = 1.64493$.
6. Integrate the standard normal *pdf* as: $\int_{-\infty}^{\tilde{z}} (2\pi)^{-\frac{1}{2}} \exp((-w^2)/2)dw = \Phi(\tilde{z})$. This gives the corresponding probability for the power method's approximation to the exponential density where in this case $1 - \Phi(\tilde{z}) = 0.49992$.
7. Plot a parametric graph of the power method approximation superimposed on the exponential density. See Figure 4.1.

Table 4.2. Sample Moments (m_i), Cumulants ($\hat{\gamma}_i$), and the c_i of the Baseline Data for the Total Number of Drinks for the Group Receiving TSF and Outpatient Treatment

Parameter Estimate[1]	*TSF (N = 311)*	*Coefficient (c_i)*
m_1	797.793890	$c_1 = -0.288170$
$m_2^{1/2}$	615.23480	$c_2 = 0.919857$
$\hat{\gamma}_3$	1.39659	$c_3 = 0.336801$
$\hat{\gamma}_4$	2.26237	$c_4 = -0.001456$
$\hat{\gamma}_5$	2.08205	$c_5 = -0.016210$
$\hat{\gamma}_6$	−10.70020[2]	$c_6 = 0.001425$

[1]See Appendix 3 for the formulae for the estimates. [2]This value had to be increased to −0.28898 to ensure a valid fifth-order power method *pdf* depicted in Figure 4.3.

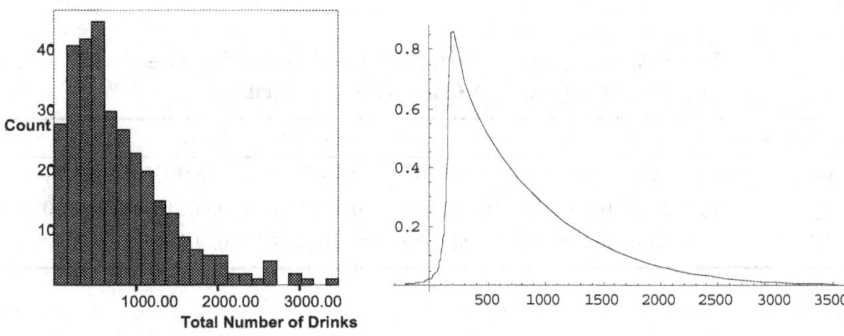

Figure 4.3. Histogram and the fifth-order power method *pdf* for the TSF group.

Table 4.3. Observed and Expected Frequencies and Chi-Square Test Based on the Fifth-Order Power Method Approximation to the Data From The TSF Treatment Group in Figure 4.3

Cum. Percentage	*Total Number of Drinks*	*Obs. Frequency*	*Exp. Frequency*
30	less than 380.05	86	93.30
50	380.05–620.50	68	62.20
70	620.50–973.41	62	62.20
75	973.41–1,094.27	17	15.55
80	1,094.27–1,238.41	18	15.55
85	1,238.41–1,418.18	15	15.55
90	1,418.18–1,660.33	16	15.55
95	1,660.33–2,045.66	15	15.55
100	2,045.66 or more	14	15.55
$\chi^2 = 1.84$	$\Pr\{\chi_3^2 \geq 1.84\} = .394$	$N = 311$	

Table 4.4. The First Six Standardized Cumulants Associated With Chi-Square Distributions With *df* = 2, 3, 4, Respectively

Distribution	γ_1	γ_2	γ_3	γ_4	γ_5	γ_6
$p(Z_1)$	0	1	2	6	24	120
$p(Z_2)$	0	1	$2\sqrt{2}/\sqrt{3}$	4	$16\sqrt{2}/\sqrt{3}$	160/3
$p(Z_3)$	0	1	$\sqrt{2}$	3	$6\sqrt{2}$	30

Table 4.5. Specified Correlations Between the Power Method Distributions

Distribution	$p(Z_1)$	$p(Z_2)$	$p(Z_2)$
$p(Z_1)$	1	0.60	0.50
$p(Z_2)$	0.60	1	0.40
$p(Z_3)$	0.50	0.40	1

Table 4.6. Power Method Coefficients for the Approximating the Chi-Square Distributions

Distribution	c_1	c_2	c_3	c_4	c_5	c_6
$p(Z_1)$	−0.307740	0.800560	0.318764	0.033500	−0.003675	0.000159
$p(Z_2)$	−0.259037	0.867102	0.265362	0.021276	−0.002108	0.000092
$p(Z_3)$	−0.227508	0.900716	0.231610	0.015466	−0.001367	0.000055

Table 4.7. Intermediate Correlation Matrix for the Standard Normal Deviates

Distribution	Z_1	Z_2	Z_3
Z_1	1	0.638318	0.538342
Z_1	0.638318	1	0.428905
Z_1	0.538342	0.428905	1

Table 4.8. Empirical Results From the Simulation for the Specified Correlations

Distribution	$p(Z_1)$	$p(Z_2)$	$p(Z_3)$
$p(Z_1)$	1	0.600	0.499
$p(Z_2)$	0.600	1	0.401
$p(Z_3)$	0.499	0.401	1

The entries are based on sample sizes of N = 10 and 25,000 repetitions.

Table 4.9. Empirical Results From the Simulation for the Specified Cumulants

Distribution	γ_1	γ_2	γ_3	γ_4	γ_5	γ_6
$p(Z_1)$	–0.000825	1.00231	2.043265	6.176354	24.56782	120.65260
$p(Z_2)$	–0.000430	1.00044	1.628754	3.945372	12.42543	50.89734
$p(Z_3)$	–0.000550	1.00072	1.407543	2.985423	8.36543	27.37690

The entries are based on sample sizes of N = 10 and 25,000 repetitions.

APPENDIX 1

The system of equations given in Headrick (2002, Equations 18, 22, B.1, B.2, B.3, B.4) is expressed in the notation developed herein as follows:

$$\gamma_1 = 0 = c_1 + c_3 + 3c_5 \tag{11}$$

$$\begin{aligned}\gamma_2 = 1 = {} & c_2^2 + 2c_3^2 + 24c_3c_5 + 6c_2(c_4 + 5c_6) \\ & + 3(5c_4^2 + 32c_5^2 + 70c_4c_6 + 315c_m^2)\end{aligned} \tag{12}$$

$$\begin{aligned}\gamma_3 = {} & 2\{4c_3^3 + 108c_3^2c_5 + 3c_2^2(c_3 + 6c_5) \\ & + 18c_2(2c_3c_4 + 16c_4c_5 + 15c_3c_6 + 150c_5c_6) \\ & + 9c_3(15c_4^2 + 128c_5^2 + 280c_4c_6 + 1575c_6^2) \\ & + 54c_5(25c_4^2 + 88c_5^2 + 560c_4c_6 + 3675c_6^2)\}\end{aligned} \tag{13}$$

$$\begin{aligned}\gamma_4 = {} & 24\{2c_3^4 + 96c_3^3c_5 + c_2^3(c_4 + 10c_6) \\ & + 30c_3^2(6c_4^2 + 64c_5^2 + 140c_4c_6 + 945c_6^2) \\ & + c_2^2(2c_3^2 + 18c_4^2 + 36c_3c_5 + 192c_5^2 + 375c_4c_6 + 2250c_6^2) \\ & + 36c_3c_5(125c_4^2 + 528c_5^2 + 3360c_4c_6 + 25725c_6^2) \\ & + 3c_2[45c_4^3 + 1584c_4c_5^2 + 1590c_5^2 + 1590c_4^2c_6 + 21360c_5^2c_6 \\ & + 21525c_4c_6^2 + 110250c_6^3 + 12c_3^2(c_4 + 10c_6) \\ & + 8c_3c_5(32c_4 + 375c_6)] + 9[45c_4^4 + 8704c_5^4 + 2415c_4^3c_6 \\ & + 932400c_5^2c_6^2 + 3018750c_6^4 + 20c_4^2(178c_5^2 + 2765c_6^2) \\ & + 35c_4(3104c_5^2c_6 + 18075c_6^3)]\}\end{aligned} \tag{14}$$

$$\begin{aligned}
\gamma_5 = {} & 24\{16c_3^5 + 5c_2^4c_5 + 1200c_3^4c_5 \\
& + 10c_2^3(3c_3c_4 + 42c_4c_5 + 40c_3c_6 + 570c_5c6) \\
& + 300c_3^3(10c_4^2 + 128c_5^2 + 280c_4c_6 + 2205c_6^2) \\
& + 1080c_3^2c5[125c_4^2 + 3920c_4c_6 + 28(22c_5^2 + 1225c_6^2)] \\
& + 10c_2^2[2c_3^3 + 72c_3^2c_5 + 3c_3(24c_4^2 + 320c_5^2 + 625c_4c_6 + 4500c_6^2) \\
& + 9c_5(109c_4^2 + 528c_5^2 + 3130c_4c_6 + 24975c_6^2)] \\
& + 30c_2[8c_3^3(2c_4 + 25c_6) + 40c_3^2c_5(16c_4 + 225c_6) \\
& + 3c_3(75c_4^3 + 3168c_4c_5^2 + 3180c_4^2c_6 + 49840c_5^2c_6 + 50225c_4c_6^2 \\
& + 294000c_6^3) + 6c_5(555c_4^3 + 8704c_4c_5^2 + 26225c_4^2c_6 \\
& + 152160c_5^2c_6 + 459375c_4c_6^2 + 2963625c_6^3)] \\
& + 90c_3[270c_4^4 + 16905c_4^3c_6 + 280c_4^2(89c_5^2 + 1580c_6^2) \\
& + 35c_4(24832c_5^2c_6 + 162675c_6^3) + 4(17408c_5^4 + 20979000c_5^2c_6^2 \\
& + 7546875c_6^4)] + 27c_5[14775c_4^4 + 1028300c_4^3c_6 \\
& + 50c_4^2(10144c_5^2 + 594055c_6^2) + 700c_4(27904c_5^2c_6 + 598575c_6^3) \\
& + 3(316928c_5^4 + 68908000c_5^2c_6^2 + 806378125c_6^4)]\}
\end{aligned} \tag{15}$$

$$\begin{aligned}
\gamma_6 = {} & 120\{32c_3^6 + 3456c_3^5c_5 + 6c_2^5c_6 \\
& + 3c_2^4(9c_4^2 + 16c_3c_5 + 168c_5^2 + 330c_4c_6 + 2850c_6^2) \\
& + 720c_3^4(15c_4^2 + 224c_5^2 + 490c_4c_6 + 4410c_6^2) \\
& + 6048c_3^3c_5(125c_4^2 + 704c_5^2 + 4480c_4c_6 + 44100c_6^2) \\
& + 12c_2^3[4c_3^2(3c_4 + 50c_6) + 60c_3c_5(7c_4 + 114c_6) \\
& + 3(24c_4^3 + 1192c_4c_5^2 + 1170c_4^2c_6 + 20440c_5^2c_6 + 20150c_4c_6^2 \\
& + 124875c_6^3)] + 216c_3^2[945c_4^4 + 67620c_4^3c_6 \\
& + 560c_4^2(178c_5^2 + 3555c_6^2) + 315c_4(12416c_5^2c_6 + 90375c_6^3) \\
& + 6(52224c_5^4 + 6993000c_5^2c_6^2 + 27671857c_6^4)] \\
& + 6c_2^2[8c_3^4 + 480c_3^3c_5 + 180c_3^2(4c_4^2 + 64c_5^2 + 125c_4c_6 + 1050c_6^2) \\
& + 72c_3c_5(327c_4^2 + 1848c_5^2 + 10955c_4c_6 + 99900c_6^2) \\
& + 9(225c_4^4 + 22824c_4^2c_5^2 + 69632c_5^4 + 15090c_4^3c_6) + 830240c_4c_5^2c_6
\end{aligned} \tag{16}$$

(Equation 16 continues on next page)

$$
\begin{aligned}
&+ 412925c_4^2c_6^2 + 8239800c_5^2c_6^2 + 5475750c_4c_6^3 + 29636250c_6^4)] \\
&+ 1296c_3c_5[5910c_4^4 + 462735c_4^3c_6 + c_4^2(228240c_5^2 + 14851375c_6^2) \\
&+ 175c_4(55808c_5^2c_6 + 1316865c_6^3) + 3(158464c_5^4 + 37899400c_5^2c_6^2 \\
&+ 483826875c_6^4)] + 27[9945c_4^6 + 92930048c_5^6 + 1166130c_4^5c_6 \\
&+ 35724729600c_5^4c_6^2 + 977816385000c_5^2c_6^4 \\
&+ 1907724656250c_6^6 + 180c_4^4(16082c_5^2 + 345905c_6^2) \\
&+ 140c_4^3(1765608c_5^2c_6 + 13775375c_6^3) \\
&+ 15c_4^2(4076032c_5^4 + 574146160c_5^2c_6^2 + 2424667875c_6^4) \\
&+ 210c_4(13526272c_5^4c_6 + 687499200c_5^2c_6^3 + 1876468125c_6^5)] \\
&+ 18c_2[80c_3^4(c_4 + 15c_6) + 160c_3^3c_5(32c_4 + 525c_6) \\
&+ 12c_3^2(225c_4^3 + 11088c_4c_5^2 + 11130c_4^2c_6 \\
&+ 199360c_5^2c_6 + 200900c_4c_6^2 + 1323000c_6^3) \\
&+ 24c_3c_5(3885c_4^3 + 69632c_4c_5^2 + 209800c_4^2c_6 \\
&+ 1369440c_5^2c_6 + 4134375c_4c_6^2 + 29636250c_6^3) \\
&+ 9[540c_4^5 + 48585c_4^4c_6 + 20c_4^3(4856c_5^2 + 95655c_6^2) \\
&+ 80c_4^2(71597c_5^2c_6 + 513625c_6^3) \\
&+ 4c_4(237696c_5^4 + 30726500c_5^2c_6^2 + 119844375c_6^4) \\
&+ 5c_6(4076032c_5^4 + 191074800c_5^2c_6^2 + 483826875c_6^4)]]\}
\end{aligned}
$$

APPENDIX 2

$$
\begin{aligned}
\text{Let } S_1 &= 54c_4^3 - 216c_3c_4c_5 + 432c_2c_5^2 + 540c_3^2c_6 - 1080c_2c_4c_6 \\
S_2 &= Sc_1^2 - 4(9c_4^2 - 24c_3c_5 + 60c_2c_6)^3 \\
S_3 &= 3c_4^2 - 8c_3c_5 + 20c_2c_6.
\end{aligned}
$$

As such, the expression for S_4, S_5, and S_6 in Equation 9 are

$$
S_4 = \frac{4c_5^2}{25c_6^2} + \frac{(\sqrt{S_2} + S_1)^{1/3}}{15c_6 2^{1/3}} + \frac{S_3 2^{1/3}}{5c_6(\sqrt{S_2} + S_1)^{1/3}} - \frac{2c_4}{5c_6}
$$

$$S_5 = \frac{1}{\sqrt{S_4}}\left(\frac{48c_4c_5}{100c_6^2} - \frac{16c_3}{20c_6} - \frac{64c_5^3}{500c_6^3}\right)$$

$$S_6 = \frac{8c_5^2}{25c_6^2} - \frac{(\sqrt{S_2}+S_1)^{1/3}}{15c_6 2^{1/3}} - \frac{S_3 2^{1/3}}{5c_6(\sqrt{S_2}+S_1)^{1/3}} - \frac{4c_4}{5c_6}$$

APPENDIX 3

The empirical distributions with the sample moments and cumulants listed in Table 3 were computed as (Headrick, 2002)

$$m_1 = \sum_{j=1}^{n} x_j / N$$

$$m_2 = \sum_{j=1}^{n} (x_j - m_1)^2 / N$$

$$\hat{\gamma}_3 = m_3 / m_2^{3/2}$$

$$\hat{\gamma}_4 = m_4 / m_2^{2/2} - 3$$

$$\hat{\gamma}_5 = m_5 / m_2^{5/2} - 10 m_3 / m_2^{3/2}$$

$$\hat{\gamma}_6 = m_6 / m_2^3 - 15 m_3 / m_2^2 - 10 m_3^2 / m_2^3 + 30$$

where $m_i = \sum_{j=1}^{n} (x_j - m_1)^i / N$ and for $i = 3,\ldots, r = 6$.

REFERENCES

Blair, R. C. (1987). *RANGEN* [Comuter software]. Boca Raton, FL: IBM.

Blair, R. C. (1981). A reaction to "Consequences of failure to meet assumptions underlying fixed effects analysis of variance and covariance." *Review of Educational Research 51*, 499-507.

Beasley, T. M. (2002). Multivariate aligned rank test for interactions in multiple group repeated measures. *Multivariate Behavioral Research, 37*, 197-226.

Beasley, T. M., & Zumbo, B. D. (2003). Comparison of aligned Friedman rank and parametric methods for testing interactions in split-plot designs. *Computational Statistics and Data Analysis, 42*, 569-593.

Bradley, J. V. (1968). *Distribution free statistical tests*. Englewood Cliffs, NJ: Prentice-Hall.

Bradley, J. V. (1982). The insidious L-shaped distribution. *Bulletin of the Psychonomic Society, 20*, 85-88.

Fleishman, A. I. (1978). A method for simulating non-normal distributions. *Psychometrika, 43*, 521-532.

Habib, A. R., & Harwell, M. R. (1989). An empirical study of the Type I error rate and power of some selected normal theory and nonparametric tests of independence of two sets of variables. *Communications in Statistics: Simulation and Computation, 18*, 793-826.

Harwell, M. R., & Serlin, R. C. (1988). An experimental study of a proposed test of nonparametric analysis of covariance. *Psychological Bulletin, 104*, 268-281.

Harwell, M. R., & Serlin, R. C. (1989). A nonparametric test statistic for the general linear model. *Journal of Educational Statistics, 14*, 351-371.

Headrick, T. C. (2002). Fast fifth-order polynomial transforms for generating univariate and multivariate non-normal distributions. *Computational Statistics and Data Analysis, 40*, 685-711.

Headrick, T. C. (2004a, June). *Distribution theory for the power method.* Paper presented at the annual meeting of the Psychometric Society, Monterey, CA. Available: http://www.siu.edu/~epse1/headrick/PowerMethod.pdf

Headrick, T. C. (2004b). On polynomial transformations for simulating multivariate non-normal distributions. *Journal of Modern Applied Statistical Methods, 3*, 65-71.

Headrick, T. C., & Beasley, T. M. (2004). A method for simulating correlated non-normal systems of linear statistical equations. *Communications in Statistics: Simulation and Computation, 33*, 19-33.

Headrick, T. C., & Rotou, O. (2001). An investigation of the rank transformation in multiple regression. *Computational Statistics and Data Analysis, 38*, 203-215.

Headrick, T. C., & Sawilowsky, S. S. (1999). Simulating correlated non-normal distributions: Extending the Fleishman power method. *Psychometrika, 64*, 25-35.

Headrick, T. C., & Sawilowsky, S. S. (2000a). Properties of the rank transformation in factorial analysis of covariance. *Communications in Statistics: Simulation and Computation, 29*, 1059-1088.

Headrick, T. C., & Sawilowsky, S. S. (2000b). Weighted simplex procedures for determining boundary points and constants for the univariate and multivariate power methods. *Journal of Educational and Behavioral Statistics, 25*, 417-436.

Headrick, T. C., & Vineyard, G. (2001). An empirical investigation of four tests for interaction in the context of factorial analysis of covariance. *Multiple Linear Regression Viewpoints, 27*, 3-15.

Headrick, T. C., & Zumbo, B. D. (2004). A method for simulating multivariate non-normal distributions with specified intraclass correlations. *Proceedings of the Statistical Computing Section, American Statistical Association* (pp. 2462-2467). Alexandria, VA: The American Statistical Association.

Hess, B., Olejnik, S., & Huberty, C. J. (2001) The efficacy of two improvement-over-chance effect sizes for two group univariate comparisons under variance heterogeneity and nonnormality. *Educational and Psychological Measurement, 61*, 909-936.

Hipp, J. R., & Bollen, K. A. (2003) Model fit in structural equation models with censored, ordinal, and dichotomous variables: Testing vanishing tetrads. *Sociological Methodology, 33*, 267.

Klockars, A. J., & Moses, T. P. (2002). Type I error rates for rank-based tests of homogeneity of regression slopes. *Journal of Modern Applied Statistical Methods, 1*, 452-460.

Kowalchuk, R. K., Keselman, H. J., & Algina, J. (2003) Repeated measures interaction test with aligned ranks. *Multivariate Behavioral Research, 38*, 433-461.

Lehmann, E. L. (1998). *Nonparametrics: Statistical methods based on ranks*. Upper Saddle River, NJ: Prentice-Hall

Lix, L. M., Algina, J., & Keselman, H. J. (2003). Analyzing multivariate repeated measures designs: A comparison of two approximate degrees of freedom procedures. *Multivariate Behavioral Research, 38*, 403-431.

Micceri, T. (1989). The unicorn, the normal curve, and other improbable creatures. *Psychological Bulletin, 105*, 156-166.

Olejnik, S. F., & Algina, J. (1987). An analysis of statistical power for parametric ANCOVA and rank transform ANCOVA. *Communications in Statistics: Theory and Methods, 16*, 1923-1949.

Pearson, E. S., & Please, N. W. (1975). Relation between the shape of population distribution and the robustness of four simple test statistics. *Biometrika*, 63, 223-241.

Project MATCH Research Group. (1993). Project MATCH: Rationale and methods for a multisite clinical trial matching patients to alcoholism treatment. *Alcoholism: Clinical and Experimental Research, 17*, 1130-1145.

Project MATCH Research Group. (1997). Matching alcoholism treatments to client heterogeneity: Project MATCH posttreatment drinking outcomes. *Journal of Studies on Alcohol, 58*, 7-29.

Rasch, D., & Guiard, V. (2004). The robustness of parametric statistical methods. *Psychology Science, 46*, 175-208.

Reinartz, W. J., Echambadi, R., & Chin, W. W. (2002). Generating non-normal data for simulation of structural equation models using Mattson's method. *Multivariate Behavioral Research, 37*, 227-244.

Sawilosky, S. S., & Blair, (1992). A more realistic look at the robustness and type I error properties of the t-test to departures from population normality. *Psychological Bulletin, 111*, 352-360.

Scheffe, H. (1959). *The analysis of variance*. New York: John Wiley & Sons.

Shieh, Y. (2000, April). *The effects of distributional characteristics on multi-level modeling parameter estimates and Type I error control of parameter tests under conditions of non-normality.* Paper presented at the annual meeting of the American Educational Research Association, New Orleans, LA.

Steyn, H. S. (1993). On the problem of more than one kurtosis parameter in multivariate analysis, *Journal of Multivariate Analysis, 44*, 1-22.

Stone, C. (2003). Empirical power and type I error rates for an IRT fit statistic that considers the precision and ability estimates. *Educational and Psychological Measurement, 63*, 566-583.

Vale, C. D., & Maurelli, V. A. (1983). Simulating multivariate nonnormal distributions. *Psychometrika, 48*, 465-471.

Wolfram, S. (2003). *The mathematica book* (5th ed.). Champaign, IL: Wolfram Media.

Zhu, R., Yu, F., & Liu, S. (2002, April). *Statistical indexes for monitoring item behavior under computer adaptive testing environment.* Paper presented at the annual meeting of the American Educational Research Association, New Orleans, LA.

CHAPTER 5

HOW AND WHY I USE REAL, MESSY DATA TO INVESTIGATE THEORY AND INFORM DECISION MAKING

Theodore Micceri

I first dealt extensively with real data during my days as a professional gambler (1975-1978), where an uncompromising bottom line (food on the table or not) forced me to recognize that many of the methods and so-called truths taught in my graduate statistics and research courses did not work effectively with real-world data. Over time, the following fundamental practices evolved, which have served well to this day: (1) obtain the largest feasible samples. (2) Conduct extensive exploratory investigations before designing decision-oriented studies (may be a literature review). (3) Replicate any study in at least two, and preferably three different environments or years (cross validate). (4) Use robust statistics where appropriate.

During my doctoral program, I managed to conduct some formal researches using real-world data which found: (1) that empirical distributions rarely begin to approximate so-called normality (Micceri, 1989); but, despite this, (2) the arithmetic mean, at least for educational and psy-

Real Data Analysis, pp. 99–103

chological measures, is a comparatively efficient location estimator (Micceri, 1990). The second finding, which completely contradicts the widely cited Princeton Robustness Study (PRS) of Andrews, Bickel, Hampel, Huber, Rogers, and Tukey (1972) occurs because the perfectly symmetrical and extremely long-tailed theoretical distributions used in the PRS never occur among the bounded empirical distributions of education and psychology. The distributions in Micceri (1989) also proved to be somewhat less extreme than those I used in Nevada. This learning added one step to my analytical practice: conduct analyses using both ordinary least squares (OLS) and robust statistics if feasible. Although this action both increases multiplicity and violates tradition, it has proven useful. Usually both statistics produce similar results, however, when they differ, investigation of those differences can prove enlightening.

In 1992, I began working as an institutional researcher (IR), which gave access to volumes of real data. As a result, some colleagues and I were able to conduct an extensive error analysis study comparing survey measures with "true" scores (Takalkar, Waugh & Micceri, 1993) where we learned (1) that surveys are very common as a source for quantitative analyses, and (2) that substantial bias (frequently 20% or more) is not unusual in survey responses. Although this result caused no change in practices, it made me even more acutely aware of how difficult it is to find quality, unbiased measures in the social sciences and supported Tukey's (1977) arguments for the use of data primarily as indicators.

SOME ISSUES WITH REAL INSTITUTIONAL RESEARCH DATA

The problems involved in conducting proper data analysis vary depending on the data, but all real-world data come saddled with impediments that can mislead the unwary. Institutional researchers at Florida State University System (SUS) institutions are blessed with more and better data sources than most IR colleagues worldwide. Nonetheless, many problems exist. First, much data are politically sensitive. For example, because funding is based on student credit hours, enrollment data records are carefully scrubbed and both double and triple checked before final recording. However, the same is not true for admissions data, and faculty activity data, other than courses taught, involves considerable guesswork.

Two important factors for institutional data are variable definition and time. There are several ways to define even something as seemingly simple as a student, and different definitions result in different counts. Further, because semesters are alive, recordings from the first day, 2 weeks later, and at the end of a semester differ substantially on every variable.

Thus, definitions must include both time and variable characteristics. This results in benchmark data.

Student variables involve many confounds. For example, 15% of new graduate students show no test scores, and institutions frequently divide up tests like the SAT and treat each part separately. Thus, if a student submits four SAT scores, the highest verbal plus the highest quantitative will be recorded as their combined SAT score, because this is the basis for admission. Another example is the part-time student classification. At semester-based schools, part-time is less than 12 hours, largely because 12 credits qualify a student for federal financial aid. Many students (perhaps 20%) enroll for 12 hours, obtain their financial aid, and then drop back to fewer courses. In the records, such students are misleadingly recorded as full-time.

The number of faculty is commonly used to indicate the institution's size, or to standardize measures for comparison between different sized institutions. Faculty effort is frequently used in financial analyses. Unfortunately, all faculty variables are politically sensitive, and can change substantially from year to year depending on the emphasis of a legislator, a university system, or an institutional president. For example, the University of Central Florida, with the same number of students as the University of South Florida, reports only half as many full-time faculty, an obvious impossibility. As the preceding shows, measures in higher education are anything but simple, and working with them requires both knowledge and creativity.

AN APPLICATION EXAPLE

This section describes the methods used in two successive studies of graduate students, both of which produced rather interesting findings and used both typical and unusual data analysis methods. The first involved an extensive multiyear investigation of 15,644 graduate students (14,065 MA/MS) on factors influencing success in graduate school (graduation). This study clearly showed that none of the variables typically used to screen students for admissions purposes (grade point average, test scores, race/ethnicity, discipline area, etc.) related in any meaningful way to success in graduate study. The only variable that did relate with higher graduation/retention rates was full-time enrollment in the first semester. The second, follow-up study which is described in more detail below, resulted when our graduate dean requested an in-depth analysis of standardized tests, because he simply could not believe that the Graduate Record Exam (GRE) subtests did not have at least some relationship with success in their related disciplines (quantitative with math intensive disciplines, verbal with language intensive disciplines).

Although much of the data used in these studies were thoroughly scrubbed and tested for internal consistency before entering the SUS archived benchmark files, for the first study, before beginning analyses, I conducted further cleaning through review of frequency distributions and scatter plot investigation of bivariate relationships among variables of interest. This resulted in the elimination of a few cases that could cause problems during analysis. Such action is wise if one desires interpretable findings, as Relles and Rogers (1977) demonstrated.

One very important issue when working with decision makers is to create clearly understandable methods and findings. Therefore, rather than deal with the uninterpretable nonlinear transformations used in logistic regression, I decided instead to expand the scale of the dependent graduation variable and make it an ordinal three-point scale (0 = attended one semester or less/1 = attended two or more semesters, and 3 = graduated) thereby avoiding the statistical limitations that associate with the traditional two-point ordinal/dichotomous variable (not graduated/graduated). This allowed the use of a both traditional OLS and rank-transform multiple regression (Conover & Iman, 1981) in place of logistic regression. Today, I would use multilevel modeling, but at that time I was unaware of its capacities.

Analyses were conducted at the college and at the department levels for large departments. All samples of 250 or more were randomly separated into two groups on which analyses were independently run (internal cross validation). The second study, which emphasized analysis at the major level, involved only masters-level graduate students due to sample sizes (too few doctoral students). Only cohorts having at least 1.67 years to graduate were included: 1990 through 1997 (which had 2 years of data).

In the second study, at the major level and looking only at subtest relationships with success, both Pearson r and Spearman r_{ranks} correlations were run between success and subtest scores. Both correlation methods produced essentially the same results in 26 departments having adequate samples (40 or more students), with the median relationship being –0.01 for quantitative and –0.03 for verbal. These zero-order correlations ranged from –0.19 to 0.12.

When informed of these findings, the dean prompted further analyses by asking whether some threshold score exists below which students have difficulty in math or language-intensive disciplines. To evaluate this, each subtest value (GRE Quantitative, GRE Verbal, GMAT) was classified into one of four groups (<400, 400-499, 500-599, ≥ 600), and the percent graduating in each group was computed. Interestingly, and surprisingly, this form of analysis disclosed negative and comparatively monotonic relationships between success and test score groups, with the lower scoring groups showing small, but consistently higher graduation rates than the higher scoring groups. At the college level, the highest graduation percentages occurred the following number of times for each group: < 400 (8 times), 400-499 (4 times), 500-599 (3 times), ≥ 600 (2 times). Almost identical results occurred at the discipline level, with one exception, Engineering. The most likely reason for this effect of lower tests and higher graduation may be that more stringent admission criteria are used for students who score lower on the tests. If true, this suggests that such criteria should be applied to all prospective students. As a result of these findings, the dean told colleges and departments that they were no longer required to use test scores for admission purposes if they did not want to. This prompted our dean of visual and performing arts to proffer profuse thanks, proved the power of data-based decision making, and stimulated Micceri (2002).

REFERENCES

Andrews, D. F., Bickel, P. J., Hampel, F. R., Huber, P. J., Rogers, W. H., & Tukey, J. W. (1972). *Robust estimates of location survey and advances*. Princeton, NJ: Princeton University Press.

Conover, W., & Iman, R. (1981). Rank transformations as a bridge between parametric and nonparametric statistics. *The American Statistician, 35*(3), 124 -134.

Micceri, T. (1989). The unicorn, the normal curve and other improbable creatures. *Psychological Bulletin, 105*(1), 156-166.

Micceri, T. (1990, April). *Feel no guilt! Your statistics are probably robust*. Paper presented at the annual meeting of the American Educational Research Association, Boston, MA. (ERIC #TM014696)

Micceri, T. (2002, June). *Evidence suggesting we should admit students who score extremely low on GRE subtests or the GMAT to graduate school programs*. Paper presented at AIR 2002 Annual Forum Paper, Toronto, Canada.

Relles, D. A., & Rogers, W. H. (1977). Statisticians are fairly robust estimators of location. *Journal of the American Statistitical Association, 72,* 107–111.

Tukey, J. (1977). *Exploratory data analysis*. Reading, MA: Addison-Wesley.

Talkalkar, P., Waugh, G., & Micceri, T. (1993, July). *A search for truth in student's answers to survey questions*. Paper presented at the AIR Annual Forum, Chicago, IL. (ERIC #ED360934)

PART II

STATISTICAL METHODS

CHAPTER 6

USING E-MAIL MESSAGES TO HELP STUDENTS PREPARE FOR A STATISTICS EXAM

Schuyler W. Huck

BACKGROUND AND PURPOSE

As typically taught, a semester-long graduate course in statistics covers a wide array of topics. A survey of online syllabi for such courses reveals that students are usually expected to learn about descriptive techniques, bivariate correlation and linear regression, sampling, probability, estimation, hypothesis testing, and various test procedures (e.g., z and t tests, one-way ANOVA, posthoc tests, and chi square tests). By the time the semester comes to a close, many students report that they are fully overwhelmed by the many concepts (e.g., kurtosis), symbols (e.g., β), test procedures (e.g., paired t), assumptions (e.g., homoscedasticity), and relationships (e.g., between n and Type II error risk) covered during the academic term.

Several researchers have sought to discover ways to help students gain better control over the content of their statistics courses. For example, Sirias (2002) investigated the use of advance organizers, Hakeem (2001) and

Real Data Analysis, pp. 107–113

Kvam (2000) examined the effect of active learning projects, Martin (2003) focused on the potential learning power of analogies, Boger (2001) studied the impact of using student-generated data, Root and Thorme (2001) asked whether community-based projects can enhance students' understanding of statistics, and Chan, Cheng, and Pritchard (2000) looked at the possible benefits of bringing real-life examples (e.g., videotapes and newspaper clippings) into the classroom.

Researchers have also investigated the effects of certain technology-related factors on student learning in statistics courses. For example, Cabilio and Farrell (2001) discussed the advantages of having a computer-based lab as a supplement to lectures, Spinelli (2001) compared the in-class use of computers versus calculators, and Leon and Parr (2000) argued that a course "home page" facilitates the learning process.

Surprisingly, no study has been conducted to assess the impact of instructor-sent e-mail messages focused on course content (see, for example, Rowell, 2004). This is surprising because (a) most graduate students read their incoming e-mail messages at least once a day, (b) instructors can easily send messages to groups of students via distribution lists or listservs, and (c) e-mail messages can be sent from instructor to student with no expense to either party.

The question posed in this investigation was simple: Will students benefit from a daily series of brief e-mail messages in which each message reviews a few previously-covered definitions, symbols, and relationships? Such e-mailed pieces of course content were construed to be (and were referred to as) "tidbits." Hence, the single objective of this study was to find out, by means of a carefully-designed experiment that was fair to all participants, whether e-mailed tidbits of information help students perform better on the final exam.

METHOD

Participating Students and Their Statistics Courses

The 52 students involved in this study were enrolled in two different master's programs offered at a large state university in the southeast region of the United States. The majority of these students were women with the participants' ages ranging from 22 to 58. None of the students was majoring in statistics, and each was enrolled simply because his/her statistics course was a curricular requirement.

One of the two courses was offered through the department of educational psychology; the other was offered through the department of audiology and speech pathology. These courses covered the same topics, used the same text, and were taught by the same instructor. The two courses had nearly identical syllabi, with exactly the same grading procedures. For all practical purposes, these two different courses were equivalent to two sections of the same course.

The Study's E-mail Messages

Thirty-one days prior to the final examination, students in both courses received an "overview" e-mail message explaining that their instructor was going to send, on a daily basis (weekend days included), an e-mail message containing five tidbits of course material. This first message pointed out that this series of e-mail messages was designed to help students (1) remain mindful of "old" course material covered earlier in the semester and (2) keep up with the "new" material that was to come. Students were encouraged to read each set of tidbits on the day it arrived, but doing so was left up to the students.

Four "rules" governed the creation of each day's set of tidbits. First, each tidbit had to be short enough to fit on one line of the computer screen. This meant each tidbit had to contain no more than 80 characters, including all punctuation and spaces. Second, each tidbit had to be tied to important course content. Third, the five tidbits sent in a single e-mail message had to deal with different sections of the reading material. Finally, tidbits sent on different days could deal with the same course concept (e.g., level of significance) but could not be repeated verbatim.

Here is the third set of tidbits that was sent to the 52 students:

1. If $M = 40$ and $SD = 6$, your z-score would be $+1.5$ if your raw score is 49.
2. A phi correlation is used when both variables are true dichotomies.
3. The two kinds of criterion-related validity: predictive and concurrent.
4. A sample is random because of the way it's selected, not how it turns out.
5. Other things held constant, a 95% CI will be narrower than a 99% CI.

The Critical Tidbits and Corresponding Test Questions

The final examination in both courses took place 4 days following the last class session of the semester. During this 3-day interval, students received the 28th, 29th, and 30th sets of tidbits. It was here, after the last class session, that the tidbits critical to this study were created and sent to students. It was deemed important to delay the study until class sessions had ended, for this prevented the instructor from doing anything in class—consciously or unconsciously—that might bias the experiment's results.

Of the last 15 tidbits sent to students, 12 were deemed "critical." They earned this status because each one of them had been randomly selected from a *pair* of tidbits. Thus, standing behind each of the 12 tidbits sent to students was a second, unsent tidbit. The previous rules for creating tidbits applied to both members of a pair. In addition, the two tidbits forming a pair had to deal with similar content, and an effort was made to make both items of each pair equally difficult. Here is one of the 12 pairs of tidbits:

a. Alpha influences but does not by itself determine Type II error risk.
b. Alpha does NOT indicate the probability that the null hypothesis is true.

Prior to selecting (at random, using a table of random numbers) one tidbit from each of the 12 pairs to send to students, a multiple-choice or true-false test question was prepared for each of the 24 tidbits. For example, the test questions prepared for tidbits "a" and "b" shown above were as follows:

a. (T/F) The level of significance determines the probability of a Type II error.
b. (T/F) Once the null hypothesis is rejected, the level of significance specifies the probability that H_0 is true.

The two test questions connected to both members of a pair of tidbits went into the 125-item final exam. Thus, 12 of the exam's 24 critical questions dealt with tidbits the students were sent while the other 12 were connected to unseen tidbits.

Data Sources and Hypotheses

To answer this study's primary question ("Do students benefit from a daily series of brief e-mail messages highlighting pieces of course content?"), two scores from the final exam were computed for each student: how he/she performed on the 12 questions tied to e-mailed tidbits, and how he/she performed on the 12 "parallel" questions tied to unseen tidbits. It was hypothesized that students would do better on the first of these two sets of questions.

RESULTS

Before using the data from the final examination to see if the e-mailed tidbits facilitated learning, the reliability of each set of critical questions was computed. Using Cronbach's method for assessing internal consistency, alpha was found equal to .56 and .45 for the questions based on tidbits that students had seen and not seen, respectively. Although these reliability estimates appear low, it should be noted that each reliability estimate was based on only 12 items. When adjusted—using the Spearman-Brown prophecy formula—to a test length of 125 items (the actual length of the final examination), the two reliabilities turn out equal to .93 and .89.

The students' scores on the final examination's two sets of critical items were subjected to both a paired *t* test and a sign test. Prior to conducting these tests, the two distributions of scores were examined and found to be similar in terms of distributional shape and variability, with no outliers present. For the sign test, a continuity correction was applied after determining that np > 5. In conducting each test, an initial alpha level of .05 was reduced to .025 (via the Bonferroni correction) because multiple tests were applied

The *t* test revealed that the 52 students, on average, earned a higher score on the 12 questions tied to tidbits they had seen (M = 8.25, SD = 2.11) than they did on the 12 questions tied to unsent tidbits (M = 6.90, SD = 1.98), $t(51) = 4.16$, $p < .001$. With 35 of the 52 students scoring higher on the first of these two sets of questions and only 11 scoring higher on the second set, a sign test also showed a statistically significant difference ($z = 3.39$, $p < .001$) between performance on the two sets of exam questions.

DISCUSSION

Although the statistical finding of the paired *t*-test was congruent with the results of the sign test, it is important to ask whether this study possesses sufficient internal validity to make the conclusions trustworthy. Because ethical considerations demanded that all 52 participants receive the same tidbits and take the same final exam, there was no traditional control group or placebo group. Nevertheless, the study's design involved three kinds of "control" that functioned to eliminate any plausible rival hypotheses. First, all critical tidbits and their corresponding test items were written *prior to* the time the two parts of each tidbit pair were randomly assigned to the "sent" and "unsent" conditions of the experiment. Second, the entire experiment took place *after* the instructor met for the last time with students to discuss course content. Finally, the test questions corresponding to the sent and unsent tidbits were interspersed throughout the 125-item final exam.

Some might be unimpressed by this study's main finding because the mean scores on the two sets of final exam questions differed by "only" 1.35 points. Nevertheless, this finding is considered by the author to be significant in a practical (as well as statistical) manner because each mean is based on just 12 questions. Extrapolated to a 125-item test (i.e., the actual length of full final exam used in this study's two courses), the benefit associated with the e-mailed tidbits would be 14.06 points!

Although the author prefers to make statements about practical significance by looking at crude summaries of raw data (such as was done in the previous paragraph by noting the difference between two sample means), some people prefer to look at standardized indices of effect size. In this study, Cohen's d turns out equal to 0.58. This estimate of effect size would be classified as "moderate" according to the generally accepted definitions of small, medium, and large effects.

The results of this study suggest that many students benefit from instructor-created e-mail messages containing tidbits of course content. Because such messages can be prepared quickly (in about 10 minutes), instructors should consider incorporating this practice into the statistics course(s) they teach. Surprisingly, the use of e-mail messages to help students learn statistics was not mentioned in Rowell's (2004) recent review of different technologies available to those who teach statistics.

REFERENCES

Boger, P. (2001). The benefit of student-generated data in an introductory statistics class. *Journal of Education for Business*, *77*, 5-8.

Cabilio, P., & Farrell, P. J. (2001). A computer-based lab supplement to courses in introductory statistics. *American Statistician*, *55*, 228-232.

Chan, L. K., Cheng, S. W., & Pritchard, Z. (2000). A new way to teach university introductory statistics courses. *Quality Progress*, *33*, 59-62.

Hakeem, S. (2001). Effect of experiential learning in business statistics. *Journal of Education for Business*, *77*, 95-98.

Kvam, P. H. (2000). The effect of active learning methods on student retention in engineering statistics. *American Statistician*, *54*, 136-140.

Leon, R. V., & Parr, W. C. (2000). Use of course home pages in teaching statistics. *American Statistician*, *54*, 44-48.

Martin, M. A. (2003). "It's like ... you know": The use of analogies and heuristics in teaching introductory statistics. *Journal of Statistics Education* [Online], *11*(2). Retrieved January 2, 2006, from www.amstat.org/publications/jse/v11n2/martin.html

Root, R., & Thorme, T. (2001), Community-based projects in applied statistics: Using service-learning to enhance student understanding. *American Statistician, 55*, 326-331.

Rowell, G. H. (2004, August). *Assessment of using technology for teaching statistics.* Presentation for the ARTIST Conference [Online]. Retrieved January 4 2006, from www.rossmanchance.com/artist/proceedings/rowell.pdf

Sirias, D. (2002). Using graphic organizers to improve the teaching of business statistics. *Journal of Education for Business, 78*, 33-37.

Spinelli, M. A. (2001). The use of technology in teaching business statistics. *Journal of Education for Business,* 77, 41-44.

CHAPTER 7

RANDOMIZATION TESTS

Statistical Tools for Assessing the Effects of Educational Interventions When Resources are Scarce

Joel R. Levin

In many educational intervention studies, a fundamental contributor to statistical conclusion invalidity (Cook & Campbell, 1979) is the mismatch between the experimental units to which the intervention is administered (often small groups or classrooms) and the statistical units on which the data analysis is based (individual students within small groups or classrooms). Because of statistical assumptions violations that typically arise from within-group nonindependence/interactivity, commonly applied inferential tests of intervention effects are problematic. In particular, such tests yield invalid outcome probabilities associated with intervention effects, which in turn lead to unwarranted conclusions and generalizations about the intervention itself (see, for example, Levin, 2005). In this chapter, I present a selected sampling of inferential statistical procedures that provide valid statistical assessments of the effects of educational interventions under scarce-resource conditions.

Real Data Analysis, pp. 115–123

Complex statistical techniques that similarly provide valid assessments of intervention effects, such as hierarchical linear modeling (e.g., Raudenbush & Bryk, 2002) and time-series analysis (e.g., McCleary & Welsh, 1992), are now readily accessible to educational researchers. Yet, the methods described in this chapter—although perhaps not as comprehensive in their analytic scope as those just mentioned—are much more straightforward insofar as they are easy for researchers to understand and apply. And, as will become apparent, each of these statistical tools: (a) derives from what is known as *permutation* (or *randomization*) statistical theory; and (b) is particularly useful in situations where a researcher's unit resources (namely, the number of individuals, small groups, classrooms, etc., for whom or which the intervention is made available) are limited.

PROBABILITY LOGIC ASSOCIATED WITH RANDOMIZATION TESTS

For the benefit of readers who are not acquainted with permutation/randomization tests and their associated probability logic, I begin by providing a brief description and simple numerical example. For a more extensive consideration of the randomization rationale, the reader should refer to applied nonparametric statistics textbooks, such as Conover (1999) and Hollander and Wolfe (1999), as well as to articles encouraging the use of randomization-based tests and their nonparametric rank analogs, such as Ludbrook and Dudley (1998) and Serlin and Harwell (2004). Also instructive is a discussion of resampling techniques, including statistical "bootstrapping" and "jackknifing" (see Efron & Tibshirani, 1998).

To make the discussion more concrete, suppose that an intervention researcher selects, or has available, 10 elementary school classrooms. Five of these classrooms are randomly assigned to receive an instructional intervention that is designed to boost students' academic performance (intervention classrooms), while students in the other five classrooms continue to receive their regular instruction (control classrooms). Following the instructional phase of the experiment, students in the 10 classrooms are administered a 50-point achievement test and the average test performance within each classroom is calculated. Of interest in this study is the mean achievement-test difference between the five intervention classrooms and the five control classrooms. The obtained mean difference is examined in the context of the distribution of all possible mean differences that can be generated by assigning the 10 obtained classroom means to two instructional conditions, assuming that five classroom means must be assigned to each condition. A statistical test is then conducted by addressing the question: How (un)likely or (im)probable is what actually occurred (i.e., the obtained intervention-control mean difference) in relation to everything that could have occurred (i.e., the distribution of all possible intervention-control mean differences, given the study's design structure and the set of means produced)? Should the result of the foregoing test be deemed statistically improbable (e.g., $p < .05$), then the researcher would conclude that the two instructional methods differ with respect to students' average achievement-test performance.

Let me now supply some hypothetical numbers for this example. With 10 classrooms, consisting of five intervention and five control, the total number of possible mean-difference assignments is given in combinatorial notation as $\binom{10}{5}$, which amounts to 252. Thus, the complete permutation distribution contains 252 possible mean differences, with the most "unlikely" outcomes—under the assumption of no intervention effect, a nondirectional alternative, and, say, a Type I error probability (α) of .05—consisting of the $.05 \times 252 = 12.6$ most extreme mean differences (or as integer values, 6 on each side of the permutation distribution). Suppose that the achievement-test means produced by the five intervention classrooms are, in decreasing order, 42.6, 41.4, 40.1, 39.8, and 37.6, and that the means produced by the five control classrooms are 39.6, 38.0, 36.7, 36.3, and 34.4. With these outcomes, the across-classrooms intervention mean is 40.3 and the across-classrooms control mean is 37.0, for an intervention-control mean difference of 3.3 points. From a permutation test standpoint, given: (1) the data-produced "population" of 10 classroom means, and (2) five classroom means associated with each condition (intervention and control), it can be determined that the mean difference actually obtained, favoring the intervention condition, is the fourth most extreme in the distribution of 252 mean differences. The most extreme mean difference of 4.1 points would occur if the score of 39.6 in the control condition were exchanged with the score of 37.6 in the intervention condition. Thus, the probability of observing a mean difference favoring the intervention condition that is as extreme as, or more extreme than, the one actually obtained is equal to $4/252 = .0159$. For a nondirectional alternative in this equal sample-size situation, the four corresponding extreme mean differences favoring the control condition must be also be incorporated, resulting in a significance probability of $8/252 = .0317$ (which is less than the a priori significance level, α, of .05). Thus, for the present set of 10 classroom means, if five of those means were randomly assigned to each condition it would be very unlikely ($p = .0317$) that a mean difference of at least 3.3 points in favor of the intervention condition could have occurred. This produces the associated conclusion that the two condition distributions differ with respect to their centers.

WHY RANDOMIZATION TESTS?

But why should researchers consider conducting randomization tests of this kind in the first place? For the just-provided intervention vs. control classrooms example, why could not a traditional two-sample t test have been conducted instead? With independent classroom means (rather than nonindependent within-classroom student scores) as the analyzed units, a reasonable case could be made here for the t test. In the face of small sample sizes, however, an assumption that the outcome measures are normally distributed in the respective populations is critical. The two-sample permutation test does not require such an assumption and, thus, is well suited to small-sample situations where normality cannot be assumed or is suspect. The present focus is on intervention research investigations based on small numbers of experimental units, or scarce resources. In what follows, then, variations on the permutation/randomization test theme are presented. The preceding randomization rationale and procedure readily extend to situations with more than two experimental conditions, as well as to within-unit (repeated-measures) designs—see Copeland's 1991 study described in the following section. As an aside, additional factors need to be taken into account when classroom (or other group) means comprise the "small" sample sizes (see, for example, Barcikowski, 1981), but those considerations do not materially affect the present discussion.

A RANDOMIZATION TEST WHEN ONLY A SMALL NUMBER OF UNITS RECEIVES THE INTERVENTION

In the experimental Wisconsin Emerging Scholars (WES) Program at the University of Wisconsin–Madison, mathematically talented students from underrepresented groups were placed in specially designed discussion sections of a first-year calculus course (Millar, Alexander, Lewis, & Levin, 1995). Although the course included a total of 1,049 students, only 28 of those students were part of the WES program and two ($n = 2$) special sections were created for them. One assessment question of interest was: How do students in these two special discussion sections compare with 1,021 students in the $n = 64$ regular sections of the course, with respect to their end-of-semester calculus achievement? To answer this question, the average course grade attained by students in each of the $2 + 64 = 66$ sections was calculated, after statistically controlling for relevant high-school achievement variables. Then, the 66 adjusted means were subjected to a two-sample permutation test, as in the preceding example. For this application, the total number of mean differences in the permutation distribution is equal to $\binom{66}{2}$, or 2,145. It was found that the mean grades for the two WES sections were the 1st and 14th highest in the set of 66 section means and the corresponding significance probability associated with the test of group (WES vs. regular section) identity was equal to .023 ($p < .05$). Note that in this example, because WES students were not randomly assigned to calculus course sections, causal attributions about the efficacy of the experimental program or its components are not warranted. Yet, it can be validly concluded that the two WES sections' comparatively higher mean grades represented a statistically unlikely outcome, in that such an extreme outcome (or outcomes more extreme) would occur only 2.3 times in 100 if the 66 obtained mean grades had been randomly assigned to sections (A conventional *t* test would be difficult to justify in this situation because of the very small number of experimental-program sections (n = 2) combined with the severe sample-size imbalance between the two section types ($n = 2$ vs. $n = 64$).

A RANDOMIZATION TEST OF STATISTICAL INTERACTIONS

Copeland (1991) was interested in determining whether teachers with and without experience in "inquiry teaching" exhibit different classroom teaching behaviors, and whether such behaviors are moderated by the assistance of microcomputers during instruction. That is, in addition to an investigation of inquiry-teaching experience differences in selected teaching behaviors, a focus was on the interaction between inquiry-teaching experience and computer use. Seven teachers (3 who were experienced in inquiry teaching and 4 who were not) each taught half of their classes in the regular manner and half with the assistance of a selected microcomputer program. Because every teacher was observed under both regular and microcomputer format situations, the within-teacher difference between the two represents the effect of the computer-use factor. More importantly for present purposes, a comparison of the three inquiry-experienced teachers and the four inquiry-inexperienced teachers with respect to that difference represents the interaction of concern. Consistent with the preceding examples, two-sample permutation tests were applied to various measures of coded teaching behaviors. On one measure, for example, although a greater amount of explicit instructing behavior was present under the regular teaching format than in the computer instructional format, the difference between the two was far greater for inexperienced teachers (mean instances of 47.9 and 23.8 for regular and computer formats, respectively, for a mean difference of 24.1) than for experienced teachers (13.3 vs. 12.4, for a mean difference of 0.9).

Because the obtained mean difference of 24.1 – 0.9 = 23.2 was the most extreme of all 35 outcomes in the permutation distribution, the significance probability associated with the critical inquiry-teaching experience by computer-use interaction is given by $p = 1/35 = .029$. In the published study, Copeland (1991, p. 444) tested this interaction using a nonparametric rank analog of the exact permutation test presented here, with the same $p = .029$ result.

RANDOMIZATION TESTS IN SINGLE-CASE TIME-SERIES EXPERIMENTS

The preceding randomization-test examples represent the exact small-sample counterparts of familiar parametric one- and two-sample statistical tests of mean differences. Less well known, perhaps, is that randomization tests can be adapted to situations where only one or a few experimental units are observed repeatedly over time, under both intervention and nonintervention conditions, in what are known in the educational and clinical research literatures as single-case designs (e.g., Kazdin, 2003; Kratochwill & Levin, 1992). To illustrate, after presenting their *regulated randomization* statistical procedure for the single-case multiple-baseline design, Koehler and Levin (1999, pp. 213-214) describe an intervention study in which mathematical story problems were presented to four college students under both standard text (baseline) and computer-based (intervention) formats. In the multiple-baseline design, a series of baseline measures is taken, followed by a series of intervention measures, with each participant (or group) phased into the intervention series sequentially at different time points. In the study described, nine time points (representing different instructional sessions) and corresponding performance measures were associated with each student, with the analyzed data consisting of the eight adjacent-measure differences (reflecting "gains" from Session t to Session $t + 1$). Consistent with the Koehler-Levin procedure, the investigator specified in advance that it would be permissible for one student's intervention (computer-based instruction) phase to begin at Session *2*, another student's at either Session 3 or *4*, another's at either Session 5 or *6*, and another's at either Session 7 or 8 (with the actual randomly determined starting session for each student shown in italics). With these design specifications, the randomization distribution consists of the 192 mean "gains" (of the four students) from all potential baseline-to-intervention sessions. The mean gain actually obtained was the third largest in the randomization distribution, resulting in a significance probability of 3/192 = .016, which indicates the benefit of the computer-based instructional approach. McKie (1998) similarly applied the Koehler-Levin procedure in demonstrating that four young children with spastic cerebral palsy were able to improve their hand grasps after wearing a newly designed thumb splint.

Additional single-case randomization designs and analyses are described by Edgington (1992) and Levin and Wampold (1999), among others. Levin and Wampold's *simultaneous start-point generalized randomization model* is a particularly attractive option for scarce-resource educational interventionists, in that it affords a scientifically credible assessment of intervention effects even with only one matched pair of experimental units (i.e., $n = 1$) in the intervention and nonintervention conditions (see, for example, Lall & Levin, 2004).

CONCLUDING COMMENTS

Randomization tests are conceptually simple and situationally versatile statistical tools. Analogous nonparametric rank tests that test for location differences in one or more populations include the Wilcoxon, Mann-Whitney, and Kruskal-Wallis (see, for example, Conover, 1999) and large-sample approximations for those tests can be performed with standard statistical software packages. Unfortunately, most commonly available statistical packages do not yet include improved nonparametric rank procedures that are robust in the face of statistical-assumption violations (e.g., Fligner & Policello, 1981).For small-sample situations (such as those described in this chapter), however, specially developed computer programs that provide exact probability calculations are needed. So are special programs required to conduct the appropriate data randomizations in nonstandard designs, such as the various single-case time-series applications alluded to here. For instance, Koehler and Levin's (2000) RegRand statistical software for Macintosh microcomputers, which was used to perform the preceding multiple-baseline analyses, is available at www.education.wisc.edu/edpsych/research/regrand/. Calculations aside, the present chapter's take-home message is simply this: Because a rich variety of scientifically and statistically valid randomization design-and-analysis strategies can be enlisted in the service of scarce-resource educational intervention assessments, researchers should begin thinking outside the conventional large-sample, large-unit box when planning their intervention studies.

REFERENCES

Barcikowski, R. S. (1981). Statistical power with group mean as the unit of analysis. *Journal of Educational Statistics*, *6*, 267-285.

Conover, W. J. (1999). *Practical nonparametric statistics* (3rd ed.). New York: Wiley.

Cook, T. D., & Campbell, D. T. (1979). *Quasi-experimentation: Design & analysis issues for field settings*. Chicago: Rand-McNally.

Copeland, W. D. (1991). Microcomputers and teaching actions in the context of historical inquiry. *Journal of Educational Computing Research*, *7*, 421-454.

Edgington, E. S. (1992). Nonparametric tests for single-case experiments. In T. R. Kratochwill & J. R. Levin (Eds.), *Single-case research design and analysis: New directions for psychology and education* (pp. 133-157). Hillsdale, NJ: Erlbaum.

Efron, B., & Tibshirani, R. J. (1998). *An introduction to the bootstrap*. (*Monographs on Statistics and Applied Probability* 57). Boca Raton, FL: CRC Press.

Fligner, M. A., & Policello, G. E., II (1981). Robust rank procedures for the Behrens-Fisher problem. *Journal of the American Statistical Association*, *76*, 162-168.

Hollander, M., & Wolfe, D. A. (1999). *Nonparametric statistical methods* (2nd ed.). New York: Wiley.

Kazdin, A. E. (2003). *Research design in clinical psychology* (4th ed.). Boston: Allyn & Bacon.

Koehler, M. J., & Levin, J. R. (1998). Regulated randomization: A potentially sharper analytical tool for the multiple-baseline design. *Psychological Methods*, *3*, 206-217.

Koehler, M. J., & Levin, J. R. (2000). RegRand: Statistical software for the multiple-baseline design. *Behavior Research Methods, Instruments, and Computers*, *32*, 367-371.

Kratochwill, T. R., & Levin, J. R. (Eds.). (1992). *Single-case research design and analysis: New directions for psychology and education*. Hillsdale, NJ: Erlbaum.

Lall, V. F., & Levin, J. R. (2004). An empirical investigation of the statistical properties of generalized single-case randomization tests. *Journal of School Psychology*, *42*, 61-86.

Levin, J. R. (2005). Randomized classroom trials on trial. In G. D. Phye, D. H. Robinson, & J. R. Levin (Eds.), *Empirical methods for evaluating educational interventions* (pp. 3-27). San Diego, CA: Elsevier Academic Press.

Levin, J. R., & Wampold, B. E. (1999). Generalized single-case randomization tests: Flexible analyses for a variety of situations. *School Psychology Quarterly*, *14*, 59-93.

Ludbrook, J., & Dudley, H. (1998). Why permutation tests are superior to *t* and *F* tests in biomedical research. *Journal of the American Statistical Association*, *52*, 127-132.

McCleary, R., & Welsh, W. N. (1992). Philosophical and statistical foundations of time-series experiments. In T. R. Kratochwill & J. R. Levin (Eds.), *Single-case research design and analysis: New directions for psychology and education* (pp. 41-91). Hillsdale, NJ: Erlbaum.

McKie, A. (1998). *Effectiveness of a neoprene hand splint on grasp in young children with cerebral palsy*. Unpublished masters thesis, University of Wisconsin–Madison, Madison, WI.

Millar, S. B., Alexander, B. B., Lewis, H. A., & Levin, J. R. (1995). *Final report on the Pilot Wisconsin Emerging Scholars Program: 1993-94*. University of Wisconsin–Madison, Madison, WI.

Raudenbush, S. W., & Bryk, A. S. (2002). *Hierarchical linear models: Applications and data analysis methods* (2nd ed.). Thousand Oaks, CA: Sage.

Serlin, R. C., & Harwell, M. R. (2004). More powerful tests of predictor subsets in regression analysis under nonnormality. *Psychological Methods*, *9*, 492-509.

CHAPTER 8

A SKIPPED MULTIVARIATE MEASURE OF LOCATION

One- and Two-Sample Hypothesis Testing

Rand R. Wilcox and H. J. Keselman

Let ξ be a measure of location for some p-variate distribution and let $\hat{\xi} = T(X_1, \ldots, X_n)$ be an appropriate estimate of ξ based on the random sample $X_1, \ldots, X_n$, where each X_i is a vector having length p. The estimator $\hat{\xi}$ is said to be affine equivariant if

$$T(X_1 A + B, \ldots, X_n A + B) = T(X_1, \ldots, X_n)A + B \tag{1}$$

where A is any nonsingular square matrix, and B is a vector having length p. So in particular, affine equivariance requires that a measure of location be transformed properly under rotations as well as changes in scale and shifts in the possible values of X. There are many robust affine equivariant measures of location in the univariate case, but typically, if they are applied to the marginal distributions in the multivariate case, they are no

Real Data Analysis, pp. 125–137

longer affine equivariant. For example, the marginal medians are not affine equivariant as noted by Donoho and Gasko (1992).

Many multivariate affine equivariant estimators have been proposed (e.g., Wilcox, in press), but very little is known about how applied researchers should test hypotheses when they are used. The problem is not finding a reasonable (theoretically sound) method, but rather knowing whether the choice of method performs reasonably well, or makes a practical difference, particularly when sample sizes are small or even moderately large. Here we focus on an approximation of an affine equivariant estimator which, however, is not itself affine equivariant. Moreover, when using another estimator that is affine equivariant, we note that the operating characteristics of the hypothesis testing method we consider are altered substantially with small to moderate sample sizes. (Controlling the probability of a Type I error, in simulations, when using an affine equivariant estimator, remains an open problem.)

Here, attention is focused on a particular type of skipped estimator with the goal of computing a confidence region for ξ or testing the hypothesis

$$H_0:\xi = 0 \tag{2}$$

This estimator is motivated by results in Wilcox and Keselman (2002) who compared the mean squared error of several estimators that have been proposed. Included were the minimum volume ellipsoid (MVE) estimator (Rousseeuw & Leroy, 1987), the minimum covariance determinant (MCD) estimator (Rousseeuw & van Driesen, 1999), a generalization of a trimmed mean proposed by Donoho and Gasko (1992), which is based in part on Tukey's notion of halfspace depth, as well as another generalization of trimmed means derived by Liu, Parelius and Singh (1999). In the simulation study conducted by Wilcox and Keselman (2002), only one estimator maintained relatively high accuracy among the multivariate distributions considered, namely the skipped estimator described in section 2. Letting ξ_j be the jth element of ξ, $j = 1, \ldots, p$, Wilcox and Keselman found a method that controls the probability of at least one Type I error when testing the p hypotheses H_0: $\xi_j = 0$. However, attempts at controlling the probability of a Type I error when dealing with the omnibus test, given by equation (2), failed. Their main strategy for testing Equation 2, which is reviewed in section 3, was to apply the general approach derived by Liu and Singh (1997) using Mahalanobis depth. This approach has been found to be effective for a wide range of situations (Wilcox, 2003, in press), but it was unsatisfactory for the problem at hand. The primary difficulty is that the actual probability of a Type I error was found to be highly unstable for the situations considered in their simulations. So, for example, if adjustments were made so that under normality, good control over the probability of a Type I error was obtained, situations were found where the actual probability of a Type I error can be well above or below the nominal level. Moreover, even altering the correlation among the marginal distributions changed the actual probability of a Type I error, and increasing p was found to affect the properties of the method as well.

When dealing with a wide range of other related problems, several unpublished studies by the first author found that replacing Mahalanobis depth by some other measure of depth mentioned by Liu and Singh (1997) provided no practical advantage. In contrast, for the situation considered here, replacing Mahalanobis depth by another measure of depth, and simultaneously making an adjustment when sample sizes are small, is found to be much more satisfactory. When sampling from a sufficiently heavy-tailed distribution, the actual probability of a Type I error was found to drop well below the nominal level when the sample size is small, so there is room for improvement. However, all indications are that Type I errors well above the nominal level can be avoided, and the actual probability of a Type I error was found to be fairly insensitive to increases in p. Also, unlike Wilcox and Keselman (2002), results on the two-sample case are reported.

DESCRIPTION OF THE ESTIMATOR

This section provides a formal description of the estimator. The basic strategy is to apply a multivariate outlier detection method to the data, remove any outliers found, and average the remaining values. It represents a simple generalization of a skipped (univariate) estimator originally proposed by Tukey which is just the sample mean after points declared outliers, using a boxplot rule, have been removed. Although the small-sample accuracy of the estimator has been compared to several other robust estimators and found to offer a distinct advantage for a wide range of situations (Wilcox & Keselman, 2002), this is not to suggest that all competing estimators have no value. Presumably this is not the case. The only point is that the choice of estimator was not arbitrary. As noted by Wilcox and Keselman (2002), a practical problem is not finding a reasonable outlier detection method for multivariate data, but rather choosing a method from among the many that have been proposed. Here, for completeness, a brief review of some proposed techniques is provided.

Rousseeuw, Ruts and Tukey (1999) suggest a method based on the notion of halfspace depth. They focus mainly on the bivariate case, but in principle the method can be used when $p > 2$; also see Liu et al. (1999) as well as Romanazzi (1997). An approach based on convex hull peeling is discussed by Zani, Riani and Corbellini (1998) but is known to be somewhat less robust than halfspace depth as shown by Donoho and Gasko (1992). Another approach, that has been studied extensively, is related to the strategy behind the MVE and MCD estimators. That is, find the ellipsoid with the smallest volume or smallest covariance determinant that encompasses at least half of the data, and use the corresponding mean and covariance matrix to detect outliers (see, e.g., Davies, 1987; Fung, 1993; Hampel, Ronchetti, Rousseeuw & Stahel, 1986; Rousseeuw & Leroy, 1987; Rousseeuw & van Driesen, 1999; Rousseeuw & van Zomeren, 1990; Tyler, 1991; for additional references, see Peña & Prieto, 2001; cf. Woodruff & Rocke, 1994.) The main paper for detecting outliers based on the MVE estimator is Rousseeuw and van Zomeren (1990). Rocke and Woodruff (1996) describe a method that uses the MVE and MCD estimators as starting values for computing S estimators of location and scatter. Poon, Lew and Poon (2000) suggest a method based in part on a Mahalanobis distance, and yet another approach was recently proposed by Viljoen and Venter (2002). One more strategy, as suggested by Stahel (1981) and Donoho (1982), is motivated by the fact that each outlier among a multivariate sample must be an extreme point based on some projection of the data. Adopting this view, Peña and Prieto (2001) focus on how far points are from the the usual sample mean, and they suggest how to choose interesting projections based on the estimated kurtosis coefficient of the projected observations.

Here, a projection-type method for detecting outliers is used. The motivation for using a projection-type outlier detection method stems in part from the so-called outside rate per observation, which refers to the expected proportion of points declared outliers based on a sample of size n. When searching for an estimator that performs nearly as well as the sample mean under normality, it seems clear that the outside rate per observation should be reasonably low when sampling is from a multivariate normal distribution. Known results on univariate outlier detection methods suggest how to control the outside rate per observation when considering projections, so this strategy is used here. This is not to suggest that all other methods should be eliminated from consideration, but for reasons to be described, the projection-type method used here has practical advantages for the problem at hand, and another convenience is that software is easily written to perform the calculations.

To reduce the number of projections considered, the strategy used by Peña and Prieto (2001) is used where attention is focused on how far a point is from the center of the data. The idea is that by projecting points onto a line that passes through the center of the data, the distances between points on the projected line can be combined with known properties of univariate outlier detection methods in a manner that is advantageous for the problem at hand. But rather than use the sample mean, as was done by Peña and Prieto, the MCD multivariate estimator, say $\hat{\xi}_m$, is used instead. (S-PLUS has a built-in function that computes $\hat{\xi}_m$.) Another difference between the projection method used here and the one used by Peña and Prieto is that they use $2p$ projections only, but we use n.

Given $\hat{\xi}m$, the remaining computational details are as follows. Fix i and for the point X_i, project all n points onto the line connecting $\hat{\xi}_m$ and X_i and let D_j be the distance between $\hat{\xi}_m$ and X_j based on this projection. More formally, let

$$A_i = X_i - \hat{\xi}_m,$$

and

$$B_j = X_j - \hat{\xi}_m,$$

where both A_i and B_j are column vectors having length p, and let

$$C_j = \frac{A_i' B_j}{B_j' B_j},$$

$j = 1, \ldots, n$. Then when projecting the points onto the line between X_i and $\hat{\xi}_m$, the distance of the jth point from $\hat{\xi}_m$ is

$$Dj = |Cj|,$$

where $|Cj|$ is the Euclidean norm of the vector Cj.

Next, a boxplot rule for detecting outliers is applied to the D_j values, but rather than the standard rule, a modification that has close similarities to one used by Carling (2000) is employed. Let $l=[n/4 + 5/12]$, where $[.]$ is the greatest integer function, and let

$$h = \frac{n}{4} + \frac{5}{12} - 1.$$

Let $D_{(1)} \le \cdots \le D_{(n)}$ be the n distances written in ascending order. The so-called ideal fourths associated with the D_j values are

$$q_1 = (1-h)D_{(j)} + hD_{(j+1)}$$

and

$$q_2 = (1-h)X_{(k)} + hX_{(k-1)},$$

where $k = n - j + 1$. Then the jth point is declared an outlier if

$$D_j > M_D + \sqrt{\chi^2_{.95,p}(q_2 - q_1)}, \quad (3)$$

where M_D is the usual sample median based on the D_j values and $\chi^2_{.95,p}$ is the .95 quantile of a chi-squared distribution with p degrees of freedom (cf. Rousseeuw & van Zomeren, 1999).

The process just described is for a single projection; for fixed i, points are projected onto the line connecting X_i to ξ_m. Repeating this process for each i, $i = 1, \ldots, n$, a point is declared an outlier if for any of these projections, it satisfies equation (3). Removing any outliers found by equation (3), and averaging the values that remain, will be called the OP (outlier-projection) estimator and denoted by $\hat{\xi}_{op}$.

Familiarity with robust methods suggests replacing the interquartile range ($q_2 - q_1$) with the median absolute deviation (MAD), which is just median of the values

$$|D_1 - M_D|, \ldots, |D_1 - M_D|$$

and declaring the jth point an outlier if

$$D_j > M_D + \sqrt{\chi^2_{.95,p}}\left(\frac{MAD}{.6745}\right) \quad (4)$$

(Equation 4 represents an approximation of the method given by equation 1.3 in Donoho & Gasko, 1992.) But as previously suggested, if we want to maintain relatively high efficiency under normality when using a skipped estimator, the outside rate per observation should be reasonably close to zero. It is common to search for a method with a rate approximately equal to .05; this usually provides good efficiency under normality. A negative feature of equation (4) is that p_n appears to be considerably less stable as a function of n. In the bivariate case, for example, it is approximately .09 with $n = 10$ and drops below .02 as n increases. So the relative accuracy of the corresponding skipped estimator varies with n. For the same situations, p_n based on Equation 2 ranged between .043 and .038. So the approached based on Equation (4) is not pursued here.

The outside rate per observation for many outlier detection methods has not been studied and addressing this issue goes beyond the scope of this paper. So, of course, some variation of the skipped estimator studied here might give improved results in some sense, but this remains to be determined.

A MEASURE OF DEPTH

Generally, any outlier detection method yields a measure of the depth of a point in a cloud of data. That is, they provide (and in fact are based on) a numerical characterization of how deeply a point is located within the data. For the projection method for detecting outliers, the numerical measure of the depth of a point is as follows. Let D_{ij} be the value of D_j, as given by equation (4), based on the ith projection, $i = 1, ..., n$. Then the depth of the jth point is taken to be

$$Q_j = maxD_{ij},$$

the maximum being taken over all $i = 1, ..., n$. That is, the depth of a point is its largest distance from the center among n projections of the data.

There are two reasons for considering Q_j as a measure of depth. The first is that compared to the halfspace depth, or the simplicial depth described for example by Liu and Singh (1997), it is easy and fast to compute. Second, it makes a practical difference versus using the more familiar Mahalanobis depth, as will be illustrated. Again, this does not mean that other measures of depth have no practical value for the problem at hand.

HYPOTHESIS TESTING

Given that we estimate location using $\hat{\xi}$, a test of H_0 can be computed using the bootstrap method in Liu and Singh (1997). For the random sample X_i, $i = 1, ..., n$, generate a bootstrap sample by resampling with replacement n vectors of observations from $X_1, ..., X_n$, and denote this bootstrap sample by X_i^*. Let $\hat{\xi}^*$ represent the estimate of ξ based on this bootstrap sample. Repeat this process B times and let $\hat{\xi}_b^*$ be the estimate of ξ based on the bth bootstrap sample, $b = 1, ..., B$. Next, taking $\hat{\xi}$, the estimate of ξ based on the original data, as the center of the cloud of bootstrap values, the projection depth of each bootstrap value, plus the depth of the null vector, is computed relative to all of the bootstrap values. If the null vector is sufficiently far from $\hat{\xi}$, reject. That is, from Liu and Singh (1997), these depths can be used to obtain an estimate of their generalized p-value.

To elaborate, the generalized p-value is computed as follows. For convenience, let $\hat{\xi}^*_{B+1}$ be the null vector. Fix b, project all B bootstrap values, plus the null vector, onto the line connecting $\hat{\xi}$ and $\hat{\xi}^*_b$ and let D^*_j be the distance between $\hat{\xi}$ and $\hat{\xi}^*_b$ based on this pr'ojection. Now

$$A_b = \hat{\xi}^*_b - \hat{\xi},$$

$$B_l = \hat{\xi}^*_l - \hat{\xi},$$

$$l = 1, \ldots, B + 1,$$

$$C_l = \frac{A'_b B_l}{B'_l B_l} B_l$$

and

$$D_l = |C_l| \, .$$

Let D_{bl} be the value of D_l based on the bth projection.
For the $B + 1$ distances just computed, b still fixed, determine the ideal fourths and the corresponding estimates of the lower and upper quartiles, say q^*_1 and q^*_2, respectively, and let $U^*_{bl} = D_{bl}/(q^*_2 - q^*_1)$. Repeating this process for all b, $b = 1, \ldots, B + 1$, the projection distance of $\hat{\xi}^*_l$ is

$$V^*_l = max U^*_{bl}, \tag{5}$$

the maximum being taken over all b. Letting $I_l = 1$ if $V^*_{B=1} \le V^*_l$, otherwise $I_l = 0$, the estimate of the Liu and Singh (1997) generalized p-value is

$$\hat{p} = \frac{1}{B} \sum_{l=1}^{B} I_l \tag{6}$$

Asymptotically, $\hat{p}$ has a uniform distribution when the null hypothesis is true, so with n sufficiently large, reject at the α level if $\hat{p} \le \alpha$.

For small sample sizes, the obvious decision rule just described does not provide adequate control over the probability of a Type I error. However, a simple modification improves matters and is based on the strategy used by Gosset to derive Student's T. That is, assume normality, determine an appropriate adjustment for a given sample size, and then use this adjustment when sampling from nonnormal distributions. For the problem at hand, adjustments were determined when all correlations are zero and it was found that this adjustment remains effective for $p = 2, 3, \ldots, 8$ Increasing ρ was found to have a small effect on the actual probability of a Type I error. In contrast, using Mahalanobis distance instead, control over the probability of a Type I error was very unstable as a function of p, n fixed. Moreover, Mahalanobis distance results in less stable control over the probability of a Type I error as the correlation among the variables changed. The small-sample adjustments used here are as follows. When testing at the .05 level, reject if $\hat{p} \le \alpha_a$, where for $n \le 20$, $\alpha_a = .02$; for $20 < n \le 30$, $\alpha_a = .025$; for $n < 30 \le 40$, $\alpha_a = .03$; for $40 < n \le 60$, $\alpha_a = .035$; for $60 < n \le 80$, $\alpha_a = .04$; for $80 < n \le 120$, $\alpha_a = .045$; and for $n > 120$, use $\alpha_a = .05$.

THE TWO-SAMPLE CASE

The method just described is readily extended to the case where two independent groups are being compared. That is, the goal is to test

$$H_0: \xi_1 = \xi_2, \tag{7}$$

where ξ_j is the population value of ξ corresponding to the jth group, $j = 1, 2$. Now, simply generate bootstrap samples from each group, compute the bootstrap estimates of ξ, say $\hat{\xi}_1^*$ and and $\hat{\xi}_2^*$ let $d^* = \hat{\xi}_2^* - \hat{\xi}_2^*$. Repeat this process B times yielding $d_1^*, \ldots, d_B^*$. Now proceed as before. That is, determine how deeply the vector $(0, \ldots, 0)$ is nested within the cloud of b values, $b = 1, \ldots, B$, again using the projection depth.

There remains the issue of how to adjust α when the sample sizes are unequal. What was found to perform relatively well was to set $n = min(n_1, n_2)$ and use α_a as defined in the one sample case.

SIMULATIONS

Simulations were used to check the small-sample properties of the proposed method. Observations were generated where the marginal distributions have a g-and-h distribution (Hoaglin, 1985) which includes the normal distribution as a special case. Both $p = 4$ and $p = 8$ were considered. More precisely, observations Z_{ij}, $i = 1, \ldots, n; j = 1, \ldots, p$ were initially generated from a multivariate normal distribution having common correlations ρ, then the marginal distributions were transformed to

$$X_{ij} = \begin{cases} \frac{\exp(gZ_{ij}) - 1}{g}\exp(hZ_{ij}^2/2), & \text{if } g > 0 \\ Z\exp(hZ_{ij}^2/2), & \text{if } g = 0 \end{cases}$$

where g and h are parameters that determine the third and fourth moments. The four (marginal) g-and-h distributions examined were the standard normal ($g = h = 0$), a symmetric heavy-tailed distribution ($g = 0$, $h = .5$), an asymmetric distribution with relatively light tails ($g = .5$, $h = 0$), and an asymmetric distribution with heavy tails ($g = h = .5$). Also, when dealing with accuracy, simulations were run with $h = 1$. This latter case might be viewed as an extreme departure from normality, but it was considered to see whether any of the estimators perform poorly when sampling from a sufficiently heavy-tailed distribution.

Table 8.1 shows the theoretical skewness (κ_1) and kurtosis (κ_2) for each distribution considered. When $g > 0$ and $h > 1/k$, $E(X^k)$is not defined and the corresponding entry in Table 8.1 is left blank. Additional properties of the g-and-h distribution are summarized by Hoaglin (1985). Some of these distributions might appear to represent extreme departures from normality, but the idea is that if a method performs reasonably well in these cases, this helps support the notion that they will perform well under conditions found in practice.

A possible objection to Table 8.1 when performing simulations is that the distribution of observations generated on a computer does not always have the theoretical skewness and kurtosis values shown. The reason is that observations generated on a computer come from a bounded interval, so the skewness and kurtosis of the distribution will be finite, even when in theory it should be infinite. Accordingly, Table 8.1 also reports the estimated skewness ($\hat{\kappa}_1$) and kurtosis ($\hat{\kappa}_2$) values based on simulations with 10,000 replications.

Table 8.1. Some Properties of the g-and-h Distribution

g	h	κ_1	κ_2	$\hat{\kappa}_1$	$\hat{\kappa}_2$
0.0	0.0	0.00	3.0	0.00	3.0
0.0	0.5	0.00	—	0.00	11,896.2
0.5	0.0	1.75	8.9	1.81	9.7
0.5	0.5	—	—	120.10	18,393.6

Table 8.2. Estimated Type I Error Probabilities, One-Sample Case, α = .05, *n* = 20

h	p	$\hat{\alpha}$	p	$\hat{\alpha}$
0.0	4	.050	8	.061
0.5	4	.005	8	.003
0.0	4	.024	8	.027
0.5	4	.002	8	.004

Table 8.3. Estimated Type I Error Probabilities, Two-Sample Case, α = .05, $n_1 = n_2 = 20$

h	p	$\hat{\alpha}$	p	$\hat{\alpha}$
0.0	4	.050	8	.079
0.5	4	.020	8	.027
0.0	4	.039	8	.069
0.5	4	.022	8	.010

Table 8.2 contains $\hat{\alpha}$, the estimated probability of making a Type I error in the one-sample case when $\rho = 0$. Results varied very little when increasing ρ to .8, so for brevity they are not reported. Generally the method performs well, the main exception being when sampling is form a heavy-tailed distribution, in which case the actual probability of a Type I error can drop well below the nominal level.

It is noted that switching to Mahalanobis distance, $\hat{\alpha}$ was considerably less stable. For example, under normality with $\rho = 0$, $\hat{\alpha} = .068$. Increasing p to 8, the estimate is .16. With $p = 4$ and $\rho = .8$, the estimate is .084. So not all practical problems are eliminated when using projection depth, but it is relatively effective and appears to avoid Type I error probabilities well above the nominal level.

Table 8.3 reports results for the two-sample case. Note that when p=8, Table 8.3 indicates that under normality, $\hat{\alpha} = .079$. Increasing n to 30, the estimate was .068. As for unequal sample sizes, the concern is that $\hat{\alpha}$ might drop substantially as one of the sample sizes increases. For $n_1 = 20$ and $n_2 = 60$, $\hat{\alpha} = .048$ under normality and $\rho = 0$. That is, the estimate barely changes when increasing n_2 from 20 to 60. (This was the reason for the suggestion on how to handle unequal sample sizes.)

CONCLUDING REMARKS

Clearly improvements on the proposed method are needed when the sample size is small, but at least it performs reasonably well compared to the more obvious alternatives. Although the method becomes too conservative in terms of Type I errors when sampling from a very heavy-tailed distribution, perhaps in realistic situations this is not a practical issue. Nonetheless, Type I error probabilities well above the nominal level can be avoided.

REFERENCES

Carling, K. (2000). Resistant outlier rules and the non-Gaussian case. *Computational Statistics & Data Analysis, 33*, 249–258.

Davies, P. L. (1987). Asymptotic behavior of S-estimators of multivariate location parameters and dispersion matrices. *Annals of Statistics, 15*, 1269–1292.

Donoho, D. L. (1982). *Breakdown properties of multivariate location estimators*. Doctoral dissertatoin, Harvard University.

Donoho, D. L., & Gasko, M. (1992). Breakdown properties of location estimates based on halfspace depth and projected outlyingness. *Annals of Statistics, 20*, 1803–1827.

Fung, W. -K. (1993). Unmasking outliers and leverage points: A confirmation. *Journal of the American Statistical Association, 88*, 515-519.

Hampel, F. R., Ronchetti, E. M., Rousseeuw, P. J., & Stahel, W. A. (1986). *Robust statistics*. New York: Wiley.

Hoaglin, D. C. (1985) Summarizing shape numerically: The g-and-h distributions. In D. Hoaglin, F. Mosteller, & J. Tukey (Eds.), *Exploring data tables, trends, and shapes* (pp. 461–515). New York: Wiley.

Liu, R. Y., Parelius, J. M., & Singh, K. (1999). Multivariate analysis by data depth: Descriptive statistics, graphics and inference. *Annals of Statistics, 27*, 783–858.

Liu, R. Y., & Singh, K. (1997). Notions of limiting P values based on data depth and bootstrap. *Journal of the American Statistical Association, 92*, 266-277.

Peña, D., & Prieto, F. J. (2001). Multivariate outlier detection and robust covariance matrix estimation. *Technometrics, 43*, 286–299.

Poon, W. -Y., Lew, S. -F., & Poon, Y. S. (2000). A local influence approach to identifying multiple outliers. *British Journal of Mathematical and Statistical Psychology, 53*, 255–273.

Rocke, D. M., & Woodruff, D. L. (1996). Identification of outliers in multivariate data. *Journal of the American Statistical Association, 91*, 1047–1061.

Romanazzi, M. (1997). A schematic plot for bivariate data. *Student, 2*, 149–158.

Rousseeuw, P. J., & Leroy, A. M. (1987). *Robust regression & outlier detection*. New York: Wiley.

Rousseeuw, P. J., Ruts, I. & Tukey, J. W. (1999). The bagplot: A bivariate boxplot. *American Statistician, 53*, 382–387.

Rousseeuw, P. J., & van Driesen, K. (1999). A fast algorithm for the minimum covariance determinant estimator. *Technometrics, 41*, 212–223.

Rousseeuw, P. J., & van Zomeren, B. C. (1990). Unmasking multivariate outliers and leverage points (with discussion). *Journal of the American Statistical Association, 85*, 633–639.

Stahel, W. A. (1981). *Breakdown of covariance estimators.* Research report 31, Fachgruppe für Statistik, E.T.H. Zürich.

Tyler, D. E. (1991). Some issues in the robust estimation of multivariate location and scatter. In W. Stahel & S. Weisberg (Eds.), *Directions in robust statistics and diagnostics, Part II* (pp 327–336). New York: Springer–Verlag.

Viljoen, H., & Venter, J. H. (2002). Identifying multivariate discordant observations: A computer-intensive approach. *Computational Statistics & Data Analysis, 40,* 159–172.

Wilcox, R. R. (2003). *Appling contemporary statistical techniques*. San Diego, CA: Academic Press.

Wilcox, R. R. (in press). *Introduction to robust estimation and hypothesis testing* (2nd ed.). San Diego, CA: Academic Press.

Wilcox, R. R., & Keselman, H. J. (2002). *Multivariate location: Robust estimators and inference.* Unpublished technical report, Deptartment of Psychology, University of Southern California.

Woodruff, D. L., & Rocke, D. M. (1994). Computable robust estimation of multivariate location and shape in high dimension using compound estimators. *Journal of the American Statistical Association, 89,* 888–896.

Zani, S., Riani, M., & Corbellini, A. (1998). Robust bivariate boxplots and multiple outlier detection. *Computational Statistics & Data Analysis 28,* 257–270.

CHAPTER 9

ROBUST STEP-DOWN TESTS FOR MULTIVARIATE GROUP DIFFERENCES

Lisa M. Lix, Ian Clara, Aynslie Hinds, and Charles N. Bernstein

Multivariate analysis of variance (MANOVA) is probably the most well-known technique for testing group differences on several response variables. However, a significant omnibus test is usually only the first step in the analysis; researchers typically wish to determine which dependent variable(s) is (are) responsible for rejection of the global hypothesis. One common approach is to conduct a univariate test on each dependent variable, applying a Bonferroni correction to control the overall rate of Type I errors to the nominal level of significance (Keselman, Wilcox, & Lix, 1998). However this approach does not account for the correlation between the measurements on successive dependent variables and can therefore result in low power to detect group differences.

If the researcher has established an a priori ordering of the dependent variables, an alternative approach is to conduct a step-down analysis (Roy, 1958; Roy & Bargman, 1958). Briefly, the dependent variables are ranked in descending order of importance and tests of group differences are conducted using an analysis of covariance (ANCOVA), in which higher-

Real Data Analysis, pp. 139–147

ranked dependent variables serve as covariates for tests on lower-ranked variables. Under the null hypothesis and assuming that the data are normally distributed, the step-down test statistics, F_k (k = 1 ,..., m) are independent and their associated p-values, p_k, are independent and uniformly distributed on the interval (0,1). The overall rate of Type I errors can be maintained at α by selecting significance levels α_1, ..., α_m such that $\alpha = 1 - \prod_{k=1}^{m} (1 - \alpha_k)$ for the set of tests. A step-down analysis reduces the multivariate problem to a series of univariate analyses, which may be easier for researchers to interpret.

Conventional step-down tests are sensitive to departures from the assumptions of a normal distribution of the dependent variables and homogeneity of group covariances (Lix & Fouladi, in press; Mudholkar & Srivastava, 2000). Robust alternatives to conventional step-down tests, which are insensitive to departures from these assumptions have demonstrated good empirical properties. This paper illustrates a step-down analysis based on robust tests using multivariate data on psychological well-being and quality of life data obtained from a clinical study of individuals with inflammatory bowel disease (IBD). Quality of life data typically do not conform to the assumptions of normality and homogeneity of group variances (Julious, George, Machin, & Stephens, 1997; Ramsey, Berry, Moinpour, Giedzinska, & Andersen, 2002; Rose, Koshman, Spreng, & Sheldon, 1999). Thus, robust tests should be routinely adopted in the analyses of these data in order to obtain valid tests of hypotheses.

DESCRIPTION OF DATA SOURCE

The data were obtained from an ongoing longitudinal study of 390 individuals with IBD. The purpose of the research is to examine the clinical, psychological, and biological effects of IBD on health outcomes. Individuals were selected for inclusion in the study cohort based on a recent (i.e., with the last 7 years) diagnosis of IBD. Entrance into the study cohort occurred between July 2002 and December 2003 and measurements are being collected every 6 months over a 5-year period. Only the baseline data were selected for the current analysis.

Researchers were initially interested in testing for differences on measures of psychological function and health-related quality of life (HRQoL) for patient groups defined by disease type and activity. Disease type has two levels: Crohn's disease and ulcerative colitis. Disease activity also has two levels: active and inactive, which are assigned based on scores for the Harvey-Bradshaw index (Harvey & Bradshaw, 1980) for Crohn's disease and the Powell-Tuck index score score for ulcerative colitis (Powell-Tuck, Brown, & Lennard-Jones, 1978). The measures selected for this numeric example are psychological well-being and mastery (Masse, Poulin, Dassa, Lambert, Belair, & Battaglini, 1998), perceived social support (Zimet, Dahlem, Zimet, & Farley, 1988), and HRQoL. The latter was evaluated using instruments that focus on disease specific HRQoL (IBDQ; Irvine, 1993) and general physical and mental HRQoL (SF-36; Ware, 1993).

DESCRIPTION OF TEST PROCEDURES

The robust step-down analysis test procedures are described in detail in Lix and Fouladi (in press). A SAS/IML program to implement this approach is available at the following URL: http://home.cc.umanitoba.ca/~lixlm. A brief description of the solution follows; it is limited to the two-group case, although the test procedures can be generalized to more than two groups (Lix, Beaumont, & Fouladi, 2005).

Consider a design with $j = 1, 2$ independent groups and $k = 1, \ldots, m$ dependent variables. Let $\mathbf{Y}_j = [y_{ijk}]$ represent the $n_j \times m$ matrix of measurements for the jth group ($i = 1, \ldots, n_j$; $\sum_{j=1}^{J} n_j = N$) and $Y = [\mathbf{Y}_1^{\mathrm{T}} \ldots \mathbf{Y}_J^{\mathrm{T}}]^{\mathrm{T}}$ where ^{T} is the transpose operator. Conventional multivariate tests assume that $\mathbf{Y}_{ij} = [y_{ij1} \ldots y_{ijm}]$ is m-variate normal with mean $\boldsymbol{\mu}_j$ and covariance matrix $\boldsymbol{\Sigma}_j = \boldsymbol{\Sigma}$, where $\boldsymbol{\mu}_j = [\mu_{j1}\, \mu_{j2} \ldots \mu_{jm}]$ is estimated by $\bar{\mathbf{Y}}_j = [\bar{Y}_{j1} \bar{Y}_{j2} \ldots \bar{Y}_{jm}]$ and $\boldsymbol{\Sigma}_j$ is estimated by $\mathbf{S}_j$.

The robust step-down tests defined by Lix and Fouladi (in press) assume neither a normal distribution nor homogeneity of group covariances. Assume that the dependent variables are arranged in decreasing order of importance with $k = 1$ representing the most important variable. Let $\mathbf{Y}_j^* = [\mathbf{y}_{j(1)} \ldots \mathbf{y}_{j(m)}]$, the ordered response matrix for the jth group, $\mathbf{Y}_{j(k)}^* = [\mathbf{y}_{j(1)} \ldots \mathbf{y}_{j(k)}]$ and $\mathbf{Y}_{j(k)}^{**} = [\mathbf{1}\mathbf{y}_{j(1)} \ldots \mathbf{y}_{j(k)}]$ where $\mathbf{1}$ is a vector of 1s. Then $\mathbf{Y}_{j(k)}^* = \mathbf{Y}_{j(k\text{-}1)}^{**} \boldsymbol{\beta}_{j(k\text{-}1)}^* + \varepsilon_{jk}$, where $\boldsymbol{\beta}_{j(k\text{-}1)}^*$ is estimated by

$$\hat{\boldsymbol{\beta}}_{j(k\text{-}1)}^* = \left(\mathbf{Y}_{j(k\text{-}1)}^{**\ \mathrm{T}} \mathbf{Y}_{j(k\text{-}1)}^{**} \right)^{-1} \mathbf{Y}_{j(k\text{-}1)}^{**\ \mathrm{T}} \mathbf{Y}_{j(k)}^* . \tag{1}$$

Let $\mathbf{U}_{j(1)} = \mathbf{y}_{j(1)}$ and $\mathbf{U}_{j(k)} = \mathbf{y}_{j(k)} - \mathbf{Y}^{*}_{j(k-1)}\hat{\boldsymbol{\beta}}^{**T}_{j(k-1)}$ where $\hat{\boldsymbol{\beta}}^{**}_{j(k-1)} = [\hat{\beta}_{j1}\hat{\beta}_{j2} \ldots \hat{\beta}_{j(k-1)}]$, that is, the vector of coefficients excluding the intercept term, for $k = 2, \ldots, m$. Mudholkar and Srivastava (2000) note that while the $\mathbf{U}_{jk}$ are not independently distributed, for N » m their dependence is negligible and they are approximately independent of $\mathbf{y}_{j(1)}, \ldots, \mathbf{y}_{j(k-1)}$.

Define the order statistics for the kth ordered dependent variable, $U_{(1)j(k)} \leq U_{(2)j(k)} \leq U_{(n_j)j(k)}$. Let $g_j = [\gamma n_j]$, where γ represents the proportion of observations to be trimmed in each tail of the distribution and $[x]$ is the greatest integer $\leq x$. The effective sample size for the jth group is $h_j = n_j - 2g_j$ if a symmetric trimming approach is adopted. The trimmed mean and Winsorized sum of squares (Yuen, 1974) for the jth group for the kth variable are denoted by $\bar{U}_{tjk}$ and ss_{wjk}, respectively. The formulae for trimmed estimators are given in several papers, including Lix and Fouladi (in press) and Keselman et al. (2003).

Yuen and Dixon (1973) and Yuen (1974) showed that when the distribution is heavy-tailed and the assumption of homogeneity of population variances is not tenable, a robust statistic for the two-group case is obtained by adopting a trimmed t statistic based on a non-pooled estimate of error variance. This nonpooled test statistic reduces to the approximate degrees of freedom statistic proposed by Welch (1938) when there is no trimming. At the kth stage in a step-down analysis, the test statistic is defined via the U statistics as

$$\tilde{t}_{t(k)} = \frac{\bar{U}_{t1(k)} - \bar{U}_{t2(k)}}{\sqrt{\dfrac{ss_{w1(k)}}{(h_1 - k)(h_1 - k + 1)} + \dfrac{ss_{w2(k)}}{(h_2 - k)(h_2 - k + 1)}}}, \tag{2}$$

which is compared to a critical value from a t distribution with degrees of freedom, $\nu_{2(k)}$, where

$$\frac{1}{\nu_{2(k)}} = \frac{c^2}{h_1 - k} + \frac{(1 - c)^2}{h_2 - k}, \tag{3}$$

$c = q_1/(q_1 + q_2)$ and $q_j = ss_{wjk}/[(h_j - k)(h_j - k + 1)]$. The p-value for the step-down statistic $\tilde{t}_{t(k)}$ is compared to the selected level of significance, α_k.

RESULTS

The IBD sample is comprised of 187 and 169 individuals with Crohn's disease and ulcerative colitis, respectively. Both groups are similar in terms of demographic characteristics, with average ages of 38.1 and 42.8 years, respectively and 59 percent females in each group. There are, however more individuals with active disease (n = 251) than inactive disease (n = 110).

Preliminary robust analyses of the IBD psychological function and HRQoL data revealed no multivariate interaction between disease type and disease activity. As well, there was no statistically significant multivariate main effect of disease type. Accordingly, we present only the analyses for the disease activity main effect. Descriptive results for each dependent variable are reported in Table 9.1. The marginal skewness (γ_1) and kurtosis (γ_2) values revealed significant departures from normality for the quality of life measures, particularly in the inactive disease group. Across all measures of psychological function and quality of life, the least-squares and trimmed means are similar, except for the disease-specific measure of HRQoL in the inactive group. These estimators are based on 20% symmetric trimming, as recommended by Wilcox (1995). The least-squares variances are substantially larger than the Winsorized variances for all measures; their ratio ranges from 1.8 to 9.0. Further analysis (not shown) revealed positive covariances among all pairs of measures, with the exception of the SF-36 measures of physical and mental function. Large differences between the least-squares and Winsorized covariances were observed for almost all pairs of measures.

The results for the step-down analyses are found in Table 9.2. Two models were considered: the first focused on the psychological measures and the disease-specific HRQoL measure, and the second captured the psychological measures as well as the generic HRQoL measures. In both analyses, the variables were ranked in descending order as follows: psy-

Table 9.1. Univariate Descriptive Analyses for Psychological Function and Health-Related Quality of Life Measures

	Inactive (n = 110)						*Active (n = 251)*					
	γ_1	γ_2	$\bar{Y}$	s^2	$\bar{Y}_t$	s_w^2	γ_1	γ_2	$\bar{Y}$	s^2	$\bar{Y}_t$	s_w^2
PWB	−0.9	0.2	84.5	184.8	86.7	89.9	−0.3	−0.6	74.8	273.4	75.5	151.3
MAST	−0.2	−0.3	20.8	14.7	20.9	5.4	−0.1	−0.2	18.6	20.5	18.7	7.6
PSS	−1.0	1.0	5.8	0.9	5.9	0.3	−1.0	1.0	5.4	1.5	5.5	0.6
IBDQ	−1.5	2.6	189.0	488.7	193.9	132.6	−0.4	−0.4	156.9	875.6	158.9	415.8
SF36P	−1.2	4.1	43.4	17.9	43.7	3.2	−0.5	−0.3	42.6	27.4	43.1	9.7
SF36M	−0.2	0.3	43.9	31.3	44.1	12.7	−0.5	0.0	42.8	37.2	43.3	15.4

Note: PWB = Psychological Well-being; MAST = Mastery; PSS = Perceived Social Support; IBDQ = Inflammatory Bowel Disease Quality of Life; SF36P = SF-36 physical functioning, SF36M = SF-36 mental functioning; γ_1 = skewness; γ_2 = kurtosis.

Table 9.2. Multivariate and Step-Down Test Results for Measures of Psychological Function and Health-Related Quality of Life

Test Procedure	*F*	*1*	*2*	*p*
Disease-Specific Quality of Life				
Conventional MANOVA	26.8	4	355	< .0001
Robust MANOVA	39.3	4	116.9	< .0001
Conventional Step-Down Tests				
1. PWB	28.3	1	358	< .0001
2. MAST	4.0	1	357	.0470
3. PSS	2.6	1	356	.1047
4. IBDQ	65.1	1	355	< .0001
Robust Step-Down Tests				
1. PWB	15.2	1	139.3	< .0001
2. MAST	7.1	1	136.7	.0088
3. PSS	0.2	1	155.8	.6410
4. IBDQ	93.7	1	99.0	< .0001
General Quality of Life				
Conventional MANOVA	7.2	5	354	< .0001
Robust MANOVA	6.5	5	110.5	< .0001
Conventional Step-Down Tests				
1. PWB	28.3	1	358	< .0001
2. MAST	4.0	1	357	.0470
3. PSS	2.6	1	356	.1047
4. SF-36P	0.4	1	355	.5200
5. SF-36M	0.2	1	354	.6500
Robust Step-Down Tests				
1. PWB	15.2	1	139.3	< .0001
2. MAST	7.1	1	136.7	.0088
3. PSS	0.2	1	155.8	.6410
4. SF-36P	32.7	1	93.6	< .0001
5. SF-36M	0.9	1	92.4	.3428

Note: Robust tests are based on trimmed/Winsorized estimators; Conventional tests are based on least-squares estimators.

chological well-being, mastery, perceived social support, and quality of life. This ordering was selected based on consultations with the investigators and previous research.

Conventional and robust step-down analyses were performed along with conventional and robust MANOVA tests for comparison. The former reduces to Hotelling's (1931) T^2 and the latter is Johansen's (1980) approximate degrees of freedom test based on trimmed estimators (Lix,

Keselman, & Hinds, 2005). For the step-down analyses, we adopted the $\alpha_k = .05/4 = .0125$ level of significance for each test.

The conventional and robust MANOVA tests were statistically significant for both models. The conventional step-down analysis produced statistically significant results for two of the four dependent variables in the disease-specific HRQoL model. However, the robust step-down analysis shows statistically significant results on all but the perceived social support measure. For the general HRQoL model a very different pattern of step-down results emerges. The conventional analysis produced statistically significant results on only one of the five dependent variables, while the robust analysis produced statistically significant results on all but two of the measures. Of particular interest is that while both of the general HRQoL measures produced non-significant results in the model based on conventional test procedures, the physical function measure was statistically significant in the model that employed robust tests.

CONCLUSIONS

A step-down analysis is one approach to test for significant differences on several dependent variables while accounting for the correlation among the measures. We have demonstrated how a robust test statistic may be obtained. The comparative results from a conventional multivariate analysis of psychological and health-related quality of life measures for a clinical cohort illustrate the effect that heavy-tailed and skewed distributions may have on statistical power to detect group differences on multiple correlated dependent variables.

We emphasize two final points. The first is that the results of a step-down analysis are specific to the ordering of variables that is adopted. Thus, a different ordering of the variables may change the assessment of statistical significance of individual variables. Second, in this analysis we have focused on testing the statistical significance of each dependent variable. However, researchers may also elect to evaluate the significance of sets of rank-ordered variables. In our data for example, the SF-36 physical health functioning and mental health functioning variables were entered into the model sequentially whereas they might have entered the model simultaneously, as described by Hollingsworth (1982).

REFERENCES

Harvey, R. F., & Bradshaw, J. M. (1980). A simple activity index of Crohn's disease activity. *Lancet, I*, 514.

Hotelling, H. (1931). The generalization of student's ratio. *Annals of Mathematical Statistics, 2*, 360-378.

Irvine, E. J. (1993). A quality of life index for IBD. *Canadian Journal of Gastroenterology*, 7, 155-159.

Johansen, S. (1980). The Welch-James approximation to the distribution of the residual sum of squares in a weighted linear regression. *Biometrika, 67*, 85-92.

Julious S. A., George, S., Machin, D., & Stephens, R. J. (1997). Sample sizes for randomized trials Measuring quality of life in cancer patients. *Quality of Life Research, 6*, 109-117.

Keselman, H. J., Wilcox, R. R., & Lix, L. M. (2003). A generally robust approach to hypothesis testing in independent and correlated groups designs. *Psychophysiology, 40*, 586-596.

Lix, L. M., Beaumont, J. L., & Fouladi, R. T. (2006). *Robust tests of means for multivariate quality of life data*. Manuscript submitted for publication.

Lix, L. M., & Fouladi, R. T. (in press). Robust step-down tests for multivariate independent group designs. *British Journal of Mathematical and Statistical Psychology*.

Lix, L. M., Keselman, H. J., & Hinds, A. (2005). Robust tests for the multivariate Behrens-Fisher problem. *Computer Methods and Programs in Biomedicine, 77*, 129-139.

Masse, R., Poulin, C., Dassa, C., Lambert, J., Belair, S., & Battaglini, M. A. (1998). Elaboration and validation of a tool to measure psychological well-being: WBMMS. *Canadian Journal of Public Health, 89*, 352-357.

Mudholkar, G. S., & Srivastava, D. K. (2000). A class of robust stepwise alternatives to Hotelling's T^2 tests. *Journal of Applied Statistics, 27*, 599-619.

Powell-Tuck, J., Brown, R. L., & Lennard-Jones, J. E. (1978). A comparison of oral prednisolone given as single or multiple daily doses for active proctocolitis. *Scandinavian Journal of Gastroenterology, 13*, 833-837.

Ramsey, S. D., Berry, K., Moinpour, C., Giedzinska, A., Andersen, M. R. (2002). Quality of life in long term survivors of colorectal cancer. *American Journal of Gastroenterology, 97*, 1228-1234.

Rose, M. S., Koshman, M. L., Spreng, S., & Sheldon, R. (1999). Statistical issues encountered in the comparison of health-related quality of life in diseased patients to published general population norms: Problems and solutions. *Journal of Clinical Epidemiology, 52*, 405-412.

Roy, S. N. (1958). Step down procedure in multivariate analysis. *Annals of Mathematical Statistics, 29*, 1177-1187.

Roy, S. N., & Bargman, R. E. (1958). Tests of multiple independence and the associated confidence bounds. *Annals of Mathematical Statistics, 29*, 491-503.

Ware, J. E., Jr. (Ed.). (1993). *SF-36 health survey: Manual and interpretation guide*. Boston: The Health Institute, New England Medical Center.

Welch, B. L. (1938). The significance of the difference between two means when the population variances are unequal. *Biometrika*, 29, 350-362.

Wilcox, R. R. (1995). Simulation results on solutions to the multivariate Behrens-Fisher problem via trimmed means. *The Statistician, 44*, 213-225.

Yuen, K. K. (1974). The two-sample trimmed *t* for unequal population variances. *Biometrika, 61*, 165-170.

Yuen, K. K., & Dixon, W. J. (1973). The approximate behavior and performance of the two-sample trimmed *t*. *Biometrika, 60*, 369-374.

Zimet, G. D., Dahlem, N. W., Zimet, S. G., & Farley, G. K. (1988). The multidimensional scale of perceived social support. *Journal of Personality Assessment, 52*, 30-41.

CHAPTER 10

DUNN-ŠIDÁK CRITICAL VALUES AND *p* VALUES

Roger E. Kirk and Joel Hetzer

The Dunn and Dunn-Šidák multiple comparison procedures are widely used to test hypotheses and construct confidence intervals for $C \geq 2$ a priori, nonorthogonal contrasts. Dunn's (1961) procedure is based on the additive Bonferroni inequality. The procedure controls the long-run average number of erroneous statements for a family of C contrasts, the per family error rate denoted by α_{PF}. The per family error rate is controlled by splitting α_{PF} among the null hypothesis tests or confidence intervals so that $\Sigma_{i=1}^{C}\alpha_{PC_i} = \alpha_{PF}$, where α_{PC_i} is the ith per contrast type I error. Researchers often assign the same type I error to all C contrasts or confidence intervals in which case $\alpha_{PC} = \alpha_{PF}/C$. A second and slightly more powerful multiple comparison procedure was proposed by Šidák (1967) and is called the Dunn-Šidák procedure. This procedure is based on a multiplicative inequality. For any set of C a priori contrasts or confidence intervals, the procedure provides an upper bound for the familywise error rate denoted by α_{FW}. This is the probability of making one or more erroneous statements for a family of C contrasts. To control the familywise

Real Data Analysis, pp. 149–153

error rate, the Dunn-Šidák procedure tests each contrast at $\alpha_{PC} = 1 - (1 - \alpha_{FW})^{1/C}$. Šidák showed that the familywise error rate for C nondependent tests is less than or equal to $1 - (1 - \alpha_{PC})^C$, which is always less than or equal to α_{PF}. For this reason, the Dunn-Šidák procedure is preferred over Dunn's procedure when $C \geq 2$.

Both the Dunn and Dunn-Šidák multiple comparison procedures use α_{PC} values that are not available in conventional t tables. Dunn (1961) prepared a table of two-tailed critical values for $\alpha_{PF} = .01$ and .05 that simplifies using the Dunn procedure. Games (1977) prepared a similar two-tailed table for the Dunn-Šidák procedure for $\alpha_{FW} = .01$, .05, .10, and .20. Tables of two-tailed critical values for the Dunn and Dunn-Šidák procedures are given in numerous textbooks: Howell (1997), Kirk (1995), Maxwell and Delaney (2004), Myers and Well (2003), and Toothaker (1991).

Researchers who test directional hypotheses or construct one-sided confidence intervals are accustomed to doubling α in a two-tailed t table to obtain the critical value for one tail. This procedure works with Dunn's table and gives one-tailed critical values for $\alpha_{PF} = .02$ and .10. However, doubling α_{FW} in Games's two-tailed table always gives one-tailed critical values, denoted by $tDS_{\alpha;\, C,\, \nu}$, that are too small. Many researchers are not aware of this problem. Suppose, for example, that a researcher wants to perform a one-tailed test with $\alpha_{FW} = .05$, $C = 5$, and error degrees of freedom = 25. Because Games's table does not contain one-tailed critical values, the researcher makes the mistake of doubling α_{FW} and looking for the critical value corresponding to $2\alpha_{FW} = 2(.05) = .10$. According to Games's table, the critical value is $tDS_{.10/2;\, 5,\, 25} = 2.466$. This critical value corresponds to testing each of the five contrasts at $\alpha_{PC} = [1 - (1 - .10)^{1/5}]/2 = .010426$. The correct one-tailed critical value is $tDS_{.05;\, 5,\, 25} = 2.476$ and corresponds to testing each contrast at $\alpha_{PC} = 1 - (1 - .05)^{1/5} = .010206$. The use of $tDS_{.10/2;\, 5,\, 25} = 2.466$ instead of the correct $tDS_{.05;\, 5,\, 25} = 2.476$ results in rejecting too many true null hypotheses and to confidence intervals that are too narrow.

Procedures for obtaining one- and two-tailed critical values for any familywise error rate, number of contrasts, and error degrees of freedom using an Excel function in Microsoft Office 2004, S-Plus, SAS, and SPSS are described next.

COMPUTATION OF CRITICAL VALUES

Excel contains the function TINV(*Probability,degrees_freedom*) that returns the inverse of student's t distribution. The function can be used to obtain one- and two-tailed critical values for the Dunn-Šidák procedure by replacing the Probability a-rgument with, respectively,

2*(1 - (1 - aFW) ^ (1/C))

1 – (1 – aFW) ^ (1/C),

where *aFW* denotes the familywise error rate for a one- or two-tailed test and *C* is the number of a priori contrasts for a set of means. The critical values also can be used to construct *C* simultaneous $100(1 - \alpha_{FW})\%$ one- and two-sided confidence intervals. Suppose that a researcher wants to obtain the one-tailed critical value for *aFW* = .05, *C* = 5, and error degrees of freedom = 25. Entering the values in the TINV function

TINV(2*(1 - (1 - .05) ^ (1/5)), 25)

yields the critical value $tDS_{.05;\,5,25} = 2.476$.

The corresponding statements to obtain one- and two tailed critical values using S-Plus are, respectively,

```
>qt(2*(1 - (1 - aFW) ^ (1/C)), df)
```

and

```
>qt(1 - (1 - aFW) ^ (1/C), df)
```

A SAS program for obtaining one-tailed critical values for the Dunn-Šidák procedure for *aFW* = .05, *C* = 5, and error degrees of freedom = 25 is as follows.

```
DATA;
INPUT aFW C df;
CV=ROUND(TINV(1 - (1 - (1 - aFW)**(1/C)), df), .001);
CARDS;
.05 5 25
;
PROC PRINT;
RUN;
```

Two-tailed critical values are obtained by replacing the CV statement with

```
CV = ROUND(TINV(1 - (1 - [(1 - aFW)**(1/C))/2, df), .001);
```

An SPSS program for obtaining one-tailed critical values for the Dunn-Šidák procedure for *aFW* = .05, *C* = 5, and error degrees of freedom = 25 is as follows.

```
data list free / aFW C df.
begin data
.05 5 25
end data.
compute CV = IDF.T(1 - (1 - (1 - aFW)**(1/C)), df).
print format CV (F5.3).
print/all.
execute.
```

Two-tailed critical values are obtained by replacing the *CV* statement with

```
CV = IDF.T(1 - (1 - (1 - aFW)**(1/C))/2, df).
```

COMPUTATION OF FAMILYWISE *p* VALUES

If a researcher has computed *C* a priori, nonorthogonal *t* statistics, the familywise *p* value, denoted by p_{FW}, can be obtained from

$$p_{FW} \leq 1 - (1 - p_1)(1 - p_2) \ldots (1 - p_C),$$

where $p_1, p_2 \ldots pC$ denote the *C* per contrast *p* values. *t*-distribution *p* values are readily obtained using the Excel the function TDIS(*x,degrees_freedom,tails*), where *x* is the numeric value at which the distribution is evaluated and *tails* = 1 gives the one-tailed *p* value and *tails* = 2 gives the two-tailed *p* value. Suppose that a researcher has obtained the following per contrast *p* values for *C* = 3 a priori, nonorthogonal contrasts: p_1 = .002362, p_2 = .034424, and p_3 = .002655. The familywise *p* value is

$$p_{FW} \leq 1 - (1 - .002362)(1 - .034424)(1 - .002655) = .039262.$$

SUMMARY

Researchers are accustomed to doubling α in a two-tailed *t* table to obtain the critical value in one tail. However, doubling α in the Dunn-Šidák two-tailed table always gives one-tailed critical values that are too small. Microsoft Office 2004 Excel, S-Plus, SAS, and SPSS computational routines are illustrated for obtaining Dunn-Šidák one- and two-tailed critical values for any familywise error rate, number of contrasts, and error degrees of freedom. Also shown is a simple procedure for determining the familywise p value for C per contrast p values.

REFERENCES

Dunn, O. J. (1961). Multiple comparisons among means. *Journal of the American Statistical Association*, *56*, 52–64.

Games, P. A. (1977). An improved t table for simultaneous control on g contrasts. *Journal of the American Statistical Association*, *72*, 531–534.

Howell, D. C. (1997). *Statistical methods for psychology and education* (4th ed). Belmont, CA: Duxbury.

Kirk, R. E. (1995). *Experimental design: Procedures for the behavioral sciences* (3rd ed). Pacific Grove, CA: Brooks/Cole.

Maxwell, S. E., & Delaney, H. D. (2004). *Designing experiments and analyzing data* (2nd ed). Mahwah, NJ: Erlbaum.

Myers, J. L., & Well, A. D. (2003). *Research design and statistical analysis* (2nd ed). Mahwah, NJ: Erlbaum.

Toothaker, L. E. (1991). *Multiple comparisons for researchers*. Newbury Park, CA: Sage.

Šidák, Z. (1967). Rectangular confidence regions for the means of multivariate normal distributions. *Journal of the American Statistical Association*, *62*, 626–633.

CHAPTER 11

CONTROLLING EXPERIMENT-WISE TYPE I ERRORS

Good Advice for Simultaneous and Sequential Hypothesis Testing

Shlomo S. Sawilowsky and Patric R. Spence

The flurry of research on controlling Type I errors in multiple testing situations in the latter half of the twentieth century produced a plethora of choices, many of which are quite powerful, as solutions to this real data analysis problem. It is surprising, therefore, that many authors (e.g., M. C. W. Braver & Braver, 1988; Braver & W. Braver, 1990a, 1990b, 1995), restrict the concern for this problem to tests conducted in parallel, thereby exempting or ignoring sequential procedures.

Two vignettes that are often excluded are (1) controlling experiment-wise Type I errors when conducting preliminary tests of underlying assumptions prior to a test of experimental outcomes, and (2) building-block tests, such as all interactions and main effects in a three-factor ANOVA. Therefore, the purpose of this chapter is to demonstrate the

Real Data Analysis, pp. 155–162

necessity of guarding against false-positives in these two situations, in addition to the typical simultaneous hypothesis testing application.

TYPE I ERRORS AND PRELIMINARY TESTS

The two examples presented here are repeated from Sawilowsky (2002). The first example pertains to the common strategy to conduct a test on variances prior to the pooled samples t test (e.g., SAS, 1990, p. 25; SPSS, 1993, pp. 254-255; SYSTAT, 1990, p. 487). If the *F* test on variances, for example, is not significant, then the researcher continues with the *t* test. However, if the *F* test is significant, then the researcher is advised to conduct the separate variances *t* test (e.g., Welch-Aspin) with modified degrees of freedom.

There is a serious problem with this approach that is universally overlooked. The sequential nature of testing for homogeneity of variance as a condition of conducting the independent samples *t* test leads to an inflation of experiment-wise Type I errors. A small Fortran program was written, compiled, and executed to demonstrate this, with the results noted in Table 11.1.

An examination of Table 11.1 highlights a number of important points:

- The experiment-wise Type I error rate, under normality, is .097 (.051 + .023 + .023) when the *t* test is conducted conditional on

Table 11.1. Type I Error and Power for the Pooled-Variances Independent Sample *T* Test Conducted Unconditionally or Conditionally on the *F* Test for Homogeneity of Variance, $\alpha = 0.050$; $n_1 = n_2 = 5$, 100,000 Repetitions

	Unconditional		*Conditional*		
Distribution	*L*	*R*	*L*	*R*	*Type I Error*
Normal					
$c = 0.0$	.025	.025	.023	.023	.051
$c = 0.95$	.000	.265	.000	.252	
$c = 2.0$	.000	.790	.000	.750	
Chi-Square ($\nu = 2$)					
$c = 0.0$	.023	.019	.015	.013	.172
$c = 1.5$	.000	.252	.000	.202	
$c = 3.5$	.000	.735	.000	.632	

Note: "*c*" = shift in location to produce approximately small or large Effect Sizes. A study of robustness with respect to Type II errors requires "*c*" to represent equal Effect Sizes across distributions, which was not done for this illustration. "L" = left tail. "R" = right tail.

the F test for homogeneity of variance. This is almost twice nominal alpha.

- The experiment-wise Type I error rate when the data were sampled from a chi-squared distribution ($\nu = 2$) is .200, which is four times nominal alpha!
- The F test on variances, as is well known, is nonrobust to departures from normality. In this case the Type I error rate for Gaussian data of 0.051 ballooned up to .172 for the chi-squared ($\nu = 2$) data. This inflation level of about 3.5 times nominal alpha means the data analyst will frequently abandon the pooled samples t test in favor of the separate variances test, when in fact, the condition of homoscedasticity holds. This problem can be ameliorated somewhat by using Levene's (1960) test, which is more robust to departures from normality.
- Conducting the t test conditioned on the F test for variances resulted in a 5% loss of power under normality, which is ill afforded in small samples applied research.
- Conducting the t-test conditioned on the F test for variances resulted in a 20% loss of power under the chi-squared ($\nu = 2$) distribution for the small effect size, and a 14% loss in power for the large effect size, which is ill afforded in small samples applied research.

Consider, as the second example, the two independent samples procedure introduced by O'Brien (1988) for situations where a treatment impacts both location and scale. It is well known that the student's t test is not efficient under these treatment outcomes. O'Brien proposed the generalized t test, which can be carried out by ordinary least squares or logistic regression. In terms of the former case, a dummy variable of 1, representing group membership, or 0, representing nonmembership, is regressed on the outcome variable, w, as well as w^2:

$$y' = \beta_0 + \beta_1 w + \beta_2 w^2 \qquad (1)$$

If β_2 is not near zero, the test for treatment effects is conducted with the usual 2 degrees of freedom F test of H_0: $\beta_1 = \beta_2 = 0$. If β_2 is near 0, however, Equation (1) is replaced with

$$y' = \beta_0 + \beta_1 w \qquad (2)$$

and the 1 degree of freedom test of H_0: $\beta_1 = 0$, an independent samples t test, is conducted. It is called a generalized t test because of the variety of levels of nominal which may be selected for testing Equation (1).

Blair and Morel (1991) examined the experiment-wise Type I error rate of conducting Equation (2) conditional on the result of Equation (1). They found the sequential conditional testing procedure resulted in Type I error inflations as high as .144 when $\alpha = 0.050$. Blair and Morel cautioned against using the procedure because the characteristics of the new procedure were not fully investigated. O'Brien responded by developing a two-thirds rule, where approximately correct Type I errors are obtained by reducing α nominal to two thirds of the desired size (Grambsch & O'Brien, 1991). Subsequently, Blair (1991) provided a table of exact critical values for O'Brien's procedure which result in correct Type I error rates.

BUILDING-BLOCK TESTS

In the second example regarding the testing of effects in ANOVA, M. C. W. Braver and Braver (1995) dismissed the issue of experiment-wise errors that would occur from an otherwise innocuous analysis of data from a three-factor ANOVA design, on the basis of comments by Keppel (1973). However, Keppel more recently wrote "most correction techniques can be adapted to the factorial design" (Keppel & Zedeck, 1989, p. 259); the issue is only that "there is little agreement among researchers *whether or not* to correct for familywise error in the detailed analysis of a factorial experiment" (p. 259, italics added).

Huck and Cormier (1996) noted "the vast majority of applied researchers do not adjust anything" because they "consider each *F* test separately" rather than a set of *F* tests (p. 381). Heiman (1992) agreed, but at least expressed it this way: "after all of the above shenanigans, we have protected our experiment-wise error" (p. 441). In any case, Huck and Cormier (1996, p. 381) noted that the familywise error rate is indeed affected by a sequence of *F* tests.

The unfortunate decision not to correct for experiment-wise Type I error is predicated on:

- the belief that the "relative lack of the sort of indiscriminate hypothesis testing often seen in the analysis of single-factor experiments, which is what has generated most of the discussion of familywise error" does not occur with three-factor experiments.
- "Factorial designs are usually undertaken when something is known about one or both of the independent variables.... The result is an experiment that is more theoretically motivated than is the typical single-factor design."

- "The analysis of a factorial should emphasize planned comparisons ... are typically few in number, which should help to moderate any concern for familywise error that a researcher might have."
- ANOVA "lean(s) heavily on the occurrence of a significant *F*, for either an interaction or a simple effect, to justify further statistical analysis—a procedure that again helps to reduce family-wise error." (Keppel & Zedeck, 1989, p. 259)

Regarding the control of Type I error in the three-factor ANOVA, M. C. W. Braver and Braver (1995) further noted that, "if one were to employ here Sawilowsky et al.'s way of figuring, the main effects would thus have experiment-wise error rate of at least .25" and concluded that "No authority, to our knowledge, expresses much concern" that the "experiment-wise error rate may exceed nominal alpha." On the contrary, many textbook authors were troubled about this and there has been considerable research activity in the social and behavioral science statistics literature on this subject.

For example, in discussing the distribution of the risk of Type I error in a three-factor ANOVA design, Marascuilo and Serlin (1988) stated, "with the inclusion of each of the two-factor interactions and the one three-factor interaction, the total risk of a Type I error is $\alpha_t \leq \alpha_a + \alpha_b + \alpha_c + \alpha_{ab} + \alpha_{ac} + \alpha_{bc} + \alpha_{abc}$. If each source of variation is tested at .05, then $\alpha_t \leq .35$" (p. 557).

Fletcher, Daw, and Young (1989) conducted a simulation study that demonstrated the deleterious effects of conducing multiple *F* tests in factorial ANOVA. They proposed relying on a significant omnibus *F* test to control the inflation of experiment-wise Type I errors. Another strategy was suggested by Stevens (1990), who used Holm's (1979) modified Bonferroni procedure. In a more extensive Monte Carlo study, Kromrey and Dickinson (1995) compared the use of no control with the omnibus *F*, Bonferroni, Holm, and Hochberg (1988) procedures for two-, three-, and four-factor ANOVA designs with varying numbers of null effects in the model. An excerpt of their findings is compiled in Table 11.2. Their simulation showed that failure to control for inflation of Type I errors resulted in an experiment-wise Type I error rate as high as .14 in two-factor ANOVA, .29 in three-factor ANOVA, and .52 in four-factor ANOVA.

The exhaustive search for significant effects in a three-factor ANOVA is analogous to the indiscriminate use of the stepwise procedure in multiple regression. Stepwise regression is clearly an ordered series of tests which first determines the variable which is the best discriminator among the groups, and after it is entered, continues to find the next best discriminator, and so forth. Thus, Stevens (1992, chapter 10) argued in favor of stepdown *F* tests, because the exhaustive search for a significant procedure

Table 11.2. Experiment-Wise Type 1 Error Rates for *F* Tests in 2-, 3-, and 4-Factor ANOVA Designs With Nominal α = 0.05

N of Factors	*N of Null Effects*	*No Control*	*Omnibus F*	*Bonferroni*	*Holm*	*Hochberg*
2	1	.05	.04	.02	.03	.03
2	2	.10	.06	.03	.04	.04
2	3	.14	.05	.05	.05	.05
3	4	.18	.14	.03	.04	.04
3	5	.22	.16	.04	.04	.04
3	6	.26	.14	.04	.05	.05
3	7	.29	.05	.05	.05	.05
4	12	.45	.35	.04	.04	.04
4	13	.48	.33	.04	.05	.05
4	14	.50	.28	.05	.05	.05
4	15	.52	.05	.05	.05	.05

Note: Excerpted from Kromrey and Dickinson (1995, Table 1, p. 58).

without a method of controlling family-wise Type I error rate "especially with small or moderate sample sizes" results in "a substantial hazard of capitalization on chance" and is "likely to produce results that will not replicate and are therefore of dubious scientific value" (p. 373).

CONCLUSION

Discussed in this chapter was the necessity of guarding against false-positives in controlling experiment-wise Type I errors when (1) conducting preliminary tests of underlying assumptions prior to a test of experimental outcomes, and (2) in the use of building-block tests. Controlling for experiment-wise Type I errors needs to be addressed when conducting both in parallel and sequential tests or procedures.

With regard to sequential tests, if the *F* test on variances is not significant, the researcher will continue with the *t* test. However, when the *F* test is significant, the researcher is advised to conduct the separate variances t test with modified degrees of freedom. The sequential nature of testing for homogeneity of variance as a condition of conducting the independent samples *t* test leads to an inflation of experiment-wise Type I errors. In reference to building-block tests, although the majority of applied researchers do not adjust anything due to considering each *F* test separately, rather than a set of *F* tests, this decision still creates a problem. Any decision made impacts experiment-wise error. Even if the researcher informally examines the first test's data to make a mental note, that decision to proceed or not to proceed affects the experiment wise-error.

REFERENCES

Blair, R. C. (1991). New critical values for the generalized *t* and generalized rank-sum procedures. *Communications in Statistics: Simulations, 20*(4), 981-994.

Blair, R. C., & Morel, J. G. (1991). On the use of the generalized *t* and generalized rank-sum statistics in medical research. *Statistics in Medicine.*

Braver, M. C. W., & Braver, S. L. (1988). Statistical treatment of the Solomon four-group design: A meta-analytic approach. *Psychological Bulletin, 104,* 150-154.

Braver, M. C. W., & Braver, S. L. (1995). Meta-analysis for Solomon-four group designs redeemed: A reply to Sawilowsky, Kelley, Blair, and Markman (1994). Unpublished manuscript.

Braver, S. L, & Braver, M. C. W. (1990a). Meta-analysis for Solomon four-group designs reconsidered: A reply to Sawilowsky and Markman. *Perceptual and Motor Skills*, *71,* 321-322.

Braver, S. L., & Braver, M. C. W. (1990b, April). Switching replications research design: What why, when, and how. Paper presented at the annual meeting of the American Educational Research Association, Boston.

Braver, S. L., & Braver, M. C. W. (1995). Unpublished manuscript.

Fletcher, H., J., Daw, H., & Young, J. (1989). Controlling multiple *F* test errors with an overall *F* test. *Journal of Applied Behavioral Science, 25,* 101-108.

Grambsch, P., & O'Brien, P. (1991).The effects of transformations and preliminary testes for non-linearity in regression. *Statistics in Medicine, 10,* 697-709.

Heiman, G. W. (1992). *Basic statistics for the behavioral sciences.* Boston: Houghton Mifflin.

Hochberg, Y. (1988). A sharper Bonferroni procedure for multiple tests of significance. *Biometrika, 75,* 800-802.

Holm, S. (1979). A simple sequentially rejective multiple test procedure. *Scandinavian Journal of Statistics, 6,* 65-70.

Huck, S. W., & Cormier, W. H. (1996). *Reading statistics and research* (2nd ed.) New York: Harper Collins.

Keppel, G. (1973). *Design and analysis: A researcher's handbook.* Englewood Cliffs, NJ: Prentice Hall.

Keppel, G., & Zedeck, S. (1989). *Data analysis for research designs: Analysis of variance and multiple regression/correlational approaches.* New York: W. H. Freeman.

Kromrey, J. D., & Dickinson, W. B. (1995). The use of an overall *F* test to control Type I error rates in factorial analyses of variance: Limitations and better strategies. *Journal of Applied Behavioral Science, 31*(1), 51-64.

Levene, H. (1960). Robust tests for equality of variance. In I. Olkin (Ed.) *Contributions to probability and statistics* (pp. 278-292). Palo Alto, CA: Stanford University Press.

Marascuilo, L. A., & Serlin, R. C. (1988). *Statistical methods for the social and behavioral sciences.* New York: W. H. Freeman.

O'Brien, P. C. (1988). Comparing two samples: extensions of the t, rank-sum, and log-rank tests. *Journal of the American Statistical Association, 83*, 52-61.

SAS. (1990). *SAS/STAT user's guide, Vol. 1.* (4th ed.) Cary, NC: SAS Institute.

Sawilowsky, S. (2002). Fermat, Schubert, Einstein, and Behrens-Fisher: The Probable Difference Between Two Means When $\sigma^1 \neq \sigma^2$. *Journal of Modern Applied Statistical Methods, 1*(2), 461-472.

SPSS. (1993). *SPSS for Windows: Base system user's guide release 6.0.* Chicago: Author.

Stevens, J. (1990). *Intermediate statistics: A modern approach.* Hillsdale, NJ: Erlbaum.

Stevens, J. (1992). *Applied multivariate statistics for the social sciences* (2nd ed.) Hillsdale, NJ: Erlbaum.

SYSTAT. (1990). *SYSTAT: The system for statistics.* Evanston, IL: Author.

CHAPTER 12

ROBUSTNESS AND POWER OF ORDINAL *d* FOR PAIRED DATA

Du Feng

Research questions concerning whether scores from one group or on one occasion tend to be higher than those from the other are usually answered by comparing mean scores of the two groups/occasions. For example, paired t test is the most frequently used test for comparing means of two matched groups, and for pre- and posttest comparisons. Parametric tests, such as paired t test, assume that variables are measured at least at the interval level, as well as assuming normality of the test variable and homogeneity of variance. However, most behavioral and social variables have only ordinal justification, and the parametric assumptions are always violated to a certain degree. It has been shown that the bulk of psychological and educational data are at least moderately and sometimes strikingly nonnormal (e.g., highly skewed, polymodal, or heavy-tailed) (O'Brien, 1988; Micceri, 1989; Wilcox, 1991). Nonnormality and heterogeneity of variance are known to inflate the actual Type I error rate and severely reduce the power of normal-based mean comparison procedures (e.g., Pearson & Please, 1975; Tan, 1982; Wilcox, 1991, 1992; Zumbo & Jennings, 2002).

Real Data Analysis, pp. 163–183

Motives for ordinal analysis have been argued elsewhere, including their suitability for many behavioral variables and research questions that are ordinal in nature, their robustness and power under departure from normality or equal variance assumptions, being invariant under monotonic transformation, and their descriptive superiority (e.g., Cliff, 1993; Long, Feng, & Cliff, 2003). An ordinal method, *d*, was proposed for answering research questions regarding central tendency of two groups or two occasions (Cliff, 1991, 1993). This method is closely related to Wilcoxon's signed rank test (WSR), but does not rely on the identical distribution assumption. Since *d* can be used on the raw scores, a rank transformation, which was found to be undesirable in designed experiment (Sawilowsky, 2000), is not necessary. It also lends itself to parameter estimations. This chapter describes the ordinal method, *d*, for analyzing paired data, and reports an empirical evaluation of the performance of *d* for paired data under various conditions. The performance of *d* in testing null hypotheses about the within-subject difference, the between-subject difference, and the combined difference, is compared to that of the traditional paired *t* test.

ORDINAL *d* FOR CORRELATED DATA

Let p represent the probability for a score drawn randomly from one group or on one occasion being higher than a random score from the other: $p = \Pr\{x_1 > x_2\}$, then, $\delta = \Pr(x_1 > x_2) - \Pr(x_1 < x_2)$. Obviously, δ is a simple transformation of a measure, $p = \Pr\{x1 > x2\}$ (Birnbaum, 1956; McGraw & Wong, 1992): $p = (\delta + 1)/2$, when there is no ties between random scores from the two groups. However, δ has advantages over p because it takes into account ties in the data (Long et al., 2003). Similarly, Vargha and Delaney (2000) proposed a generalization of the "common language effect size statistic" (CL) which was suggested by McGraw and Wong (1992), in order to take into account ties between the two groups scores. They called the generalization "*A* measure of stochastic superiority," which was defined as $A = \Pr\{x1 > x2\} + .5 \Pr\{x1 = x2\}$. It was noted that A is simply a linear transformation of δ: $A = (\delta + 1)/2$ (Vargha & Delaney, 2000). δ is between −1.0 and 1.0 when there is no tie.

The sample estimate of δ, called *d*, compares the proportion of times a score from one group or on one occasion being higher than a score from the other. Cliff (1993) described the calculation of *d* as involving comparison of each of the scores on one occasion to each of the scores one the other occasion. A "dominance variable" d_{ij} is defined as: $d_{ij} = \mathrm{sign}(x_i - x_j)$, where x_i represents any observation on the first occasion, x_j in the second. The row averages of d_{ij} is called d_i, the column averages d_j. For dependent data, the within-subject (or within-pair) difference (δ_w) is distinguished from the between-subject (or between-pair) difference (δ). The unbiased sample estimate of δ_w is the average within-subject dominance:

$$d_w = \Sigma\, d_{ii}/n. \tag{1}$$

When there are no ties in the paired observations, d_w would be equivalent to the Friedman (1937) statistic.

δ is estimated by the average between-subject dominance, d_b:

$$d_b = \underset{i \neq j}{\Sigma\Sigma}\, dij/n(n-1) \tag{2}$$

It has been suggested that inferences about δ (or the equivalent, p) should be based on the sample estimate of its variance rather than the identical distribution assumption (Birnbaum & McCarty, 1958; Cliff, 1993; Fligner & Policello, 1981; Zaremba, 1962). The sampling distributions of d_b and d_w are asymptotically normal (since they are averages scores), with means δ and δ_w, and sampling variances σ^2_{db} and σ^2_{dw}, respectively. An unbiased estimate of σ^2_{db} was shown (Cliff, 1993) to be

$$s^2_{db} = \frac{(n-1)^2(\Sigma d^{*2}_{i.} + \Sigma d^{*2}_{.i} + 2\Sigma d^*_{i.} d^*_{i.}) - \Sigma\Sigma d^{*2}_{ij} - \Sigma\Sigma d^*_{ij} d^*_{ij}}{n(n-1)(n-2)(n-3)}, \tag{3}$$

where $d^*_{i.} = d_{i.} - d_b$ and $d^*_{ij} = d_{ij} - d_b$. Here, $d_{i.}$ and $d_{.i}$ both have i as subscript since they refer to the same set of scores. The unbiased estimate of σ^2_{dw} was derived in a similar way:

$$s^2_{dw} = \Sigma(d_{ii} - d_w)^2/(n-1) \tag{4}$$

The CI for δ and δ_w can be formed with s_{db} and s_{dw}, respectively, and hypotheses about δ and δ_w can be tested. In addition, a combination effect of δ and δ_w can be tested by testing H_0: $\delta + \delta_w = 0$. Since these two statistics are not independent, the test of the combined effect involves their covariance cov(d_w, d_b). Cliff (1993) showed that the unbiased estimate of this covariance is

$$\mathrm{Est}[\mathrm{cov}(d_w, d_b)] = \frac{\Sigma_i(\Sigma_j d_{ij} + \Sigma_j d_{ji})d_{ii} - 2n(n-1)d_b d_w}{n(n-1)(n-2)}. \tag{5}$$

The variance of the sum of the two dominance variables d_w and d_b is

$$\text{var}(d_w + d_b) = \sigma^2_{dw} + \sigma^2_{db} + 2\text{cov}(d_w, d_b). \quad (6)$$

The square root of the above can be used to construct a CI for $(\delta + \delta_w)$, and to test H_0: $\delta + \delta_w = 0$.

An asymmetric CI for δ, compensating for the positive correlation between the independent *d* and its variance, was shown to improve the performance of *d* for independent groups (Feng & Cliff, 2004). Here, a similar asymmetrically adjusted CI for δ is applied for correlated data, with the upper and lower limits calculated as:

$$\delta = \frac{d - d^3 \pm t_{\alpha/2} s_d (1 - 2d^2 + d^4 + t^2_{\alpha/2} s^2_d)^{1/2}}{1 - d^2 + t^2_{\alpha/2} s^2_d}. \quad (7)$$

When *d* is 1.0, s_d reduces to zero, and the CI would reduce to a point. In that situation, the upper bound for the CI for δ is 1.0, and the lower bound is calculated by

$$d = (n - Z^2_{\alpha/2})/(n + Z^2_{\alpha/2}) \quad (8)$$

When $d = -1.0$, the solution is the negative of Equation (8).

DISTRIBUTIONAL BEHAVIOR OF ORDINAL *d*

Feng and Cliff (2004) reported a Monte Carlo evaluation of *d* for independent data, and found it to behave well, using the aforementioned improved confidence interval (CI). Other researchers found similar results for CI for $\Pr\{x_1 > x_2\}$ based on sample estimations (Halperin, Gilbert, & Lachin, 1987; Mee, 1990; Ury, 1972). Delaney and Vargha (2002) reported that modifications of CI for δ consisting of using Welch-like *dfs* improved performance of *d* (Delaney & Vargha, 2002). However, no simulation studies have been conducted to evaluate *d* for paired data. This chapter reports a Monte Carlo evaluation of *d* for paired data in small ($n = 10$) to large samples ($n = 100$), under normal and nonnormal population conditions with different degrees of correlation (ρ), and compares *d* with paired *t* for the same samples.

METHODOLOGY

The Simulation Procedure

A Monte Carlo study was carried out in a variety of situations. In simulating the data, six factors were manipulated: form, mean, variance, and skewness of the parent distributions, correlation between paired populations, and sample size. In order to represent psychological and behavioral variables frequently found in practice, which not only have a variety of distributions (often skewed), but also are sometime bounded at one or both ends, four types of distributions were simulated: normal, skewed, chi-square (one-side bounded), and beta (two-side bounded) distributions. Within each family of distributions, certain combinations of means and variances were selected so that δ ranged from .3 to .8. The selection of effect sizes, in terms of δ, conforms to Cohen's (1988) guidelines for small, medium, and large effects for comparable location models.

Samples were taken repeatedly from a large number of paired populations. Then, statistical inferences about δ, δ_w, and $\delta + \delta_w$ were computed based on each selected pair of samples, and two-sided d_b, d_w, $d_b + d_w$, and paired t tests were performed at the .05 significance level. Subroutines of IMSL library were called by FORTRAN programs to generate the populations and samples. Another FORTRAN program was written to compute statistical inferences about δ, δ_w, and $\delta + \delta_w$ for two paired groups and to perform d and paired t tests.

Two thousand random samples were drawn under each distributional situation. With this number of replications, when looking at the proportion of rejection of the H_0 (or the $1 - \alpha$ CI coverage proportion) at $\alpha =$ .05 level, a .01 difference would be significant. With 2,000 replications and .05 Type I error rate for the proportions test, the power of the test to detect a departure of $\alpha \pm \frac{1}{2}\alpha$, which was defined by Bradley (1978) as "liberal" tolerance criterion for robustness of Monte Carlo experiments, is above .9; the power to detect a departure of $\alpha \pm \frac{1}{4}\alpha$, the "intermediate" criterion (Robey & Barcikowski, 1992), is .7 (Cohen, 1988; Robey & Barcikowski, 1992).

Distributional Situations Examined

Normal Distributions

The IMSL routine RNNOA was used to obtain independent standard normal variates with 10,000 random observations in each group. The normal distributions selected had μ of 0, 1, 2, or 3, and σ^2 of 1, 4, or 9. While all pairs of groups with these means and variances were considered, only a subset of them, representing typical results, are reported in this chapter. With symmetric distributions, the null hypotheses for the *d* analyses, H_0: $\delta = 0$, H_0: $\delta_w = 0$, and H_0: $\delta + \delta_w = 0$, are true when the null hypothesis regarding mean difference (μ_d) for the paired *t* test, $H_0 : \mu_d = 0$, is true.

Skewed Distributions

Skewed distributions were obtained by transforming the simulated standard normal variate using the *g* transformation: e^{gz-1}/g (Hoaglin, 1985), where *Z* is *N*(0, 1), and *g* controls the skewness of the resulting variate. The parameter *g* was manipulated to yield skewness of 2, and –2. These skewed variates also have higher kurtosis (about 8.0) than the normal variates. Since the skewed data were compared with the nonskewed ones as well, and we wanted to separate the effect of skewness from the effect of kurtosis in such cases, the symmetric (skewness = 0) distributions were obtained by transforming the standard normal distributions using the *h* transformation: $Ze^{hZ\ 1/2}$ (Hoaglin, 1985) to match the skewed ones in terms of kurtosis. The skewness of the two comparison groups was in pairs of approximately (0:0), (0:2), (2:2), and (2:–2).

Given the levels of mean, variance, and skewness, there can be 54 different kinds of combinations for each group, and the number is squared when two groups are involved. However, only some representative combinations were selected, and a subset of these are reported here. Unlike in the normal case, for skewed data, the null hypotheses regarding δ, δ_w, and $\delta + \delta_w$ and the null hypothesis regarding μ_d are not necessarily all true or all false, although effects are quite small. Cases when all H_0's are true or false, as well as when one of them is true while the others are false, were examined.

Chi-Square Distributions

One-side bounded data were simulated with chi-square distributions. The *df* of the selected chi-square distributions ranged from 2 to 20. Certain combinations of the population groups were selected so that the effect size, δ, δ_w, and $\delta + \delta_w$ fell into the low (.3) to high (.8) range. Several chi-square variates were rescaled by multiplying by constants in order to obtain the desired effect sizes.

Beta Distributions

Two-side bounded data were generated according to beta distributions with the first parameter (*p*) and the second parameter (*q*) ranging from 1 to 14. Again, certain population groups were selected for comparison, so that δ ranged from .3 to .8.

The null cases for one-side or two-side bounded data were those when the two groups had identical chi-square or beta distributions. For the non-null cases, again, the populations compared could have equal or unequal variance, skewness, and kurtosis. For nonnormal data, four nonnull situations were considered: when two groups were (a) the same in shape (skewness and kurtosis) and scale (variance); (b) the same in shape but different in scale; (c) the same in scale but different in shape; and (d) different in shape and scale.

Correlation Between the Paired Populations

For each type of distribution, let X represent one set of 10,000 random numbers generated, and ω for a set of 10,000 random numbers generated for a standard normal variate. Then, another set of observations, represented by Y, which is correlated with X, was obtained by the following transformation:

$$Y = \rho X + (1 - \rho^2)^{1/2}\omega, \tag{9}$$

where ρ is the correlation between X and Y. ρ was .3, .5, and .8.

The correlated variates, X and Y, were then rescaled to obtain desired mean and variance combinations. In estimating power and CI coverage, δ ranged from .25 to .82, and δ_w ranged from .33 to 1.0. $\sigma_1{:}\sigma_2$ was manipulated at (1:1), (1:2.25), (1:4), and (1:9) for normal and skewed populations, and within a similar range for bounded distributions. These sets of 10,000 transformed and rescaled observations were treated as populations, from which samples were randomly drawn. The procedure for inducing correlations between the bounded populations changed the mean, variance, skewness, and kurtosis of the original variables. Properties of the bounded distributions actually used in simulation are summarized in Table 12.1. Skewness (τ_1) is measured with $\mu_3/\mu_2^{2/3}$, and kurtosis (τ_2) with μ_4/μ_2^2, where μ_k is the k-th moment about the mean.

Sample Size

Sample size, particularly differences in sample size, can profoundly affect the behavior of location comparisons. For each pair of populations, observations were simulated with small (n = 10), moderate (n = 30), and large (n = 100) sizes. Both d and paired t tests were performed for the same data at the α = .05 significance level.

Table 12.1. Some Characteristics of the Paired Bounded Distributions

Group 1				*Group 2*				
μ	σ	τ_1	τ_2	μ	σ	τ_1	τ_2	ρ
One-side Bounded: Null Cases								
3.3	2.4	1.6	6.8	3.3	2.4	1.5	6.7	.3
4.0	2.8	1.4	5.8	4.0	2.8	1.4	6.0	.5
5.9	4.3	1.7	8.2	5.9	4.4	1.6	6.9	.8
One-side Bounded: Nonnull Cases								
2.0	1.0	1.0	4.3	1.6	1.0	1.2	5.2	.3
5.0	3.2	1.2	4.8	2.7	1.0	.8	4.3	.3
11.0	4.8	.9	4.4	5.0	3.2	1.3	5.5	.3
2.4	1.0	.9	4.1	2.0	1.0	1.1	4.9	.5
8.0	4.0	1.0	4.6	5.0	1.7	.7	3.7	.5
15.5	5.9	.8	4.1	8.0	4.0	1.0	4.3	.5
24.0	6.9	.6	3.4	21.0	6.5	.6	3.5	.8
20.0	6.3	.6	3.6	15.0	3.9	.5	3.3	.8
44.0	10.8	.5	3.5	27.0	7.2	.6	3.4	.8
Two-side Bounded: Null Cases								
.29	.05	.9	4.5	.29	.05	.9	4.5	.3
.30	.06	.5	3.6	.30	.06	.5	3.5	.5
.29	.09	.2	2.8	.29	.09	.1	2.8	.8
Two-side Bounded: Nonnull Cases								
.38	.11	.6	3.0	.32	.08	.6	3.5	.3
.45	.11	.2	2.6	.35	.10	.6	3.3	.3
.50	.15	.0	2.1	.30	.07	.3	3.4	.3
.54	.08	-.1	2.9	.50	.08	.0	2.8	.5
.36	.08	.3	3.1	.30	.07	.4	3.4	.5
.50	.13	.0	2.6	.29	.08	.1	2.7	.5
.33	.10	.1	2.7	.29	.09	.1	2.7	.8
.69	.13	−.1	2.5	.56	.13	.0	2.5	.8
.56	.13	.0	2.4	.33	.13	.2	2.7	.8

Evaluation Criteria

Three criteria were used to evaluate the statistics: empirical Type I error rate, power, and CI coverage. The Type I error rate was estimated by the proportion of rejection at .05 level, out of 2,000 replications, in each null case. Power was estimated by the proportion of rejection *in the right* direction at the .05 level in nonnull cases. The CI coverage probability was estimated by the proportion that the CI generated by each method covers the corresponding population parameter.

RESULTS

A total of 72 null cases were simulated in studying empirical Type I error rate, and 378 nonnull cases were simulated in studying power and CI coverage. Results for typical combinations are reported in this chapter in order to represent the range of the aforementioned factors.

Empirical Type I Error Rate

With the asymmetric CI's for δ, δ_w, and $\delta + \delta_w$, d appeared to be robust in terms of actual probability of a Type I error. See Table 12.2 for results on the probability of a Type I error for the d statistics and the paired t under some representative distributions examined. In fact, for all four types of distributions considered, along with all levels of correlation between the populations, d maintained an empirical Type I error rate at the nominal a level (.05) when the sample size was as large as 30, with a few exceptions when it tended to be a little bit conservative. This method was rather conservative (its actual α level was much lower than .05) when the sample size was small ($n = 10$), no matter what form the distributions took. More specifically, d_w and $d_b + d_w$ had empirical α levels at .017 to .031 when $n = 10$, for normal and nonnormal variables. The population correlation did not show any effect on the significance levels of d_w and $d_b + d_w$ when other factors were controlled. The empirical α level of d_b, on the other hand, was a decreasing function of ρ: it was less conservative when the correlation between the two groups was low (.3), and became more conservative as ρ increased.

The paired t test also appeared to behave well in terms of probability of controlling Type I errors. It maintained an empirical Type I error rate at the nominal level for all sample sizes, all types of distributions, and all levels of population correlation considered. In short, under normality, the heterogeneity of variances did not have an effect on either d or t in terms of probability of a Type I error.

Empirical Power

Table 12.3 shows the empirical power of the d and t statistics for some typical conditions considered. As expected, for the same two-group comparisons, the power of d_b, d_w, $d_b + d_w$, and t all increased when the sample size was increased, and/or when the population correlation level was increased. It appeared that the sample size had a stronger effect on the d statistics than on the paired t (i.e., when the sample sizes increased, the

Table 12.2. Empirical Type I Error Rate of *d* and Paired *t*, $\alpha = .05$

	$n = 10$				$n = 30$				$n = 100$			
ρ	d_b	d_w	d_b+d_w	t	d_b	d_w	d_b+d_w	t	d_b	d_w	d_b+d_w	t
Normal Distributions ($\mu_1 = \mu_2 = 0.0$; $\sigma_1 = \sigma_2 = 1.0$)												
.3	.034⁻	.016⁻	.023⁻	.051	.041	.043	.042	.052	.058	.058	.048	.057
.5	.024⁻	.022⁻	.024⁻	.051	.043	.042	.040	.049	.055	.049	.050	.052
.8	.007⁻	.021⁻	.025⁻	.049	.038⁻	.043	.045	.045	.041	.055	.051	.052
Skewed Distributions ($\mu_1 = \mu_2 = 0.0$; $\sigma_1 = \sigma_2 = 1.0$; $sk_1 = sk_2 = 2.0$)												
.3	.026⁻	.019⁻	.026⁻	.038⁻	.042	.040	.041	.036⁻	.051	.060	.049	.047
.5	.021⁻	.017⁻	.022⁻	.040	.034⁻	.048	.041	.041	.047	.051	.045	.054
.8	.005⁻	.018⁻	.021⁻	.044	.051	.052	.051	.045	.036⁻	.049	.040	.047
Chi-square Distributions ($df_1 = df_2 = 2.0$)												
.3	.030⁻	.019⁻	.031⁻	.041	.051	.051	.051	.058	.045	.051	.045	.051
.5	.023⁻	.019⁻	.026⁻	.040	.040	.041	.039⁻	.051	.049	.057	.047	.048
.8	.010⁻	.023⁻	.029⁻	.041	.052	.043	.045	.054	.047	.058	.051	.045
Beta Distributions ($p_1 = p_2 = 1.0$; $q_1 = q_2 = 10.0$)												
.3	.027⁻	.021⁻	.030⁻	.045	.045	.049	.049	.046	.045	.049	.039⁻	.042
.5	.016⁻	.020⁻	.023⁻	.040	.043	.038⁻	.041	.055	.041	.054	.041	.047
.8	.003⁻	.021⁻	.024⁻	.048	.046	.041	.046	.047	.047	.056	.051	.054

Note: + At least two standard deviations above .05, computed as if $\alpha = .05$; - At least two standard deviations below .05, computed as if $\alpha = .05$.

Table 12.3. Empirical Power of d and Paired t, $\alpha = .05$

				$n = 10$				$n = 30$				$n = 100$			
ρ	$\sigma_1{:}\sigma_2$	d	δ_w	d_b	d_w	d_b+d_w	t	d_b	d_w	d_b+d_w	t	d_b	d_w	d_b+d_w	t
Normal Distributions ($\mu_1 = \mu_2 = 0.0$; $\sigma_1 = \sigma_2 = 1.0$)															
.3	2:3	.427	.492	.321	.212	.262	.444	.891	.770	.857	.928	.997	.989	1.0	.998
.5	2:1	.336	.423	.230	.186	.215	.387	.767	.673	.740	.867	.999	.996	.998	.999
.8	2:1	.342	.542	.266	.298	.320	.532	.915	.882	.906	.977	1.0	1.0	1.0	1.0
Equally Skewed Distributions ($sk_1 = sk_2 = 2.0$)															
.3	2:1	.327	.444	.236	.196	.231	.299	.721	.694	.739	.822	.999	.998	.999	1.0
.5	3:2	.490	.665	.535	.460	.525	.610	.983	.970	.980	.974	1.0	1.0	1.0	1.0
.8	3:1	.808	.890	.970	.892	.949	.969	1.0	1.0	1.0	1.0	1.0	1.0	1.0	1.0
One Skewed and One Symmetric Distributions ($sk_1 = 2.0$, $sk_2 = 0.0$)															
.3	2:1	.333	.392	.218	.146	.191	.306	.757	.573	.680	.866	.998	.986	.994	1.0
.5	2:1	.332	.452	.235	.197	.252	.407	.935	.699	.832	.976	1.0	.998	1.0	1.0
.8	3:1	.767	.989	.997	.998	1.0	.997	1.0	1.0	1.0	1.0	1.0	1.0	1.0	1.0
Oppositely Skewed Distributions ($sk_1 = 2.0$, $sk_2 = -2.0$)															
.3	2:3	.358	.445	.266	.181	.243	.438	.792	.682	.766	.976	.999	.996	.998	1.0
.5	3:1	.764	.943	.977	.967	.980	.988	1.0	1.0	1.0	1.0	1.0	1.0	1.0	1.0
.7	2:1	.245	.622	.126	.409	.424	.616	.923	.957	.962	.997	1.0	1.0	1.0	1.0
Chi-Square Distributions															
.3	1:1	.280	.346	.164	.111	.148	.208	.581	.466	.543	.535	.985	.956	.979	.966
.5	1:1	.262	.382	.152	.117	.155	.250	.670	.549	.637	.678	.993	.977	.989	.991
.8	1.6:1	.485	.771	.675	.679	.740	.905	1.0	.999	1.0	1.0	1.0	1.0	1.0	1.0
Beta Distributions															
.3	1.4:1	.286	.329	.153	.106	.138	.245	.592	.410	.510	.690	.991	.933	.975	.998
.5	1:1	.304	.421	.209	.169	.216	.343	.790	.660	.748	.841	.999	.993	.998	1.0
.8	0.9:1	.786	.965	.996	.983	.993	1.0	1.0	1.0	1.0	1.0	1.0	1.0	1.0	1.0

Note: μ_d is 1.0 to 3.0 for normal and skewed distributions.

increase in the power of d was larger than that of t), whereas the degree to which the population groups were correlated had a stronger effect on t than on d. Unequal variances, unequal skewnesses, or boundedness did not seem to have a substantial effect on the power of either d or t statistic for the conditions simulated in this study, given that at similar levels of effect size, the power of each test was similar whether the population groups were normal or skewed, had equal or unequal variance, and were bounded or not.

Comparing d_b, d_w, and $d_b + d_w$, ρ appeared to have a stronger effect on d_w and $d_b + d_w$ than on d_b in terms of power, and the sample size effect was more obvious with d_b and $d_b + d_w$ than d_w. When $n = 10$, for all distributional situations considered, d_b showed higher power than the other two when ρ was in the low range (about .3), but the power of $d_b + d_w$ and d_w increased at a greater rate as ρ increased; and when ρ became high (about .8), $d_b + d_w$ and d_w showed higher power than d_b. When $n = 30$, no matter ρ was low, moderate, or high, d_b and $d_b + d_w$ usually had similar power, which was higher than that of d_w. When n was increased to 100, at any level of the effect size and for any ρ, all of the statistics tested had a power that was equal to, or very close to, the maximum level 1.0, so comparisons are moot.

Comparing the d statistics with the paired t, in general, t showed higher power than d in small samples. This difference in power was seen for all forms of distributions studied, but it was a little bit larger for normal data, and smaller when nonnormality, skewness, or boundedness was involved. It is seen in Table 12.3 that when the $n = 10$, the paired t demonstrated highest power among the statistics examined, which was followed by d_b when $\rho = .3$, or by $d_b + d_w$ when $\rho = .8$. However, it should be noted that a direct power comparison between d and t is not always valid, because the two statistics usually had different actually α level and different CI coverage as well (see later for more details). The power advantage of t became less obvious when the sample sizes increased to 30. In fact, the power of d was sometimes about the same as, or slightly higher, than that of t with moderate sample sizes (e.g., with equally skewed, one skewed and one symmetric, and chi-square distributions). When $n = 100$, d and t had similar power—approximately 1.0.

Coverage of CI

Table 12.4 presents typical results on the empirical probability of the CI coverage of the tests. In general, with the asymmetric CI's for δ, δ_w, and $\delta + \delta_w$, the d method performed well in terms of probability of the CI coverage. Its empirical CI coverage tended to be higher than the $1 - \alpha$

nominal level (.95) in small samples, and became closer to the nominal level as the sample size got larger, independent of the form of the population distributions, the variance ratio, skewness, boundedness of the groups, and the correlation between the paired groups. It was practically maintained at the $1 - \alpha$ level whenever n was increased to 100. The paired t test, however, was affected by the skewness of the population groups, the variance ratio between them, and probably the interaction between these two factors, in terms of the coverage probability of the CI for μ_d.

Comparing the three CI's for within-subject/within-pair difference, group difference, and the combined difference, the former two had a better (at or above $1 - \alpha$) probability of coverage than the third. The estimated probability that falls within its CI was rarely significantly below .95, and it never dropped below .925 under all distributional conditions considered in this study. It is seen from Table 12.4 that even with $n = 10$, the CI coverage for δ was almost always at or above the nominal level. The few exceptions took place when δ was quite high (above .7) and n was small (10). When the sample sizes were increased to 30 or more, this CI coverage probability was usually maintained at the .95 level.

The behavior of d_w was less consistent in terms of the probability of its CI coverage than d_b. In small samples, d_w tended to yield a coverage well above .95. When $n = 30$, this coverage was still observed to be significantly higher than .95 for half of the cases. Similar results were found occasionally even when n was as large as 100. On the other hand, there were a few cases, usually when δ_w was close to 1.0, in which the same CI coverage dropped below the .95 level. This lack of coverage happened when $n = 10$, 30, and 100.

The effect size and the degree of ρ seemed to interact and influence on the CI coverage for $\delta + \delta_w$. For all types of the distributions examined, this coverage was usually maintained at the nominal level when $\delta + \delta_w$ and were both in their low range, or both high. It tended to be relatively low when ρ was small and $\delta + \delta_w$ was high, or when ρ was large and $\delta + \delta_w$ was in the low range. In small samples, there were a few cases when the empirical coverage of CI for $\delta + \delta_w$ dropped slightly below .9, but it improved substantially (got closer to $1 - \alpha$) as a function of n.

As mentioned above, the paired t test was affected by the form (especially skewness) of the populations, their variance ratio, and the interaction between these two factors, in terms of CI coverage for μ_d. The paired t performed well for normal data; it yielded CI coverages at the $1 - \alpha$ level no matter what the sample size, ρ, and the variance ratio between the populations were, as long as they were normally distributed. For skewed variables, though, t generally provided inadequate CI coverage for μ_d, particularly in small samples. When the two paired groups were equally skewed (skewness $\approx$ 2.0), or one was skewed and the other was symmetric,

Table 12.4. Empirical Probability of CI Coverage of *d* and Paired *t*, $\alpha = .05$

				$n = 10$				$n = 30$				$n = 100$			
ρ	$\sigma_1{:}\sigma_2$	d	δ_w	d_b	d_w	$d_b + d_w$	t	d_b	d_w	$d_b + d_w$	t	d_b	d_w	$d_b + d_w$	t
Normal Distributions ($\mu_1 = \mu_2 = 0.0$; $\sigma_1 = \sigma_2 = 1.0$)															
.3	2:3	.427	.492	.963$^+$	.979$^+$	.942	.957	.964$^+$	.960	.956	.952	.955	.953	.953	.946
.5	2:1	.336	.423	.963$^+$	.993$^+$	.951	.951	.962$^+$	.966$^+$	.957	.954	.956	.961$^+$	.951	.954
.8	2:1	.342	.542	.967$^+$	.988$^+$	.924$^-$	.953	.961$^+$	.951	.953	.947	.956	.957	.950	.955
Equally Skewed Distributions ($sk_1 = sk_2 = 2.0$)															
.3	2:1	.327	.444	.960	.994$^+$	.947	.938$^-$	.961$^+$	.966$^+$	.966	.947	.947	.951	.941	.952
.5	3:2	.490	.665	.955	.984$^+$	.892-	.961$^+$	.953	.967$^+$	.942	.950	.942	.951	.946	.945
.8	3:1	.799	.961	.967$^+$	.981$^+$	.953	.911$^-$	.955	.974$^+$	.939$^-$	.932$^-$	.949	.942	.933$^-$	.946
One Skewed and One Symmetric Distributions ($sk_1 = 2.0$, $sk_2 = 0.0$)															
.3	2:1	.333	.392	.962$^+$	.988$^+$	.957	.932$^-$	.965$^+$	.974$^+$	.965$^+$	.933$^-$	.947	.945	.948	.947
.5	2:1	.332	.452	.961$^+$	.996$^+$	.947	.874$^-$	.943	.956	.943	.903$^-$	.952	.966$^+$	.961$^+$	.936$^-$
.8	3:1	.767	.989	.940	.943	.941	.912$^-$	.945	.985$^+$	.950	.925$^-$	.955	.979$^+$	.956	.947
Oppositely Skewed Distributions ($sk_1 = 2.0$, $sk_2 = {}^-2.0$)															
.3	2:3	.358	.445	.964$^+$	.993$^+$	.945	.930$^-$	.957	.971$^+$	.961$^+$	.935$^-$	.956	.952	.948	.945
.5	3:1	.764	.943	.954	.967$^+$	.967$^+$	.914$^-$	.944	.941	.940	.919$^-$	.953	.982$^+$	.948	.944
.7	2:1	.245	.622	.993$^+$	.977$^+$	.891$^-$	.885$^-$	.941	.970$^+$	.947	.913$^-$	.951	.943	.949	.939$^-$
Chi-Square Distributions															
.3	1:1	.280	.346	.973$^+$	.980$^+$	.967$^+$	.957	.961$^+$	.971$^+$	.962$^+$	.948	.956	.962$^+$	.958	.952
.5	1:1	.262	.382	.971$^+$	.988$^+$	.959	.947	.961$^+$	.962$^+$	.964$^+$	.953	.956	.963$^+$	.959	.950
.8	1.6:1	.485	.771	.969$^+$	.980$^+$	.933$^-$	.949	.951	.986$^+$	.947	.948	.953	.941	.943	.951
Beta Distributions															
.3	1.4:1	.286	.329	.963$^+$	.974$^+$	.964$^+$	.947	.959	.968$^+$	.961$^+$	.951	.951	.946	.951	.951
.5	1:1	.304	.421	.961$^+$	.989$^+$	.953	.950	.955	.958	.960	.958	.955	.952	.948	.944
.8	0.9:1	.786	.965	.944	.983$^+$	.955	.943	.960	.986$^+$	.950	.949	.951	.974$^+$	.947	.957

Note: + At least two standard deviations above .95, computed as if $\alpha = .05$; - At least two standard deviations below .95, computed as if $\alpha = .05$.

the coverage of the CI for μ_d was consistently significantly below .95 when σ_1:σ_2 was 2 or greater and $n = 10$. When the two groups were oppositely skewed, the paired *t* test always provided a CI with inadequate coverage for μ_d, even when the population groups were homogeneous in variance, if the sample size was not large. This lack of coverage was improved to some extent when *n* was increased to 30 and 100, but not completely. In fact, in all but one case, the *t* consistently yielded a CI coverage below $1 - \alpha$ with samples of 30 when the two groups were skewed to opposite directions.

Boundedness, one-sided or two-sided, did not seem to affect the performance of the paired *t* in terms of controlling the probability of CI coverage, though. It performed equally as well with chi-square and beta variates as under normality.

SUMMARY

The *d* method was found to behave quite well in terms of Type I error rate and CI coverage, but it generally produced less power than the paired *t* test with the continuous data simulated in this study. This ordinal method tended to be conservative in terms of controlling Type I errors (seemingly at the expense of a slight loss of power), particularly in small samples, for all distributional conditions considered. The paired *t* test also performed well as far as the Type I error rate was concerned; its actual level was maintained at .05 under all conditions. Power of both *d* and *t* was influenced by sample size and the population correlation, but not by other factors investigated (e.g., variance, skewness, and boundedness of the paired groups). The *d* method, in general, is robust in terms of probability of the CI coverage, whereas paired *t* is not (it is affected by the population variance and skewness, and probably their interaction as well). Comparing the *d* statistics for detecting the within-subject difference, the group difference, and the combined difference, d_b seemed to be the best choice in most cases (unless the two groups were very highly correlated in their populations). Its Type I error rate was at or below α; its coverage was at or above $1 - \alpha$; and its power was mostly equal to or greater than that of d_w and $d_b + d_w$.

Comparability of the Findings

A purpose of this study was to evaluate the relative performance of *d*, in comparison to paired *t*, in normal and nonnormal populations for correlated data. The findings based on simulations generally show that both *d* and *t* have good control over the actual probability of a Type I error under the conditions considered. This result is similar to that of a comparable study by Blair and Higgins (1985) in that they found that the WSR test produced actual levels in reasonable aggreement with the nominal levels throughout all the normal and nonnormal distributions (representing symmetric, skewed, and heavy- and light-tailed shapes) they considered. However, the same researchers found the *t* test to be markedly conservative in terms of Type I error rate under some mixture distributions (e.g., mixed normal and mixed exponential) and the heavy-tailed Cauchy distribution, and somewhat conservative under the lognormal and the chi-square distributions (Blair & Higgins, 1985). Wilcox (1992) also found that the paired *t* test can be rather conservative in case of contamination (heavy-tailedness). Zumbo and Jennings (2002) showed that the paired *t* test was fairly robust for a range of symmetrically contaminated data, but had inflated Type I error rate when contamination was asymmetric. There is some difference between the distributions considered in the current study and those in the previous ones. For example, the distributions compared in the present study may differ not only in location, but also in scale and/or shape, whereas Blair and Higgins (1985) only considered shift in location. Besides, this study did not include very heavy-tailed distributions as the other ones did.

In general, the *d* method provided CI's with good coverage probability regardless of the form, variance ratio, and skewnesses of the populations compared, or the correlation between them. It was usually maintained at the nominal level even when *n* was as small as 10, with few exceptions (see Table 12.4). The power of *d* is not affected by nonnormality, heterogeneity of variance, skewness, or kurtosis of the compared groups. This "robust" feature of *d* is expected since this statistic does not assume equal variance or equal skewness. These findings on the *d* analysis for dependent data are consistent with findings of our previous study on *d* for independent groups (Feng & Cliff, 2004).

The finding of the good performance of *d* in terms of CI coverage is particularly important. This is because, as many researchers have pointed out (e.g., Cohen, 1990, 1994), in a science that aims to be quantitative, the ability to provide an accurate range of possible values for the parameter to be estimated is more important than the ability to make a simple dichotomous decision about whether or not the null hypothesis should be rejected. The paired *t*, however, is not robust to unequal variances and unequal skewnesses in terms of CI coverage. Comparable prior research on CI for the mean difference in paired data is not available.

Under the conditions tested here, nonnormality, unequal variance, or unequal skewness did not show a substantial effect on the power of the paired *t*. However, as mentioned before, there are other simulation studies showing that nonnormality can have a great impact on the power of the paired t test (Blair & Higgins, 1985; Wilcox, 1992; Zumbo & Jennings, 2002). Wilcox (1992) simulated contaminated normal data and showed that contamination (heavy-tailedness) can greatly reduce the power of t regardless of the extent to which the population groups might be correlated. Zumbo and Jennings (2002) found the power of paired t to be greatly affected by outliers when the effect size was small, especially when the small effect size was paired with sample sizes. The difference in our findings from the above mentioned other studies may lie in that the variances of the data used for simulation were controlled in the present study, but not in the other ones. For example, the contaminated normal data can have variances much larger than the normal data. Hence the variance of the mean difference can be much larger as well, resulting in low power for the t test and very long CI for μ_d. Power of d, on the other hand, should not be affected since the variances of the d_i variables would not change in case of contamination or heavy-tailedness as σ^2_{ud} does.

For the continuous data simulated in this study, the paired t test shows a small to moderate power advantage over d_b, and d_b usually has higher power than d_w (which is equivalent to the Friedman test when there are no ties in the paired observations) and than $d_b + d_w$. However, direct comparisons of power estimates by t and d tests are not valid since the true levels of these tests are not the same. Adjustment of the power estimates for Monte Carlo simulations was suggested by some researchers (Zhang & Boos, 1994). More important, as stated above, the probability of CI coverage is perhaps more of a concern than power in evaluating the robustness of the tests. It is noted that the power advantage of t should be considered for only in those cases when it also provides accurate CI for μ_d, and this substantially limits the situations where t shows power advantage. It is also noted that the power advantage of the paired t over d statistics is larger normal data with equal variance, and smaller for nonnormal (e.g., skewed) data. This suggests that the ordinal d might be less affected in terms of power by nonnormality, and skewness in particular, than the paired t.

Other Factors That Affect the Performance of *d* and *t*

For all statistics tested, using normal or nonnormal data, under each selected effect size, the performance of the tests were better when the sample sizes were larger. This is accounted for by the central limit effect. However, the performance of d seemed to improve more than that of the paired t as n increased. For instance, the above-mentioned power advantage of the paired t over d became less obvious, or disappeared, when the sample size increased, suggesting that the power of d increases faster than that of t with the increase of n. As mentioned before, the d tended to produce conservative actual levels in small samples. It seems that this conservativeness with small n is associated with a slight loss of power. This finding is similar to results of another study comparing the WSR test to paired t, which found the magnitude of the WSR's power advantage often increased with sample size (Blair & Higgins, 1985).

It was seen that for the same two-group comparisons, the power of both d and t tests increased when the correlation increased. This power increase with ρ is expected for the paired t test, since for two dependent random variables, the variance of their difference is a function of their correlation. The sampling variance of the mean difference is determined by the variances of the two dependent variables and their correlation: $(\sigma_x^2 + \sigma_y^2 - 2\rho\sigma_x\sigma_y)/n$. As ρ approaches 1, the variance of the sample mean difference decreases, which in turn leads to higher power for the paired t test. In other words, the more correlated the two paired groups are, the more power when testing H_0: $\mu_d = 0$. As Cliff (1993) pointed out, the sampling variance of d_b has similar properties as that of the difference between means with correlated data. If n is large, the only difference is that in the case of d_b, the determining variances and covariances (or correlation) are of $d_{i.}$ and $d_{.i}$ rather than the raw scores. It is a fact that when the correlation between the original variables is high, the correlation between the d_i variables is high in magnitude as well. This explains why at the same level of effect size, power of d_b increases with ρ. It should be noted, though, the power increase of d_b is not as fast as that of t. Not surprisingly, power of d_w also increases with ρ, since δ_w itself increases as ρ approaches 1 with the simulated data. However, power of d does not increase as fast as t.

CONCLUSION

This simulation study has shown that with the asymmetric CI's, the ordinal d for correlated data has good distributional behavior in general, in small, moderate, and large samples in terms of actual level, power, and probability of CI coverage for normal and non-normal populations. It tends to be conservative in terms of actual level in small samples. Its relative power tends to be lower than that of the paired t, but it can be noted that many of the conditions where t has the power advantage are those where its CI coverage is lower than the nominal level, thus its advantage is largely spurious. The paired t test was found to be robust in terms of Type I error rate for the data simulated, but not robust in terms of CI coverage.

Comparing the *d* statistics for detecting the within-subject difference, the group difference, and the combined difference, d_b seems to be the best choice in most cases. This ordinal method is robust to nonnormality of the population distributions; its sampling behavior is not influenced by the variance ratio and the correlation between the populations, or by their skewnesses.

The *d* has attractive characteristics as a description of location difference. It is a direct numerical reflection of the tendency for scores in one group to lie generally above those of another. It is also invariant under monotonic scale transformations, so conclusions about location need less qualification. The additional fact that its sampling behavior has to be rated as good seems to lead to a conclusion that it is the method of choice for location comparison in many situation.

ACKNOWLEDGMENT

I wish to thank Dr. Norman Cliff for his suggestions and guidance in the completion of this project.

REFERENCES

Birnbaum, Z. W. (1956). On a use of the Mann-Whitney statistic. In J. Neyman (Ed.), *Proceedings of the third Berkeley Symposium on Mathematical Statistics* (pp. 13-17). Berkeley, CA: University of California Press.

Birnbaum, A. W., & Mccarty, R. C. (1958). A distribution-free upper confidence bound for Pr {Y < X}, based on independent samples of X and Y. *Annual Mathematical Statistics, 29*, 558-562.

Blair, R. C., & Higgins, J. J. (1985). Comparison of the power of the paired samples *t* test relative to that of Wilcoxon's signed-ranks tests under various population shapes. *Psychological Bulletin, 97*, 119-128.

Bradley, J. V. (1978). Robustness? *British Journal of Mathematical and Statistical Psychology, 31*, 144-152.

Cliff, N. (1991). Ordinal methods in the study of change. In L.M. Collins & J. Horn (Eds.) *Best methods for the analysis of change* (pp. 34-46). Washington, DC: American Psychological Association.

Cliff, N. (1993). Dominance statistics: Ordinal analyses to answer ordinal questions. *Psychological Bulletin, 114*, 494 -509.

Cohen, J. (1988). *Statistical power analysis for the behavioral sciences* (2nd ed.). Hillsdale, NJ: Erlbaum.

Cohen, J. (1990). Things I have learned (so far). *American Psychologist, 45*, 1304-1312.

Cohen, J. (1994). The earth is round ($p < .05$). *American Psychologist, 49*, 997-1003.

Delaney, H. D., & Vargha, A. (2002). Comparing several robust tests of stochastic equality with ordinally scaled variables and small to moderate sized samples. *Psychological Methods, 7*, 485-503.

Feng, D., & Cliff, N. (2004). Monte Carlo evaluation of ordinal *d* with improved confidence interval. *Journal of Modern Applied Statistical Methods, 3*(2), 322-332.

Fligner, M. A., & Policello, G. E., II (1981). Robust rank procedure for the Behrens-Fisher problem. *Journal of the American Statistical Association, 76*, 162-168.

Friedman, M. (1937). The use of ranks to avoid the assumption of normality in the analysis of variance. *Journal of the American Statistical Association, 32*, 675-701.

Halperin, M., Gilbert, P. R., & Lachin, J. M. (1987). Distribution-free confidence intervals for $\Pr(X_1 < X_2)$, *Biometrics, 43*, 71-80.

Hoaglin, D. C. (1985). Summarizing shape numerically: The g&h distributions. In D. C. Hoaglin, F. Mosteller, & J. W. Tukey (Eds.) *Exploring data tables, trends, and shapes* (pp. 461-513). New York: Wiley.

Long, J. D., Feng, D., & Cliff, N. (2003). Ordinal analysis of behavioral data. In J. Schinka, W. Velicer, and I. B. Weiner (Eds.), *Comprehensive handbook of psychology, Vol. 2: Research methods in psychology* (pp. 635-662). New York: Wiley.

McGraw, K. O., & Wong, S. P. (1992). A common language effect size statistic. *Psychological Bulletin, 111*, 361-365.

Mee, R. W. (1990). Confidence intervals for probabilities and tolenrance regions based on a generalization of the Mann-Whitney statistics. *Journal of the American Statistical Association, 85*, 793-800.

Micceri, T. (1989). The Unicorn, the normal curve, and other improbable creatures. *Psychological Bulletin, 105*, 156-166.

O'Brien, P. C. (1988). Comparing two samples: Extension of the *t*, rank-sum, and log-rank tests. *Journal of the American Statistical Association, 83*, 52-61.

Pearson, E. S., & Please, N. W. (1975). Relation between the shape of population distribution and the robustness of four simple statistics. *Biometrika, 62*, 223-241.

Robey, R. R., & Barcikowski, R. S. (1992). Type I error and the number of iteration in Monte Carlo studies of robustness. *British Journal of Mathematical and Statistical Psychology, 45*, 283-288.

Sawilowsky, S. S. (2000). Review of the rank transform in designed experiments. *Perceptual & Motor Skills, 90(2)*, 489-497.

Tan, W. Y. (1982). Sampling distribution and robustness of *t*, *F* and variance ratio of two samples and ANOVA models with respect to departure from normality. *Communications in Statistics: Theory and Computation, 11*, 2485-2511.

Ury, H. K. (1972). On distribution-free confidence bounds for $\Pr\{Y < X\}$. *Technometrics, 14*, 577-581.

Vargha, A., & Delaney, H. D. (2000). A critique and improvement of the CL common language effect size statistics of McGraw and Wong. *Journal of Education and Behavioral Statistics, 25*, 101-132.

Wilcox, R. R. (1991). Why can methods for comparing means have relatively low power, and what can you do to correct the problem? *Current Directions in Psychological Science, 1*, 101-105.

Wilcox, R. R. (1992). Comparing the medians of dependent groups. *British Journal of Mathematical and Statistical Psychology, 45*, 151-162.

Zaremba, S. K. (1962). A generalization of Wilcoxon's test. *Monatshefte fur Mathematik, 66*, 359-370.

Zhang, J., & Boos, D. D. (1994). Adjusted power estimates in Monte Carlo experiments. *Communications in Statistics-Simulation and Computation, 23*, 165-173.

Zumbo, B. D., & Jennings, M. J. (2002). The robustness of validity and efficiency of the related samples *t*-test in the presence of outliers. *Psicologica, 23(2)*, 415-450.

CHAPTER 13

FACTORIAL ANOVA IN SPSS

Fixed-, Random-, and Mixed-Effects Models

Richard G. Lomax and Stacy Hughey Surman

Since its inception, ANOVA has been a popular solution for reducing the experiment-wise error rate problematic in the use of multiple *t* tests. In the behavioral sciences, factorial ANOVA models are quite popular in terms of assessing mean differences in an experimental or quasi-experimental design. Here we consider the simplest factorial ANOVA model, the two-factor model, where we refer to the factors as Factor A and Factor B. In some cases, factors are known as fixed-effects factors, where the levels of the factor are specifically selected by the researcher. Here only those particular levels of interest are selected for the experiment; results can only be generalized about those selected levels, and thus the same levels would be involved in replications. Some typical fixed-effects factors include specifically selected textbooks for review, socioeconomic level, marital status, age group, gender, or weight.

In some cases, factors are known as random-effects factors, where the levels of the factor are randomly selected from some population of levels. Here one can generalize results from the randomly selected sample of levels back to the population of levels, and thus different levels could be

Real Data Analysis, 185–189

involved in replications. Some typical random-effects factors include randomly selected depression therapies, subjects (e.g., people, animals, corporations), time (e.g., hours, days), medication included in a drug study, or instructional materials.

In a two-factor situation, four different models are possible. Model I is where A and B are both fixed, known as a fixed-effects model. Model II is where A and B are both random, known as a random-effects model. Model III is where A is fixed and B is random, known as one type of a mixed-effects model. Model IV is where A is random and B is fixed, known as another type of a mixed-effects model.

The purpose of this chapter is to (a) describe in detail the nature of these four models and how proper *F* ratios ought to be formed, and (b) compare the results of the proper *F* ratios with those generated by SPSS for each model using an example dataset.

PROPER *F* RATIOS OF THE FOUR MODELS

The proper *F* ratios described in this chapter are based on the expected mean squares as detailed in texts such as Hays (1994), Kirk (1994), and Lomax (2001). From these expected mean squares (not shown for space reasons, but provided in each text), the proper *F* ratios are developed as follows:

Model I: Fixed-Effects Model

$F_A = MS_A / MS_{with}$
$F_B = MS_B / MS_{with}$
$F_{AB} = MS_{AB} / MS_{with}$

Model II: Random-Effects Model

$F_A = MS_A / MS_{AB}$
$F_B = MS_B / MS_{AB}$
$F_{AB} = MS_{AB} / MS_{with}$

Model III: Mixed-Effects Model (A Fixed and B Random)

$F_A = MS_A / MS_{AB}$
$F_B = MS_B / MS_{with}$
$F_{AB} = MS_{AB} / MS_{with}$

Model IV: Mixed-Effects Model (A Random and B Fixed)

$F_A = MS_A / MS_{with}$

$F_B = MS_B/MS_{AB}$
$F_{AB} = MS_{AB}/MS_{with}$

RESULTS

In this section, we utilized SPSS with a particular data set (Lomax, 2001, p. 349) for each of the four models. Factor A has four levels, factor B has two levels, and the number of observations per cell is four; thus the example is an equal n model. The purpose of this analysis was to determine whether SPSS yielded the proper F ratios for each of the four models. Specifically we used the univariate part of the General Linear Model (GLM) module from SPSS 12 (although the multivariate part yielded the same results as did SPSS 13).

The first step was to compute the *MS* terms in various ways (e.g., SPSS, SAS, hand computations), all of which resulted in the exact same *MS* values as follows (reported here to three places): MS_A = 246.198; MS_B = 712.531; MS_{AB} = 7.281; MS_{with} = 11.531. The second step was to compute the F values, (a) by hand using the *MS* values to generate the proper F ratios, and (b) from SPSS by inserting the factor name into the appropriate fixed-factor and random-factor dialog boxes in SPSS GLM. The user assumes these dialog boxes yield the proper F ratios. For each model, the proper F ratios generated by hand and the F ratios generated by SPSS are shown in Table 13.1.

The results indicate that when both factors are either fixed (Model I) or random (Model II), SPSS correctly yields the same results as the proper F ratios. However, when one factor is fixed and one factor is random (i.e., mixed-effects Models III or IV), SPSS does not yield the same results as the proper F ratios. This is because SPSS uses the interaction as the error term (or denominator) for all main effects in a mixed-effects model, regardless of whether that main effect is fixed or random. Thus in any two factor mixed-effects model, one of the main effect F values will be incorrectly calculated by SPSS, although the interaction F ratios will always be correct. We have replicated these results with other two-factor datasets and have always arrived at the same conclusion about SPSS (e.g., Kirk, 1994, p. 367).

In fact SPSS actually indicates to the user which of the error terms is used in factorial models. The superscripts in the *MS* column (e.g., [b]) of the SPSS ANOVA summary table indicate which error terms are used for each F (whether correct or not). Here is the table (Table 13.2) for mixed-effects Model III (A fixed and B random) using the Lomax (2001) example:

Table 13.1. Proper *F* Ratios and SPSS Generated *F* Ratios of Four Models for Example Data

Proper F ratio	*SPSS F ratio*
Model I:	
$F_A = MS_A/MS_{with} = 246.198/11.531 = 21.350$	$F_A = 246.198/11.531 = 21.350$
$F_B = MS_B/MS_{with} = 712.531/11.531 = 61.791$	$F_B = 712.531/11.531 = 61.791$
$F_{AB} = MS_{AB}/MS_{with} = 7.281/11.531 = 0.631$	$F_{AB} = 7.281/11.531 = 0.631$
Model II:	
$F_A = MS_A/MS_{AB} = 246.198/7.281 = 33.813$	$F_A = 246.198/7.281 = 33.813$
$F_B = MS_B/MS_{AB} = 712.531/7.281 = 97.858$	$F_B = 712.531/7.281 = 97.858$
$F_{AB} = MS_{AB}/MS_{with} = 7.281/11.531 = 0.631$	$F_{AB} = 7.281/11.531 = 0.631$
Model III:	
$F_A = MS_A/MS_{AB} = 246.198/7.281 = 33.813$	$F_A = 246.198/7.281 = 33.813$
$F_B = MS_B/MS_{with} = 712.531/11.531 = 61.791$	$F_B = 712.531/7.281 = 97.858$*
$F_{AB} = MS_{AB}/MS_{with} = 7.281/11.531 = 0.631$	$F_{AB} = 7.281/11.531 = 0.631$
Model IV:	
$F_A = MS_A/MS_{with} = 246.198/11.531 = 21.350$	$F_A = 246.198/7.281 = 33.813$*
$F_B = MS_B/MS_{AB} = 712.531/7.281 = 97.858$	$F_B = 712.531/7.281 = 97.858$
$F_{AB} = MS_{AB}/MS_{with} = 7.281/11.531 = 0.631$	$F_{AB} = 7.281/11.531 = 0.631$

Note: *Situations where the SPSS *F* ratios are incorrect.

Table 13.2. Tests of Between-Subjects Effects

Dependent Variable: dv

Source		*Type III Sum of Squares*	*df*	*Mean Square*	*F*	*Sig.*
a	Hypothesis	738.594	3	246.198	33.813	.008
	Error	21.844	3	7.281[b]		
b	Hypothesis	712.531	1	712.531	97.858	.002
	Error	21.844	3	7.281[b]		
a * *b*	Hypothesis	21.844	3	7.281	.631	.602
	Error	276.750	24	11.531[c]		

b. *MS*(*a* * *b*)
c. *MS*(Error)

DISCUSSION

In order to avoid an increased likelihood of a decision error (i.e., Type I or Type II) resulting from incorrect *F* ratios, the user of mixed-effect ANOVA models has two methods of correction available when using

SPSS. One option is that once *MS* values have been computed by SPSS, *F* ratios can then be easily calculated by hand to arrive at the correct values of the main effects. Of course the user has to remember to apply the hand correction in each application.

A second option is to construct the appropriate *F* ratios with user-supplied SPSS syntax. This correction allows the user to write and reuse syntax for future mixed-effect ANOVA models. For example, if factor A is fixed and factor B is random, then the syntax should include the following commands to produce the proper *F* ratios:

```
/RANDOM = factorb

/DESIGN = factora VS 1, factorb VS WITHIN, factora BY factorb = 1 VS WITHIN
```

Here VS indicates which error term the effect of interest is tested against (VS means versus or against). The interaction is defined as the "1" error term. Thus the interaction is used as the error term for factor A, while within is used as the error term for both factor B and the interaction.

Mixed-effect ANOVA models will continue to be of great use for data analysis in the behavioral sciences. With the ever-increasing use of statistical software, it is of the utmost importance that a fail-safe be in place to assess results produced by such packages for accuracy. Whether using hand calculations or syntax, it is simple to make the appropriate correction and arrive at the proper *F* ratios with SPSS.

REFERENCES

Hayes, W. L. (1994). *Statistics* (5th ed.). Belmont, CA: Wadsworth.

Kirk, R. E. (1994). *Experimental design: Procedures for the behavioral sciences* (3rd ed.). Belmont, CA: Wadsworth.

Lomax, R. G. (2001). *An introduction to statistical concepts for education and behavioral sciences*. Mahwah, NJ: Erlbaum.

CHAPTER 14

ANOVA

Effect Sizes, Simulating Interaction Versus Main Effects, and a Modified ANOVA Table

Shlomo S. Sawilowsky

The fifth edition of the American Psychological Association's (APA, 2001) *Publication Manual* contains a number of changes to the standard ANOVA table. Among the changes are inducements to report obtained p values and include η, a measure of effect size.

The revision to the APA style manual was influenced considerably by Thompson (1996; see Thompson & Vacha-Haase, 2000). He recommended that effect sizes, "can and should be reported and interpreted in all studies, regardless of whether statistical tests are reported. AERA [the American Educational Research Association] should venture beyond the APA, and require" (Thompson, 1996, p. 29) reporting of effect sizes.

The importance of reporting effect sizes associated with statistically significant results should not be underestimated. I proposed an encyclopedia to serve as a repository of statistically significant effect sizes (Sawilowsky 1996, 2003a). It would permit the calculation of the minimum sample size to design an experiment based on science instead of prestidigitation.

Real Data Analysis, pp. 191–212

However, it is untenable to report effect sizes for nonsignificant results. Sawilowsky and Yoon (2001) demonstrated this by examining effect sizes for studies that are not significant. A Monte Carlo study with 10,000 repetitions was conducted on scores randomly obtained from a Gaussian distribution and assigned to two groups with $n_1 = n_2 = 10$. A two-sided independent samples t test was conducted with $\alpha = 0.05$. The magnitude of the average effect size for 95% of the replications that failed to reject the null hypothesis was $|0.34|$, which is not near zero. See further the discussion in Sawilowsky (2003b, 2003c). The publication of individual nonsignificant results will create the false impression that there exists what Cohen (1988) described as a small to medium treatment effect.

Thus, the APA guideline will promote confusion. The important a priori hypothesized effect size, which is related to prospective power and sample size determination, will become confused with the misleading a posteriori obtained effect size, which is related to retrospective power. Zumbo and Hubley (1998) pointed out, "It is not generally viable to compute retrospective power, particularly when one has not rejected the null hypothesis" (p. 385).

As is most often the case when erroneous statistical practice is promulgated, the culprit is in misunderstanding or ignoring the hypothesis being tested. For example, with $k = 3$ groups, the null hypothesis is H_0: $\mu_1 = \mu_2 = \mu_3$ in the one-way ANOVA; the H_o generalizes to factorial ANOVA and ANCOVA.

A failure to reject decision, based on the evidence from the sample, indicates that observed differences are not statistically different from zero. Based on the sample, the observed differences should be viewed as zero. Similarly, η, the effect size, is not statistically significantly different from zero (i.e., no effect). Citing η is legitimate only when the null hypothesis is rejected, as noted by Cohen (1988)

> the null hypothesis always means the effect size is zero ... [but] when the null hypothesis is false, it is false to some specific degree, i.e., the effect size (ES) is some specific nonzero value in the population. (p. 10)

This discussion should not be confused with the issue of whether or not a study should be published if the results are not significant. An examination of a supposed effective intervention that, in fact, is not effective is certainly highly publishable. This is fundamentally different from publishing quantities associated with nonsignificant results, such as the magnitude of the effect size or the p value.

Thompson (1996) and Thompson and Vacha-Haase (2000) wanted the inclusion of effect sizes and their corresponding p values for nonsignificant results because of their desire to promote meta-analytic studies.

Although not supportive of meta-analysis (see, e.g., Knapp & Sawilowsky, 2001a, 2001b), Sawilowsky and Markman (1990a, 1990b) and Sawilowsky, Kelley, Blair, and Markman (1994) stated that if a meta-analysis is to be conducted, it *must* include studies that are significant and are not significant. This pertains to a researcher who is conducting the original studies for the purpose of a meta-analysis; not someone who is data mining archival studies to put together a meta-analysis. There is no support for confusing readers of statistical material by inundating them with nonsignificant η's and their respective p values.

This concept is restated with the following parable. The government wanted to test the effectiveness of a certain type of fertilizer called Beautiful-Essence™ (universally known as Be-Es™). Unfortunately, the government didn't have a single plot of land large enough to test it. So, the study was conducted across various smaller plots of land scattered around the country, even though they had different combinations of soil, moisture, and sunlight conditions.

The results were diverse, with some studies indicating statistically significant increase in comparative growth, while others were not statistically significant. In order to get the bigger picture, a meta-analysis was conducted over all the experiments, including those with nonsignificant results. Suppose there was no overall effect. No harm was done in preserving the nonsignificant results, because they were only known to the meta-analyst.

In contradistinction, suppose the study was conducted by individual, independent researchers at each location. There is nothing within the framework of meta-analysis that precludes the joining of studies conducted independently. Yet, the presentation and dissemination of the effect sizes associated with nonsignificant studies would be misleading. The moral of the parable is that it is OK to study Be-Es™, not create more of it.

FACTORIAL ANALYSIS OF VARIANCE (ANOVA)

Factorial ANOVA provides methodology to analyze experimental designs with one dependent variable and two or more independent variables. The independent variables may be fixed, random, or mixed. The discussion here pertains to the fixed effects model.

A 2 × 2 factorial ANOVA layout presents the following seven nonnull outcomes of interest:

- interaction only
- interaction and A and B main effects

- interaction and A main effect, but no B main effect
- interaction and B main effect, but no A main effect
- A and B main effect, but no interaction effect
- A main effect, but no interaction effect and no B main effect
- B main effect, but no interaction effect and no A main effect

The classical factorial ANOVA table appears Table 14.1.

The fifth edition of the APA style manual has recommended changes to the standard ANOVA table, as mentioned above. Regardless of the merits of the proposed changes, it is worthwhile to delve into the question of whether or not this table should be read from the top down (i.e., A, B, and then A × B) or from the bottom up (i.e., A × B, and then A and B). I recommend a divergent view on the process of interpreting the table. The presentation and interpretation should commence with most complex effect, and only if it is not statistically significant should the simple effects be interpreted.

Therefore, in a major break with statistics textbooks authors, consider the modification to the ANOVA output, as indicated in Table 14.2. Notice that the A × B effect is not only placed above the A and B effects, but it is separated from them. The A and B effects are depicted as being on equal footing and within the same level of analysis. The reasons and supports for this will now be discussed.

Table 14.1. ANOVA Table

Source	*SS*	*df*	*Mean Square*	*F*
A				
B				
A×B				
Error				
Total				

Table 14.2. New ANOVA Table

Source	*SS*	*df*	*Mean Square*	*F*
A × B				
A				
B				
Error				
Total				

Simulating Main and Interaction Effects

The dependent variable is the motivating force behind univariate research. Main effects refer to the manner in which the dependent variable is expressed, or becomes revealed, via the frame of reference of the independent variable(s). Alternatively, a dependent variable may be explained by simultaneous but entirely orthogonal independent variables. Interaction effects refer to a more sophisticated and realistic condition in which the dependent variable can only be revealed through two (or more) interacting independent variables.

In considering the realm of applied problems in educational and psychological research, main effects should be regarded as two-dimensional components in a three-dimensional universe. Only in the most basic and pristine condition will simple independent variables be of interest, or for that matter, be considered as the sole effect producing (in the sense of expressing or revealing) outcomes. The applied world of social and behavioral science research is replete with complexities far beyond simple variables and their effects.

A significant interaction indicates, with an associated level of probability, that a new variable or construct exists which is more than the sum of its parts. When two simple variables interact, a new variable comes into being, which might share none, some, or all of the characteristics of either or both simple variables. It is through this new variable that the dependent variable becomes revealed.

A postmortem dissection of an interaction will likely be futile. Attribution fails because the main effects, in contradistinction with the simple variables from which they purport to emanate, are likely not real. It will also fail because even perchance they are real, the main effects are essentially hopelessly intertwined, immaterial, and uninteresting in the presence of the interaction. Moreover, in the latter case, the main effects may be acting jointly but not proportionately, or jointly and proportionately. In situations where main effects are working jointly but not interactively, it would be expected that a test for interaction would not be significant, and subsequent tests for both of the two main effects would be significant, if indeed they do so individually in single factor designs.

A frequently repeated definition of interactions is that the effect of one variable depends on the level of the other variable. However, this explains a potential usefulness of an interaction; it is not a definition of what is an interaction.

Consider a balanced 2 × 2 randomized design, where N variates are randomly selected from the standard normal distribution ($\mu = 0, \sigma = 1$) and randomly assigned to cells. The row, column, and diagonal means of these scores will be zero, as noted in Figure 14.1.

Suppose an A main effect is to be modeled. If the treatment model was shift in location, this could be achieved by adding a constant c to each of the scores in cells A_1B_1 *and* A_1B_2. Thus, $\overline{A_1} = 1$, and $\overline{A_1} > \overline{A_2}$. This indicates the presence of a significant A main effect, as in Figure 14.2. However, $\overline{B_1} = \overline{B_2} = \frac{1}{2}$, indicating there is no B main effect, and, $\overline{A_1B_2}, \overline{A_2, B_1} = \overline{A_1B_1}, \overline{A_2, B_2} = \frac{1}{2}$, indicating there is no A × B interaction effect.

The B main effect could be modeled in a similar fashion. The presence of both an A and B main effect is modeled in Figure 14.3. Starting with the previous figure, c is also added to each of the scores in A_1B_1 and A_2B_1. For convenience, only the means of the cells, after c has been added to each score, is depicted.

Clearly, $\overline{A_1} > \overline{A_2}$ and $\overline{B_1} > \overline{B_2}$, but $\overline{A_1B_2}, \overline{A_2, B_1} = \overline{A_1B_1}, \overline{A_2B_2}$, so there is no interaction effect. An interaction effect can also be modeled, however, in the same fashion. Consider a crossover interaction, which is commonly referred to as a disordinal interaction (Figure 14.4). This can be modeled by making $\overline{A_1B_1} = \overline{A_2B_2} = 1$ and $\overline{A_1B_2} = \overline{A_2B_1} = -1$ (Figure 14.5).

There is no A main effect because the means of both columns are zero. There is no B main effect because the means of both rows are zero. Yet,

	A1	A2		$\overline{A_1B_2}, \overline{A_2, B_1} = 0$
B1	x_1 . . . $x_{n/4}$	$x_{(n/2)+1}$ . . . $x_{3n/4}$	$\overline{B_1} = 0$	
B2	$x_{(n/4)+1}$ . . . $x_{n/2}$	$x_{(3n/4)+1}$ . . . x_n	$\overline{B_2} = 0$	
	$\overline{A_1} = 0$	$\overline{A_2} = 0$		$\overline{A_1B_1}, \overline{A_2, B_2} = 0$

Figure 14.1. Random selection and assignment in a 2 × 2 ANOVA layout.

	A_1	A_2	$\overline{A_1B_2}, \overline{A_2B_1} = \frac{1}{2}$
B_1	$x_1 + 1$	$x_{(n/2)+1}$	$\overline{B_1} = (1 + 0)/2 = ½$
	. + 1	.	
	. +1	.	
	. +1	.	
	$x_{n/4} + 1$	$x_{3n/4}$	
B_2	$x_{(n/4)+1} + 1$	$x_{3(n/4)+1}$	$\overline{B_2} = (1 + 0)/2 = ½$
	. + 1	.	
	. + 1	.	
	. + 1	.	
	$x_{n/2} + 1$	x_n	
	$\overline{A_1} = (1+1)/2 = 1$	$\overline{A_2} = (0+0)/2 = 0$	$\overline{A_1B_1}, \overline{A_2B_2} = \frac{1}{2}$

*Because c = 1 is added to every score in the A_1 cells, the mean of A_1 is 1. Because nothing is added to the scores in the A_2 cells, its mean is 0.

Figure 14.2. Modeling an A main effect in the 2 × 2 layout with c =1*.

	A_1	A_2	
B_1	1+1	1	$^3/_2$
B_2	1	0	½
	---	---	
	$^3/_2$	½	

Figure 14.3. Modeling A and B main effect in the 2 × 2 layout.

the two simple variables together produce the A × B interaction. This is not an illusion. The main effects cannot be acting jointly, for individually they are null. The two simple variables are, however, interacting to produce A × B in such a fashion that a postmortem dissection of main effects reveals nothing in terms of what the interaction is, how it came into being, or why it exists in the manner in which it does.

It is similarly possible to model the presence of an A main effect, B main effect, and an A × B interaction simultaneously, as in Figure 14.6. Or, consider just one main effect and an interaction, as indicated in Figure 14.7.

There is no B main effect in the above example. This is guaranteed on the basis of a shift in location model because c was not added to each vari-

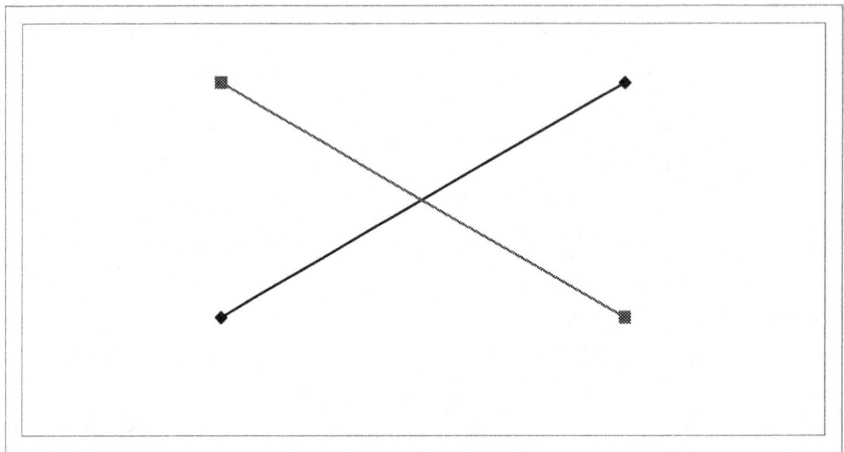

Figure 14.4. Disordinal (crossover) A × B interaction.

	$\underline{A_1}$	$\underline{A_2}$		(-1+(-1))/2=-1
$\underline{B_1}$	1	-1	(1+(-1))/2=0	
$\underline{B_2}$	-1	1	((-1)+1)/2=0	
	—	—		
	(1+(-1))/2=0	(-1+1)/2=0		(1+1)/2=1

Figure 14.5. Modeling an A × B disordinal interaction in a 2 × 2 ANOVA layout.

	$\underline{A_1}$	$\underline{A_2}$		0
$\underline{B_1}$	1+1+1	1-1	$^3/_2$	
$\underline{B_2}$	1-1	1	½	
	—	—		
	$^3/_2$	½		2

Figure 14.6. Modeling three nonnull effects in the 2 × 2 ANOVA layout.

	A_1	A_2		-1
B_1	1+1	-1	1	
B_2	1-1	1	1	
	—	—		
	$^3/_2$	0		$^3/_2$

Figure 14.7. Modeling an A main effect and an interaction effect 2 × 2 ANOVA layout.

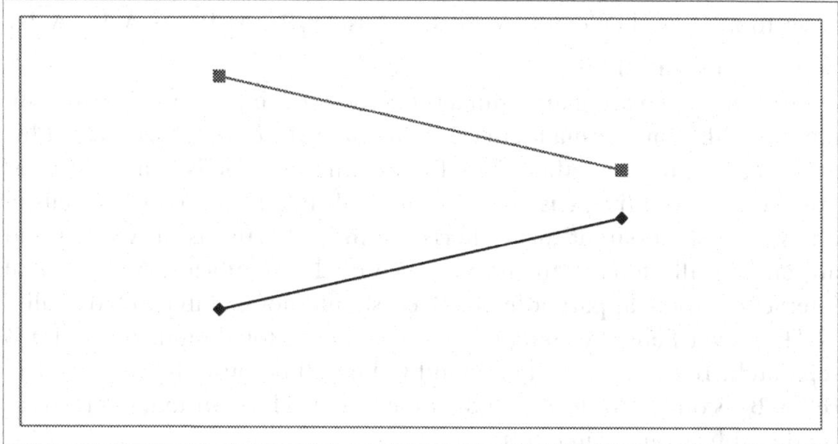

Figure 14.8. Ordinal (noncrossover) A × B interaction.

ate in the A_1B_1 and A_1B_2 cells, and thus $B_1 = B_2$. Nevertheless, the A × B interaction exists in the presence of the significant A main effect and non-significant B main effect.

Now, consider ordinal (noncrossover) interactions, as in Figure 14.8. First, it is important to agree on when a main effect is present. In the shift in location model above, an A main effect was considered to be present by deliberately modeling its presence by adding c to each score in *both* cells of the A_1 column, but not to the scores in the A_2 column. Similarly, a B main effect was modeled by adding the constant to the scores in *both* cells of the B_1 row, but not to the scores in the B_2 row.

The simplest method for producing an ordinal interaction is accomplished by adding c to the scores in cell A_1B_1 alone. This is a specific

	$\underline{A_1}$	$\underline{A_2}$		0
$\underline{B_1}$	1	0	½	
$\underline{B_2}$	0	0	0	
	$\overline{½}$	$\overline{0}$		½

Figure 14.9. Modeling an ordinal interaction in the 2 × 2 ANOVA layout.

example of a general method of adding c to A_1B_1, and k × c to A_2B_1, where $0 \leq k \leq \infty$. In this case where shift in location is being investigated, k is set to zero. (Other methods exist.) Thus, $\overline{A_1B_2}, \overline{A_2,B_1} > \overline{A_1B_1}, \overline{A_2B_2}$ as noted in Figure 14.9.

However, in creating an ordinal (noncrossover) interaction in this fashion, nonnull A and B main effects suddenly surface! But, this can not be, as the agreed-upon methodology for creating an A or B main effect has not been invoked (i.e., c is added to *both* cells in a column, or *both* cells in a row). These apparent main effects are indeed artifacts of ANOVA and are entirely illusionary. In the presence of the significant A×B ordinal interaction, these apparent main effects should not be interpreted at all.

This is verifiable by conducting two single factor designs on A and B separately. Both effects will be found to be null because the value of 1 in cell A_1B_1 is only introduced via the interaction. Thus, ordinal interactions produce phantom main effects.

Letters with Norman Anderson

I had a series of correspondences with Professor Norman Anderson from 1996–1997 (Sawilowsky, 1998). This occurred when he sent me several chapters, for comment, of his subsequently published, critically acclaimed book on research design and analysis (Anderson, 2001).

Question 1: Are Interactions Illusionary?

Amidst the exchange, the question arose with regard to the interpretation of interaction effects, with Professor Anderson maintaining that main effects are real, but interaction effects are illusionary. As explained here, I hold the opposite.

Professor Anderson did not mince words over the illusion of interactions. He referred to them as residuals. He called for reform in teaching statistics whereby interactions are taught as something illusionary, artifacts, and if perchance real, surely unimportant.

Professor Anderson illustrated his point of view with the example of two investigators, P and Q, *who observe the same behavior* of a rat learning to traverse an alley for a reward of food. The experimental design is a 2 × 2 factorial layout with $N = 1$, with one observation per cell. The two independent variables are Hunger Motivation (high vs. low) and Food Reward (high vs. low).

Researcher P recorded the time in seconds (s) it takes the rat to run the alley. The experiment was repeated for a total of four trials, with each trial representing one of the four treatment conditions. Researcher Q observed the same experiments, but measured speed in traversing the alley. Their results are compiled in the left and right panels of Table 14.3, respectively. Professor Anderson called these data asymptotic, meaning the rat's effort is recorded after sufficient experience with each condition such that its performance has stabilized.

There are four simple effects that can be studied in a 2 × 2 factorial layout: high hunger–reward, high hunger–low reward, low hunger–high reward, and low hunger–reward. With $N = 1$, these simple effects can be examined through graphical displays and visual analyses after the tradition of Skinner (1956), Sidman (1960), and Kazdin (1973). With $N > 1$ but still small, the randomization test can be used to test their statistical significance. However, there is no randomization test of the interaction for $N = 1$, as noted by Edgington (1995), Todman and Dugard (2001), and others.

ANOVA can be used as a test for interaction with success (if underlying assumptions are met) in an experiment as small as $N = 8$ ($n = 2$ per cell), but it cannot be used with $N = 1$. The nonparametric Friedman test (Friedman, 1937), based on the Sign test, is appropriate for $N = 4$ and one observation per cell, but it assumes no interaction is present.

Hartlaub, Dean, and Wolfe (1999) reported on a Monte Carlo study of the problem of testing for interactions in the two-way layout with one observation per cell. They examined aligned-ranks tests adapted from

Table 14.3. Two Researcher's Measurement of the Same Experiment

	Researcher P Time (Seconds)		*Researcher Q Speed (1/Time)*	
	Hunger Motivation		*Hunger Motivation*	
Food Reward	*High*	*Low*	*High*	*Low*
High	2	3	3/6	2/6
Low	3	6	2/6	1/6

Tukey (1949), de Kroon and van der Laan (1981), and adapted from Wolfe, Dean, and Hartlaub (1990). The adaptation of the latter procedure was based on the Blair-Sawilowsky Salter-Fawcet adjusted rank transform (Sawilowsky & Blair, 1990; Fawcett & Salter, 1984). Only the Hartlaub, Dean, and Wolfe (1999) test had acceptable Type I error rates when data were nonnormally distributed, but even this test inflated to 0.1 with = 0.05 for exponentially distributed data in higher order two-way layouts, such as the 5 × 9 layout.

Suppose in the current case, however, each entry is considered to be the cell mean, meaning that it refers to the average of a number of replications (or so-called asymptotic results) for the rat. Thus, if it can be assumed that the entry is reduced to the mean for shorthand purposes, (similar to that in Figure 14.3), then the interpretation of the ANOVA test interaction proceeds as usual.

The $\overline{A_1B_2}$ and $\overline{A_2B_1}$ diagonals for the left panel are 4 and 3 in Figure 14.3, respectively, indicating an interaction effect. The rat takes less time (i.e., runs faster) even for little food reward if its hunger motivation is high, or conversely, if it isn't motivated by food, it runs slower even if there is a large food reward.

However, the $\overline{A_1B_2}$ and $\overline{A_2B_1}$ diagonals for the right panel are both 1/3, indicating there is no interaction effect. This means that the food reward has the same effect, regardless of the rat's hunger motivation, because its speed (i.e., how fast it runs) will be the same. Thus, Professor Anderson concluded the supposed interaction is illusionary.

Challenges to Professor Anderson's Interpretation

Professor Anderson's position is that because the interaction was made to apparently disappear, interactions are not real. However:

1. The simplest explanation for the different results is P and Q aren't measuring the same construct. The metric of time is seconds (s), but the metric of speed is, for example, meters per second (m/s).

2. In taking the reciprocal, a well-known transformation was performed that resulted in making a nonnull interaction effect appear to be null, as the marginals for the left panel are 8 and 6, but are 4/6 and 4/6 in the right panel. Unfortunately, this transformation also changed the magnitude of the unstandardized main effects from .56 (5/9) each to 1.67 (.4167/.25). Even worse, the sign was also changed from A_1 (5) < A_2 (9) and B_1 (5) < B_2 (9), to A_1 (.4167) > A_2 (.25) and B_1 (.4167) > B_2 (.25). This is prima facie evidence that the construct of interest was changed,

which frequently happens when using transformations. Thus, why should P and Q achieve the same results?

The construct speed is not the reciprocal of the construct of time, although their coefficients are indeed equal when distance is taken to be unity. For example, let d = distance, t = time, and s = speed, and restrict the discussion to an object moving in a straight line. In this situation $d = t \times s$, and if distance is unity, then $1 = t \times s$, dividing both sides by t yields $\frac{1}{t} = s$. However, if $d \neq 1$, this relationship does not hold. For example, if $d = 2$ the coefficient of speed is equal to *twice* the coefficient of the reciprocal of time.

Moreover, what is the meaning of reciprocals of typical psychology and education constructs? What is the meaning of the inverse of a *MMPI-2* subscale score, a *Tennessee Self-Concept* subscale score, or *Attribution-Style Questionnaire* subscale score? What is the meaning of the inverse of a *Scholastic Achievement Test* verbal score, a *Strong-Campbel Interest Inventory* score, or a *School Attitude Measure* score? What is the meaning of the inverse of days absent, grade point average, or fraction of free lunch entitlement?

Interactions can be made to apparently vanish with other types of well-known transformations, such as logarithmic, hyperbolic sine, or squaring the above-mentioned inverse, but how frequently in social and behavioral sciences would anyone be interested in the resulting metric and therefore the meaning of such transformed scores? And more importantly, in which of these cases is the meaning of the construct unchanged by taking the reciprocal?

3. According to Professor Anderson's explanation, P concludes the rat's *time* will be differentially affected based on food motivation: if hunger motivation is high the time will be minimized regardless of the level of food reward, but if hunger motivation is low, the time will change drastically depending on the level of food reward. Q concludes there is no interaction between food motivation and level of reward in terms of *speed*. Thus, increasing the level of food reward will not have differential effects based on whether there is high or low food motivation.

Which is the variable of interest, time or speed? Researchers should think very carefully in selecting the variable of interest. In this case, is the concern with elapsed time taken to traverse the alley, or, is it with the speed of traversing the alley? Nor or these the only choices. A sprint coach might be interested in *acceleration*, whereas an endurance coach might be interested in *average speed*, discussed below.

In kinematics, the physics of motion of objects, the *average velocity* is defined as change in *displacement* (i.e., new position minus original position) per unit of time (i.e., final time minus original time). If the rat traverses a 1 meter long alley from west to east in 2 seconds, the average velocity is $\frac{1\text{m} - 0\text{m}}{2\text{s}} = \frac{1\text{m}}{2\text{s}} = .5\text{m/s}$, east. Velocity is a vector quantity that is direction-aware, and therefore it is reported with a magnitude (.5m/s) and direction (east or E.). Interestingly, if the rat were to run furiously back and forth many times, returning to the origin as its final destination, the average velocity would be (0, Origin).

Professor Anderson probably foresaw the problem of displacement from the origin, which could lead to zero velocity even after strenuous activity on the part of the rat. That could be why the experiment was set up in a straight alley, which would preclude the rat from going in all directions.

The trial depicted by the upper right quadrant of the left panel in Table 14.4 indicates the rat traversed the alley with an average velocity of (.5m/s, E.). The magnitude part of average velocity is called *speed.* Speed is a scaler quantity, meaning it is not direction-aware. Thus, the rat's speed would be .5m/s.

However, even in a straight alley, the rat could reverse its direction, and backtrack as far as the origin. Is Q really concerned with speed, or *average speed*? Averaging speed, which is a scaler quantity, produces a scaler quantity that is defined as distance (i.e., total distance regardless of direction) divided by time.

The track record of the three rats is compiled in Table 14.4. All three rats completed the trip from the origin to the end of the alley, a distance of 1m, and did so in 2 seconds. The average velocity was (.5m/s, E.), and hence, the speed of all three rats was .5m/s.

However, the average speed was markedly different. Rat 1's average speed was $\frac{|.2| + |.2| + |.2| + |.2| + |.2|}{2\text{s}} = \frac{1\text{m}}{2\text{s}} = .5\text{m/s}$. Rat's 2 and 3 average speed were $\frac{|.4| + |-.2| + |.4| + |-.3| + |.7|}{2\text{s}} = \frac{2\text{m}}{2\text{s}} = 1\text{m/s}$ and $\frac{|.8| + |-.8| + |.8| + |-.8| + |1.0|}{2\text{s}} = \frac{4.2\text{m}}{2\text{s}} = 2.1\text{m/s}$, respectively.

A closer inspection of the three rat's behavior reveals markedly different interpretations from that provided by Professor Anderson. In a state of high food motivation when presented with high food reward, the first rat proceeded to traverse the alley at a rapid pace, as explained by Professor Anderson. The second rat, however, went about half-way, returned half of that purchase, regained the same amount of real estate as initially ventured, returned half again as much as initially, and then made a break for the food. The third rat's behavior is classic approach-avoidance, rising to the brink of success, sinking back to the gutter, reaching again for the

Table 14.4. Track Record of Three Rats With High Hunger Motivation–High Food Reward

	Rat 1		*Rat 2*		*Rat 3*	
Time (Seconds)	*Position (Meters)*	Δ	*Position (Meters)*	Δ	*Position (Meters)*	Δ
0	0		0		0	
.4s	.2m	+.2	.4m	+.4	.8m	+.8
.8s	.4m	+.2	.2m	−.2	0	−.8
1.2s	.6m	+.2	.6m	+.4	.8m	+.8
1.6s	.8m	+.2	.3m	−.3	0	−.8
2.0s	1m	+.2	1m	+.7	1m	+1.0
Average velocity	.5m/s, E.		.5m/s, E.		.5m/s, E.	
Speed	.5m/s		.5m/s		.5m/s	
Average speed	.5m/s		1m/s		2.1m/s	

clouds, having a major bout with recidivism, and then bringing home the prize. Yet, the *speed* of all three rats is the same.

Professor Anderson's Response

In an effort to present a balanced perspective, here is Professor Anderson's response (January 25, 1997, personal correspondence):

> The time-speed example from my 1961 paper remains valid. Both are monotone measures of a latent variable of response strength. But what we seek is a linear measure.
>
> (Your puzzlement about the effects reversing themselves under the reciprocal transformation clears up once it is realized that the latent variable is at issue, not the observable measure.)

Question 2: How Should the ANOVA Table Be Read: Top Down or Bottom Up?

A second question that arose pertaining to the role of interactions was with regard to the question of how an ANOVA table should be read: from the top down, or the bottom up?

Professor Anderson reads the traditional ANOVA table from the top down, consistent with his position that main effects are real and interactions are illusionary. Only in the absence of main effects, from his perspective, would it be productive to examine interactions. Similarly, in a higher order layout (e.g., 2 × 2 × 2), he would proceed to interpret main effects, followed by lower order interactions, and finally the higher order interaction.

However, I maintain the classical ANOVA table should be read from the bottom up in the classical ANOVA table, because in the presence of a significant A × B × C interaction, the lower order interactions and main effects are uninteresting, if not illusionary. Only in the absence of a higher order interaction does it make sense to proceed further in interpreting the lower order interactions. Moreover, only in the absence of lower order interactions does it make sense to proceed to interpret the main effects, because if there is a significant interaction, the main effects are uninteresting, if not illusionary. That is why Kempthorne (1975) wrote, "The testing of main effects, without additional input, is an exercise in fatuity" (p. 483).

Moreover, this perspective will ameliorate the problems that arise in more sophisticated experiments, such as the A × B × C layout. The usual step-wise approach is to conduct four tests of interactions (i.e., A × B × C, A × B, A × C, B ×C) and three main effects (i.e., A, B, C). This is an exercise in the search for Type I errors (see, e.g., Kromrey & Dickinson, 1995). Professor Anderson resorted to an unsystematic partial analysis, which appears to require clairvoyance on the part of the researcher, to determine a subset of effects that should be tested. Instead, taking the approach of reading the classical ANOVA table from the bottom up provides the stopping rule that once a higher order effect is significant, the conducting of statistical tests ceases at that level of complexity.

Professor Anderson's Response

Again, for a balanced presentation, here is Professor Anderson's response (January 25, 1997, personal correspondence):

> Statistically, interactions are defined as residuals from an additive model, that is, as nonadditives. Whether these statistical residuals have empirical meaning cannot be decided without empirical theory.
>
> No empirical foundation is known for assuming the additive model. Unless it has empirical relevance, any decisions are arbitrary. Without a substantive foundation, the ANOVA model cannot provide empirical conclusions.
>
> Please note that the point about model dependence of interaction is recognized by ... preeminent statisticians.

Table 14.5. New 2×2×2 Factorial ANOVA Table

Source	SS	df	MS	F
A × B × C				
A × B				
A × C				
B × C				
A				
B				
C				
Error				
Total				

A×B×C Layouts: More Than Two Independent Variables

Following the redesign of the A×B ANOVA table, the A×B×C ANOVA table appears in Table 14.5. Consistent with the prior discussion, the first effect to be interpreted is the higher order A × B × C interaction, should it be statistically significant. If it is not, then the explanation of effects continues to the next level, where all three lower order interactions are examined. The discussion concludes in the presence of at least one significant lower order interaction. If the four interactions are null, then and only then should the interpretation step down to the three main effects.

Underlying Assumptions of Factorial ANOVA

It seems fitting to conclude a chapter on the practical application of ANOVA with a brief review on the impact of violating underlying assumptions. The probability associated with the ANOVA *F* statistic is accurate, and the power to find a false null hypothesis is maximized, when underlying assumptions of the ANOVA have been met. The primary assumption, as with all tests in the Neyman-Pearson (1931) paradigm of statistics, is that the population was sampled randomly; or at least there was random assignment of either participants to treatments, or treatments to participants. In addition, there are three assumptions specific to the *F* test:

- independence (i.e., components that contribute variance are additive)
- homoscedasticity (homogenous variances)
- normality

I add a fifth consideration that is nearly universally overlooked. It is most important to stress that testing for ordinal interactions (Figure 14.8) in factorial ANOVA can be more severely debilitating than testing for disordinal interactions (Figure 14.7) when underlying assumptions are violated (Sawilowsky, 1985).

The literature on the behavior of the ANOVA *F* test in the presence of violations of underlying assumptions is amazingly vast, considerably controversial, and only recently conclusive. Most of what is known regarding the operating characteristics of the ANOVA *F* test parallels work on the robustness of the t test, and most of that work was based on Monte Carlo studies.

The violation of independence is a recipe for disaster in terms of Type I errors. There is no statistic that can overcome a true lack of independence, either within or between scores. Heteroscedasticity, or heterogeneous variances within or between groups, is quite debilitating in terms of Type I errors (e.g., Randolph & Barcikowski, 1989). This is especially so, in no particular order, when (a) sample sizes are unequal, (b) cells with the smaller n's have the larger variances, (c) accompanied by other violations of assumptions, and (d) the degree of nonhomogeneity increases.

The work of Norton (1952, as cited in Lindquist, 1953), Boneau (1960), and Glass, Peckham, and Sanders (1972) was responsible for a half century of indiscriminate usage of the ANOVA *F* test despite the prevalence of nonnormally distributed data. Either it was believed that the *F* test was immune to nonnormality, or it was believed that nonnormally distributed data was rare. Both perspectives are false (Pearson & Please, 1975; Tan, 1982; Micceri, 1986, 1989; Sawilowsky, Blair, & Micceri, 1990; for conditions where departures from population normality are tolerated, see Sawilowsky & Blair, 1992). Bradley (1968) was one of the first to forewarn about the potentially deleterious effects of nonnormality on the ANOVA *F* test.

Unfortunately, Bradley (1968) did not emerge as the victor from this debate in the opinion of the applied statistics community, even though he was correct. This probably occurred because his arguments were focused primarily on robustness with respect to Type I errors. His opponents' position was problems only arose with ridiculously small α levels, or bizarre distribution shapes (e.g., Glass et al., 1972). (An apparent unspoken reason was the erroneous presumption there was equal probability that the Type I error would decrease from nominal α, as opposed to increase from nominal α, and who would complain about making fewer Type I errors than initially agreed upon?)

Regarding the positions of Bradley (1968) versus Glass et al. (1972), Blair (1980) and Blair and Higgins (1981) opined that "resolution of these two diverging points of view is not easy, primarily because there are no commonly agreed upon standards as to what constitutes robustness and what does not" (p. 125). However, the debate finally did come to a sudden and definite close after the effects of nonnormality on statistical power was introduced into the argument by Blair (1980), Blair and Higgins (1980a, 1980b, 1981, 1985), and Blair, Higgins, and Smitely (1980).

Earlier, Scheffé (1959) pointed out to a deaf audience that, "the question of whether *F* tests preserve against nonnormal alternatives the power calculated under normal theory should not be confused with that of their efficiency against such alternatives relative to other kinds of tests" (p. 351). This statement pertains to the Type II error properties of the test.

Suppose the power of the *F* test was computed under normality for a certain α level, sample size, and effect size, with a resulting rate of rejection of the null hypothesis at .15. Approximately the same power level would be obtained even if the statistic was computed under the same conditions, with the exception that the population was changed from normality to any nonnormal shape (e.g., uniform, exponential, mixed normal). This characteristic means the ANOVA *F* test is robust with respect to Type II errors. This was the major defense of the *F* test in the presence of nonnormality by Glass et al. (1972).

Nevertheless, Scheffè's unheeded point was that as wondrous as this property seems, it is irrelevant because once normality has been violated some other competing statistic could obtain far greater power levels. The Monte Carlo work by Blair (1980) and Blair and Higgins (1981) conclusively demonstrated this point.

For example, a nonparametric alternative conducted under the same conditions, and being sensitive to same hypothesis being testing with the parametric test, might have a power level of .99. The impact of this tremendous increase directly translates to a considerably smaller sample size necessary to detect a false null hypothesis as compared with its parametric counterpart. To illustrate with commonly occurring skewed distributions (e.g., exponential), if the classical parametric statistic required a cell n = 40, the preferred nonparametric test would only require, approximately, a cell n = 10 to detect the same shift in location treatment effect (Sawilowsky & Blair, 1992). Demonstration of this power advantage, via Monte Carlo methods, has changed the course of modern applied statistics.

> I recently presented a poster at the Society for Clinical Trials. They are concerned with, for example, the impact of adding 10 patients to a trial. The MRI [magnetic resonance imaging] and doctor's fees can amount to $20,000 per patient. I showed, keeping the power level constant, what happens to the required sample size in terms of how much smaller samples need to be when using nonparametric rank tests. There was considerable excitement; people were running around hollering and waving their arms to come view the poster. (Blair, cited in Sawilowsky, 2004, p. 532).

REFERENCES

Anderson, N. H. (2001). *Empirical direction in design and analysis*. Mahwah, NJ: Erlbaum.

American Psychological Association. (2001). *Publication manual of the American Psychological Association* (5th ed.). Washington, DC: Author.

Blair, R. C. (1980). *A comparison of the power of the two independent means t test to that of the Wilcoxon's rank-sum test for samples of various populations*. Unpublished doctoral dissertation, University of South Florida, Tampa, FL.

Blair, R. C., & Higgins, J. J. (1980a.) A comparison of the power of the *t* test and the Wilcoxon statistics when samples are drawn from certain mixed normal distributions. *Evaluation Review, 4*, 645-656.

Blair, R. C., & Higgins, J. J. (1980b). A comparison of the power of the Wilcoxon's rank-sum statistic to that of student's *t* statistic under various non-normal distributions. *Journal of Educational Statistics, 5*, 309-335.

Blair, R. C., & Higgins, J. J. (1981). A note on the asymptotic relative efficiency of the Wilcoxon rank-sum test relative to the independent means *t* test under mixtures of two normal distributions. *British Journal of Mathematical and Statistical Psychology, 34*, 124-128.

Blair, R. C., & Higgins, J. J. (1985). Comparison of the power of the paired samples t test to that of Wilcoxon's signed-ranks test under various population shapes. *Psychological Bulletin, 97*, 119-128.

Blair, R. C., Higgins, J. J., & Smitley, W. D. S. (1980). On the relative power of the *U* and *t* tests. *British Journal of Mathematical and Statistical Psychology, 33*, 114-120.

Boneau, C. A. (1960). The effects of violations of assumptions underlying the *t* test. *Psychological Bulletin, 57*, 49-64.

Bradley, J. V. (1968). *Distribution-free statistical tests*. Englewood Cliffs, NJ: Prentice-Hall.

Cohen, J. (1988). *Statistical power analysis for the behavioral sciences* (2nd ed.). Hillsdale, NJ: Erlbaum.

de Kroon, J., & van der Laan, P. (1981). Distribution-free test procedures in two-way layouts: A concept of rank-interaction. *Statistica Neerlandica, 35*, 189-213.

Edgington, E. S. (1995). *Randomization tests* (3rd ed.). New York: Marcel Dekker.

Fawcett, R. F., & Salter, K. C. (1984). A Monte Carlo study of the *F* test and three tests based on ranks of treatment effects in randomized block designs. *Communications in Statistics, B13*, 213-225.

Friedman, M. (1937). The use of ranks to avoid the assumption of normality implicit in the analysis of variance. *Journal of the American Statistical Association, 32*, 675-701.

Glass, G. V., Peckham, P. D., & Sanders, J. R. (1972). Consequences of falure to meet assumptions underlying the fixed effects analyses of variance and covariance. *Review of Educational Research, 42*, 237-288.

Hartlaub, B. A., Dean, A. M., & Wolfe, D. A. (1999). Rank-based test procedures for interaction in the two-way layout with one observation per cell. *Canadian Journal of Statistics, 27*, 863-874.

Kazdin, A. E. (1973). Methodological and assessment considerations in evaluating reinforcement programs in applied settings. *Journal of Applied Behavior Analysis, 6*, 517-531.

Kempthorne, O. (1975). Fixed and mixed models in the analysis of variances. *Biometrics, 31*, 473-486.

Knapp, T. R., & Sawilowsky, S. S. (2001a). Constructive criticisms of methodological and editorial practices. *The Journal of Experimental Education, 70*, 65-79.

Knapp, T. R., & Sawilowsky, S. S. (2001b). Strong arguments: Rejoinder to Thompson. *The Journal of Experimental Education, 70*, 94-95.

Kromrey, J. D., & Dickinson, W. B. (1995). The use of an overall *F* test to control Type I error rates in factorial analyses of variance: Limitations and better strategies. *Journal of Applied Behavioral Science, 31*(1), 51-64.

Lindquist, E. F. (1953). *Design and analysis of experiments in psychology and education.* Boston: Houghton Mifflin.

Micceri, T, (1986, November). *A futile search for that statistical chimera of normality.* Paper presented at the 31st annual convention of the Florida Educational Research Association, Tampa.

Micceri, T. (1989). The unicorn, the normal curve, and other improbable creatures. *Psychological Bulletin, 105*, 156-166.

Neyman, J., & Pearson, E. S. (1931). On the problem of *k* samples. Bulletin international de l'Académie Polonaise des Sciences et des lettres (Cracovié), *Sciences mathématiques, Série A*, 460-481.

Pearson, E. S., & Please, N. W. (1975). Relation between the shape of population distribution and the robustness of four simple test statistics. *Biometrika, 63*, 223-241.

Randolph, E. A., & Barcikowski, R. S. (1989, November). *Type I error rate when real study values are used as population parameters in a Monte Carlo study.* Paper presented at the 11th annual meeting of the Mid-Western Educational Research Association, Chicago.

Sawilowsky, S. S. (1985). *Robust and power analysis of the 2 ×2 ×2 ANOVA, rank transformation, random normal scores, and expected normal scores transformation tests.* Unpublished doctoral dissertation, University of South Florida, Tampa, FL.

Sawilowsky, S. S. (1996, April). *Encyclopedia of educational and psychological effect sizes and distribution shapes*. Paper presented at the annual meeting of the American Educational Research Association, New York.

Sawilowsky, S. (1998, Winter). *Reading the ANOVA table—Top down or bottom up? Letters with Norman Anderson*. Invited presentation at the Detroit Chapter of the American Statistical Association, Farmington Hills, MI.

Sawilowsky, S. S. (2003a). A different future for social and behavioral science research. *Journal of Modern Applied Statistical Methods, 2*(1), 128-132.

Sawilowsky, S. S. (2003b). You think you've got trivials? *Journal of Modern Applied Statistical Methods, 2*(1), 218-225.

Sawilowsky, S. S. (2003c). Trivials: The birth, sale, and final production of meta-analysis. *Journal of Modern Applied Statistical Methods, 2*(1), 242-246.

Sawilowsky, S. S. (2004). A conversation with R. Clifford Blair on the occasion of his retirement. *Journal of Modern Applied Statistical Methods, 3*(2), 518-566.

Sawilowsky, S., & Blair, R. C. (April, 1990). *A test for interaction based on the rank transform.* Presented at the annual meeting of the American Educational Research Association, Boston.

Sawilowsky, S. S., & Blair, R. C. (1992). A more realistic look at the robustness and type II error properties of the *t* test to departures from population normality. *Psychological Bulletin, 111,* 353-360.

Sawilowsky, S. S., & Markman, B. S. (1990a). Another look at the power of meta-analysis in the Solomon four-group design. *Perceptual and Motor Skills, 71,* 177-178.

Sawilowsky, S. S., & Markman, B. S. (1990b). Rejoinder to Braver and Walton Braver. *Perceptual and Motor Skills, 71,* 424-426.

Sawilowsky, S. S., & Yoon, G. (2001, August). The trouble with trivials ($p > .05$). Paper presented at the 54th session of the International Statistical Institute, Seoul, Korea.

Sawilowsky, S. S., Blair, R. C., & Micceri, T. (1990). A PC Fortran subroutine library of psychology and education data sets. *Psychometrika, 55,* 729.

Sawilowsky, S., Kelley, D. L., Blair, R. C., & Markman, B. S. (1994). Meta-analysis and the Solomon four-group design. *The Journal of Experimental Education, 62,* 361-376.

Scheffé, H. (1959). *The analysis of variance.* New York: Wiley.

Sidman, M. (1960). *Tactics of scientific research: Evaluating experimental dat in psychological research.* New York: Basic Books.

Skinner, B. F. (1956). A case history in scientific method. *American Psychologist, 11,* 221-233.

Tan, W. Y. (1982). Sampling distributions and robustness of *t, F,* and variance-ratio in two samples and ANOVA models with respect to departure from normality. *Communications in Statistics, A11,* 2485-2511.

Thompson, B. (1996). AERA editorial policies regarding statistical significance testing: Three suggested reforms. *Educational Researcher, 25,* 26-30.

Thompson, B., & Vacha-Haase, T. (2000). Psychometrics is datametrics: The test is not reliable. *Educational and Psychological Measurement, 60,* 174-195.

Todman, J. B., & Dugard, P. (2001). *Singe-case and small-n experimental designs: A practical guide to randomization tests.* Mahway, NJ: Erlbaum.

Tukey, J. W. (1949). One degree of freedom for non-additivity. *Biometrics, 5,* 232-242.

Wolfe, D. A., Dean, A. M., & Hartlaub, B. A. (1990). Nonparametric rank-based test procedures for the presence of interaction I: No replications. *Communications in Statistics, A19,* 4355-4382.

Zumbo, B. D., & Hubley, A. M. (1998). A note on misconceptions concerning prospective and retrospective power. *The Statistician, 47*(2), 385-388.

CHAPTER 15

ANCOVA AND QUASI-EXPERIMENTAL DESIGN

The Legacy of Campbell and Stanley

Shlomo S. Sawilowsky

Two of the most frequently cited references on the utility of quasi-experimental design are Campbell and Stanley (1963) and Cook and Campbell (1979). The latter defined quasi-experimental design as

> experiments that have treatments, outcome measures, and experimental units, but do not use random assignment to create the comparisons from which treatment-caused change is inferred. Instead, the comparisons depend on nonequivalent groups that differ from each other in many ways other than the presence of a treatment whose effects are being tested. (Cook & Campbell, 1979, p. 6)

Campbell and Stanley suggested the use of quasi-experimental designs for the "many natural social settings" (p. 34) in which there is no ability to randomly expose participants to experimental stimuli. Some commonly

Real Data Analysis, pp. 213–238

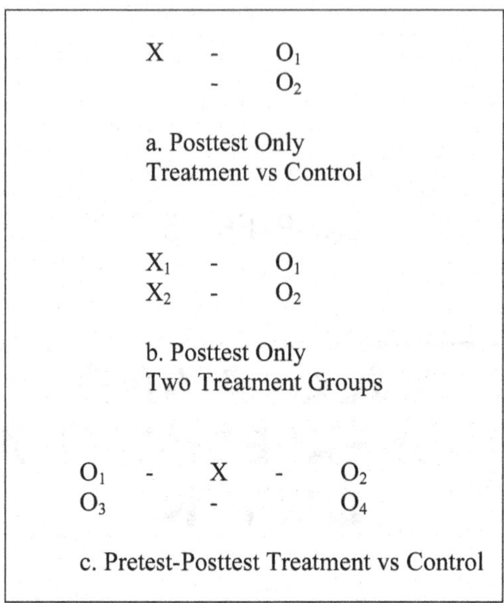

X - O_1
- O_2
a. Posttest Only
Treatment vs Control
X_1 - O_1
X_2 - O_2
b. Posttest Only
Two Treatment Groups
O_1 - X - O_2
O_3 - O_4
c. Pretest-Posttest Treatment vs Control

Figure 15.1. Quasi-experimental designs.

encountered examples of quasi-experimental designs are depicted in Figure 15.1. Note the absence of symbols (typically "R") representing random selection and random assignment.

The inability to randomly assign participants to a treatment group is quite common in social and behavioral science research. Clinicians, teachers, social workers, therapists, scholars, doctoral and master's students, and funded researchers are frequently permitted access to the classroom, hospital, or clinic for research purposes, only to find that the treatment and control groups available must be limited to intact groups. Having participated on over seven dozen doctoral committees, I have heard many unsatisfactory attempts to support the possibility that the two intact groups are as random as can be expected in field research. In perusing the applied research literature, the reader is inundated with a variety of heuristic arguments from authors struggling to find base-line equality among intact groups.

The advantages of randomization are well documented in the research and statistics literature. It is the best way to control for initial differences between the treatment and control group, both for variables that have been documented to confound the research outcome and for those variables unknown to the researcher or as yet undiscovered in the literature. *There is no substitute for randomization.* The statistics literature is replete with the failure or limitation of techniques such as matching (caliper, nearest available, stratified, frequency, mean), regression, econometric simultaneous modeling, latent-variable modeling, and other techniques which seek to correct for initial differences and selection bias in nonrandomized studies.

Interestingly, Campbell and Stanley (1963) warned researchers and students about "a feeling of hopelessness with regard to achieving experimental control [that] leads to the abandonment of such efforts in favor of more informal methods of investigation" (p. 34). (It may be postulated that this statement was intended to encourage researchers to remain within the quantitative research paradigm, as historically, that time period represented the nadir in relations between quantitative and qualitative methodologists.) Their proposed solution strategy was to promote the use of quasi-experimental design.

However, their essential defense of quasi-experimental design was that it is "deemed worthy of use where better designs are not feasible" (p. 34). In other words, the support for the use of quasi-experimental design is not based on its intrinsic worth; rather, it was positioned as an approach to be used when better designs are not possible. This notion was echoed by Anderson, Auquier, Hauck, Oakes, Vandaele, and Weisberg (1980, p. 36), who listed the following reasons for conducting a quasi-experiment: a) it might be unethical to randomly assign the treatment, b) it might not be logistically possible to conduct a randomized study, and c) a randomized study might be too expensive. Note these reasons pertain to potential limitations of conducting a randomized study. None of these reasons address strengths of quasi-experimental designs.

If the choice of quasi-experimental design is so precarious, the question arises as to the worthiness of the results. A typical defense of results garnered from quasi-experimental design was advanced by Vockell and Asher (1995):

> a quasi-experiment, on the other hand, lacks some of these controls and attempts to compensate with reasoning like this: "If this threat were a problem, it would show up at this point in my observations. My results contradict this, and so I am going to assume that this threat is not a serious factor." Quasi-experiments, in other words, may rely on a lengthy series of inferences, whereas true experiments are based on simple, straightforward statistical probability. (p. 286)

(They pointed out, however, that given a choice the researcher should choose a true experimental design.)

Moreover, the reasoning process for accepting results from a quasi-experimental design appears to be as follows. If the results are statistically significant, at the very least it demonstrates the need to conduct a true experiment. If a quasi-experiment is not significant, however, a prudent researcher would still be wise to retain the initial hypothesis until evidence from a true experiment is available. Finally, if a quasi-experiment has been replicated a number of times, surely the results may be considered in aggregate form, yielding conclusions that can be given as much weight as if the results were obtained from a true randomized experiment. Reasoning such as this appears in many textbooks on research design (e.g., Leary, 1995, p. 284).

In the absence of randomization, Anderson et al. (1980) posed and answered this question:

> Does this mean that the investigator should discard the idea of doing a study at all if randomization is not feasible? Similarly, when reviewing the results of previous studies, should the reviewer discard all those with non-randomized designs? We think not. (p. 43)

PURPOSE

Monte Carlo simulations were conducted in order to explicate what happens in three quasi-experimental designs commonly employed in social and behavioral science research. The designs examined are a (I) posttest only treatment group versus control group, (II) posttest only two treatment groups, and (III) pretest-posttest treatment vs control group where the pretest is a covariate measure of some construct which is highly correlated with the dependent variable. These designs are depicted in Figure 15.1, parts a, b, and c, respectively.

Methodology for Designs I and II

To examine the first two designs (the methodology for the third design, which is dissimilar to these two designs, is discussed separately below), a Fortran program was written for the Pentium-based microcomputer. The smooth symmetric data set with light tails (similar to the normal or bell curve) identified by Micceri (1989) as occurring, albeit rarely, in psychology and education research was sampled with replacement to simulate many repetitions of a study conducted with a treatment and control group. (This data set, along with seven more prevalent data sets identified by Micceri, 1986, are available in Sawilowsky, Blair, & Micceri, 1990. Histograms and summary statistics on these data sets are available in Sawilowsky & Blair, 1992.)

Many Monte Carlo studies have been conducted on theoretically and mathematically expedient distributions, but Micceri (1989) noted practical advantages for using real data sets. Although most data sets in applied research are skewed or multimodal/lumpy, the smooth symmetric data set was selected in order to control for the effects of violations of population normality on the parametric test examined. The sample size was $n_1 = n_2 = 30$, which is typical of educational research conducted in the classroom. Nominal α was set at 0.05.

In order to examine the posttest-only treatment versus control group design, 60 scores were randomly selected from the data set. Thirty scores were then randomly assigned to a treatment group and 30 scores were similarly placed in a control group. An independent samples t test was conducted on the difference in the means between the two groups, and the results were recorded. This simulation was then repeated 1 million times. The proportion of rejections of the null hypothesis of no difference between the treatment and control group means was calculated. As expected with a true randomized experimental design, the Type I error rate was within sampling error of 0.05.

Next, a treatment was modeled as a shift in location, by adding a constant or treatment effect of $.1\sigma - 2.0\sigma$ (.1). For example, because the standard deviation of the data set is 4.91, a treatment effect size (ES) of $.1\sigma = .491$. (The effect size is the standardized difference between the treatment and control group: ES $= (\mu_1 - \mu_2)/\sigma$, where σ is the pooled standard deviation of the treatment and control group.) The experiment was repeated for each level of the treatment effect. A quasi-experimental design was modeled in a similar fashion as the true randomized experimental design, except that a constant was added to either the treatment or control group to simulate initial differences between the two groups. The magnitude of the initial difference was modeled at $.2\sigma - .8\sigma$ (.3).

The simulation methodology for Design II, the posttest only two treatment group design depicted in Figure 15.1 part b, differs from the above stated procedures in that a treatment effect was added to both treatment groups. The magnitude of the difference in treatment effectiveness between the two groups was modeled at $.2\sigma - .8\sigma$ (.3). The conditions studied for this design, as well as the previous design, are summarized in Table 15.1.

RESULTS FOR DESIGNS I AND II

Design I: Posttest Only Treatment vs. Control Group

The resulting power curve for the true randomized experimental design is presented in Figure 15.2 as the smooth line without any markers. Figure 15.2 also contains results for the quasi-experimental design.

Table 15.1. Treatment Conditions Studied for th Post-Only Treatment Versus Control Design (I) and the Posttest only Two Treatment Group Design (II)

	Treatment Magnitude		*Initial Difference*	
D	*Treatment Group*	*Control Group*	*Treatment Group*	*Control Group*
I	$.1\sigma - 2.0\sigma\ (.1\sigma)$	0	$2\sigma - .8\sigma\ (.3\sigma)$	0
	$.1\sigma - 2.0\sigma\ (.1\sigma)$	0	0	$2\sigma - .8\sigma\ (.3\sigma)$
	Treatment Group 1	*Treatment Group 2*	*Treatment Group 1*	*Treatment Group 2*
II	$.1\sigma - 2.0\sigma\ (.1\sigma)$	$[.1\sigma - 2.0\sigma\ (.1\sigma)] - .2\sigma$	$2\sigma - .8\sigma\ (.3\sigma)$	0
	$.1\sigma - 2.0\sigma\ (.1\sigma)$	$[.1\sigma - 2.0\sigma\ (.1\sigma)] - .5\sigma$	$2\sigma - .8\sigma\ (.3\sigma)$	0
	$.1\sigma - 2.0\sigma\ (.1\sigma)$	$[.1\sigma - 2.0\sigma\ (.1\sigma)] - .8\sigma$	$2\sigma - .8\sigma\ (.3\sigma)$	0
	$.1\sigma - 2.0\sigma\ (.1\sigma)$	$[.1\sigma - 2.0\sigma\ (.1\sigma)] - .2\sigma$	0	$2\sigma - .8\sigma\ (.3\sigma)$
	$.1\sigma - 2.0\sigma\ (.1\sigma)$	$[.1\sigma - 2.0\sigma\ (.1\sigma)] - .5\sigma$	0	$2\sigma - .8\sigma\ (.3\sigma)$
	$.1\sigma - 2.0\sigma\ (.1\sigma)$	$[.1\sigma - 2.0\sigma\ (.1\sigma)] - .8\sigma$	0	$2\sigma - .8\sigma\ (.3\sigma)$

Note: D = Design (see Figure 15.1).

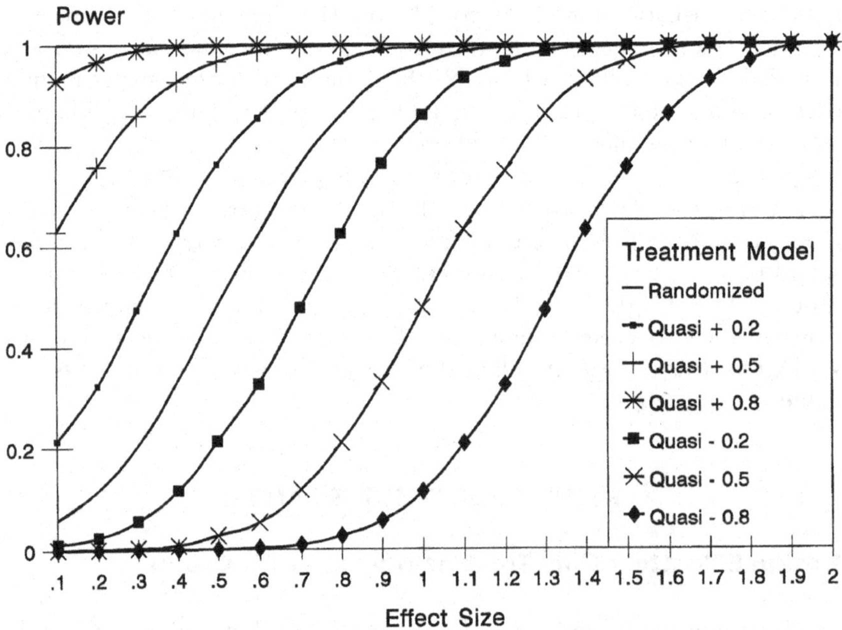

Figure 15.2. One-tailed power, smooth symmetric distribution, $n_1 = n_2 = 30$, $\alpha = 0.05$, 1 million repetitions.

The curve labeled Quasi+.2 indicates the mean of the treatment group was initially .2σ larger than the control group. The curve labeled Quasi-.2 indicates the mean of the treatment group was initially lower than the control group by that amount. The remaining series were constructed in a similar fashion.

Cohen (1988) stated that .2σ is considered a small effect size, .5σ is medium, and .8σ is large. In order to interpret Figure 15.2, consider the effect size of typical variables in educational psychology, as noted by Bloom (1984), Walberg (1986), and others. In terms of student achievement, a typical small treatment effect might be the use of advance organizers; another example would be peer group influence. A medium treatment effect would be home environment intervention, and a large treatment effect might be cooperative learning, or perhaps graded homework (Vockell & Asher, 1995, p. 361).

Type I Errors (False Positives)

Suppose two intact groups are chosen for a quasi-experimental study of a known nonsense treatment. Results for a true randomized experimental would indicate a rejection rate of 0.05, meaning that 5 times out of 100 a Type I error (false positive) will be made, incorrectly indicating a significant treatment effect. However, as noted in Figure 15.2, if the treatment group has an initial difference of .8σ, which might occur due to the nature of quasi-experimental design, the probability that the researcher will incorrectly conclude the nonsense treatment is effective is about 93 times out of a hundred.

Similarly stated, if 100 independent researchers replicated this experiment, there would be seemingly irrefutable evidence (statistically significant results would be reported by 93 of 100 independent researchers) of the effectiveness of this treatment. Cohen (1988) considered an effect size of .8 to be "grossly perceptible" (p. 27), so consider smaller differences. A medium level of initial difference would be rejected in 63 of the research studies, and a small level of initial difference would lead to a rejection of the null hypothesis of no difference between group means in 21 of one hundred studies. Hence, there will be the likelihood of a prolific number of published articles in the literature on the effectiveness of the nonsense treatment.

Mispecification of Treatment Magnitude

The overstatement or understatement for small, medium, and large treatment effects with small, medium, and large initial differences between the treatment and control group obtained through the use of a quasi-experimental design are summarized in Table 15.2. The magnitude of overstatement or understatement of the effectiveness of a treatment for

Table 15.2. Summary of the Statistical Power of Quasi-Experimental Design for a Variety of Treatment Effect Sizes and Initial Differences Between the Treatment and Control Group, $n_1 = n_2 = 30$, $\alpha = 0.05$

	Model						
ES	*R*	$Q+.2\sigma$	$Q+.5\sigma$	$Q+.8\sigma$	$Q-.2\sigma$	$Q-.5\sigma$	$Q-.8\sigma$
.2σ	.12	.32	.76	.97	.02	0.0	0.0
.5σ	.48	.76	.97	1.0	.21	.03	0.0
.8σ	.86	.97	1.0	1.0	.63	.21	.03

Note: ES = effect size; R = randomized design; Q ± *x*σ = quasi-experimental design with initial differences of ± *x*σ. Results are based on a real smooth symmetric data set.

Table 15.3. Magnitude of Overstatement (+) and Understatement (–) of the Power of Quasi-Experimental Design for a Variety of Treatment Effect Sizes and Initial Differences, $n_1 = n_2 = 30$, $\alpha = 0.05$

	Model					
ES	$Q+.2\sigma$	$Q+.5\sigma$	$Q+.8\sigma$	$Q-.2\sigma$	$Q-.5\sigma$	$Q-.8\sigma$
.2	2.67	6.37	8.08	–6.0	–∞	–∞
.5	1.58	2.02	2.08	–2.78	–16.0	–∞
.8	1.13	1.16	1.16	–1.37	–4.10	–28.67

Note: ES = effect size; Q ± *x* = quasi-experimental design with initial differences of ± .xσ. Results are based on a real smooth symmetric data set.

these conditions are compiled in Table 15.3. An inspection of Table 15.3 indicates that when the treatment group is initially different by only a small amount (i.e., .2σ), the quasi-experimental design leads to overestimating the treatment by a factor of about 2.7; if the control group was initially different by the same magnitude, the estimate of the effectiveness of the treatment is understated by a factor of six.

Variation on a Theme: Design I with a Comparison Group

Consider a slight modification of Design I, where a control group is replaced with a comparison group. Whereas a control group has no intervention, a comparison group receives the usual intervention. Typically, the purpose for using this design is dissatisfaction due to the known lack of effectiveness of the usual intervention. This design differs from that of Design II, where both treatment groups receive interventions that are known to be effective and the hypothesis being tested is which of the two treatments is more effective.

Simulations were conducted in a fashion similar to that above for ES = .25σ - 2.0σ (.25) and the results are compiled in Figure 15.3. Because both

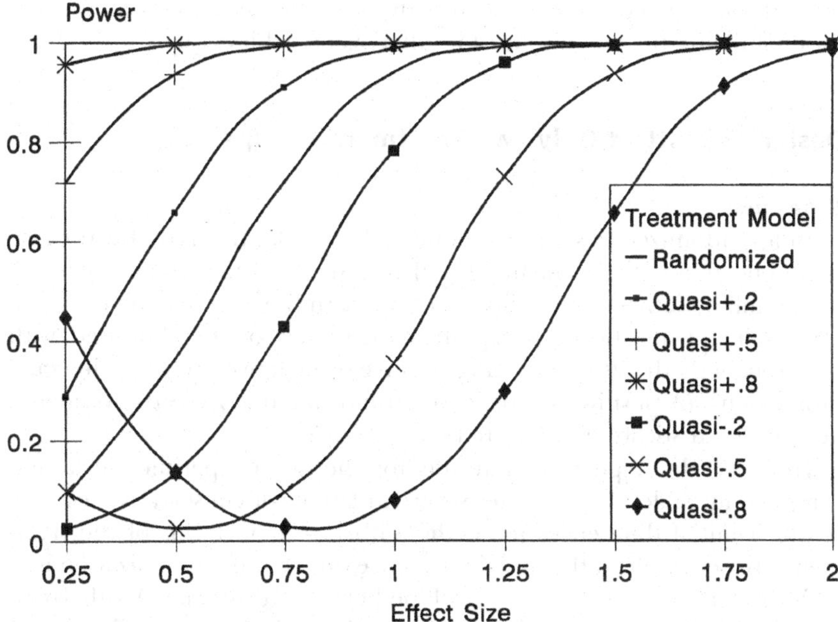

Figure 15.3. Two-tailed power, smooth symmetric distribution, $n_1 = n_2 = 30$, $\alpha = 0.05$, 1 million repetitions.

groups are receiving an intervention (the treatment and comparison group receive the new and the usual intervention, respectively), two-tailed power curves are presented in Figure 15.3.

The deleterious situation previously noted in Figure 15.2 has degenerated further. For example, examine the power curve for the quasi-experimental design when the comparison group has an initial difference of .8α. The researcher would incorrectly conclude the usual intervention is more successful than the new treatment, despite the former's historically poor performance, when the ES favoring the new treatment is low.

This is referred to as a Type III error (Kaiser, 1960), which is defined as an incorrect decision of direction following a two-tailed test. When the ES favoring the new treatment reaches about .38, the new and usual treatments incorrectly appear to be of equal success, and as the ES further increases, the power curves for the randomized and quasi-experimental design cross each other.

The falsehood of replications obtained from quasi-experimental studies should now be clear. Results from 196 million t tests conducted on data sampled with replacement from the real social science data set demonstrate that replicating the same poor design has little chance of contributing accurate evidence for or against the effectiveness of a treatment, or for quantifying the magnitude of its effectiveness if it exists.

Design II: Posttest Only Two Treatment Groups

Robustness

In a randomized design with nominal $\alpha = 0.05$, the Type I error rate should be .025 for both the upper tail and the lower tail. Under the truth of the null hypothesis of no difference between the two treatment groups, the obtained t statistic will be significant five times out of a hundred, with the probability that the sign being positive or negative occurring in equal proportions. (A positive t statistic would indicate that $\mu_1 > \mu_2$, whereas a negative t statistic would indicate that $\mu_2 > \mu_1$.)

However, the Type I error results for the quasi-experimental design compiled in Table 15.4 indicates severe inflations or conservativeness as a result of initial differences (even though $\mu_1 = \mu_2$ in terms of the treatment). For example, if the initial difference due to nonrandomization is .8 in favor of Treatment Group 1, the Type I error rate associated with Treatment Group 1 inflates by a factor of 17.3, from .025 to .867. The Type I error rate associated with Group Two becomes conservative, with a rejection rate of .000 instead of the correct .025.

The one-tail power results for the two treatment groups are depicted in Figure 4. Results for the randomized design appear as in the previous figures as the line without any markers. The remaining series represent obtained power curves for the quasi-experimental design where the initial difference favors Treatment Group 1 by $.2\sigma - .8\sigma$ (.3) (denoted as T1 + .2, T1 + .5, and T1 + .8, respectively), and where the initial differ-

Table 15.4. Type I Errors for a Two Treatment Group Quasi-Experimental Design; $n_1 = n_2 = 30$; Nominal = 0.05; 1 Million Repetitions

$\Delta T1$	$T1$	$T2$	$\Delta T2$	$T1$	$T2$
$.2\sigma$	.114	.002	$.2\sigma$	.004	.111
$.5\sigma$	.477	.000	$.5\sigma$	.000	.477
$.8\sigma$	.867	.000	$.8\sigma$	.000	.864

Note: In a randomized design, with nominal $\alpha = 0.05$, the correct upper and lower tail rejection rate is .025 when the null hypothesis of no difference between treatment groups is true. ΔT1 = magnitude of initial difference due to quasi-experimental design favoring Treatment Group 1, ΔT2 = magnitude of initial difference due to quasi-experimental design favoring Treatment Group 2, T1 = rejection rate for Treatment Group 1, T2 = rejection rate for Treatment Group 2.

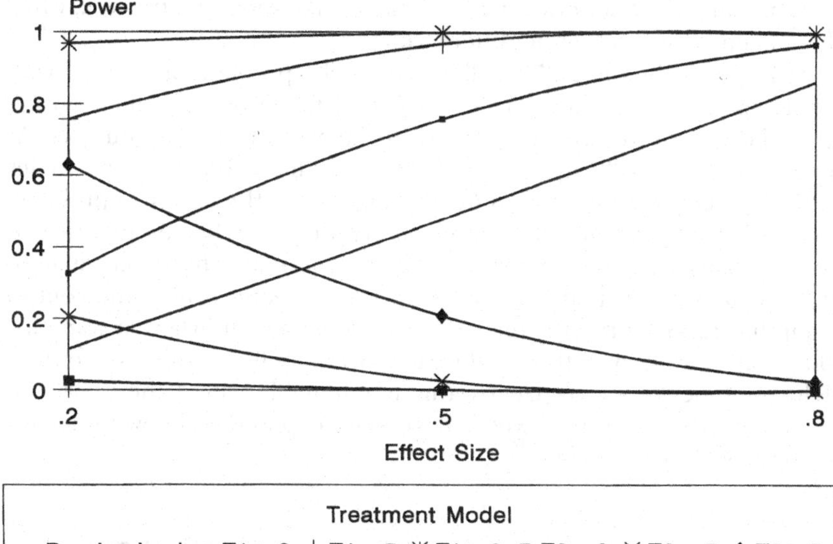

Figure 15.4. One-tailed power, smooth symmetric distribution, $n_1 = n_2 = 30$, $\alpha = 0.05$, 1 million repetitions.

ence due to the nonrandomized design favors Treatment Group 2 by the same amount (denoted as T2 + .2, T2 + .5, and T2 + .8, respectively).

The information contained in Figure 15.4 can be summarized in two parts. First, the three power curves above the power rates obtained for a randomized study are overestimates of the effectiveness of Treatment 1 as compared with Treatment 2. For example, with a true ES = .2σ, the *t* test should result in rejecting the null hypothesis of no difference between the two treatment groups with power of .114. When the level of initial difference is as high as .8, the rejection rate inflates by a factor of 7.6 to .863. Even if the initial difference is as low as .2, the inflated rejection rate is tripled to .342.

Second, consider the same situation, except the initial difference is in the opposite direction of the treatment effect (i.e., Treatment 1 is more effective, but the initial differences favor Treatment 2). If the ES = .2 and the initial difference is .8 , the researcher will incorrectly conclude that Treatment 2 is significant (power = .617), when in fact Treatment 1 is superior. In other words, if this situation confronted 100 independent researchers, instead of an overall conclusion supporting the notion that Treatment 1 is more effective (14 experiments favoring Treatment 1, while the remainder indicating no difference), the conclusion would be that Treatment 2 is superior (62 experiments favoring Treatment 2, while the remainder indicating no difference).

As indicated by these 378 million t tests, the problems associated with quasi-experimental design are exacerbated in the two treatment group case where both groups are exposed to known effective treatments. As noted above, Vockell and Asher (1995) presumed that the researcher could "compensate with reasoning like this: 'If this threat were a problem, it would show up at this point in my observations.'" Whereas an astute or possibly clairvoyant researcher might be able to make this determination in the context of a treatment versus a control group (where the control group has received no treatment), or to a lesser extent where a comparison group has received the usual treatment which historically is known to yield poor performance, clearly this is untenable where there are two treatment groups, both of which have been exposed to known effective treatments.

Design III: Pretest-Posttest Treatment Versus Control Group

Methodology For Design III

The study of this quasi-experimental design is approached from the frame of reference of classical measurement theory. A score obtained on a test as is comprised of two components,

$$x_i = t_i + \varepsilon_i \tag{1}$$

where t_i refers to a person's "true score," and ε_i refers to an error component. Error represents those random influences that inflate or deflate a test score, but are unrelated to the true score. The ε_i are generally taken to have a mean of zero (Gulliksen, 1950). Classical measurement theory, as expressed in Equation (1), can be expanded to include other stable components that do not represent a person's true score:

$$x_i = t_i + c_{1i} + c_{2i} + \ldots + c_{ki} + \varepsilon_i \tag{2}$$

where c_{1i}, c_{2i}, ... c_{ki} represent the various components of this type that contribute to the obtained score of the ith person.

An example of a potential c_i in education is test-wiseness. It has been defined as an examinee's ability to use the characteristics or format of a test to obtain a higher score (Millman, Bishop, & Ebel, 1965). In an academic skills test, it is independent of the student's knowledge of the subject matter. Test-wiseness can be seen in students who have had extensive experience with a particular type of test. For example, students taking multiple-choice tests may learn to look for clues that will allow them to eliminate plausible yet incorrect distracters. Other examples of c_i are discussed by Bajtelsmit (1975), Diamond and Evans (1972), Hall, Follman, and Fisher (1987), Kirkland and Hollandsworth (1980), Rowley (1974), Sarnacki (1979), Stanley (1971), and Wigdor and Garner (1982). In the context of the pretest in Design III, c_i could take the form of any covariate that is highly correlated with the dependent variable.

Simulation techniques are used to demonstrate the effects of making adjustments with a pretest covariate in the nonrandomized pretest-posttest treatment versus control group design (III) for situations where the null hypothesis is true or when it is false. The single-factor ANCOVA used is based on the general linear model

$$y_{ij} = \mu + \alpha_j + \beta(x_{ij} - \bar{x}) + \varepsilon_{ij} \quad (3)$$
$$i = 1, \ldots, n$$
$$j = 1, \ldots, m$$

where μ is the grand mean, is the effect due to the treatment, β is the regression of y on x, ε refers to the error component, n is the number of subjects, and m is the number of groups.

Many years ago, Anderson (1963), Lord (1969), and others objected to the use of ANCOVA with intact groups. Nevertheless, McMillan and Schumacher (1989) pointed out that "ANCOVA is used frequently with intact groups, without randomization" (p. 368), although they did not condone the practice. Indeed many textbook authors opined the opposite of Anderson and Lord, advising researchers to employ ANCOVA for data obtained for naturally occurring or intact groups.

For example, Gall, Borg, and Gall (1996) stated, "Analysis of covariance is useful ... because the researcher cannot always select comparison groups that are matched with respect to all relevant variables except the one that is the main concern of the investigation" (p. 395). Similarly, Crowl (1993) stated, "There are numerous situations in which it is appropriate to use analysis of covariance. In educational research, however, one of the most common situations is a quasi-experimental design in which two intact groups are to be compared on some measure" (p. 219). Similarly, the rationale of Best and Kahn (1993) for using ANCOVA in a pretest-posttest quasi-experimental design: "Because this design may be the only feasible one, the comparison is justifiable" (p. 151). Other textbook authors who expressed this view include Fraenkel and Wallen (1993, p. 325), Gay (1987, pp. 290-291), Sprinthhall, Schmutte, and Sirois (1991, p. 146), and Wiersma (1995, p. 384).

There are numerous objections in using ANCOVA with intact groups. Stevens (1992) pointed out, "First, even the use of several covariates will *not* equate intact groups. The groups may still differ on some unknown important variable(s). Also, note that equating groups on one variable may result in accentuating their differences on other variables" (p. 336). Other difficulties mentioned by Stevens (1992, pp. 336 - 338) include the following:

- ANCOVA adjusts the posttest means to what they would be if all the groups had started out equal on the covariate(s), even if groups that were equal on the covariate(s) do not exist in the real world
- meeting assumptions of linearity and homogeneity of regression slopes are unlikely with intact groups
- the presence of differential growth (for example, suppose natural growth is greater in the treatment group than in the control group) may lead to a significant ANCOVA, but it will not be clear if the difference is due to the treatment, differential growth, or both
- measurement error may further bias the treatment effect.

Stevens (1992) concluded,

> Given all the above problems, the reader may well wonder whether we should abandon the use of covariance when comparing intact groups. But, other statistical methods for analyzing this kind of data (such as matched samples, gain score ANOVA) suffer from many of the same problems, such as seriously biased treatment effects. The fact is that inferring cause-effect from intact groups is treacherous, regardless of the type of statistical analysis. (p. 338)

Note that the logic of this conclusion amounts to supporting the use of ANCOVA with intact groups, despite the enumeration of its many flaws, because other statistics suffer from the same difficulties.

In a pretest-posttest design, consideration must be given to the nature of the pretest. The simplest approach is to administer an exact copy or a parallel form of the posttest. However, this may increase the factor jeopardizing internal validity called testing, which is the "effects of taking a test upon the scores of a second testing" (Campbell & Stanley, 1963, p. 5). Vockell and Asher (1995) noted,

> With regard to achievement tests, pretesting is a problem because an initial test may familiarize the students with the type or the actual content of the test questions they will have to deal with on the posttest and therefore artificially inflate their scores. In cases where the pretest and posttest are identi-

> cal, such familiarity with the measurement process may even be more useful to uninformed students that the instructional lesson itself. (p. 234)

In a randomized experiment, this difficulty could be ameliorated by employing the Solomon Four-group design, where the effects of the pretest can be quantified. Another way to lesson the effect of the pretest on the posttest is to use some other pretest measure, but one that represents a covariable that is highly correlated with the outcome variable. (In studies of attitudes and personality, however, it should be noted that even in this case the pretest may still sensitize the participant.)This approach is adopted in the two vignettes described below.

Vignette 1: Unsuccessful Adjustment When H_0 Is True

A researcher wants to determine if a new method of teaching arithmetic skills produces greater student learning outcomes, as measured by scores on an arithmetic test. The researcher uses two previously formed classes as a control/comparison group (Class A) and a treatment group (Class B) in a quasi-experimental design. The pretest is a standardized mathematics test that is given every year at the school. The posttest is a criterion-referenced test that was developed to accompany the curriculum. Content validation evidence supporting the use of the pretest is obtained from considerable congruence of the test blueprints for the pretest and the posttest.

Suppose that the pretest measures arithmetic skills with a greater emphasis on word problems as the medium of presentation, but the posttest assesses arithmetic skills by stressing calculation problems. Both tests measure arithmetic ability, but they do so with a slightly different emphasis on the form of problem presentation. This difference is well known to mathematics educators; the example was chosen only for illustrative purposes. There might be other components not shared by these tests, such as reasoning ability and so forth, which are less readily apparent.

Suppose further that the two classes have approximately the same arithmetic skills, but Class A has higher mean reading ability than does Class B, which occurred due to the quasi-experimental design. Table 15.5, which characterizes the data set for the use vignettes discussed below, reflects this by indicating that reading components (c) of the covariate scores for Class A were sampled from a population with a mean of one while those for Class B had a population mean of zero. In this example reading ability is taken to be independent of arithmetic skill and is extraneous to the experiment.

Table 15.5. Characteristics of Data Sets Used In Vignettes 1 and 2

		Score		*μ, σ*		
Vignette	*Class*	*dep*	*cov*	*t*	*c*	*tr*
1	A	$t_i + \varepsilon_{1i}$	$t_i + c_i + \varepsilon_{2i}$	0;1	1;1	0.0
	B	$t_i + \varepsilon_{1i}$	$t_i + c_i + \varepsilon_{2i}$	0;1	0;1	0.0
2	A	$t_i + \varepsilon_{1i}$	$t_i + c_i + \varepsilon_{2i}$	0;1	1;1	0.0
	B	$t_i + tr + \varepsilon_{1i}$	$t_i + c_i + \varepsilon_{2i}$	0;1	0;1	–0.5

Note: dep = dependent variable; cov = covariate; μ, α (t) = mean and standard deviation of true score; μ, α (c) = mean and standard deviation of component score; tr = treatment effect; ε = error component.

Dependent and covariate measures for the two classes are made up of true and error score components only, and thus the column *c* reflects the fact that the scores contained no other components. True scores for Class A were sampled from a population with a mean of 1.0, while those for Class B came from a population with a mean of zero. The last column shows that no treatment effect (in the form of a constant to produce a shift in location parameter) was added to the scores of either group. The ε_{1i} and ε_{2i} for all examples were sampled from distributions with a mean of zero and variance of 1. All data sets were composed of 70 observations (35 per class) with random variates being sampled from normal populations with means and variances as shown in the table.

In order to simplify this demonstration, Table 15.6 shows the various models based on Equation (3) that were used in this example and subsequent analyses. Least squares regression models (with intercepts) were used for all analyses. In Table 15.6, dep and cov represent, respectively, the dependent and covariate variables. In the models, *grp* is a dummy vector (1 or 0) representing group membership, and *int* is the product of *cov* and *grp*.

The test of β_1 in (a) and β_3 in (b) results in p values of .000 and .949, respectively. This indicates a relationship between the covariate and dependent variables and leaves as tenable the hypothesis of homoge-

Table 15.6. Least Squares Models Used in Vignette Analyses

Model Designation	*Model*
(a)	dep = $\beta_0 + \beta_1$cov + $\beta_2$grp
(b)	dep = $\beta_0 + \beta_1$cov + $\beta_2$grp + $\beta_3$int
(c)	dep = $\beta_0 + \beta_1$grp

Notes: dep = dependent variable, cov = covariate, grp = group membership, int = product of covariate and group membership.

neous regressions for the two classes. Of primary interest is the test of β_2 in (a) which yields a p value of .027, leading to the incorrect conclusion that a treatment effect is present in the data. In this vignette, the correct conclusion of no treatment effect is obtained by the test on β_1 in (c) (i.e., an independent samples t test) which gives $p = .857$.

The quasi-experimental design led to the erroneous conclusion of effectiveness of the new instructional method. The explanation is straightforward: the covariate adjustment was made on the basis of the difference in reading levels of the two classes. But, reading level is unrelated to the dependent variable in this example and is therefore irrelevant to the study.

Vignette 2: Unsuccessful Adjustment When H_0 Is False

The data used in this example are the same as those above, with the exception that a treatment effect (modeled with a constant of $-.5\sigma$) was added to the dependent variable scores of the students in Class B with scores being the same as those used in the previous example. Conclusions reached on the two preliminary tests are the same as those reached in the previous vignette. The test of β_2 in (a) is nonsignificant with $p = .814$, while that of β_1 in (c) yields $p = .021$. In this case, the model with the covariate failed to detect the presence of the treatment effect. It was detected, however, when information from the pretest was removed from the analysis.

SCIENCE OR ART?

Is quasi-experimental design science or art? Leary (1995) noted,

> For many years, most behavioral scientists held a well-entrenched bias against quasi-experimental designs. For many, the tightly controlled experiment was the benchmark of behavioral research, and anything less than a true experiment was regarded with suspicion. Most contemporary behavioral researchers tend not to share this bias against quasi-experimentation, recognizing that the limitations of quasi-experimental designs are compensated by some notable advantages. (pp. 284-285)

I find the phrases "bias against quasi-experimental design" and "bias against quasi-experimentation" ironic. Moreover, the veracity of quasi-experimental design is a double-edge sword. When the results confirm a certain hypothesis, a notable advantage has arisen. However, it also affords the opportunity to dismiss results of a study that do not conform to previously established beliefs.

In fact, a high degree of scrutiny is directed toward quasi-experimental designs when the study results do not match up with politically-held beliefs. For example, consider the much discussed Follow Through Variation Study (Abt Associates, 1977; also see Cicirelli, 1969). This was an extension to the Project Head Start, which included a variety of programmatic innovations implemented over a decade and funded by the American taxpayers at the level of nearly $US 0.5 billion. The research design was a nonrandomized pretest-posttest design. Why was a quasi-experimental design employed? "Because of political urgency, the Head Start evaluators could not wait several years to retest the students. The researchers had to use an ex post facto design to compare groups created after the treatment" (Dooley, 1995, p. 216).

Standardized measures, such as the *Metropolitan Achievement Test Battery* and the *Coopersmith Self-Image Inventory* were administered. The results of the study indicated that the control group performed better than the treatment group for many interventions in the program, and where the treatment groups did performed better, they only obtained negligible advantages over the control group. Best and Kahn (1993) remarked that, "it is unlikely that any large-scale study has been scrutinized so extensively concerning research design, procedures employed, and the interpretation of the data. There have been critiques of the evaluations and critiques of the critiques, with sharp disagreements on most aspects of the study" (pp. 152-153).

The primary reason given as the explanation of the politically unacceptable results of the study was "because experimental treatments were not randomly selected and control groups were not randomly assigned, mismatching resulted and comparisons were really made between different populations" (Best & Kahn, 1993, p. 153). While critics of Head Start point to these studies to support the position that "compensatory education does not work," "critics of the Head Start evaluation have said that evaluation was in error" because "the nonequivalent control group made the program look ineffective" (Kidder, 1981, p. 95; see also Campbell & Erlebacher, 1970).

Huitema (1980, p. 123), among others, discussed different levels of quasi-experimental design. The randomly assigned groups design (pp. 136-137) where intact groups are assigned to the treatment or comparison group but the unit of analysis is the student is more defensible than the nonequivalent groups design (pp. 143-146) where subjects are selected from different populations. Although the designers of the Follow Through Variation Study had intended to invoke the former, Best and

Kahn's cited critics of the study maintained the dismal results were obtained because the latter was inadvertently invoked.

In another example, consider the Casa Blanca nonequivalent treatment vs control group study on desegregation via busing and its impact on educational achievement (Singer, Gerard, & Redfearn, 1975). In the mid to late 1960s, students in one segregated Riverside, California school were bused to an integrated school, while another segregated school was allowed to remain segregated. Statewide standardized achievement tests were administered after the ensuing school year. Results showed the treatment group (desegregated) performed no better than the control group (not desegregated).

Whereas the results of a study are supposed to be attributed to the intervention, because the outcome was socially undesirable in this case, the researchers were forced to assert that the outcome was due to the design. Yet, Dooley (1995) raised every potential threat to internal validity identified by Campbell and Stanley (1963) (e.g., maturation, outside events, selection maturation interaction) and found satisfactory defenses to each challenge. (Dooley noted that the literature on desegregation and achievement in studies where there is "random assignment of experimental and control groups" demonstrates the "beneficial effects of busing" [p. 221] in terms of academic achievement.)

Indeed, when results conform to politically or socially expedient beliefs, design considerations employed to answer rival hypotheses seeking to explain the outcome of the study are carefully examined, and subsequently (if not summarily) justified. Many authors of social and behavioral research textbooks demonstrate this process by reprinting a quasi-experimental design on some topic that was previously published in the literature. Then, the authors commence a point-by-point challenge of each of the threats to internal validity discussed by Campbell and Stanley (1963), applying logic, common sense, and a well-grounded knowledge of the literature to answer each threat.

Unfortunately, the reader will oftentimes confront statements such as "Luckily, the two groups were about the same on ...," "It was insightful of the researcher to anticipate ...," or "Fortunately, the researchers were able to obtain ..." and other such phrases. This suggests success (and hence, replication) depends heavily on the personal charisma of the researcher, a characteristic more likely associated with art than science.

MONTE CARLO VERSUS META-ANALYSIS

No attempt has been made in this Monte Carlo study to catalog the types of bias prevalent, determine how frequently initial differences arise, or quantify the magnitude of differences among intact groups in quasi-experimental studies in social and behavioral sciences. In my opinion, such an undertaking would be naïve. The insidiousness of bias is that in the absence of randomization it is unknowable. It can never been known in terms of confounding variables the researcher is aware of, or in terms of confounding variables the researcher is not aware of. See Sawilowsky (2004) for a Monte Carlo demonstration on how randomization controls bias, even with samples as small as $n = 2$.

Meta-analytic methods have been used to compare the effect size obtained from randomized and nonrandomized experiments for some variables (e.g., Colditz, Miller, & Mosteller, 1988). Lipsey and Wilson (1993) summarized more than 70 meta-analytic studies which contained estimates of the ES obtained from randomized and nonrandomized studies on the same variables. The average difference in effect size between the two methodologies was only about .05 (ES = .46 for randomized studies vs. ES = .41 for nonrandomized studies). Nevertheless, an inspection of the comparisons in the individual studies prompted them to conclude that nonrandomized studies "may result in a treatment estimate quite discrepant" (p. 1193) from a randomized study.

Heinsman and Shadish (1996) used meta-analysis to compare 51 randomized studies with 47 nonrandomized studies of a variety of variables, including "Scholastic Aptitude Test coaching, ability grouping of students within classrooms, pre-surgical education of patients to improve post-surgical outcome, and drug abuse prevention with juveniles" (p. 154). A summary of the effect sizes indicated an average ES = .28 for the randomized studies versus an ES = .03 for the nonrandomized studies, which is substantially different from the findings of Lipsey and Wilson (1993).

Heinsman and Shadish defended these results by "projecting effect sizes using predictor variables that equate studies at an ideal or reasonable level" for both methodologies. They projected an average ES = 1.01 for the 51 randomized studies and an ES = 1.00 for the 47 nonrandomized studies, a difference in average effect size of only .01, which is in better agreement with the findings of Lipsey and Wilson (1993).

However, consider the list of conditions for their projection: (1) "both groups use passive control groups, internal control groups, and matching," (2) "exact computation of d [ES]" is assumed, (3) there is "no attrition" of participants in the studies, (4) only "standardized treatments" are used, (5) studies "were published," (6) studies "had pretest effect sizes of zero," (7) there were "N = 1,000 subjects per study," (8) neither methodologies "allow for self-selection of subjects into conditions," and (9) only "outcomes based on self-reports and specifically tailored to treatment" were used (p. 162). Their remarkable conclusion was that "nonrandomized experiments are more like randomized experiments if one takes confounds into account" (p. 162)!

CONCLUSION

It should be pointed out that the parameters of this study were deliberately chosen to be most favorable to the researcher: (a) A deliberate attempt was made to sample with replacement from a real data set that, although implausible, nevertheless exhibited features most amenable to the statistical tests invoked. The real data set used in Design I and II was symmetric with light tails, presenting only minimal deviation from the population normality assumption which the t test is dependent upon. The results would be even worse than those presented in this study if data sets with heavy tails or skew had been sampled, (b) The scores used in Design III were obtained without measurement error, (c) A sample of size $n = 30$ was used, which is typical in education research. However, many published studies in social work, psychology, and health care have much smaller sample sizes, which would further diminish the power of statistics to detect treatment effects.

Other well known problems were ignored, such as (d) extrapolation (which assumes the regression line for the intact data set has the same slope as would a random sample, because if it does not, then "the interpretation of the ANCOVA results is speculative," Werts & Linn, 1971, p. 97), and (e) regression artifact, which can lead to the inappropriate conclusion that "(1) treatment effects exist (when they don't), (2) no treatment effects exist (when they do), (3) a particular treatment is helpful (when it is actually harmful), and (4) a particular effect is harmful (when it is actually helpful)" (Huitema, 1980, p. 14).

It may be concluded that an illegitimate use of quasi-experimental design is conducting research to bolster a particular belief. If a controversial hypothesis is being tested, a savvy (albeit unethical) researcher could employ this design with little risk in maintaining the previously established belief. The quasi-experiment is deemed successful if the results are favorable, and "a notable advantage has arisen." If the results are not favorable, however, the researcher can minimize the results by simply calling attention to the flaws inherent in quasi-experimental design.

A legitimate use of quasi-experimental design might be to relegate this methodology to doctoral studies as a learning tool designed to approximate the process of conducting a randomized experiment. Many doctoral studies are already severely limited by extremely small sample sizes, thereby diminishing the ability of statistical procedures in detecting differences among groups. This directly impacts the importance of the findings of the study. Thus, the focus of doctoral studies would be on demonstrating knowledge and skills of the process of disciplined inquiry (as opposed to experimental design), instead of a focus on the findings of the study.

Hyman (1995) suggested that to merely point out what is wrong with methodological studies or procedures is less constructive than to suggest solutions. Given the premise that restrictions preclude applied or field researchers from conducting true randomized experimental designs, perhaps a reasonable, if not inexpensive, solution might be to change the unit of analysis in these studies from the student to the classroom. See Glendening (1977) for further comments on changing the unit of analysis.

Huitema (1980) discussed an example where classes selected from 10 schools were randomly assigned to participate either as a treatment or a comparison group. In this situation, statements regarding the effectiveness of the treatment would be restricted to classes, not made about students. The potential lack of statistical power was noted due to the reduced degrees of freedom because the class is the unit of analysis, and hence, $N = 10$. However, it was pointed out that statistical power is regained due to the fact that "the error mean square is generally smaller than is the case with individual units," (Huitema, 1980, p. 136).

The notion of changing the unit of analysis in applied research might be considered too costly in terms of expense, time, and effort. Also, the suggestion might arise to simply abandon the quantitative approach altogether, and instead, adopt a qualitative design. My response is (1) the cost of answering a research question should always be taken into consideration, and in any case, consider all the research funds that will be available that are currently ill-spent on quasi-experiments, and (2) a qualitative design should be selected on the basis of a qualitative research and the merits of the qualitative design, not the demerits of a quantitative design.

The flaws in using quasi-experimental designs are an open secret in social and behavioral science research. The seriousness of these flaws, moreover, appears to be greatly underestimated. The rationale supporting the effective use of quasi-experimental design presumes personal qualities rarely in the possession of researchers.

Reconsider the question raised above on whether or not a researcher should abandon the notion of conducting a study if randomization is not possible; or whether or not in reviewing studies should those based on nonrandomized designs be discarded. On the basis of the simulations presented here, I think so. Why? If the outcome of a quasi-experimental study is publishable (i.e., politically and socially acceptable), the results ascend to the level of a true randomized experimental design. If the outcome is not desirable, however, the results are discounted due to the flawed design. This is the legacy of Campbell and Stanley (1963).

APPENDIX

Some material on Design III was initially written by R. C. Blair and accepted for publication in a prestigious statistics journal in the early 1980s. A change in editorship led to the manuscript being withdrawn. Professor Blair gave me the material to revise, and I presented as part of a larger paper (Blair & Sawilowsky, 1991).

Subsequent development on this chapter was conducted in 1994-1995 with the assistance of a Wayne State University Career Development Chair Award. Eventually, the material evolved into a manuscript that was accepted for publication as a peer-reviewed chapter in a prestigious social science yearbook. It was to appear in 1999, but due to technical difficulties, the yearbook was never published. In 2005, the copyright was reassigned back to me.

During the quarter-century history of bringing this chapter to print, Professor Donald T. Campbell passed away (May 6, 1996). His obituary appeared in a Sunday edition of the *New York Times*:

> For a generation, virtually no respectable researcher this side of the chemistry lab has designed or carried out a reputable scientific study without a thorough grounding in what Dr. Campbell called quasi-experimentation, the highly sophisticated statistics-based approach he invented to replicate the effects of the truly randomized scientific studies that are all but impossible in the slippery and unruly world of human interactions. (May 12, 1996, p. y 17)

REFERENCES

Abt Associates. (1977). *Education as experimentation: A planned variation model*. Cambridge, MA: Author.

Anderson, N. H. (1963). Comparison of different populations: Resistance to extinction and transfer. *Psychological Bulletin, 70*, 162-179.

Anderson, S., Auquier, A., Hauck, W., Oakes, D., Vandaele, W., & Weisberg, H. I. (1980). *Statistical methods for comparative studies: Techniques for bias reduction*. New York: Wiley.

Bajtelsmit, J. W. (1975). *Development and validation of an adult measure of secondary cue-using strategies on objective examinations: The test of obscure knowledge (TOOK)*. Annual Meeting of the Northeastern Educational Research Association, Ellenville, New York.

Best, J. W., & Kahn, J. V. (1993). *Research in education* (7th ed.). Boston: Allyn & Bacon.

Blair, R. C., & Sawilowsky, S. (1991, October). *Confounding covariates in nonrandomized studies.* Paper presented at the annual meeting of the Mid-Western Educational Research Association, Chicago.

Bloom, B. S. (1984). The search for methods of group instruction as effective as one-to-one tutoring. *Educational Leadership, 41*, 4-17.

Campbell, D. T., & Stanley, J. C. (1963). *Experimental and quasi-experimental designs for research*. Chicago: AERA.

Campbell, D. T., & Erlebacher, A. (1970). How regression artifacts in quasi-experimental evaluations can mistakenly make compensatory education look harmful. In J. Hellmuth (Ed.), *The disadvantaged child: Vol. 3. Compensatory education: A national debate* (pp. 185-210). New York: Brunner/Mazel.

Cicirelli, V. G. (1969). *The impact of Head Start: An evaluation of the effects of Head Start on children's cognitive and affective development.* Clearinghouse for Federal Scientific and Technical Information, U.S. Department of Commerce, National Bureau of Standards, Institute for Applied Technology, PB 184 328.

Cohen, J. (1988). *Statistical power analysis for the behavioral sciences* (2nd ed.). Hillsdale, NJ: Erlbaum.

Colditz, G. A., Miller, J. N., & Mosteller, F. (1988). The effect of study design on gain in evaluation of new treatments in medicine and surgery. *Drug Information Journal, 22*, 343-352.

Cook, T. D., & Campbell, D. T. (1979). *Quasi-experimentation: Design & analysis issues for field settings*. Chicago: Rand McNally.

Crowl, T. K. (1993). *Fundamentals of educational research*. Madison, WI: WCB Brown & Benchmark.

Diamond, J. J., & Evans, W. J. (1972). An investigation of the cognitive correlates of test-wiseness. *Journal of Educational Measurement, 9*, 145-150.

Dooley, D. (1995). *Social research methods* (3rd ed.). Englewood Cliffs, NJ: Prentice Hall.

Fraenkel, J. R., & Wallen, N. E. (1993). *How to design and evaluate research in education* (2nd ed.). New York: McGraw-Hill.

Gall, M. D., Borg, W. R., & Gall, J. P. (1996). *Educational research: An introduction* (6th ed.) White Plains, NY: Longman.

Gay, L. R. (1987). *Educational research: Competencies for analysis and application* (4th ed.). New York: Merrill.

Glendening, L. K. (1977). *Operationally defining the assumption of independence and choosing the appropriate unit of analysis*. Unpublished doctoral dissertation, Michigan State University, East Lansing, MI.

Gulliksen, H. (1950). *Theory of mental tests.* Hillsdale, NJ: Erlbaum.

Hall, B. W., Follman, J. C., & Fisher, S. K. (1987). *An examination for affective correlates of test-wiseness.* Paper presented at the annual meeting of the National Council on Measurement in Education, Washington, DC.

Heinsman, D. T., & Shadish, W. R. (1996). Assignment methods in experimentation: When do nonrandomized experiments approximate answers from randomized experiments? *Psychological Methods, 1*, 154-169.

Huitema, B. E. (1980). *The analysis of covariance*. New York: John Wiley Sons.

Hyman, R. (1995). How to critique a published article. *Psychological Bulletin, 118*(2), 178-182.

Kaiser, H. G. (1960). Directional statistical decisions. *Psychological Review, 67*, 160-167.

Kidder, L. H. (1981). *Sellitz, Wrightsman, and Cook's research methods in social relations* (4th ed.). New York: Holt, Rinehart, and Winston.

Kirkland, K., & Hollandsworth, J. G. (1980). Effective test taking: Skills-acquisition versus anxiety-reduction techniques. *Journal of Consulting and Clinical Psychology, 48*, 431-438.

Leary, M. R. (1995). *Introduction to behavioral research methods* (2nd ed.). Pacific Grove, CA: Brooks/Cole.

Lipsey, M. W., & Wilson, D. B. (1993). The efficacy of psychological, educational, and behavioral treatment: Confirmation from meta-analysis. *American Psychologist, 48*, 1181-1209.

Lord, F. (1969). Statistical adjustments when comparing pre-existing groups. *Psychological Bulletin, 72*, 336-337.

McMillan, J. H., & Schumacher, S. (1989). *Research in education: A conceptual introduction*. Glenview, IL: Scott, Foresman.

Micceri, T. (1986, November). *A futile search for that statistical chimera of normality.* Paper presented at the annual meeting of the Florida Educational Research Association, Tampa, FL.

Micceri, T. (1989). The unicorn, the normal curve, and other improbable creatures. *Psychological Bulletin, 105*(1), 156-166.

Millman, J., Bishop, C. H., & Ebel, R. L. (1965). An analysis of test-wiseness. *Educational and Psychological Measurement, 25*, 707-726.

Rowley, G. L. (1974). Which examinees are favored by the use of multiple choice tests? *Journal of Educational Measurement, 11*, 15-23.

Sarnacki, R. E. (1979). An examination of test-wiseness in the cognitive test domain. *Review of Educational Research, 49*, 252-279.

Sawilowsky, S. (2004). Teaching random assignment: Do you believe it works? *Journal of Modern Applied Statistical Methods, 3*(1), 221-226.

Sawilowsky, S., & Blair, R. C. (1992). A more realistic look at the robustness and Type II error properties of the *t* test to departures from population normality. *Psychological Bulletin, 111*, 352-360.

Sawilowsky, S., Blair, R. C., & Micceri, T. (1990). A PC FORTRAN subroutine library of psychology and educational data sets. *Psychometrika, 55*, 729.

Singer, H., Gerard, H. B., & Redfearn, D. (1975). Achievement. In H. B. Gerard & B. Miller (Eds.), *School desegregation: A longitudinal study.* New York: Plenum Press.

Spinthhall, R. C., Schmutte, G. T., & Sirois, L. (1991). *Understanding educational research*. Englewood Cliffs, NJ: Prentice Hall.

Stanley, J. C. (1971). Reliability. In R. L. Thorndike (Ed.), *Educational measurement*. Washington, DC: American Council on Education.

Stevens, J. (1992). *Applied multivariate statistics for the social sciences* (2nd ed.). Hillsdale, NJ: Erlbaum.

Vockell, E. L., & Asher, J. W. (1995). *Educational research* (2nd ed.). Englewood Cliffs, NJ: Merril.

Walberg, H. J. (1986). Synthesis of research on teaching. In M. C. Wittrock (Ed.), *Handbook of research on teaching* (3rd ed., pp. 214-229). New York: Macmillian.

Werts, C. E., & Linn, R. L. (1971). Analyzing school effects: ANCOVA with a fallible covariate. *Educational and Psychological Measurement, 31*, 95-104.

Wiersma, W. (1995). *Research methods in education: An introduction* (6th ed.). Boston: Allyn & Bacon.

Wigdor, A. K., & Garner, W. R. (1982). *Ability testing: Uses, consequences, and controversies*. Washington, DC: National Academy Press.

PART III

MEASUREMENT

CHAPTER 16

THINKING ABOUT ITEM RESPONSE THEORY FROM A LOGISTIC REGRESSION PERSPECTIVE

A Focus on Polytomous Models

Amery D. Wu and Bruno D. Zumbo

The purpose of this chapter is to describe the conceptual bridge between item response theory (IRT) and logistic regression (LogR) by describing the essential similarities and differences between these two statistical frameworks. In so doing, we foster knowledge translation from psychometrics to those disciplines extensively using LogR (e.g., sociology, health care, and epidemiology) hence increasing the use of IRT. Therefore, the goal of this chapter is to advance the use of item response theory in real data analyses settings. Furthermore, it becomes apparent early on in this chapter that IRT is a special case of LogR, hence one can not only use LogR as a perspective to describe IRT to novices but also as a way of IRT specialists gaining insight into complex models such as polytomous IRT and their assumptions.

Real Data Analysis, pp. 241–269

It should be noted that we are not suggesting that we have built the bridge between LogR and IRT but rather that we are describing this bridge and using it as a way of getting from one vantage point to the other. The chapter is organized in three major sections traveling along the bridge from LogR to IRT. The first section is a brief overview of the family of logistic regression models. The second section describes the bridge between LogR and IRT. In the third section, IRT is described from the vantage point of LogR with particular attention to how these IRT models are constructed and their assumptions. This description of IRT will focus, in particular, on organizing and articulating the variety of polytomous IRT models because polytomous data are commonly found in day-to-day research settings yet polytomous IRT is seldom applied. It becomes apparent throughout that the LogR perspective brings a useful organizing framework and allows one to fully appreciate the range of IRT models and their assumptions.

A BRIEF OVERVIEW OF THE FAMILY OF LOGISTIC REGRESSION MODELS

The use of LogR has greatly increased during the last decade and become routinely available in statistical packages (Hosmer & Lemeshow, 2000; Peng, Lee, & Ingersoll, 2002), especially in areas like medicine, health science and epidemiology. The goal of LogR is to model categorical outcome variables by regressing on some explanatory variable(s) (Hosmer, & Lemeshow, 2000). LogR is an engine for modeling *categorical* outcome variables that are unlikely to meet the demanding assumptions of least squares regression. LogR only assumes "conditional independence" which means that the error terms are uncorrelated and that a linear relationship between the explanatory variable and the logit outcome variable (as discussed later).

Generally speaking, categorical outcome variables can be classified into two kinds: (1) *nominal*, if the variation between/among the possible outcomes is in the form of "types" such as types of learning strategies, and (2) *ordinal*, if the possible outcomes can be logically "ordered" such as grades. Under each of the nominal or ordinal form, the outcomes variable may take up two or more categories. When there are only two categories, the outcome variable is referred to as binary; and polytomous if there are three or more categories. Because there are only two possible outcomes for a binary variable, the distinction between whether a binary outcome variable is nominal or ordinal is usually regarded as irrelevant. For this reason, the majority of the textbooks and statistical software often organize LogR analyses into three sections: binary LogR, ordinal LogR,

Table 16.1. Classification of LogR and IRT Models

Number of Categories for the Outcome Variable	*LogR Models*	*IRT Models*
2 (binary)	Binary LogR	Binary IRT (1, 2, or 3 PL)
More than 2 (polytomous)		
Ordinal	Ordinal LogR	PC (1PL), RS (1PL), GR (2PL)
Nominal	Multinomial LogR	NR (2PL)

Note: LogR = logistic regression, IRT = item response theory, PL = parameter logistic, PC = partial credit, RS = rating scale, GR = graded response, and NR = nominal response.

and multinominal LogR. When the outcome variable is binary, one can simply apply binary LogR regardless of whether the outcome variable is nominal or ordinal. When the outcome variable is polytomous, one can apply multinomial LogR if the outcome variable is nominal, or ordinal LogR if ordered. Table 16.1 is a summary of our above description of the LogR models—we will return to Table 16.1 when we describe the IRT models and connect them to their corresponding LogR models. The first column of Table 16.1 classifies the three types of LogR by the number of outcome variable categories. Note that polytomous LogR models can also be applied to binary outcome variables and yields the same results. This is because a binary outcome variable can be seen as a special case of polytomous variable with only two categories.

BINARY LOGISTIC REGRESSION

A simple LogR with one explanatory variable and one binary outcome variable can be expressed as a probability function

$$P(u = 1|X) = \frac{\exp[c + \alpha X]}{1 + \exp[c + \alpha X]} \tag{1}$$

where u is a discrete random variable that takes up the sample space of "1" (a.k.a., case; success) or "0" (a.k.a., noncase; failure); X is an explanatory variable; the "exp" denotes the operator[1] that returns e (the base of natural logarithms) raised to a power; c and α are the intercept and the regression coefficient, respectively, for the linear regression in the logit form discussed below. The expression $P(u = 1|X)$ can be read as "the probability of success/case given X, for example, the probability of having lung cancer given that one smokes."

Readers may have noticed that we used somewhat different notation from those of most textbooks; this is because our notation will serve to maintain the consistency in our later discussion of IRT models. To estimate the regression coefficients, LogR makes use of the maximum likelihood method where one maximizes the likelihood function given the data at hand. For mathematical and practical simplicity, however, one actually minimizes the –2 log likelihood function. The Wald statistic and its associated p value are used to test the significance of individual coefficients. The amount of reduction in –2 log likelihood minimized by adding the explanatory variable compared to the base model that includes only the intercept term serves as a model fit statistics. In other words, a perfect fitting model will minimize the starting –2 log likelihood (a.k.a., deviance) to 0. A variety of effect size measures such as Nagelkerke R-square and Pseudo R-square were proposed to mimic "the percentage of variance explained" in linear regression.

Modeling the occurrence of a certain outcome is related to another key feature of LogR: the nonlinear relationship between the "probabilistic" outcome variable and the explanatory variable. The nonlinear relationship for a binary LogR is often characterized by a monotonically increasing S-shaped curve. Note that the modeled variable, $P(u = 1|X)$, in Equation 1 can be transformed by taking the natural logarithm of the odds (i.e., the ratio of probability of outcome being 1 to the probability of not being 1), and yields

$$\text{Logit} = \ln\left[\frac{P(u = 1|X)}{1 - P(u = 1|X)}\right] = c + \alpha X, \tag{2}$$

or simply

$$\text{Logit} = c + \alpha X, \tag{3}$$

where α is analogous to the regression coefficient and c to the intercept in linear regression. Two things should be noted here. First, LogR does not model the raw response (i.e., 0 and 1); instead, it models the probability or the logit. Second, the logit is assumed to be linear in its coefficients and is continuous ranging from $-\infty$ to $+\infty$. The transformed logit regression models given in Equation 2 or 3 have many of the desired properties of a linear regression model, and hence, the LogR model is regarded as a type of *generalized linear model*.

POLYTOMOUS LOGISTIC REGRESSION: MULTINOMIAL AND ORDINAL

For binary LogR, there are only two possible outcomes, 0 and 1. Modeling the probability of outcome "1" occurring, P, is sufficient because the probability of "0" occurring is simply $1 - P$. In contrast to binary LogR, multinomial and ordinal LogR involve more than two possible outcomes; therefore, require simultaneously fitting multiple regression curves. As a general rule, for an outcome variable that consists of $J + 1$ categories, J regression analyses will be entailed. Here J is the maximum coding of the outcome categories when the coding of the possible outcomes begins with 0. For example, an outcome variable that is measured on five ordered categories such as strongly disagree, disagree, neutral, agree, and strongly agree and is coded as 0, 1, 2, 3, and 4 will have a maximum coding of J equals to 4. Hence, four regression lines will be fitted for the $J + 1 = 5$ response categories. This systematic notation of "J" is capable of providing a lot of information about the specification of a model including the coding for the possible outcomes (i.e., 0, 1, ..., J), maximum value for outcome coding (J), number of outcome categories ($J + 1$), and number of regression analyses involved (J). Hence, this notation will be used throughout the rest of this chapter.

There are numerous ways of specifying the probabilities for the $J + 1$ outcomes occurring (see Agresti, 2002, chapter 7). For nominal outcomes, multinomial LogR involves a *direct* method of specifying $P(u = j|X), j = 0, 1, 2, \ldots, J$, which means that the probability is obtained directly by a divide-by-total procedure such that

$$P(u = j|X) = \frac{\exp[c_j + \alpha_j X]}{\sum_{j=0}^{J} \exp[c_j + \alpha_j X]}, \qquad (4)$$

with $c_0 = 0$ and $\alpha_0 = 0$. For ordinal outcomes, the most common method for specifying the probabilities for the $J + 1$ outcomes is an *indirect* (a.k.a., difference) method using the *cumulative logit* (see O'Connell, 2006 for other ordinal LogR models). Namely, the ordered categories are contrasted into J dichotomies such that responding in $u \leq j$ is contrasted with $u > j$. For example, suppose that the outcome variable has four ordered categories coded as 0, 1, 2, and 3, three ($J = 3$) regression analyses will be entailed and are achieved by contrasting the ordered outcomes into three dichotomies: (i) 0 versus 1, 2, and 3 (ii) 0 and 1 versus 2 and 3 (iii) 0, 1, and 2 versus 3. This cumulative contrasting is most widely used and the cumulative probability is written as

$$P(u \leq j|X) = \frac{\exp[c_j + \alpha X]}{1 + \exp[c_j + \alpha X]}, \text{ or} \tag{5}$$

$$Logit = \ln\left[\frac{P(u \leq j|X)}{P(u > j|X)}\right] = c_j + \alpha X. \tag{6}$$

Note that there is no subscript for the α slopes across the cumulative logits. This is because the slopes, most commonly, are assumed to be equal (i.e., parallel) in cumulative logit LogR. This *equal slopes assumption* in (5) and (6) is also referred to as *proportional odds assumption* (Agretsi, 2002, p. 275). The cumulative logit LogR is the default model in SPSS and SAS and is the mostly commonly applied LogR model for ordinal outcomes. Because ordinal LogR models the cumulative probabilities, the probability of a specific category occurring must be written as a difference between two adjacent cumulative probabilities such that

$$P(u = j|X) = P(u \leq j|X) - P(u \leq j - 1|X). \tag{7}$$

Later in our discussion readers will see that one of the ordinal IRT models, the Graded Response model, is built on very similar conceptual frameworks and assumptions in expressing the probabilities of examinees' specific response to test item.

To reiterate our brief introduction on LogR: The goal of LogR is to model the nonlinear probabilistic relationship between a categorical outcome variable and the explanatory variable(s). The logit form of the regression is assumed to be linear in its regression coefficients: intercept and slope, and can be classified as a generalized linear model. There are three major classes of LogR models: binary, ordinal and multinomial. The choice of which model to apply depends on the metric, nature, and number of the categorical outcome variable. For polytomous LogR models, J regression analyses are entailed for the $J + 1$ possible outcomes and the probability of an individual outcome can be obtained by direct or indirect specification. In addition to logit linear and conditional independence, the proportional odds ordinal LogR assumes equal slopes across the cumulative logits. These backbones of LogR foreshadow our discussions on IRT as a special form of LogR in the next section. Readers interested in LogR should consult Hosmer and Lemeshow (2000), Menard (2001), O'Connell (2006) or Peng et al. (2002) for more details.

DESCRIBING THE BRIDGE BETWEEN LOGR AND LOGISTIC IRT

Although IRT and LogR seem to share little in common on the surface, the embryo of using logistic regression groundwork in developing IRT can be traced back to Birnbaum (1968) and Rasch (1960). However, users of neither methods have explicitly described the affiliation between the two methods, and, consequently, there has been a lack of conceptual and organizational framework linking these two popular methods. In addition, we believe, that IRT is used less often in day-to-day research practice because it is often portrayed as a distinct method from what is widely known, such as LogR and regression modeling.

How is IRT connected to and distinct from LogR? In broad strokes, IRT and LogR are both branches of generalized linear models except that the explanatory variable in IRT is a *latent variable*, as opposed to an *observed variable* in LogR. For this reason, IRT is referred to as, to be more precise, a *generalized linear latent model*. Another major distinction, which is also related to the construction of the latent explanatory variable, is that IRT simultaneously model a number of categorical outcome variables. In LogR language, IRT runs multiple regression analyses at the same time. We will further explain these two distinctions in our subsequent discussions. However, at this point, it is more important to foreshadow that IRT is connected to LogR because they share the same framework and mechanism. These commonalities include the purpose, the assumptions, the shapes of the regression curve, the coding system, the specification of the probability, the estimation method, as well as the classification and choice of major IRT models explained hereafter.

IRT is defined as a model-based measurement theory that aims to specify a mathematical function relating the probability of an examinee's response on a test item to an underlying ability (van der Linden & Hambleton, 1996). Often, the choice of the mathematical functional form is a logistic curve. Namely, IRT uses a logistic curve to depict the nonlinear probabilistic relationship, Item Characteristic Curve (ICC, see Figure 16.1), between examinees' item response and their ability. Here, *ability*, often denoted as θ, is a generic term used in IRT literature to represent the underlying characteristic, construct, or trait being measured. Hence, in a regression sense, IRT intends to regress a categorical outcome variable, *item response*, onto the explanatory variable, the examinees' ability. In addition to the conditional independence assumption, the relationship between the logit-transformed item response and ability is assumed to be linear. In this sense, IRT uses the logistic function to model an item response and can be regarded as a type of generalized linear model.

However, note that what makes IRT distinct from a typical LogR is the nature of the explanatory variable. Normally, the explanatory variable in a LogR is an observed variable where data is obtained from the direct observation of the sampling units, whereas the explanatory variable in IRT, θ, is a *continuous latent variable*—an unobserved variable that must be created and estimated. This continuous latent variable θ, in short, is constructed by exploiting the *joint probability distributions* of the examinees' responses to a studied item and the rest of the test items. Therefore, when building an IRT regression model, one must simultaneously estimate the explanatory variable, which is the *person parameter* θ and the regression coefficients, which are the *item parameters*. As a side note, there exists an analogy between least squares regression and normal theory factor analysis. That is, one can simply conceive of factor analysis as multivariate ordinary least squares regressions with the latent continuous explanatory variable(s) (i.e., factor, also called the latent variable) being the predictor(s), which are created by accounting for the inter-correlations among the observed continuous variables. Despite these two major differences, the same principles of classification and choice of models apply to IRT. Binary IRT model is designed for binary item response. When item response is polytomous, nominal response IRT model is the choice if response categories are nominal, otherwise ordinal IRT model.

LOGISTIC IRT AS A SPECIAL CASE OF LOGR

Binary Logistic IRT

In this chapter, the notation used to describe IRT models will follow those of Embretson and Reise (2000). For the purpose of easy illustration, we will restrict the subsequent discussions of LogR and IRT to only one explanatory variable. Often, the number of sufficient item parameters assumed to aptly fit the data classifies IRT models (a.k.a., 1PL, 2PL and 3PL, etc.). In LogR language, the number of (item level) regression coefficients needed to accurately describe the relationship between examinees' ability and the item responses classifies IRT models. The binary logistic IRT model given below includes three parameters (i.e., 3PL) and is in the most general form,

$$P(u_i = 1 | \theta, \alpha_i, \beta_i, \gamma_i) = \gamma_i + (1 - \gamma_i)\frac{\exp[\alpha_1(\theta - \beta_1)]}{1 + \exp[\alpha_i(\theta - \beta_i)]}, \tag{8}$$

where

i = i^{th} item; 0, 1, ..., I
u_i = the item response of an examinee to item i (0 or 1)
θ = the ability level of an examinee

α_i = the discrimination (a.k.a., slope) for item i
β_i = the threshold (a.k.a., difficulty) for item i
γ_i = the lower asymptote (a.k.a., pseudo-chance) for item i.

Note that we have not indexed θ. Instead, we treat it as a random vector with dimension equal to the sample size N. Figure 16.1 shows the ICC for a hypothetical item with item parameters $\alpha = 1.5$, $\beta = 0.5$, and $\gamma=0.1$. One can see that the x-axis is the latent continuous ability θ scaled to a mean of 0 and standard deviation of 1. The probability of $u = 1$ shown on the y-axis given the item parameters is a function of examinees' θ. The discrimination parameter, α, is related to the slope at the point of inflection of the ICC indicating how precise or sensitive an item is in discriminating an examinee with high ability from one with low ability. The pseudo-chance parameter, γ, is located at the point on the y-axis with which the lower asymptote intersects. The pseudo-chance parameter indicates the chance of endorsing or getting an item right with no or little of the ability being measured (e.g., $\theta = -3$). The threshold parameter, β, is the value on the θ continuum with which the vertical line drawn from the inflection point intersects. The threshold value indicates how much ability examinees would need to have a $(1 + \gamma)/2$ chance of endorsing or getting an item right (i.e., 0.5 for 1PL and 2 PL models because $\gamma = 0$).

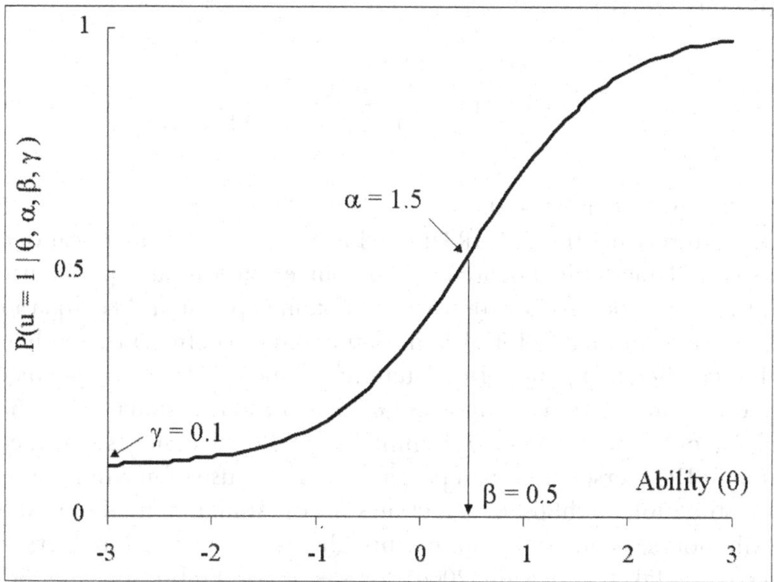

Figure 16.1. Item Characteristic Curve (ICC) for binary item response.

Note that the structure of Equation 8 looks very similar to that of the simple binary LogR given in Equation 1, the only difference is that the IRT model is more elaborate in two ways: First, a latent variable θ is involved, and second, a larger number of coefficients (i.e., item parameters) are specified. The term "$(\theta - \beta_i)$" represents the discrepancy between how much ability an examinee possesses and how much ability an examinee should possess to have a $(1 + \gamma_i)/2$ chance of endorsing or getting item i right (i.e., item threshold). Hence, one can understand Equation 8 as "regressing the probability of getting an item right onto the term $(\theta - \beta_i)$."

One can easily construct the 1PL and 2PL IRT models by removing the unnecessary parameters in Equation 8. To show the connection between LogR and IRT, a 2PL model for item i is shown below by removing the γ_i parameter,

$$P(u = 1|\theta, \alpha, \beta) = \frac{\exp[\alpha(\theta - \beta)]}{1 + \exp[\alpha(\theta - \beta)]}. \tag{9}$$

In Equation 9, if we treat $(\theta - \beta)$ as our explanatory variable by relabeling it with X and add a zero intercept term, c, we get a variation of the basic LogR Equation 1,

$$P(u = 1|X) = \frac{\exp[c + \alpha X]}{1 + \exp[c + \alpha X]}, \tag{10}$$

where $X = (\theta - \beta)$, and $c = 0$.

One can see that the 2PL IRT model in Equation 10 is identical to the binary LogR model in Equation 1. Of course one can also perform the logit transformation to Equation 10 and obtain expressions like Equations 2 and 3 and show that 2PL IRT logit is linear in its coefficients, and hence can be classified as a generalized latent linear model. These simple mathematical manipulations demonstrate that unidimensional IRT (i.e., involving only one θ) indeed is a simple LogR model. Same as LogR, estimation of IRT person and item parameters makes use of maximum likelihood estimation methods, or sometimes Bayes estimation methods, which we will not explain in detail in this chapter. Interested readers are referred to Baker and Kim (2004) for details or Embretson and Reise (2000) and Hambleton, Swaminathan, and Rogers (1991) for a concise introduction.

In summary, IRT uses LogR function to characterize the nonlinear relationship between the probability of a categorical item response and a continuous latent variable θ by estimating the necessary item parameters. Given that IRT is a type of LogR, one way of classifying the IRT models is to follow Table 16.1, which is organized by the number of response categories. Focusing on column three of Table 16.1 one is able to map our subsequent discussions on the commonly used polytomous IRT models.

POLYTOMOUS LOGISTIC IRT

Apparent in the labeling, polytomous IRT models refer to modeling item responses that take up three or more categories. Following our earlier classification of LogR in Table 16.1, there are two divisions of polytomous IRT models classified by the metric nature of the item response: ordinal or nominal. However, to better understand our discussion of the two divisions of polytomous IRT models, we need to preface our discussion by looking at the similarities with and differences between binary and polytomous IRT models and some common features of the various polytomous IRT models.

Same as binary LogR, binary IRT models require only one regression analysis, $P(u = 1)$, to describe the probabilistic relationship. This is because the probability of the only other outcome, $P(u = 0)$, is simply equal to $1 - P(u = 1)$ as in Figure 16.1. In fact, in the logit form of the regression equation as in Equation 2 and 3, it is written as the ratio of $P(u = 1)$ to $P(u = 0)$ to uniformly express the linear relationship. However, for the same reason as we discussed on polytomous LogR, polytomous IRT models involve multiple response categories. Consequently, one has to model multiple relationships for each item. In other words, for each item in a test, a series of multiple Category Characteristic Curves (CCCs) will be modeled (Dodd, 1984). Modeling multiple relationships is often done by some kind of contrasting among the response categories as we discussed in LogR: the maximum code and the number of analyses entailed are equal to J for the $J + 1$ categories when the lowest category is coded as 0. In other words, within each item, it takes J steps (i.e., thresholds) for an examinee to stride from the lowest response category, 0, to the highest, J. Note that the number of response categories does not have to be equal across items. Another important notion is needed to prime our polytomous IRT discussions. For polytomous IRT models, there is a hierarchical structure of parameters involved. *At the test level,* a polytomous IRT will simultaneously model a number of items and their corresponding item parameters may or may not vary across items. *At the item level,* in the meantime, a polytomous IRT will simultaneously model a number of response categories within each item, and their corresponding parameters may or may not vary across categories.

In sum, historically, a variety of polytomous IRT models were developed to appropriately describe the multiple probabilistic relationships varying in these regards: (1) the metric nature of the item response, (2) the methods of contrasting among the $J + 1$ multiple response categories, (3) within an item, how the parameters are assumed across response categories, and (4) within a test, how the parameters are assumed across items. The first three points are analogous to LogR whereas the last point is unique to IRT. Obviously, modeling polytomous IRT is far more complex than the binary models. What are the justifications and payoffs for choosing the more complex polytomous models over the binary models? Ostini and Nering (2005) and van der Ark (2001) listed three major reasons for preference for polytomous items over binary items. First, polytomous responses provide more precise information than binary responses. As a result, fewer items are typically needed to achieve the same degree of reliability. Second, some psychological constructs are often measured on rating scales. Last, certain kinds of item responses (i.e., those that are naturally ordered) are better characterized on an ordinal scale. For these reasons, polytomous IRT is believed to be a statistically more malleable and practically useful for polytomous responses. However, because of its statistical complexities in applications and interpretations, polytomous IRT models are less often discussed than they should have been. Therefore, by using the conceptual framework of LogR, we hope our discussions will disentangle the complexities and elucidate understanding of the polytomous IRT models. Before proceeding, therefore, readers may wish to review the aforementioned similarities and distinctions between LogR and IRT as in Table 16.2, which is a summary of the above description.

The following remarks provide an overview of four commonly applied polytomous IRT models: three IRT models for ordinal responses and one IRT model for nominal responses. Readers are directed to de Ayala (1993), Embretson and Reise (2000), Ostini and Nering (2005), van der Ark (2001), or Van der Linden & Hambleton (1996) for more technical details and alternative models. Also, acknowledging the inconsistency and complexity in the notation and terminology used in the polytomous IRT literature, we attempt to synthesize the discrepancies in the terminology and minimize the number of necessary notations needed to express across various polytomous IRT models. For this notation system to work, the coding of polytomous response categories should follow the coding system we mentioned throughout our earlier discussions.

Table 16.2. Similarities and Distinctions Between LogR and Logistic IRT

Similarities	*LogR*	*IRT*
Purpose	Modeling categorical outcome variable	Modeling categorical item response
Model assumption	Conditional independence Logit linear	Conditional independence Logit linear (1PL, 2PL)
Outcome category coding	0, 1, …, J for $J + 1$ categories	0, 1, …, J for $J + 1$ categories
Probability modeling	Direct or indirect	Direct or indirect
Regression function	Logistic	Logistic
Estimation method	Maximum likelihood	Maximum likelihood (or Bayes)
Classification	Binary, ordinal, nominal	Binary, ordinal, nominal
Distinctions	*LogR*	*IRT*
Explanatory variable	Observed categorical or continuous	Latent continuous
Number of outcome variables	Modeling one outcome variable at a time	Modeling multivariate items simultaneously
Parameter assumption	Only across response category assumption	Both across item and across response category assumptions

ORDINAL ITEM RESPONSE

Partial Credit Model (PC)

Self-evident in the labeling, the 1PL partial credit model was originally developed by Masters (1982) to model partial credits assigned to examinees, who respond to test items involving multiple steps. For example, an item may instruct examinees to resolve the height of a triangle as the first step and then resolve the area of the triangle as the second step. One partial credit will be assigned to an examinee who only correctly solves the first step; two full credits will be assigned to an examinee who correctly solves both steps; and no credit will be assigned if an examinee does not successfully solve the first step given that one is unlikely to successfully solve the second step without correctly solving the first. Using our coding system, each examinee will receive a score, $u = 0, 1,$ or 2. The maximum value J and the number of logistic regression analyses entailed are equal to 2 for the $J + 1 = 3$ response categories. In PC models, the probabilistic relation is specified as a *direct* IRT model like the multinomial LogR. As described in LogR introduction, the probability of getting a particular credit (i.e., category) is written directly as an exponential divided by the sum of all the exponentials that can possibly appear in the numerator (Embretson & Reise, 2000, p. 105) as below:

$$P_{ij}(\theta) = \frac{\exp\left[\sum_{j=0}^{u_i} (\theta - \beta_{ij})\right]}{\sum_{j=0}^{J}\left[\exp \sum_{j=0}^{J} (\theta - \beta_{ij})\right]}, \tag{11}$$

$\sum(\theta - \beta_{ij}) = 0$ when $u_i = 0$, $P_{ij}(\theta)$ = the probability of $u = j$ for item i given θ.

An example will make Equation 11 more accessible. If the ith item is scored on a scale of 0, 1, 2, and 3, the probability of $u = 2, J = 3$ would have a numerator of $\text{Exp}[(\theta - \beta_0) + (\theta - \beta_1) + (\theta - \beta_2)]$ and a denominator of $\text{Exp}[(\theta - \beta_0)] + \text{Exp}[(\theta - \beta_0) + (\theta - \beta_1)] + \text{Exp}[(\theta - \beta_0) + (\theta - \beta_1) + (\theta - \beta_2)] + \text{Exp}[(\theta - \beta_0) + (\theta - \beta_1) + (\theta - \beta_2) + (\theta - \beta_3)]$. In words, for item i, the numerator is the exponential of the cumulative $(\theta - \beta_j)$ up to $j = u$, and the denominator is always the same, which is the sum of all the possible numerators. As one can see in Equation 11, PC models assume that only the step parameters β_{ij} (i.e., threshold) is needed to specify the probabilistic relationship between the multiple response categories and θ, and are interpreted as thresholds for transition from one category to the next. The step parameters are located at the intersection points between two adjacent CCCs indicating where on the θ continuum the response of one category becomes relatively more likely than the previous category (see Figure 16.2). Readers should be cautious not to interpret step parameters as the point on the θ continuum where an examinee has a 50% of responding above a category threshold. Using the example of the area of a triangle, the PC model requires that the steps within an item be completed in sequence, although the steps need not be equally difficult, nor be ordered by the levels of difficulty. When the step difficulties are not ordered (see the example in Embretson & Reise, 2000, p. 109), a *reversal* is said to exist (Dodd & Koch, 1987). In PC models, the slopes (i.e., the discrimination) for the CCCs across the response categories are assumed to be equal and fixed at 1, hence drop out of Equation 11. De Ayala (1993) showed that the Rasch model (binary, 1PL, $\alpha_i = 1$) is simply a special case of the PC model with two response categories. Like the Rasch model, packaged with the equal discrimination assumption, PC models have the advantage of using the total score as a sufficient statistic for estimating examinees' θ score. Because only the β_{ij} parameter is estimated, the sample size required to obtain quality item and category parameters is smaller than the 2PL polytomous IRT models discussed later. However, the assumption of equal slopes (i.e.m discrimination) across items and category parameters, at the same time, restricts the use of PC models in practice. For this reason, Muraki (1992, 1993) proposed the Generalized Partial Credit model (GPC) where item discrimination parameters are allowed to vary across items.

To illustrate a PC model, we used the item parameters of Table 5.5 in Embretson and Reise (2000, p. 108). The item parameters were estimated based on 350 undergraduate students who responded to the 12 items on the neuroticism scale of the Neuroticism Extroversion Openness Five-Factor Inventory (NEO-FFI) (Costa & McCrae, 1992). These items were scored on a 0 to 4 scale (0 = *strongly disagree*; 1 = *disagree*; 2 = *neutral*; 3 = *agree*; 4 = *strongly agree*). Figure 16.2 shows the CCCs and the four threshold parameters for item two: "I feel inferior to others." Note that the threshold parameter β_1 between item categories 0 and 1 is the intersection of the two CCCs and is located at the point –1.763 on the θ continuum. In addition, the four thresholds divide the θ continuum into five intervals and each interval encompasses the θ range where a specific response category is more likely. For example, if a respondent has a θ value between –1.673 and 0.080, as shown in Figure 16.2, he or she will be estimated to endorse "1" more likely than other response categories.

Rating Scale Model (RS)

Extended from the PC models, Andrich (1978a, 1978b) proposed a 1PL polytomous IRT model to accommodate the rating scale type of responses. In performance or achievement tests, it is logical that a test item requires multiple steps for completion, and the step difficulty would differ across steps and across items. However, it is reasonable to assume that the threshold values would remain very similar across items for an attitude rating scale with common anchors such as 0 = strongly disagree, 1 = disagree, 2 = neutral, 3 = agree, and 4 = strongly agree. Namely, a set of ordered *J*-step parameters (i.e., category thresholds) is well suited for all items in a measure. For this reason, a step threshold β_{ij} in the RS model is decomposed into two parts, β_i and δ_j, where $\beta_{ij} = \beta_i + \delta_j$. For each item, there is one β_i threshold parameter that is allowed to vary across items. The set of δ_js are the category level parameters and are fixed to be the same for all items in a test. If one substitutes $\beta_i + \delta_j$ for β_{ij} in Equation 11 for the PC model, one would get the expression as below:

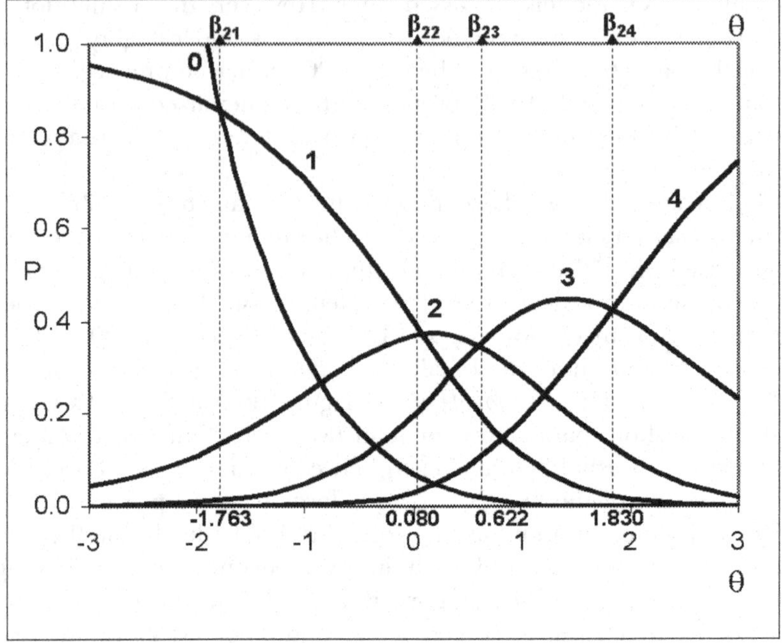

Figure 16.2. Category Characteristic Curves for the PC Model.

$$P_{ij}(\theta) = \frac{\exp\left[\sum_{j=0}^{u_i} [\theta - (\beta_i + \delta_j)]\right]}{\sum_{j=0}^{J}\left[\exp \sum_{j=0}^{J} [\theta - (\beta_i + \delta_j)]\right]}, \tag{12}$$

where $\sum[\theta - (\beta_i + \delta_j)] = 0$ when $u_i = 0$.

The interpretation for the parameters β_{ij} is the same as that of the PC model; They are thresholds for transition from one category to the next and are located at the intersection points between two adjacent CCCs, indicating where on the θ continuum the response of one category becomes relatively more likely than the previous category. Figure 16.3 illustrates the CCCs for a RS model using our earlier example item 2. We see that, for item two, β_2 = 0.300, and the set of δs are: δ_1 = −1.600; δ_2 = 0.224; δ_3 = −0.184; δ_4 = 1.560. This set of four δs was estimated and fixed for all the items in the scale despite that item threshold parameters, β_i, are free to vary across items such as 0.300 estimated for our example item 2. Using $\beta_{ij} = \beta_i + \delta_j$, we yield threshold values for item two: $\beta_{21} = -1.300$; $\beta_{22} = 0.524$; $\beta_{23} = 0.116$; $\beta_{24} = 1.860$. One can see that the RS model is more restricted than the PC model because it assumes the set of category thresholds is equal across items in addition to equal discrimination assumption in the PC model.

As with the PC model, the conditional probability of endorsing a particular point on the rating scale can be obtained through direct operation specified in Equation 12. The RS and PC models share the same advantages and drawbacks because they are both 1PL models assuming item and category discrimination parameters to be "1." One additional limitation of the RS model is that it is not suitable for test items with different response formats. However, for the same reason, the RS model has the advantage of being more parsimonious because it entails even fewer parameter estimates than the PC model. Another advantage is that this set of identical categorical threshold estimates could provide some information on the psychological distances between the scale points for the underlying construct being measured.

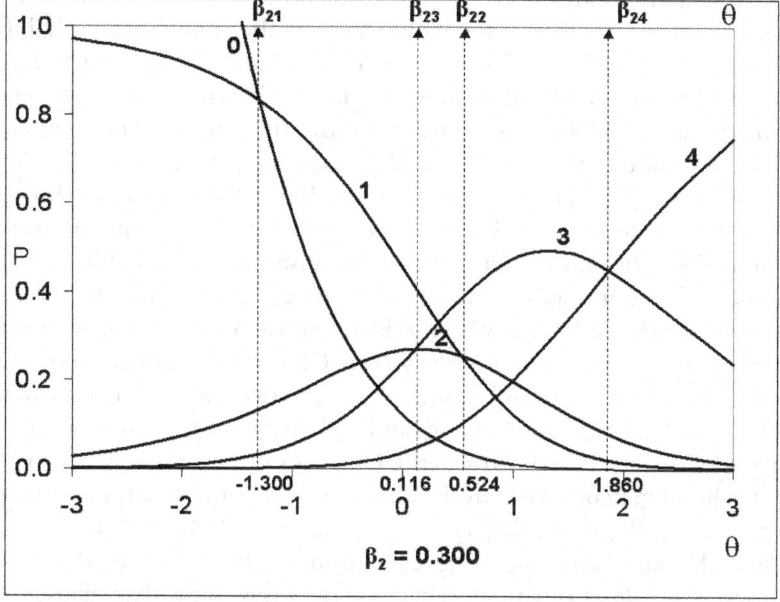

Figure 16.3. The Category Characteristic Curve for the RS model.

Graded Response Model (GR)

Samejima (1969, 1996) developed the 2PL GR models for ordered categorical response. In the GR model, the response categories are contrasted with J dichotomies such that responding in $u_i < j$ is contrasted with $u_i \geq j$. For instance, an item with 5 score points, 0, 1, 2, 3, and 4, would have four contrasting dichotomies as: (1) 0 versus 1, 2, 3, and 4; (2) 0 and 1 versus 2, 3, and 4; (3) 0, 1, and 2, versus 3 and 4; (4) 0, 1, 2, and 3, versus 4. Consequently, the GR model specifies the probability in terms of responding in u_i or higher ($u_i \geq j$) in relation to θ scores. In other words, for each of the J dichotomies, a probabilistic relationship will be modeled. Embretson and Reise (2000) referred to the J curves as Operating Characteristic Curves (OCCs) and can be written as,

$$P(u \geq j|\theta) = \frac{\exp[\alpha_i(\theta - \beta_{ij})]}{1 + \exp[\alpha_i(\theta - \beta_{ij})]}, \qquad j = 0, \ldots, J, \tag{13}$$

where $P(u \geq j|\theta)$ is the probability of responding in a particular category score j or higher on item i. Hence, the probability of responding in the lowest category or higher, $P_{i0}(\theta)$, is equal to 1. Note that the contrasting and probability modeled are opposite to those of LogR we introduced earlier where $u \leq j$ is contrasted with $u > j$ and the cumulative probability of $P(u \leq j|X)$ is modeled. However, the logic for contrasting the $J + 1$ outcomes using J cumulative dichotomies remains the same. The β_{ij} parameter in the GR model is the threshold indicating the θ level needed to make a response that is equal to and greater than the threshold j with a 50% probability for item i (see Figure 16.4). In the GR model, the discrimination parameters α_i are always allowed to differ across items. However, the slopes may or may not vary across response categories within an item. When α_i is constant across the response categories, it is referred to as a *homogeneous* GR model and when α_i is not constant across response categories, it is referred to as a *heterogeneous* GR model. Homogeneous GR models are more commonly applied in practice and are conceptually equivalent to the cumulative logit LogR, where the slopes are assumed to be parallel. Figure 16.4 illustrates the OCCs for our example item 2 based on the homogeneous GR Model. The corresponding parameters are: $\alpha_2 = 1.42$ and $\beta_{21} = -2.07$; $\beta_{22} = -0.22$; $\beta_{23} = 0.93$; $\beta_{24} = 2.42$.

As in the cumulative logit LogR for ordinal outcomes, the GR models are viewed as *indirect* IRT models because the probability of an examinee's response to a particular category $P_{i(jth)}(\theta)$, hence the CCC, is obtained by,

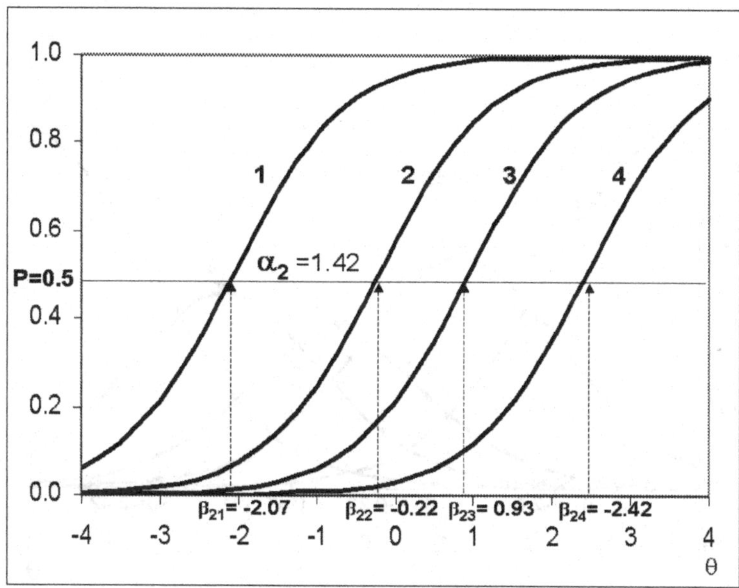

Figure 16.4. Operating Characteristic Curves for the graded response model.

$$P_{i(jth)}(\theta) = P_{ij}(\theta) - P_{i(j+1)}(\theta). \tag{14}$$

For example, the probability of endorsing category 2 would be: $P_{2nd}(\theta) = P_2(\theta) - P_3(\theta)$. In this sense, the GR model is also referred to as a "*difference*" model (Embretson & Reise, 2000; Thissen & Steinberg, 1986). Note that the homogeneous GR model is analogous to the equal slopes model in ordinal LogR in terms of (a) equal slopes assumption across response categories and (b) indirect specification of the probability. Figure 16.5 illustrates the CCCs for our example item 2. Note that the middle point of two adjacent threshold parameters β_{ij} and $\beta_{i(j+1)}$ in the CCCs depicts the point on the θ continuum where the probability of *j*th category peaks on the CCCs. One can see that the CCC for category1 peaks at the midpoint of β_{21} and β_{22}, and is equal to $\frac{(-2.07)+(-0.22)}{2} = -1.145$, which indicates the θ level needed to have the maximum probability of endorsing category 1 (i.e., disagree).

Readers may have noticed that, all the three ordinal IRT models we have introduced assume equal slopes across response categories. However, the GR model differs from the PC and RS models in three aspects: (1) PC and RS model fix the values of the category slopes to be 1, whereas

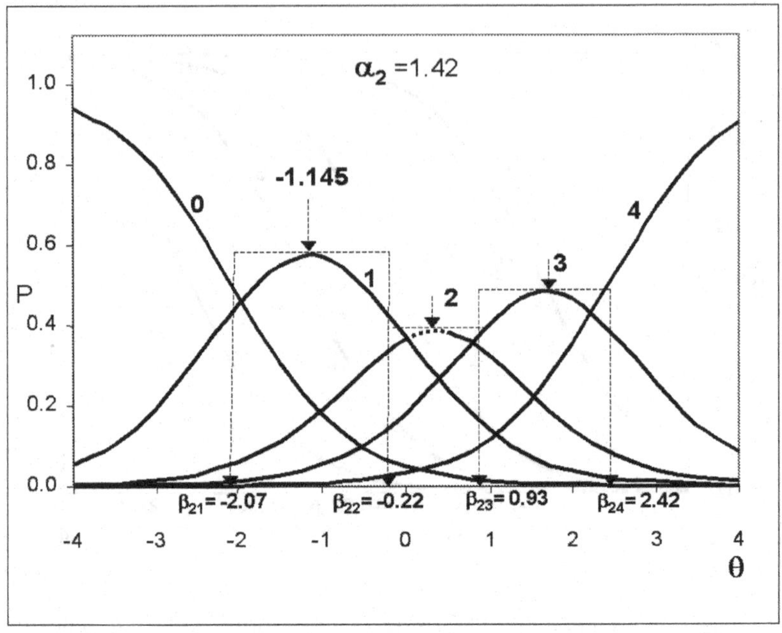

Figure 16.5. Category Characteristic Curve for the GR model.

the GR model allows the category slopes to be estimated or fixed at values other than 1 within each item, (2) the discrimination parameters are allowed to differ across items such as our example item 2 being estimated at 1.42, (3) items within a test need not have the same number of response categories like the RS model (i.e., J does not have to the same for all items), and (4) the β_{ij} in a GR model are always ordered such that $\beta_{(j+1)} > \beta_j$.

De Ayala (1993) showed that 2PL binary IRT models are simply a special case of GR models with two response categories. One of the advantages of the GR model is that the item discrimination parameters, unlike PC, GPC, and RS models, are allowed to vary across items. This advantage is welcomed by a set of test items that are likely to have differential discrimination power as in the attitude or personality measures. In addition, the GR model has the flexibility to accommodate test items with different response formats. Notice that a modified graded response model was developed by Muraki (1990, 1992) to model a Likert-type response format where the items are of the same number of response categories. One of the drawbacks of the GR model is the indirect calculation of the CCCs.

NOMINAL ITEM RESPONSE

Nominal Response Model (NR)

Bock (1972) proposed a 2PL polytomous IRT model characterizing item responses that were on a nominal scale. His initial intention was to model the alternatives in multiple-choice items. Conventionally, multiple-choice items are scored into a dichotomization of correct or incorrect and modeled accordingly. The NR model argued that the information provided by examinees' wrong responses by choosing a certain distracter is not all the same and should not be treated uniformly as "incorrect." Modeling an item's incorrect response to distracters may provide more information about an examinee's level of ability. The NR model is a direct probability model and can be written as:

$$P_{ij}(\theta) = \frac{\exp(c_{ij} + \alpha_{ij}\theta)}{\sum_{j=0}^{J} \exp(c_{ij} + \alpha_{ij}\theta)}, \tag{15}$$

where $\sum \alpha_{ij} = \sum c_{ij} = 0$ or $\alpha_{i0} = c_{i0} = 0$.

The α_{ij} parameters are interpreted the same way as the discrimination parameters in the ordinal IRT, and c_{ij} are the intercept parameters of the nonlinear response function associated with jth category of item i. Specifically, c and α are the intercept and the slope, respectively, for the linear regression in the logit form. Readers should be cautious not to interpret the c parameter in the same manner as one would interpret the γ parameter in the 3PL binary model, which actually indicates the pseudo-chance parameter of an item. For each item, as usual, there are J threshold parameters (a.k.a., location parameter in the logit linear literature) that are often assumed to be unordered, although there are occasions where data indicates that they are, in fact, ordered. Because Equation 15 is invariant with respect to translation of the logit, the constraint on $\sum \alpha_{ij} = \sum c_{ij} = 0$ or $\alpha_{i0} = c_{i0} = 0$ is needed as an anchor to solve the identification problem. One can see that the expression and identification restriction in Equation 15 are almost identical to that in Equation 4 for multinomial LogR except that IRT is subscribed by "i" indicating that "I" items are simultaneously modeled. De Ayala (1992) showed that the threshold parameters could be obtained by,

$$\beta_{ij} = \frac{c_{(j-1)} - c_j}{\alpha_j - \alpha_{(j-1)}}. \tag{16}$$

The β_{ij} parameters are analogous to the step difficulty of the PC model and are located at the intersection of adjacent CCCs. In fact, all the divide-by-total or direct methods (e.g., PC model and RS model) can be shown to be special cases of the nominal response model (Embreston & Reise, 2000; Thissen & Steinberg, 1986). The NR model is the most general specification of polytomous IRT models. This means that it has the least assumptions made about the number of item and category parameters as well as the order of the category thresholds. Namely, both the threshold and discrimination parameters are free to vary across items and across categories except for the identification restrictions. Like other polytomous IRT models, the NR model can also be applied to binary item response. To illustrate, we borrowed the example of Tatsuoka (1983) in de Ayala (1993): a multiple-choice item with three options (i.e., two distracters). Using our notation system, J equals to 2, where the first option was coded as "0," second as "1," and third as "2." The J is also the maximum code indicating that there are $J + 1 = 3$ options. This item is a mathematics addition problem asking "–6 – 10 = ?" with three alternatives: (a) –16, (b) –4, and (c) 4. Figure 16.6 shows the values for α were $\alpha_0 = -0.75$, $\alpha_1 = -0.25$, and $\alpha_2 = 1.0$ and, although not shown, the values for c were $c_0 = -1.5$; $c_1 = -0.25$; $c_2 = 1.75$. Using Equation 16, we yielded $\beta_1 = -2.5$ and $\beta_2 = -1.6$. The advantage of the NR model is that it is the most flexible model for the different types of item responses. Its limitation, for the same reason, is that it is less parsimonious to specific types of item responses.

SUMMARY

A brief introduction to LogR was given in terms of the purpose, assumptions, functional forms, when to use which LogR models, and its nature as a generalized linear model. Building on this introduction, we showed that IRT is a special form of LogR with the explanatory variable being a continuous latent variable constructed by accounting for the joint distributions among the test items. In IRT, the probabilistic relationship between examinees' responses to an item and their latent ability estimates is described by a nonlinear logistic function characterized by the item parameters. In addition to binary IRT, two branches of polytomous IRT models were described: ordinal and nominal. For ordinal item responses, the Partial Credit model, the Rating Scale model, and the Graded Response model were described. These models differ in the manner of

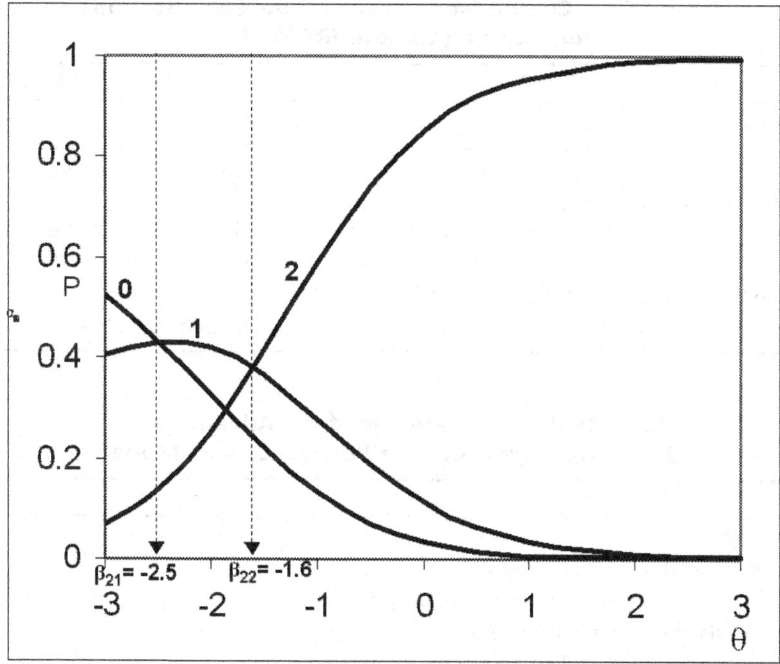

Figure 16.6. Category Characteristic Curves for the nominal response model.

how item and category parameters are constructed and how the probability is modeled. Table 16.3 summarizes the features of the four polytomous IRT models discussed in this chapter and Table 16.4 compares their advantages and disadvantages.

Closing Remarks and Filling in the Portrait of IRT From a LogR Perspective

Although we have focused on the connection between LogR and IRT, it is important to note that there is one important difference between these two methodologies. That is, because the predictor variable is a latent variable logistic IRT models, as compared to LogR, require a large sample size to achieve unbiased person and item parameter estimates. In addition, a large number of items are also needed to guarantee unbiased person parameter estimation and small sample-to-sample variation in theta estimates. An insufficient number of examinees or items will lead to an inappropriate specification of the statistical relationship. In the case of

Table 16.3. Comparisons of the Model Specifications for Four Polytomous IRT Models

Model	*PC (1PL)*	*RS (1PL)*	*GR (2PL)*	*NR (2PL)*
Across items				
α	Fixed at 1	Fixed at 1	Free	Free
β	Free	Free	Free	Free
Within an item				
α	Fixed at 1	Fixed at 1	Fixed / Free	Free
β	Free	Free, Equal across items	Free & Ordered	Free
Contrasting coding	j vs. all	j vs. all	$u \geq j$ vs. $u < j$	j vs. all
Probability modeling	Direct	Direct	Indirect	Direct

Table 16.4. Comparisons of the Advantages and Disadvantages for Four Polytomous IRT Models

Models	*PC*	*RS*	*GR*	*NR*
Advantages				
Total score is sufficient for ability estimates	✓	✓		
Requiring (relatively) smaller sample size than 2PL models	✓	✓		
Accommodating tests with different response formats	✓		✓	✓
Providing the psychological distance of the measured construct		✓		
Item discrimination is allowed to vary			✓	✓
Flexibility to all types of item responses				✓
Disadvantages				
Equal discrimination restricts use in practice	✓	✓		
Requiring (relatively) larger sample size than 1PL models			✓	✓
Not suitable for test items with different response formats		✓		
Indirect specification of probability			✓	
Less parsimonious to specific types of items responses				✓

small sample sizes and short tests or scales, practitioners should consider using nonparametric IRT models in which no prespecified functional form, such as LogR, would be imposed to describe the relationship between the item response and the ability score (see, e.g., Sijtsma & Molenaar, 2002).

The parametric logistic IRT framework described herein should be increasingly utilized in day-to-day measurement research and data analysis in the health, social, and behavioral sciences because of its versatility and practicality in solving many problems in measurement and testing such as measurement bias, item parameter drift, test score equating, and computer adaptive testing (Embreston & Reises, 2000; Hambleton et al.,

1991). These advantages of IRT models, especially when compared to classical test theory, reside in the fundamental premise that IRT measurement models generate item-independent person parameters and person-independent item parameters. However, these advantages are not guaranteed by simply fitting an IRT model to the response data. Rather, they are subject to the empirical assessment of parameter invariance of the specified model (Hambleton et al., 1991; Rupp & Zumbo, 2004), a cornerstone principle, yet often misunderstood element of IRT.

At this point, it is appropriate to say a few words about invariance in IRT models and its implications for IRT practice in terms of item bias, item drift, computer adaptive testing, and equating/linking of test versions or forms. Invariance is a population property dictating that the values of the parameters of a statistical model are identical across the subpopulations or the test conditions for which the test items are designed. Parameter invariance is often construed in applications and the applied literature as a magical yet mythical property; however, in fact, it is a universal phenomenon of all model based regression-like analyses such as least square regression, logistic regression, structural equation modeling, and IRT models (Breithaupt & Zumbo, 2002; Zimmerman & Zumbo, 2001; Zumbo & Rupp, 2004). Simply put, if a model is correctly specified (i.e., the regression function is correct for the population), then the regression parameters are invariant across the subpopulations or test conditions. IRT parameter invariance, hence, cannot be explicitly tested because it is a theoretical property in the population. At best, it may be indirectly and empirically tested by the model-data fit and by examining whether the parameters remain invariant across different calibration samples after the parameters are put on the same metric. In other words, IRT person parameter invariance and item parameter invariance hold if the set of parameters calibrated on one data is the linear transformation of those calibrated on the other (Rupp & Zumbo, 2003, 2004, in press). This exercise of linear transformation is necessary because the metrics of the IRT person and item parameters are often set arbitrarily from calibration to calibration. Note that the latent predictor, θ, is constructed from the joint distribution of the items in a scale and hence has no inherent mean or variance (i.e., metric).

Therefore, the versatile IRT day-to-day applications will succeed only if the model fits the data well and parameter invariance hold true. Following the same premise, IRT based investigation of differential item functioning, in essence, can be regarded as a statistical method for detecting item bias through the examination of lack of invariance where item parameters are variant across subpopulations such as gender or ethnic groups. The same logic applies to the investigation of item parameter drift where the initial parameters of items in an item pool show drift in a later calibration after prolonged use. Also, because of the item-independent person parameter property, a result of IRT parameter invariance, computer adaptive testing is able to assign unbiased ability scores to examinees regardless of what items in the item pool are administered to the examinees. When used to equate test scores, IRT naturally overcomes the problems of incomparability in scores of examinees taking different tests. If an IRT model fits the data well, examinees' ability scores are made directly comparable by the item-independent invariance property.

The invariance property is of less importance in LogR, even though the same premise still holds. This is because most researchers utilize LogR primarily for the explanatory purpose of statistically testing whether a set of predictors contributes to the explanation of the variation in the outcome variable. Thus, one is more concerned about whether the proportion of deviation (i.e., −2 log likelihood) explained away by the chosen predictors is just a result of sampling capitalization, rather than whether the specified model is correct in the population. In other words, LogR modellers make fewer demands on the perfect model-data fit and do not expect the model to explain away all the variation in the outcome variable; a close enough approximation of the population model would suffice. In contrast, conventional IRT is utilized as a measurement model that adopts a "model fitting" perspective which dictates that a single latent ability variable, theta, is the sole drive for people's responses and should be sufficient to account for nearly all the variation in people's responses and hence the model is expected to fit the data nearly perfectly so that the beneficial applications of IRT parameter invariance will succeed. Currently, IRT modellers have moved ahead from the simple conventional IRT models to more expanded models. For example, whether it be binary or polytomous, multidimensional IRT models (i.e., more than one single latent ability variables) have been developed to more aptly describe examinees' item responses (see, e.g., Ackerman, 1992; Embreston & Reise, 2000, p. 82). Also latent class (i.e., discrete grouping variable) IRT models have been developed where examinees are assigned to latent classes that serve as the explanatory variable for the item responses.

Finally, we believe that the future of IRT, in many ways, will move from the traditional "response fitting" measurement approach to a more explanatory approach. For example, this could be done by framing the IRT models under the generalized linear and nonlinear mixed effects models, a model with random coefficients in which the fixed and/or random effects enter the model nonlinearly (e.g., Rijmen, Tuerlinckx, de Boeck, & Kuppens, 2003) where items are nested within the examinees and one or more latent ability variables are treated as random effects, and multiple examinee-level predictors can now be incorporated into the extended model. Also the beneficial property of IRT parameter invariance follows naturally under this generalized linear and nonlinear mixed effects framework: the specified IRT model, within transformation, is the same model (i.e., item parameters are fixed) at various levels of the random variable, theta, when the model fits the data. In moving toward a more "explanatory" modeling strategy, measurement and psychometrics are becoming more than just a descriptive or normative process but rather one that tells the researcher why and how item responses arise. This is a relatively new avenue in IRT (De Boeck & Wilson, 2004; Lu, Thomas, & Zumbo, 2005) and more generally to a new perspective on validity and the practice of validation in measurement (Zumbo, 2005).

ACKNOWLEDGEMENT

We would like to thank Zhen Li and Siok Leng Ng for helpful and detailed comments on an earlier draft of this manuscript.

NOTE

1. Please note that exp(x) is the same function as e^x, where e is about 2.718.

REFERENCES

Ackerman, T. A. (1992). A didaction explanation of item bias, item impact, and item validity from a multidimensional perspective. *Journal of Educational Measurement, 29,* 67-91.

Agretsi, A. (2002). *Categorical data analysis*. New York: Wiley.

Andrich, D. (1978a). Application of a psychometric model to ordered categories which are scored with successive integers. *Applied Psychological Measurement, 2,* 581-94.

Andrich, D. (1978b). A rating formulation for ordered response categories. *Psychometrika, 43,* 561-73.

Baker, F. B., & Kim, S. (2004). *Item response theory: Parameter estimation techniques*. New York: Marcel Decker.

Birnbaum, A. (1968). Some latent trait models and their use in inferring an examinee's ability. In F. M. Lord & M. R. Novick (Eds.), *Statistical theories of mental test scores* (pp. 397-479). Reading, MA: Addison-Wesley.

Bock, R. D. (1972). Estimating item parameters and latent ability when responses are scored in two or more nominal categories. *Psychometrika, 37,* 29-51.

Breithaupt, K., & Zumbo, B. D. (2002). Sample invariance of the structural equation model and the item response model: a case study. *Structural Equation Modeling, 9,* 390-412.

Costa, P. T., & McCrae, R. R. (1992). *The revised NEO personality inventory (NEO-PI-R) and NEO five-factor inventory (NEO-FFI) professional manual*. Odessa, FL: Psychological Assessment Resources.

De Ayala, R. J. (1992). The nominal response model in computerized adaptive testing. *Applied Psychological Measurement, 16*, 327-43.

De Ayala, R. J. (1993). An introduction to polytomous item response theory models. *Measurement and Evaluation in Counselling and Development, 25*, 172-189.

De Boeck, P., & Wilson, M. (2004). *Explanatory item response models: A generalized linear and nonlinear approach*. New York: Springer.

Dodd, B. G. (1984). Attitude scaling: A comparison of the graded response and partial credit latent trait models. (Doctoral dissertation, University of Texas at Austin, 1984). *Dissertation Abstract International, 45*, 2074A.

Dodd, B. G., & Koch, W. R. (1987). Effects of variations in item step values on item and test information in the partial credit model. *Applied Psychological Measurement, 11*, 371-84.

Embretson, S. E., & Reise, S. P. (2000). *Item response theory for psychologists*. Mahwah, NJ: Erlbaum.

Hambleton, R. K., Swaminathan, H., & Rogers, H. J. (1991). *Fundamentals of item response theory*. Newbury Park, CA: Sage

Hosmer, D. W., & Lemeshow, S. (2000). *Applied logistic regression* (2nd ed.). New York: Wiley.

Lu, I. R. R., Thomas, D. R., & Zumbo, B. D. (2005). Embedding IRT in structural equation models: A comparison with regression based on IRT scores. *Structural Equation Modeling, 12*, 263-277.

Masters, G. N. (1982). A Rasch model for partial credit scoring. *Psychometrika, 47*, 149-174.

Menard, S. (2001). *Applied logistic regression analysis* (2nd ed.). Newbury Park, CA: Sage.

Muraki, E. (1990). Fitting a polytomous item response model to Likert-type data. *Applied Psychological Measurement, 14*, 59-71.

Muraki, E. (1992). A generalized partial credit model: Application of an EM algorithm. *Applied Psychological Measurement, 16*, 159-176.

Muraki, E. (1993). Information functions of the generalized partial credit model. *Applied Psychological measurement, 17*, 351-363.

O'Connell, A. A. (2006). *Logistic regression models for ordinal response variables*. Thousand Oaks, CA: Sage.

Ostini, R., & Nering, M. L. (2005). *Polytomous item response theory model*. Thousand Oaks, CA: Sage.

Peng, C. J., Lee, K. L., & Ingersoll, G. M. (2002). An introduction to logistic regression analysis and reporting. *The Journal of Educational Research, 96*, 3-14.

Rasch, G. (1960). *Probabilistic models for some intelligence and attainment tests* (G. Leunbach, Trans.). Copenhagen: The Danish Institute for Educational Research.

Rijmen, F., Tuerlinckx, F., De Boeck, P., & Kuppens, P. (2003). A nonlinear mixed model framework for item response theory. *Psychological Methods, 8*, 185-205.

Rupp, A. A., & Zumbo, B. D. (2003). Which model is best? Robustness properties to justify model choice among unidimensional IRT models under item parameter drift. *Alberta Journal of Educational Research, 49*, 264-276.

Rupp, A. A., & Zumbo, B. D. (2004). A note on how to quantify and report whether IRT parameter invariance holds: When Pearson correlations are not enough. *Educational and Psychological Measurement, 64*, 588-599. {*Errata, (2004) Educational and Psychological Measurement, 64*, 991}.

Rupp, A. A., & Zumbo, B. D. (in press). Understanding parameter invariance in unidimensional IRT models. *Educational and Psychological Measurement*.

Samejima, F. (1969). Estimation of latent ability using a response pattern of graded scores. *Psychometrika Monograph, No. 17*.

Samejima, F. (1996). The graded response model. In W. J. van der Linden & Hambleton, R. K. (Eds.), *Handbook of modern item response theory*. New York: Springer.

Sijtsma, K., & I. W., Molenaar. (2002). *Introduction to nonparametric item response theory*. Thousand Oaks, CA: Sage.

Tatsuoka, K. K. (1983). Rule space: An approach for dealing with misconceptions based on item response theory. *Journal of Educational Measurement, 20*, 345-354.

Thissen, D., & Steinberg, L. (1986). A taxonomy of item response models. *Psychometrika, 51*, 567-77.

van der Ark, L. A. (2001). Relationships and properties of polytomous item response theory. *Applied Psychological Measurement, 25*, 273-282.

van der Linden, W. J., & Hambleton, R. K. (1996). *Handbook of modern item response theory*. New York: Springer.

Zimmerman, D. W., & Zumbo, B. D. (2001). The geometry of probability, statistics, and test theory. *International Journal of Testing, 1*, 283-303.

Zumbo, B. D. (2005). *Reflections on validity at the intersection of psychometrics, scaling, philosophy of inquiry, and language testing*. Samuel J. Messick Memorial Award Lecture, LTRC 27th Language Testing Research Colloquium, Ottawa, Canada.

Zumbo, B. D., & Rupp, A. A. (2004). Responsible modeling of measurement data for appropriate inferences: Important advances in reliability and validity theory. In D. Kaplan (Ed.), *The SAGE Handbook of Quantitative Methodology for the Social Sciences* (pp. 73-92). Thousand Oaks, CA: Sage Press.

CHAPTER 17

SOME PRACTICAL USES OF ITEM RESPONSE TIME TO IMPROVE THE QUALITY OF LOW-STAKES ACHIEVEMENT TEST DATA

Steven L. Wise and Xiaojing Kong

All researchers are aware that the value of a given data analysis is dependent on the quality of the data analyzed. Although statistical methods are often used to identify and potentially remove questionable data (e.g., analysis of outliers), there are many instances in which such data are difficult to identify. This is particularly true when the data come from achievement tests used to measure the examinee proficiency. Whenever tests are administered under low-stakes conditions—for which there are few, if any, consequences for examinees based on their performance—it is likely that some examinees will not give good effort. For these examinees, the test data will typically underestimate their true proficiency levels, and the validity of their test scores will be diminished.

In practice, identification of the examinees who did not give good effort is challenging. We have found, however, that when computer-based

Real Data Analysis, pp. 271–276

tests (CBTs) are used, collection of item response time can provide valuable information that can be used to identify and ameliorate instances of low effort.

Schnipke and Scrams (2002) studied the behavior of examinees at the end of speeded high-stakes multiple-choice tests. They observed that as time was running out, some examinees switched from *solution behavior* (i.e., trying to work out the answers) to *rapid-guessing behavior* (i.e., quickly and unsystematically entering answers). Rapid-guessing behavior can be identified by (a) short item response times and (b) answers with accuracy rates close to that expected by random responding.

We recently discovered that rapid-guessing behaviors can also be found in the data from unspeeded low-stakes CBTs (Wise & Kong, 2005). Moreover, we found that rapid guessing can occur throughout a test and not just toward the end as Schnipke and Scrams (2002) had observed. Figure 17.1 shows the frequency distribution of examinee response times for one item we studied. It is bimodal, exhibiting the characteristic frequency "spike" for very short response times (in this case, less than 5 seconds) that Schnipke and Scrams observed. A 5-second threshold is indicated in Figure 17.1 which corresponds to the end of the frequency spike. The time threshold can be used to differentiate solution from rapid-guessing behavior, and this classification of item responses is the central idea

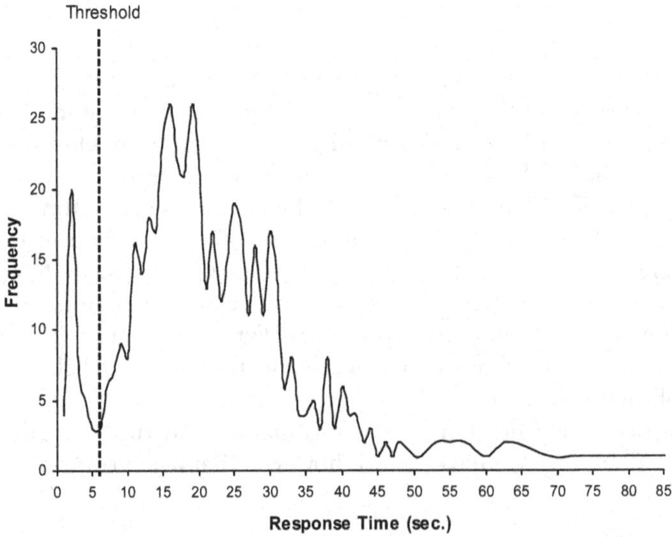

Figure 17.1. Distribution of examinee response times for a multiple-choice achievement test item.

underlying several methods for obtaining test data whose validity is less compromised by low examinee effort.

RESPONSE TIME EFFORT

We then developed a response time-based index that we believed would measure the effort given by examinees. Response time effort (RTE) scores are based on the conceptualization that a test session consists of a series of examinee-item encounters. In each encounter, the examinee makes a choice to engage in either solution or rapid-guessing behavior, which is reflected by the time the examinee takes to respond to the item. Thus, for item i, there is a threshold, T_i, that represents the response time boundary between rapid-guessing behavior and solution behavior. Given an examinee j's response time, RT_{ij}, to item i, a dichotomous index of item solution behavior, SB_{ij}, is computed as

$$SB_{ij} = \begin{Bmatrix} 1 \text{ if } RT_{ij} \geq T_i, \\ 0 \text{ otherwise} \end{Bmatrix} \tag{1}$$

The index of overall response time effort for examinee j to the test is given by

$$RTE_j = \frac{\sum_{i=1}^{k} SB_{ij}}{k}, \tag{2}$$

where k = the number of items in the test.

RTE scores range from zero to one, and represent the proportion of test items for which the examinees exhibited solution behavior. We investigated the characteristics of the *RTE* scores obtained from the administration of an 80-item university assessment test. It was found that *RTE* scores were highly reliable, and validity evidence was found that provided strong support for our hypothesis that these scores reflect examinee effort. Thus, *RTE* values near one indicate strong examinee effort to a test, and the farther a value falls below one, the less effort the examinee expended.

RTE scores can provide a researcher with useful information regarding the effort given by examinees. In addition, researchers can study the pattern of the dichotomous SB_{ij}s across items for an examinee to explore if that examinee's effort changed during the testing session. Figure 17.2

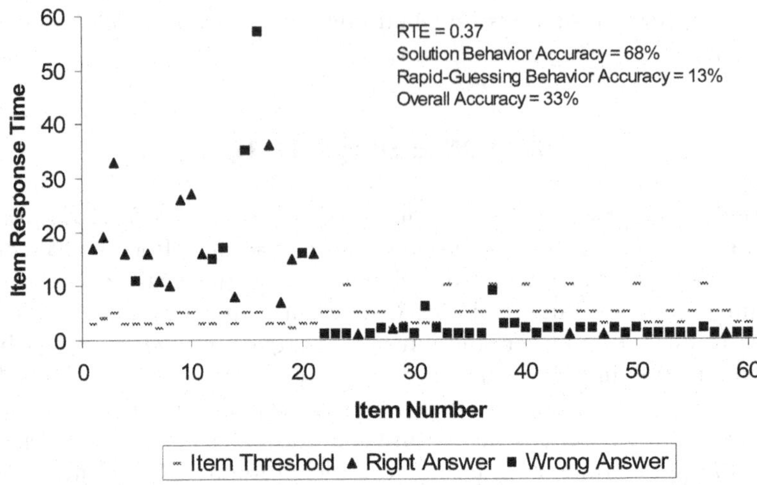

Figure 17.2. Item response times for an examinee who appeared to change testing strategies in midtest.

shows the item-by-item response times for an examinee on a 60-item test. This examinee consistently exhibited long response times (indicating solution behavior) for the first 21 items, after which the response times became very short (indicating rapid-guessing behavior). These attributions about their response strategies are reinforced by the relative accuracy of responses. During the first 21 items the examinee passed 68% of the items; afterward, accuracy fell to 13%. Thus, inspection of Figure 17.2 reveals a dramatic change in test-taking strategy during the testing session.

How might researchers use this information to improve the quality of their data? They might deem as untrustworthy the data from any examinees with RTE scores below some criterion value (say, .90) and delete these examinees from the sample (a process termed *motivation filtering*). Alternatively, they might view as salvageable all item responses that reflected solution behavior.

EFFORT-MODERATED ITEM RESPONSE THEORY

As was shown in Figure 17.2, the accuracy rates for solution and rapid-guessing behavior will typically be markedly different. Moreover, under solution behavior the probability of a correct response typically increases with examinee proficiency, and would be effectively modeled by a monotonically increasing function such as that represented under a traditional item response theory (IRT) model. In contrast, under rapid-guessing behavior the probability of a correct response remains near the level expected by chance regardless of examinee proficiency, which can be modeled by a flat item response function with a constant probability of a correct response across the range of proficiency. Thus, the functional relationship between examine proficiency and the probability of a correct response will be very different under the two response strategies.

These two item response functions can be combined into a single model that is moderated by response strategy. Assuming that the value of SB_{ij} is a function of examinee effort to the item, we can form an *effort-moderated item response model*. For example, suppose that solution behavior is represented by the three-parameter logistic (3PL) IRT model, and rapid-guessing behavior is represented by a constant-probability model specified as $P_i(\theta) = d_i$, where d_i is the reciprocal of the number of response options for item i. In this case, the effort-moderated model would be:

$$P_i(\theta) = (SB_{ij})\left(c_i + (1 - c_i)\left(\frac{e^{Da_i(\theta - b_i)}}{1 + e^{Da_i(\theta - b_i)}}\right)\right) + (1 - SB_{ij})(d_i) \tag{4}$$

In essence, because SB_{ij} takes only the values 0 or 1, the effort-moderated model specifies two distinct item response functions—one for solution behavior and one for rapid-guessing behavior. Wise and DeMars (2006) showed that, relative to a traditional IRT model, the effort-moderated model showed superior model fit, more accurately estimated both item parameters and test information, and yielded proficiency estimates with higher convergent validity. Their results suggest that the effort-moderated model may be preferable to the standard IRT models when rapid-guessing behavior is present.

CONCLUSIONS

By collecting item response time during CBT administration, researchers will be able to identify rapid-guessing behavior, which is indicative of low examinee effort. This information can be effectively used to identify and remove the data from examinees who did not exhibit a minimally acceptable level of effort. Alternatively, classification of each examinee-item interaction as reflecting solution or rapid-guessing behavior can permit more accurate modeling of examinee-item interactions. This will improve the quality of test score data and, consequently enhance score validity.

REFERENCES

Schnipke, D. L., & Scrams, D. J. (2002). Exploring issues of examinee behavior: Insights gained from response-time analyses. In C. N. Mills, M. T. Potenza, J. J. Fremer, & W. C. Ward (Eds.), *Computer-based testing: Building the foundation for future assessments* (pp. 237-266). Mahwah, NJ: Erlbaum.

Wise, S. L., & DeMars, C. D. (2006). An application of item response time: The effort-moderated IRT model. *Journal of Educational Measurement, 43,* 19-38.

Wise, S. L., & Kong, X. (2005). Response time effort: A new measure of examinee motivation in computer-based tests. *Applied Measurement in Education, 18,* 163-183.

CHAPTER 18

USING MOVING AVERAGES TO DETECT EXPOSED TEST ITEMS IN COMPUTER-BASED TESTING

Ning Han and Ronald Hambleton

INTRODUCTION

Exposed test items are a major threat to the validity of computer-based testing (CBT). In this chapter, an exposed test item is an item that is administered to an examinee taking a test and then shared by the examinee directly or indirectly with other examinees before they take the test. Historically, paper and pencil tests have maintained test security by (1) closely monitoring test forms (including their printing, distribution, administration, and collection), and (2) regularly introducing new test forms. However, because of the necessity of daily use of item banks with examinees in a computer-based testing environment, standard methods for maintaining test security with paper-and-pencil administrations are no longer applicable. Failure to adequately solve the item security problem with computer-based testing will guarantee the demise of this approach for high-stakes assessment.

Much of the research for limiting item exposure with computer-based tests has focused on finding ways to minimize item usage: Expanding the

Real Data Analysis, pp. 277–286

number of test items in a bank (either by hiring extra item writers and/or using item generation methods and algorithms) (see Pitoniak, 2002), establishing conditional item exposure controls (see, for example, Revuelta & Ponsoda, 1998; Stocking & Lewis, 1998; Yi & Chang, 2003), rotating item banks, expanded initiatives to reduce sharing of test items on the internet (see, for example, the work of Caveon and other test security companies like them in finding Web sites where test items are passed on to examinees), shortening test administration windows, and modifying test designs (with the intent of reducing the number of items that examinees are administered, without loss of measurement precision).

A very different approach to addressing the problem is to focus attention on the generation and use of item statistics that can reveal whether test items have become known to examinees prior to seeing the items in the test they are administered (Lu & Hambleton, 2004; Segall, 2001; Zhu & Liu, 2002). If these exposed items can be spotted statistically, they can be deleted from the item bank and the damage of exposed test items in tests can be minimized. Along these lines, several item statistics have been proposed (see, e.g., Han, 2003; Han & Hambleton, in press; Lu & Hambleton, 2004).

Han (2003) proposed the concept of "moving averages" for detecting exposed test items. The moving average is a form of average which has been adjusted to allow for periodic and random components of time series data. A moving average is a smoothing technique used to make the long term trends of a time series clearer. Item performance can be monitored over time (i.e., after each item administration to an examinee), and changes in item performance can be noted and used to identify potentially exposed test items. Preliminary research has been encouraging (Han & Hambleton, in press). In this chapter, several moving average item statistics will be introduced and an example of an exposed test item will be provided.

MOVING AVERAGES

Moving averages are widely used in the stock market to predict the trend of stock prices. The definition and computations of moving averages are:

Given a sequence of values $\{x_1, x_2, \ldots, x_t, \ldots\}$ and a window size $K > 0$, the k-th moving average of the given sequence is defined as follows:

$$y_1 = \frac{1}{k}(x_1 + \ldots + x_k)$$

$$y_2 = \frac{1}{k}(x_2 + \ldots + x_{k+1})$$

$$\vdots$$

$$y_{n-k+1} = \frac{1}{k}(x_{n-k+1} + x_{n-k+2} + \ldots + x_n)$$

Moving average is a form of averages that has been adjusted to allow the long-term trends of time series data to be clearer. One property of the moving average is that moving averages with a small window size respond to the trend faster than the ones with a big window size. That is to say, the larger the value of k is, the more stable the moving averages are, but then they become less sensitive to changes that may be taking place. When k is chosen to be large (say, 1,000), the change of one element or a few elements will not affect the moving averages significantly. On the other hand, when k becomes small (say, 50 to 100), minor changes of a few elements or of even one element will result in immediately noticeable changes in moving averages. In the stock market, a series of moving averages with different window sizes of k are usually computed for a stock (e.g. 5 days, 10 days, 30 days, a half year, a year, etc.) to forecast the changes of the stock prices. If the trend of the stock price is going up, the short-term moving averages will increase before the long-term moving averages do so as well.

When a variable, like the scores of examinees taking a CBT, is observed at a sequence of time intervals, this sequence of data is called time series data. The essential difference between time series data and the random samples of observations that are discussed in the context of most other statistical methods is that data points taken over time may have internal structure (such as a trend or periodic variation) that should be accounted for. The underlying trend usually is difficult to see because of the presence of periodic variation and random error. Moving average is a powerful tool that can be used to eliminate these components and random errors from time series data.

Unlike in conventional paper-and-pencil tests, where a single test is administrated to a whole population of examinees at the same time therefore "time" is not an interesting variable, in CBT a string of examinees take a test successively. Sometimes "time" may affect the test results dramatically (if examinees share information about the items they saw on the test). Therefore, the scores of examinees or observed examinee performance are time series data. There may be trend, periodic variation, and other variations underlying the data. For example, if an item bank is over exposed, examinees taking the test at later points in time may take advantage of the knowledge of item bank to get higher scores. There will be an increasing trend underlying the score series.

Consider first that over time it is reasonable to assume that the examinee distribution of ability is about the same. If the examinees taking a CBT are treated as a time series sequence $\{x_1, x_2, \ldots, x_t, \ldots\}$ where x_t is the ability of the t-th examinee, this sequence should have a similar mean and standard deviation over time. In other words, there should be no significant increasing or decreasing trend in this sequence. The scores of the examinees would look like they are being randomly drawn from a fixed distribution with a common location and common standard deviation.

To apply this method in CBT programs, one promising way is to compute and display the moving average of the examinees' score sequence. If this pattern keeps unchanged we can be reasonably confident (though not certain) that the item bank is secure. If the pattern begins to increase, and significantly so, we might conclude that the item pool is compromised, or we may question the assumption that the examinee ability distribution over time is stable.

For every item in the bank, similar moving averages of the response sequence can be computed in the same way (a more suitable name is perhaps moving p values). A similar interpretative rule like the one considered above can be applied also. Therefore, instead of judging an item by how many times the item has been seen during test administration, an item might be removed from the bank if there is a sizeable shift in the time series of item performance.

A criterion to judge if an item or a pool is secure can be set up by simulation when the distribution of the examinee population is known or can be assumed to be known. For each window size k, a great number of simulations can be conducted on an item pool. The moving averages with a specific window size k are computed based on these simulations. The empirical distribution or the confidence interval of the moving averages can then be obtained under the assumption that the only variation is random. If the observed distribution differs from the simulated one significantly, the test administrators can infer that something unexpected has happened. In the case of p values, the confidence bands too can be determined based on the knowledge that the approximate sampling error of the p-value is the square root of $p(1 - p)$/window size (sample size on which the p-value is based). In our previous research, detection of potentially exposed items can be detected with reasonable accuracy with as few as about 100 examinees (see, Han & Hambleton, in press).

DETECTION OF EXPOSED TEST ITEMS BASED ON MOVING AVERAGES

Moving *P*-Values

Mathematically, a moving average of the item scores equals the item p value estimated on this set of examinees. Therefore the moving averages sequence of the item scores will be called "moving p values." For an example, see Figure 18.1. Here, the time-series plot shows that as the number of examinees continues to take the test, the item statistic with some selected window size (e.g., the last 200 examinees) remains fairly flat, and

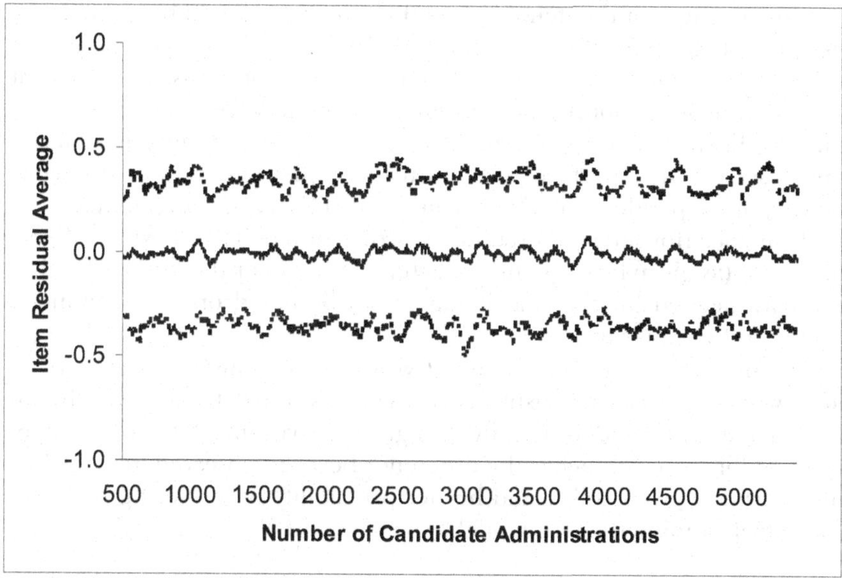

Figure 18.1. Item residual plot over time with a window size of 200. Confidence bands based on empirical results from simulation studies with no exposure are also shown.

does not fall outside the range of expected values assuming only examinee ability and the vagaries of random sampling of examinees and measurement error in examinee responses are impacting on item performance. The approach also assumes that the ability distribution itself remains more or less the same over time. In Figure 18.1, there is no evidence of item exposure.

Obviously, the assumption of equivalent ability scores over time is too strong in many testing programs. Examinee abilities are very likely to increase or decrease over time. High ability examinees may show up in the beginning of the test period while low ability examinees may show up later, or vice-versa, for example. The moving p value sequence is dependent on the ability distribution of the examinees therefore will be useless in detecting item exposure in this case because item performance differences and ability differences may be confounded. We need to look for some item statistics which are free of the ability distribution.

Item Residuals Based Upon IRT Modeling of the Data

A natural item index is the item b value under the IRT framework (Hambleton, Swaminathan, & Rogers, 1999). Obvious if we compute the moving averages of the item b values the sequence should be stable if the item is not exposed. But monitoring the moving averages of the item b values over examinees will involve too many calibrations. An excellent variation involves plotting instead, the average item residual over examinees with window size k, where examinee item performance is adjusted for expected item performance. Instead of plotting examinee performance, the dependent variable becomes the difference between item level performance (for binary scored items, scores of 0 or 1) and expected performance (as given by the item characteristic curve for the item). The ability score needed for the calculation would be based on the examinee's overall test performance.

The probability that an examinee with a given ability level answers an item with given characteristics correctly is assumed to be given by an underlying IRT model—usually a logistic curve—in IRT. So, an item residual for the examinee is the difference between observed item performance with a given ability and his/her probability of answering this item correctly assuming the IRT model to be true:

$$r_{ij} = x_{ij} - p_{ij}$$

where i denotes the item and j denotes the examinee. x_{ij} is the observed score of the examinee on this item. p_{ij} is the probability that the examinee answers the item correctly under the IRT model. Figure 18.2 shows the residual scores for two examinees who differ in ability. In Figure 18.2, the examinee with the lower ability score answers the item correctly; while the higher ability examinee does not. The dependent variable in the time series analysis would be the residuals that are shown. What is plotted is the average item residual over the most recent k examinees. Figure 18.3 shows a plot of item residuals over the last k examinees and the exposure of the test item is easily seen. The confidence bands for the item residual statistic have been smoothed in the figure.

If we compute the moving average of the item residuals for a certain item and a group of examinees, the moving average sequence should be stable as long as the sample size is large enough. Actually, it is expected that the moving average sequence should have an average close to zero. However, if an item is exposed, the chances of giving correct answers to the disclosed items have been increased because some examinees have prior knowledge to the items, especially for those examinees with lower ability levels. Consequently, with more examinees answering the items correctly than expected, therefore, the moving average of item residuals will have higher positive values. This property makes item residuals potentially quite useful in spotting exposed test items and our research suggests that they are (Han & Hambleton, in press).

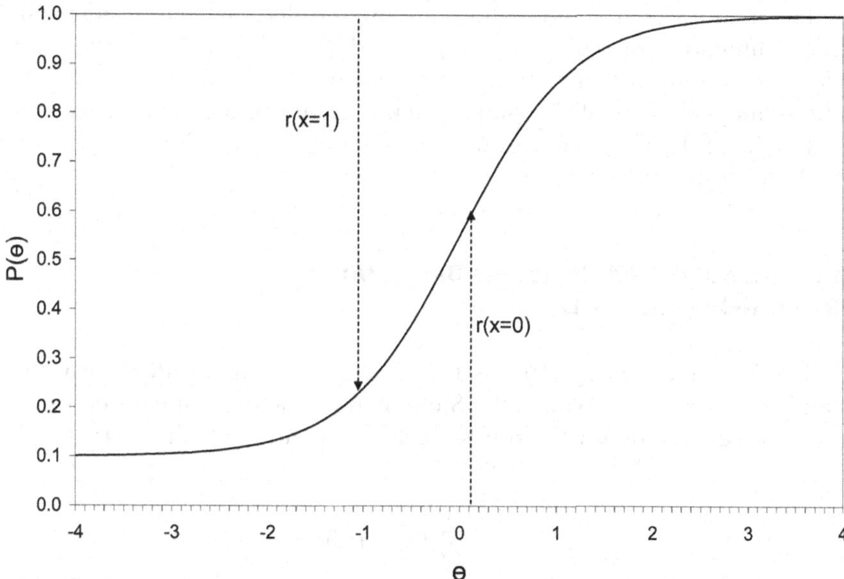

Figure 18.2. Item residuals for a low ability examinee (who answers the item correctly) and a higher ability examinee (who answers the item incorrectly), respectively.

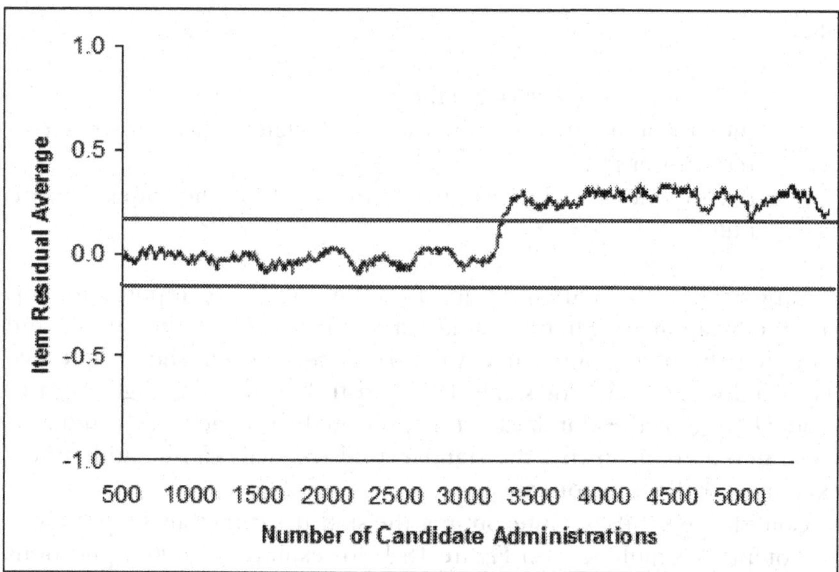

Figure 18.3. Example of an item residual plot over time that indicates an exposed test item. The horizontal (smoothed) bands provide the expected range due to random fluctuations in the item statistic only.

The item residual defined above are often called raw item residuals in IRT. A limitation of raw item residuals is that they do not take the sampling error into account (Hambleton, Swaminathan, & Rogers, 1999). The numerical value of the statistic depends on the trait level, and so it may be helpful if these raw residuals were standardized prior to averaging them over examinees.

Item Standardized Residuals Based Upon IRT Modeling of the Data

Standardized item residual is the ratio of the raw residual over the standard error. Wang, Wingersky, Steffen and Zhu (1998) suggested using the Z_c index to monitor the fitness of the item and model in CBT:

$$Z_c = \frac{\sum_{j=1}^{N} (x_{ij} - P_{ij})}{\sqrt{\sum_{j=1}^{N} P_{ij}(1 - P_{ij})}}$$

where

x_{ij} = is the binary score variable for item i of examinee j,
P_{ij} = the probability that examinee j, with the latent trait θ_j, gives a correct answer to item i,
N = the sample size (i.e., window size) on which the index is computed.

Suppose that there are a group of examinees, Z_c is computed for this group of examinees. Then by adding a new examinee to the sample and dropping the oldest one a new value is obtained while the sample size (i.e., window size) stays the same. This statistic has the advantage over raw residuals in that the standard error associated with each raw residual is taken into account so that the standardized residuals can be added over examinees without major concern.

Confidence bands for interpreting the statistics can easily be produced via computer simulation: In Figure 18.1, for example, 1,000 replications were carried out and the approximate 2.5, 97.5 percentiles were determined along with the mean of the 1,000 item residual statistics). What was used to approximate the percentiles was the mean + two standard deviations and the mean – two standard deviations. These extremes were used in the flagging of deviant test items (i.e. detecting of exposed items). Whenever an item statistic exceeds these boundaries, either a type I is made (if no exposure is present) or exposure is detected (if exposure is present).

CONCLUSIONS

Our experience with a number of statistics to detect exposed items, especially item residuals and standardized residuals, suggests that these statistics are quite effective at detecting the most problematic exposed items (i.e., those that are difficult and discriminating test items) with window sizes as small as 100 to 200 examinees, and also, shifts in ability distributions over time, even substantial ones, do not complicate the detection process with statistical methods that incorporate the ability scores into the process.

REFERENCES

Hambleton, R. K., Swaminathan, H., & Rogers, H. J. (1991). *Fundamentals of item response theory.* Newbury Park, CA: Sage.

Han, N. (2003). *Using moving averages to assess test and item security in computer-based testing* (AICPA Technical Report, Series Two). Ewing, PA: American Institute of Certified Public Accountants.

Han, N., & Hambleton, R. K. (in press). Improving test validity by detecting exposed test items. In C. L. Wild & R. Ramaswamy (Eds.), *Improving testing: Applying quality tools and techniques*. Mahwah, NJ: Erlbaum.

Lu, Y., & Hambleton, R. K. (2004). Statistics for detecting disclosed items in a CAT environment. *Metodologia de Las Ciencias del Comportamiento, 5*(2), 225-242.

Pitoniak, M. (2002). *Automatic item generation methodology in theory and practice* (Center for Educational Assessment Research Report No. 444). Amherst: University of Massachusetts, Center for Educational Assessment.

Revuelta, J., & Ponsoda, V. (1998). A comparison of item exposure control methods in computerized adaptive testing. *Journal of Educational Measurement, 35*, 311-327.

Segall, D. O. (2001, April). *Measuring test compromise in high-stakes computerized adaptive testing: A Bayesian strategy for surrogate test-taker detection.* Paper presented at the meeting of the National Council on Measurement in Education, Seattle, WA.

Stocking, M. L., & Lewis, C. (1998). Controlling item exposure conditional on ability in computerized adaptive testing. *Journal of Educational and Behavioral Statistics, 23*, 57-75.

Wang, M. M., Wingersky, M., Steffen, M., & Zhu, R. (1998). *Preliminary operational item monitoring procedures.* Unpublished manuscript. Princeton, NJ: Educational Testing Service.

Yi, Q., & Chang, H. H. (2003). A-stratified CAT design with content blocking. *British Journal of Mathematical and Statistical Psychology, 56,* 359-378.

Zhu, R., Yu, F., & Liu, S. (2002, April). *Statistical indexes for monitoring item behavior under computer adaptive testing environment.* Paper presented at the meeting of the American Educational Research Association, New Orleans.

CHAPTER 19

AN EMPIRICAL CALIBRATION OF THE EFFECTS OF MULTIPLE SOURCES OF MEASUREMENT ERROR ON RELIABILITY ESTIMATES FOR INDIVIDUAL DIFFERENCES MEASURES

Frank L. Schmidt and Huy Le

Psychological measurement and measurement theory are fundamental tools that make progress in psychological research possible. Estimating relationships between constructs is essential to the advancement of psychological theories. Because of measurement error, the relationships between specific measures (observed relationships) underestimate the relationships between the constructs (true score relationships). To estimate true score relationships the observed relationships are often adjusted for the effect of measurement error; and for these true score relationship estimates to be accurate the adjustments need to be precise.

There are three major error processes that are relevant to all psychological self-report measurement: random response error, transient error,

Real Data Analysis, pp. 287–292

and specific factor error. Depending on which of these sources of error variance are taken into account when computing reliability estimates, the magnitude of the reliability estimates can vary substantially, which can lead to erroneous interpretations of observed relationships between psychological constructs (Schmidt & Hunter, 1999; Thorndike, 1951).

An important class of measurement errors that is often overlooked is transient error (Becker, 2000; Thorndike, 1951). Transient errors are defined as longitudinal variations in responses to measures that are produced by random variations in respondents' psychological states across time. If transient errors indeed exist, ignoring them in the estimation of the reliability of a specific measure leads to overestimates of reliability.

The research presented here investigates the implications of transient error in the measurement of important individual differences variables. Specifically, we examine how the type of reliability most frequently used in research, coefficient of equivalence (CE), is inflated by transient error.

The CE, often estimated by coefficient alpha, assesses the magnitude of measurement error produced by specific factor and random response error but not by transient error. Another type of reliability which is much less known is coefficient of equivalence and stability (CES). The CES is computed by correlating two parallel forms of a measure, each administered on *a different occasion*. The CES is the only type of reliability coefficients that estimates the magnitude of the measurement error produced by all three error processes. Thus, it is the most appropriate reliability to be used to correct for measurement error.

In many cases parallel forms of the same measure may not be available. For such cases, we derive the following formula that allow us to estimate the CES of a scale from the coefficient of equivalence and stability of its half-scale (ces) that was obtained either from (a) administering the scale on two distinct occasions and then splitting it post hoc to form parallel half-scales, or (b) splitting the scale into parallel halves then administering each half on each separate occasion:

$$\text{CES} = 2\ \text{ces}/(1 + \text{ce}), \tag{1}$$

with CES being the coefficient of equivalence of the full scale which we want to estimate; ces being the coefficient of equivalence and stability of the half-scale; and ce being the coefficient of equivalence of the half-scale.

Knowing the CES we can estimate the extent to which CE overestimates reliability: subtracting CES from CE yields the proportion of observed variance produced by transient error processes (Feldt & Brennan, 1989).

$$\text{TEV} = \text{CE} - \text{CES}. \tag{2}$$

TEV is the ratio of transient error variance to observed score variance for the measure in question.

METHOD

We conducted a study on 167 students at a Midwestern university. All participants were requested to complete two laboratory sessions separated by an interval of approximately 1 week. Measures were organized into two distinct questionnaires, each included one of a pair of parallel forms of measures for each construct studied (described below) in this project. Each participant received different questionnaires in his/her two different sessions.

We measured general mental ability (GMA), the Big Five personality traits, self-esteem, self-efficacy, positive affectivity, and negative affectivity. The measures are shown in Table 19.1.

There were only two of the measures used having parallel forms available (Wonderlic Personnel Test and Texas Social Behavior Inventory, 1988). For the other measures, we split them into halves to form parallel half-scales.

ANALYSES

We estimated the CE and the CES for the measures. For those with parallel forms, the CE values were estimated by averaging the coefficient alphas of the forms; the CES values were the correlations between the parallel forms administered on different occasions. For those measures without parallel forms, their half-scale coefficient of equivalence (ce) were estimated by averaging coefficient alphas of the half-scales; their half-scale coefficients of equivalence and stability (ces) were the correlations between the parallel half-scales of the same measures administered on two different occasions. The Spearman-Brown formula was then used to estimate the coefficient of equivalence of the full scales (CE) from those of the half-scales (ce). The CES of the full scales was estimated from those of the half-scales (ces) by use of Equation 1. Finally, we estimated the TEV by subtracting the CES from CE (Equation 2).

With limited sample size, all the reliability and error variance estimates are affected by sampling error. We used Monte-Carlo simulation procedure to estimate the standard errors of the estimates. One thousand datasets were simulated based on the results (i.e., CE, CES, and TEV estimates) obtained from the previous analysis. For each dataset, the same

Table 11.1. Standard Errors for the Reliability Coefficients and Transient Error Variance Estimates

Construct	*Measure*	*CE*	SE_{CE}[a]	*CES*	SE_{CES}[b]	*TEV*	SE_{TEV}[c]	*% Over-estimate*[d]
GMA	Wonderlic Test[g]	.79	.020	.74	.035	.05	.029	6.7%
Conscien-tiousness	PCI[h]	.88	.013	.78	.042	.10	.039	13.0%
	Goldberg's IPIP[i]	.93	.008	.89	.022	.04	.019	4.5%
	Average	*.91*	*.008*[e]	*.84*	*.024*[e]	*.07*	*.022*[e]	*8.3%*
Extraversion	PCI[h]	.81	.020	.83	.039	.00[f]	.038	0.0%
	Goldberg's IPIP[i]	.92	.009	.88	.025	.04	.022	4.5%
	Average	*.86*	*.011*[e]	*.86*	*.023*[e]	*.02*	*.022*[e]	*2.2%*
Agreeable-ness	PCI[h]	.85	.017	.80	.041	.05	.039	6.3%
	Goldberg's IPIP[i]	.88	.014	.87	.030	.01	.027	1.1%
	Average	*.87*	*.011*[e]	*.84*	*.025*[e]	*.03*	*.024*[e]	*3.6%*
Neuroticism	PCI[h]	.85	.016	.74	.048	.11	.045	14.9%
	Goldberg's IPIP[i]	.93	.008	.86	.027	.07	.025	8.1%
	Average	.89	*.009*[e]	*.80*	*.028*[e]	*.09*	*.026*[e]	*11.3%*
Openness	PCI[h]	.81	.023	.87	.045	.00[f]	.045	0.0%
	Goldberg's IPIP[i]	.88	.013	.90	.028	.00[f]	.027	0.0%
	Average	*.85*	*.013*[e]	*.89*	*.027*[e]	*.00*	*.026*[e]	*0.0%*
GSE	Sherer's GSE[j]	.89	.013	.83	.035	.05	.032	6.0%
Self-esteem	TSBI[k]	.85	.015	.80	.029	.05	.023	6.3%
	Rosenberg[l]	.84	.019	.79	.044	.05	.043	6.3%
	Average	*.85*	*.012*[e]	*.80*	*.026*[e]	*.05*	*.024*[e]	*6.3%*
Positive affectivity	PANAS[m]	.82	.022	.63	.065	.19	.062	30.2%
	MPI[n]	.91	.011	.81	.033	.09	.031	11.1%
	Diener et al.[o]	.86	.018	.74	.045	.12	.044	16.2%
	Average	*.86*	*.010*[e]	*.73*	*.029*[e]	*.13*	*.027*[e]	*17.8%*
Negative affectivity	PANAS[m]	.83	.021	.78	.047	.05	.046	6.4%
	MPI[n]	.90	.011	.80	.036	.09	.033	11.2%
	Diener et al.[o]	.90	.012	.69	.049	.21	.046	30.4%
	Average	*.88*	*.009*[d]	*.76*	*.026*[d]	*.11*	*.024*[e]	*14.5%*

Notes: $N = 167$, [a]Standard error of the CE estimates; [b]Standard error of the CES estimates; [c]Standard error of the TEV estimates. [d]Percent that CES is over-estimated by CE; [e]Standard error of the averaged estimates. [f]The estimated ratio of transient error variance to observed score variance is negative for these measures. Since variance proportion cannot be negative, zero is the appropriate estimate of its population value. [g]Wonderlic Personnel Test, Forms I and II (Wonderlic Personnel Test, 1998); [h]Personal Characteristic Inventory (Barrick & Mount, 1995); [i]Goldberg's IPIP big five (Goldberg, 1997); [j]Sherer's Generalized Self-Efficacy Scale (Sherer, Maddux, Mercandate, Prentice-Dunn, Jacobs, & Rogers, 1982); [k]Texas Social Behavior Inventory, Forms A and B (Helmreich & Stapp,1974); [l]Rosenberg Self-esteem Scale (Rosenberg, 1965); [m]PANAS (Watson, Clark, & Tellegen, 1988); [n]Multidimensional Personality Index (Watson & Tellegen, 1985); [o]Diener & Emmons's short scale (Diener & Emmons, 1985).

analysis procedure described in the previous section was carried out to estimate the CE, CES, and TEV. Standard deviations of the distributions of these estimates provide the standard errors of interest.

RESULTS

Table 19.1 shows the results of the study. As can be seen, estimates of the CES are generally smaller than the CE estimates, indicating that transient error exists in scores obtained with the measures used in this study. For GMA, the CE overestimated the reliability of the measure by 6.7%; for the Big Five personality measures, the extent of the overestimation varied between zero and 14.9% across the ten measures. The estimated TEV is negative for measures of Openness to Experience and for the PCI measure of Extraversion. Because proportion of variance cannot be negative by definition, negative values must be attributed to sampling error, so we considered the TEV of these measures to be zero.

For the generalized self-efficacy construct, the CE of the Sherer, Maddux, Mercandante, Prentice-Dunn, Jacobs, and Rogers (1982) measure overestimated reliability by 6%. The overestimation was 6.3% for both measures of self-esteem. The findings indicate that the proportion of transient error component is quite large for measures of affectivity, averaging (across the three affectivity inventories) 13% for positive affectivity, and 11% for negative affectivity.

Table 19.1 also shows the standard errors of the CE, CES, and TEV. Of special interest are the standard errors of the TEV. These values are relatively large compared to the TEV estimates due to the modest sample size of the study. Nevertheless, the fact that the 90% confidence intervals of the majority of the TEV estimates (12 cases out of 20 measures included in the study) do not cover the zero point indicates the existence of transient error in those measures.

CONCLUSION

The primary implication of these findings is that the nearly universal use of the CE (typified by coefficient alpha) as the reliability estimate for measures of important and widely used psychological constructs leads to overestimates of scale reliability. The over-estimation of reliability occurs because the CE does not capture transient error. The present study contributes to the literature on measurement by calibrating empirically the effect of transient error on the measurement of important constructs from the individual differences area, and by formulating a simple method of computing the CES—the reliability coefficient that takes into account random response, transient, and specific-factor error processes.

The finding that transient error indeed has nontrivial effects calls for more comprehensive treatment of measurement errors in empirical research. Studies like this one specifically designed to estimate the CES of measures of important psychological constructs can provide the needed reliability estimates to be subsequently used to correct for measurement error in observed correlations between measures. The cumulative development of such a database for the CES estimates of measures of widely used psychological constructs can thus enable substantive researchers to obtain unbiased estimates of construct-level relationships among their variables of interest, while minimizing the research resources needed.

REFERENCES

Barrick, M.R., & Mount, M.K. (1995). *The Personal Characteristics Inventory Manual.* Unpublished manuscript, University of Iowa, Iowa City.

Becker, G. (2000). How important is transient error in estimating reliability? Going beyond simulation studies. *Psychological Methods, 5,* 370-379.

Diener, E., & Emmons, R.A. (1985). The independence of positive and negative affect. *Journal of Personality and Social Psychology, 47,* 1105-1117.

Feldt, L. S., & Brennan, R. L. (1989). Reliability. In R. L. Linn (Ed.), *Educational measurement* (3rd ed., pp. 105-146). New York: Macmillan.

Goldberg, L. R. (1997). A broad-bandwidth, public-domain, personality inventory measuring the lower-level facets of several five-factor models. In I. Mervielde, I. Deary, F. De Fruyt, & F. Ostendorf (Eds.), *Personality psychology in Europe* (Vol. 7, pp. 7-28). Tilburg, Netherlands: Tilburg University Press.

Rosenberg, M. (1965). *Society and the adolescent self-image.* Princeton, NJ: Princeton University Press.

Schmidt, F. L., & Hunter, J. E. (1999). Theory testing and measurement error. *Intelligence, 27,* 183-198.

Sherer, M., Maddux, J. E., Mercandante, B., Prentice-Dunn, S., Jacobs, B., & Rogers, R. W. (1982). The self-efficacy scale. *Psychological Reports, 76,* 707-710.

Watson, D., Clark, L. A., & Tellegen, A. (1988). Development and validation of brief measures of positive and negative affect: The PANAS scales. *Journal of Personality and Social Psychology, 54*(6), 1063-1070.

Watson, D., & Tellegen, A. (1985). Toward a consensual structure of mood. *Psychological Bulletin, 98,* 219-235.

Wonderlic Personnel Test, Inc. (1998). Wonderlic Personnel Test & Scholastic Level Exam, User's Manual.

CHAPTER 20

LATENT STRUCTURE OF ATTITUDES TOWARD ABORTION

C. Mitchell Dayton

Attitudes toward abortion in the United States are often portrayed in terms that suggest the existence of a prevailing trend that can be tracked in much the same manner as a presidential election Thus, we hear assertions that the majority of Americans favors such-and-such position on abortion. In contrast to this, the premise of this chapter is that there are distinguishable subpopulations with well-defined attitudes toward abortion that can be characterized and tracked over time using latent variable methods. Rather than simple proabortion and antiabortion groups, there is evidence for four dominant latent classes that have changed in prevalence relatively little over the 26-year span of General Social Survey (GSS) data that were studied. According to one's biases, these four latent classes can be aggregated in various ways to portray the population as either pro-abortion or antiabortion, although reality is a good deal more complex.

Items dealing with attitudes toward abortion have been included in the GSS for many years and six items that appeared 21 times in the period from 1972 through 1998 were selected for analysis. These abortion data are in public-access databases maintained by the National Opinion Research Center in Chicago, Illinois at the Web site http://

Real Data Analysis, pp. 293–298

webapp.icpsr.umich.edu/GSS/. In the GSS, these items are presented with the introduction:

"Please tell me whether or not *you* think it should be possible for a pregnant woman to obtain a *legal* abortion if ..."

This introduction was followed by specific statements:

A: The woman's own health is seriously endangered by the pregnancy
B: She became pregnant as a result of rape
C: There is a strong chance of serious defect in the baby
D: The family has a very low income and cannot afford any more children
E: She is not married and does not want to marry the man
F: She is married and does not want any more children

Response options comprised Yes, No, Don't Know and No Answer, but only the Yes, No responses were considered as nonmissing in the present analyses. Counts and percents for data aggregated over the years 1972 through 1998 are presented in Table 20.1. Complete data were available for 27,151 respondents.

For variables with categorical responses such as Yes/No or Agree/Disagree, latent class analysis (LCA) may be viewed as a method for clustering respondents into homogeneous subgroups. Each subgroup (i.e., latent class) is characterized by a unique set of conditional probabilities for, say, a Yes response. However, a distinctive feature of LCA is that membership in these subgroups is probabilistic rather than deterministic. Thus, a respondent with any one of the possible patterns of Yes/No responses to the six items could be associated with any of the latent classes, although this likelihood is greater for some classes than for others. The mathematical model for LCA, estimation procedures and various applications may be found in Dayton (1999).

Table 20.1. Counts and Percents for Responses to Abortion Items

	Yes		*No*	
Item	*Count*	*%*	*Count*	*%*
Woman's health seriously endangered	27,187	90.1	2,985	9.9
Pregnant as result of rape	24,691	82.8	5,125	17.2
Strong chance of serious defect	24,487	81.5	5,553	18.5
Low income—can't afford more children	14,487	48.6	15,322	51.4
Not married	13,450	45.2	16,331	54.8
Married—wants no more children	13,204	44.2	16,675	55.8

Models with one to seven latent classes were fit to frequencies for the $2^6 = 64$ unique response patterns for the six abortion items based on the total group of 27,151 respondents. Using a min(BIC) criterion, a five-class model was selected as the best approximating model. The profiles for the five latent classes in Figure 20.1 are based on output from the program, Latent Gold (Vermunt & Magidson, 2000). Note that the vertical axis represents the estimated probability for a Yes response and that the estimated sizes of the classes (i.e., latent class proportions) are shown in parentheses in the legend. Latent class 5 has very small prevalence (about 1%) and can be interpreted as an "undecided" or "indifferent" group. The four-class solution results in a latent class structure that is essentially the same as the first four classes from the five-class solution (Figure 20.2).

The four latent classes may be interpreted as follows:

Latent Class 1: Strongly pro-abortion with no restriction based on the factors in the survey items; this class is estimated to represent about 41% of respondents.

Latent Class 2: Quite strongly pro-abortion for health of mother, cases of rape or serious defect in baby but even more strongly anti-abortion for reasons that can be viewed as social; this class is estimated to represent about 28% of respondents.

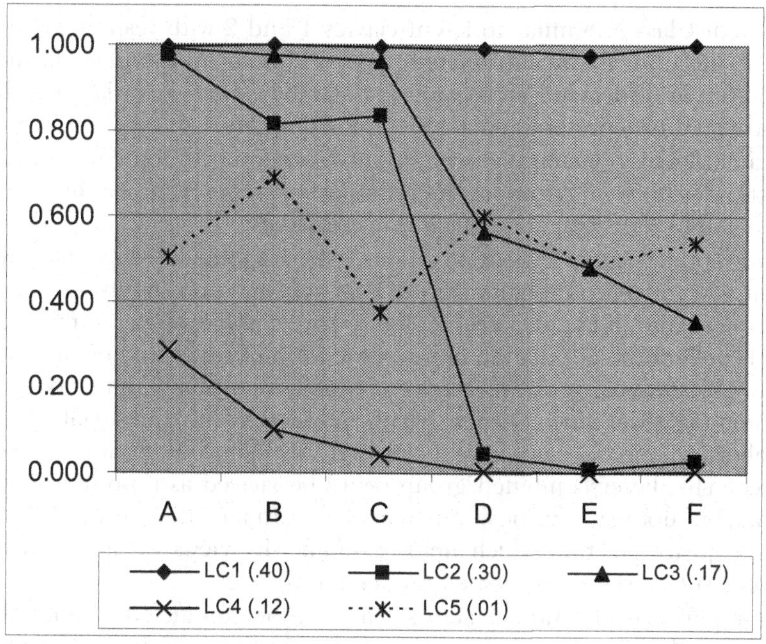

Figure 20.1. Profiles for five-class latent class solution.

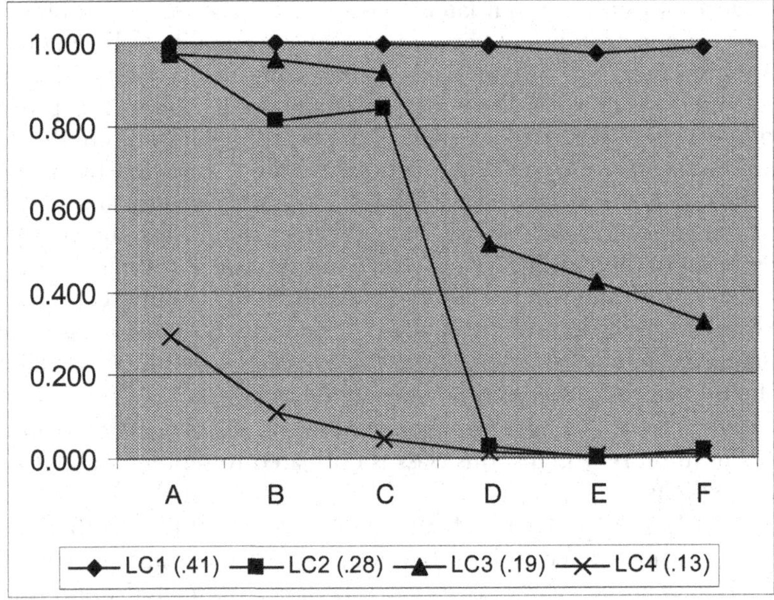

Figure 20.2. Profiles for four-class latent class solution.

Latent Class 3: Similar to latent classes 1 and 2 with respect to being pro-abortion for the health-related reasons in items A, B and C but more moderate or undecided for reasons that can be viewed as social; this class is estimated to represent about 19% of respondents.

Latent Class 4: Generally strongly anti-abortion with some moderation of attitudes for item A and less moderation for items B and C; this class is estimated to represent about 13% of respondents.

Note that if latent classes 1, 2 and 3 are combined, we estimate that about 88% of the population favors abortion in some circumstance. On the other hand, if latent classes 2, 3 and 4 are combined, we estimate that nearly 60% of the population favors some form of restriction on abortion. Finally, if latent classes 2 and 3 are combined, we estimate that about 47% of the population distinguishes sharply between health and social reasons for abortion and does not have a consistent pro-abortion or anti-abortion stance. This latter combined group could be viewed as representing the modal, but not majority, position on abortion. In fact, there is no unequivocal majority position which helps explain why views on abortion can become such a polarizing issue in American society.

Comparisons of attitudes across years can be conducted in a number of ways including by use of year as a stratification variable or by treating year as a covariate. Given the large number of years, 21, the covari-

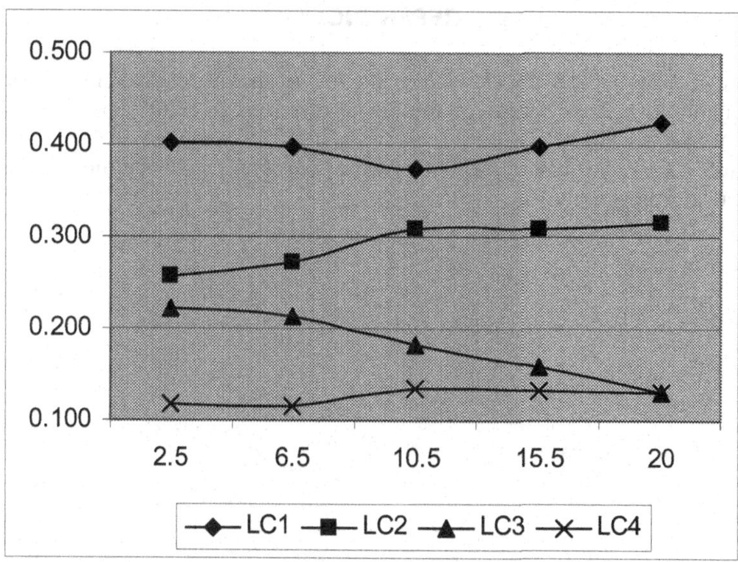

Figure 20.3. Latent class proportions as a function of year of survey.

ate approach is more parsimonious and, as it turns out, yields estimates that are very similar to those based on stratification. For the covariate model, the proportions in the latent classes are assumed to be a multivariate logistic function of the year of the survey whereas the conditional probabilities for the six abortion items are assumed to be constant across years (i.e., a partially homogeneous model is assumed; Dayton, 1999). Once again, Latent Gold was used to estimate the parameters in the covariate model and based on a min(BIC) strategy, the covariate model is a better approximating model than its counterpart that does not include year as a covariate. For simplicity, years were divided into five groups and associated latent class proportions are shown in Figure 20.3 (note that mid-points of unequal sized intervals are displayed). Although there is a good deal of consistency over time, the main trend appears to be a declining prevalence for latent class 3 with the change being more or less equally distributed among the remaining three latent classes. One might speculate that latent class 3 is becoming marginalized and that the dominant pattern that is emerging is one with a pro-abortion class, a much smaller antiabortion class and a class that sharply distinguishes between what might be called "health" and "social" reasons for abortion.

REFERENCES

Dayton, C. M. (1999). *Latent class scaling analysis* (Sage University Papers Series on Quantitative Applications in the Social Sciences, 07-126). Thousand Oaks, CA: Sage.

Vermunt, J. K., & Magidson, J. (2000). *Latent Gold: User's guide*. Belmont, MA: Statistical Innovations.

PART IV

DATA ANALYSIS

CHAPTER 21

HIERARCHICAL LINEAR MODELS AND THE ESTIMATION OF STUDENTS' MATHEMATICS ACHIEVEMENT

Kathrin A. Parks and Dudley L. Poston, Jr.

In the social sciences, many of the concepts and data structures are hierarchical. That is, the dependent variables are intended to describe the behavior of individuals, but the individuals themselves are grouped into larger units, known as contexts, such as families, schools, neighborhoods, counties, states, nations, and so forth. Moreover, many social science theories hypothesize that the individual outcome behavior will be influenced by both the person's characteristics and those of the contexts. For instance, "one of the basic problems of sociology is to relate properties of individuals and properties of groups and structures in which the individuals function" (de Leeuw, 2002, p. xix). If one wishes to test such theories, then the independent variables the researcher is interested in employing should refer both to the characteristics of the individuals and those of the higher order units.

This kind of thinking is not new. Indeed, DiPrete and Forristal (1994) have written that "the idea that individuals respond to the social context

Real Data Analysis, pp. 301–313

is a defining claim of the sociological discipline, which is found in Marx's work on political economy, in Durkheim's studies of the impact of community on anomia and suicide, in Weber's research on how the religious community shapes economic behavior, and in Merton's work on communities, relative deprivation, and social comparison theory" (p. 331). But the correct statistical estimation methodology is new.

Multilevel research is also important in the field of education, where students are grouped in classes, and both students and the classes have characteristics of interest. Students' academic performance, for example, is thought to be influenced by characteristics of the students, as well as by characteristics of the schools. The basic problem then is how to relate the properties of the individuals and the properties of the schools in which the individuals are located.

A good example is research by Entwisle, Alexander, and Olson (1994) pertaining to the gender gap in mathematics. The authors analyzed a data set of Baltimore school children in which the children were nested in schools and neighborhoods. Using multilevel models, they showed that the gender gap in mathematics between high-scoring males and females, favoring males, is due in large part to the greater responsiveness of boys' mathematics skills to neighborhood resources.

Multilevel investigations are sometimes referred to as hierarchical models, multilevel models, mixed-effects models, random-effects models, random-coefficient regression models, covariance components models, or hierarchical linear models. In this chapter we refer to such statistical models as hierarchical models.

What kinds of statistical techniques might be used to take into account hierarchical structure? In the past there were mainly two procedures, both of which have problems; one involves disaggregation, and another involves aggregation. The first technique is to disaggregate all the contextual level variables down to the level of the individuals. If one were examining the effects of country characteristics on the fertility behavior of women from different countries, the characteristics of the countries would all be assigned to the individual women, and the analysis would then proceed at the individual level, perhaps using a linear model such as ordinary least squares (OLS) regression. The main problem with this approach is that if we know that women are from the same country, then we also know that they have the same values on the various country characteristics. "Thus we cannot use the assumption of independence of observations that is basic for the use of classic statistical techniques" (de Leeuw, 2002, p. xx) because women are not randomly assigned to countries, or in the case of education research, schoolchildren are not randomly assigned to schools or to classrooms. If one disaggregates the context data down to the individuals, the women in the same countries and the students in the same classrooms will be more similar to one another than to women in other countries and to students in other classrooms. The women in the different countries and the students in the different classrooms will be independent, but the women in the same countries and the students in the same classrooms will have similar or the same values on many variables. "Some of these variables will not be observed, which means that they vanish into the error term of the linear model, causing correlation between disturbances (de Leeuw, 2002, p. xx).

An alternate technique is to aggregate the individual-level characteristics up to the contextual level and to conduct the analysis at the aggregate level. In the case of the above examples, one would aggregate, that is, average, the women characteristics on educational attainment and on fertility up to the country level of analysis and then conduct the analysis among countries, using OLS. Or one would aggregate the student characteristics up to the class or school level of analysis and conduct an OLS analysis among the classes or among the schools. Perhaps one could weight the variables by class or by school size. The main problem here is that one discards all the within-group (i.e., within-country, or within-school/classroom) variation, which could well mean that as much as 80-90% of the variation could be thrown away before the analysis begins.

To illustrate, in Poston's (2002) analysis of the earnings patterns of male Asian immigrants to the United States, he found that only around 7% of the variance in annual earnings occurred between country-groups of Asian men, and that, thus, around 93% of the variance occurred at the individual level, that is, within country-groups of Asian male workers. Had he aggregated the individual characteristics of the Asian men up to the level of their countries, he would have thrown away over 90% of the variation in income before starting his analysis.

If one aggregates the individual data up to the level of the context, information thus is frequently wasted. Also, it is often the case that the relations between the aggregate (the country or the school) variables are stronger and sometimes even different from their relationships at the individual level of the woman or student. Moreover, the interpretation of the results could be distorted, if not fallacious, if one endeavors to interpret the aggregate relationships at the individual level (Robinson, 1950).

There are major statistical problems with the methods of disaggregation and aggregation. Both are statistically incorrect approaches for modeling an individual behavior using characteristics of the individuals and their contexts as the independent variables. In this paper we show how a statistically correct hierarchical linear model (HLM) may be employed. As an example to illustrate the application of HLM we extend research of Raudenbush and Bryk (2002) and model students' mathematical performance (the dependent variable) using as independent variables several characteristics of the student and several characteristics of the students' schools.

We show that the use of HLM enables us to examine mathematics achievement at two levels. We will see how student characteristics influence their mathematics achievement and how school characteristics influence mean mathematics achievement. We will examine the interactions between the school characteristics and the effects of the student characteristics on their levels of mathematics achievement. "HLM is a powerful tool that permits a separation of within-school from between-school phenomena and allows the simultaneous consideration of the effects of school factors not only on school means but also on structural relationships within schools" (Raudenbush & Bryk, 1986, p. 13).

DATA AND VARIABLES

The data used in this chapter are from a subset of data from the High School and Beyond Survey (HS&B) of 7,185 students who are nested in 160 high schools in the United States. Of these schools, 90 are public, and 70 are private Catholic schools (Bryk, Lee, & Holland, 1993, p. 61). The dependent variable is the mathematics achievement scores of the students in the 160 schools. This is a measure of an individual student's mathematics achievement in the senior year. Mathematics achievement is a desired focus of student achievement, because "(1) mathematics is the academic area most influenced by schooling and least affected by home factors (Murnane, 1975), (2) mathematics is the longest and most reliable of the six HS&B achievement tests (Heyns & Hilton, 1982), and (3) the best information about specific courses students have taken is available in this subject area" (Lee & Bryk, 1989, p. 179).

We use five independent variables to model mathematics achievement (Table 21.1). Three are measured at the level of the individual student, and two are measured at the level of the school. They are the following:

(1) Female

This is a dummy variable scored 1 if the student is female, and 0 if male.

(2) Race

This is a dummy variable coded 1 if the student is black or Hispanic, and 0 if not.

(3) Socioeconomic status (*SES*)

This variable is a standardized measure determined from socioeconomic characteristics of the students' parents. The scale includes various aspects of socioeconomic status, such as the parents' education level, occupation, and income.

(4) High minority percentage (*HIMINTY*)

This is a school-based measure of the percentage of minorities enrolled in an individual school. It is a dummy variable scored 1 if the school has more than 40% minority enrollment and 0 if 40% or less minority enrollment

(5) Academic Tracking (*PRACAD*)

This is a school-level measure of the proportion of students in the school in an academic track.

Table 21.1 shows descriptive information for the dependent variable and the five independent variables. The students' mean mathematics achievement score is 12.8. Almost one third of the students are minority, and just over one half are females. Socioeconomic status is measured in standardized units, so its mean is zero. On average each school has 51 percent of its students in an academic track, and 28% of the schools have more than 40% minority enrollment.

ANALYSIS OF VARIANCE

To begin the analysis, we first conducted an analysis of variance (ANOVA) to enable us to "determine the total amount of variability in the outcome (senior-year mathematics achievement) within and between schools"

Table 21.1 Descriptive Data: 7,185 Students Nested in 160 Schools

Variable Name	*N*	*Mean*	*SD*	*Minimum*	*Maximum*
Minority status (*MINORITY*)	7,185	0.27	0.45	0.00	1.00
Female gender (*FEMALE*)	7,185	0.53	0.50	0.00	1.00
Socioeconomic Status (*SES*)	7,185	0.00	0.78	−3.76	2.69
Mathematics achievement (*MATHACH*)	7,185	12.75	6.88	−2.83	24.99
Proportion of the school with students in an academic track (*PRACAD*)	160	0.51	0.26	0.00	1.00
Whether the school is more than 40% minority (*HIMINTY*)	160	0.28	0.45	0.00	1.00

Note: Data source obtained from the 1982 High School and Beyond Survey.

(Byrk & Raudenbush, 1992, p. 104). If the school level variance does not equal zero, this means that there is variance in mathematics achievement across the 160 schools, and is an indication that multilevel modeling is an appropriate methodology.

The Level-1 or student equation predicting mathematics achievement, Y_{ij}, for the i-th student in the j-th school, with no independent variables, is the following (Raudenbush & Bryk, 2002, pp. 69-70):

$$Y_{ij} = \beta_{0j} + r_{ij} \tag{1}$$

This equation models student achievement in each school with just an intercept, β_{0j}, which in this case is the mean of mathematics achievement for the school; r_{ij} is the error for the i-th student in the j-th school.

The Level-2, or the school level equation, with each school's mean mathematics achievement, β_{0j}, is modeled as a function of the grand mean on mathematics achievement plus a random error, and is the following:

$$\beta_{0j} = \gamma_{00} + u_{0j} \tag{2}$$

These two equations are combined into one individual-level equation, and estimated via HLM, as follows:

$$Y_{ij} = \gamma_{00} + u_{0j} + r_{ij} \tag{3}$$

The maximum likelihood estimates of the variance components are as follows. At the Level-1 or student level, the variance is $\text{Var}(r_{ij}) = \sigma^2 =$ 39.15. At the Level-2 or school level, the variance of the true school means around the grand mean, referred to as τ_{00}, is 8.61. These estimates indicate that most of the variation in student mathematics achievement occurs at the student level, that is, within schools, although there is a substantial proportion of variance in the dependent variable between schools.

To be specific, we may estimate the intraclass correlation, which in this case represents "the proportion of variance in Y between schools" (Raudenbush & Bryk, 2002, p. 71), using this formula:

$$\begin{aligned} \rho &= \tau_{00} / \tau_{00} + \sigma^2 \\ &= 8.61 / (8.61 + 39.15) \\ &= 0.18 \end{aligned} \tag{4}$$

This means that 18% of the variance in student mathematics achievement occurs between schools, and that 82% (100% – 18%) of the variance occurs at the student level, that is, within schools. These are the variances we will endeavor to explain, or account for, in our modeling (Raudenbush & Bryk, 2002, pp. 69-71).

THE HIERARCHICAL LINEAR MODEL

The ANOVA indicates there is a significant amount of variance in mathematics achievement at the school level. We now introduce the hierarchical linear model to be used to model these variances. The model is adapted and extended from equations presented in Raudenbush and Bryk (2002, chapters 2 and 4).

The relationship between the three student-level independent variables, namely *MINORITY, FEMALE*, and *SES* and the student-level outcome of mathematics achievement (*MATHACH*) is:

$$Y_i = \beta_0 + \beta_1(MINORITY)_i + \beta_2(FEMALE)_i + \beta_3(SES)_i + r_i \quad (5)$$

The intercept, β_0, is the expected mathematics achievement of a student whose values on the independent variables are zero, that is, they are not minority, they are not female, and their SES is zero. The slope, β_1, is the expected change in mathematics achievement if the student is a minority. The slope, β_2, is the expected change in mathematics achievement if the student is a female. And the slope, β_3, is the expected change in mathematics achievement associated with a one unit increase in SES. The error term, r_i, represents a unique effect associated with person i. It is assumed that r_i is normally distributed. We center the three student level independent variables so that the intercept may be interpreted as average mathematics achievement.

Equation 5 is a typical microlevel equation, which predicts the same expected achievement β_0 for all students on the basis of their values on the three independent variables; and it furthermore specifies the effects of the three independent variables on mathematics achievement (β_1, β_2, and β_2) to be the same for all students. In other words, the effects in this model are equal for all students; they are fixed.

Let us move beyond Equation 5 to an equation in which the four effects (the intercept and the three slopes) are random, and not fixed. We noted above that the data used here consist of a random sample of 160 schools in which the 7,185 students are nested. Thus we will estimate the mathematics achievement Equation 5 above for each of the 160 schools as follows:

$$Y_{ij} = \beta_{0j} + \beta_{1j}(MINORITY)_{ij} + \beta_{2j}(FEMALE)_{ij} + \beta_{3j}(SES)_{ij} + r_{ij} \quad (6)$$

Note that the intercept and the three slopes have been subscripted with j. Thus the four effects, β_{0j}, β_{1j} , β_{2j}, and β_{3j}, are now varying across the schools. We now present level-2 or school-based equations in which we use the two school characteristics of whether or not the school has more than 40% minority (*HIMINTY*) and the proportion of the students in the school in an academic track (*PRACAD*) to predict each of these four effects.

The four school level equations thus are the following:

$$\beta_{0j} = \gamma_{00} + \gamma_{01}\,(HIMINTY)_j + \gamma_{02}\,(PRACAD)_j + u_{0j} \qquad (7)$$

$$\beta_{1j} = \gamma_{10} + \gamma_{11}\,(HIMINTY)_j + \gamma_{12}\,(PRACAD)_j + u_{1j} \qquad (8)$$

$$\beta_{2j} = \gamma_{20} + \gamma_{21}\,(HIMINTY)_j + \gamma_{22}\,(PRACAD)_j + u_{2j} \qquad (9)$$

$$\beta_{3j} = \gamma_{30} + \gamma_{31}\,(HIMINTY)_j + \gamma_{32}\,(PRACAD)_j + u_{3j} \qquad (10)$$

Equations 7 through 10 are then combined with Equation 6 to yield the following HLM equation:

$$\begin{aligned} Y_{ij} = {} & \gamma_{00} + \gamma_{01}(PRACAD)_j + \gamma_{02}(HIMINTY)_j + \\ & \gamma_{10}\,(MINORITY_{ij}) + \gamma_{11}(PRACAD)_j\,(MINORITY_{ij}) + \\ & \gamma_{12}(HIMINITY)_j\,(MINORITY_{ij}) + \gamma_{20}\,(FEMALE_{ij}) + \\ & \gamma_{21}(PRACAD)_j\,(FEMALE_{ij}) + \gamma_{22}(HIMINITY)_j\,(FEMALE_{ij}) + \\ & \gamma_{30}(SES_{ij}) + \gamma_{31}(PRACAD)_j\,(SES_{ij}) + \gamma_{32}(HIMINITY)_j\,(SES_{ij}) + \\ & u_{0j} + u_{1j}\,(MINORITY)_{ij} + u_{1j}\,(FEMALE)_{ij} + u_{1j}\,(SES)_{ij} + \\ & u_{2j}\,(MINORITY)_{ij} + u_{2j}\,(FEMALE)_{ij} + u_{2j}\,(SES)_{ij} + r_{ij} \end{aligned} \qquad (11)$$

Equation 11 is a statistically correct multilevel equation estimating the student outcome on mathematics achievement, Y_{ij}, as a function of the following:

- the overall intercept, γ_{00}, which in this case is the grand mean on mathematics achievement across the schools,
- the main effect of (school's) academic track (*PRACAD*), γ_{01},
- the main effect of (school's) high minority (*HIMINTY*), γ_{02},
- the main effect of (student's) minority status (*MINORITY*), γ_{10},
- the main effect of (student's) female status (*FEMALE*), γ_{20},
- the main effect of (student's) SES (*SES*), γ_{30},
- and six cross-level interactions involving
  - *PRACAD* with MINORITY slope, γ_{11},
  - *PRACAD* with *FEMALE* slope, γ_{21},
  - *PRACAD* with *SES* slope, γ_{31},

- *HIMINTY* with *MINORITY* slope, γ_{12},
- *HIMINTY* with *FEMALE* slope, γ_{22}, and
- *HIMINTY* with SES slope, γ_{32}, plus

a random error,

$$u_{0j} + u_{1j}\,(MINORITY)_{ij} + u_{1j}\,(FEMALE)_{ij} + u_{1j}\,(SES)_{ij} + u_{2j}\,(MINORITY)_{ij} + u_{2j}\,(FEMALE)_{ij} + u_{2j}\,(SES)_{ij} + r_{ij}$$

The HLM regression results for Equation 11 are reported in Table 21.2. This HLM model includes three student level variables (*MINORITY, FEMALE,* and *SES*) and two school level variables (*PRACAD* and *HIMINTY*). As discussed previously, *PRACAD* is the proportion of students in the academic track and *HIMINTY* is whether or not the school had a minority population of over 40%.

We look first at the direct effects of the student level variables. The HLM regression results in Table 21.2 indicate that student's minority status, γ_{10}, is negatively related to mathematics achievement. Minority students on average have mathematics achievement scores 3.05 points lower than white students ($t = -11.47$). Female students on average have mathematics achievement scores that are 1.10 points lower than male students, γ_{20}, ($t = -5.76$). A third direct effect pertains to the student's socioeconomic status (*SES*), γ_{30}. With each increase in a unit of SES, the student's mathematics score on average increases by 1.91 points ($t = 15.89$). The HLM regression results shown in Table 21.2 make evident the fact that student level characteristics do indeed have statistically significant effects on mathematics achievement.

We next consider the direct effects of the school level variables. In Table 21.2, we see that *PRACAD* is positively related to mathematics achievement and is highly significant, $\gamma_{01} = 7.81$, $t = 21.18$. On average, with every increase of .01 in the proportion of students in the academic track, mathematics achievement increases by .08 points. There is also a significant negative relationship between *HIMINTY* and mathematics achievement, $\gamma_{02} = -2.36$, $t = -11.35$. Schools over 40% minority have mathematics achievement scores on average that are 2.36 lower than schools with less than 40% minority.

Last, we examine the three cross-level interactions that are statistically significant. The school characteristic *PRACAD*, that is, the proportion of students in the academic track, has significant influences on two of the three student-level slopes, namely the minority slope, γ_{11}, and the SES slope, γ_{31}. With each increase in *PRACAD* of .01, the minority-mathematics achievement slope increases by .02 ($t = 2.54$). In schools with a large

Table 21.2. HLM Regression Results Predicting Math Achievement

	Effect	*SE*	*t statistic*
Direct Effects			
Intercept (γ_{00})	12.608	.093	135.644
MINORITY (γ_{10})	–3.053	.266	–11.471
FEMALE (γ_{20})	–1.099	.191	–5.755
SES (γ_{30})	1.909	.120	15.893
Academic Track (*PRACAD*) ($\gamma 01$)	7.808	.369	21.176
High Minority (*HIMINTY*) (γ_{02})	–2.359	.208	–11.351
Interaction Effects			
Academic track (*PRACAD*) on:			
MINORITY slope ($\gamma 11$)	2.529	.994	2.543
FEMALE slope (γ_{21})	.896	.829	1.081
SES slope (γ_{31})	–1.014	.485	–2.089
High minority (*HIMINTY*) on:			
MINORITY slope (γ_{12})	.335	.534	.627
FEMALE slope (γ_{22})	.207	.441	.471
SES slope (γ_{32})	–0.935	.264	–3.546

proportion of students in the academic track, the disadvantageous effect of minority status on mathematics achievement is lessened as follows: with each increase of .01 in *PRACAD*, the SES-mathematics achievement slope decreases by .01. In other words, SES is converted into mean mathematics achievement in schools with a high proportion of students in the academic track at a rate .01 less than in schools with a lower proportion of students in the academic track. Therefore, the potentially advantageous effects of high SES are decreased in schools with a high proportion of students in the academic track, and vice versa. The one cross-level interaction involving the school variable of 40% or more minorities (*HIMINTY*) is with the SES slope, γ_{32}. In high minority schools, SES is converted into mathematics achievement at a rate .94 lower than in low minority schools. Again, the advantageous effects of SES decline in schools with over 40% minority student enrollment.

CONCLUSION

In this chapter we were concerned with modeling an individual level dependent variable using as predictors characteristics of both the individuals and their contexts. We used as an example the estimation of mathematics achievement of schoolchildren. This dependent variable was estimated using three student characteristics and two school characteristics.

We noted that the disaggregating of the school characteristics down to the student level, and the aggregating of the student characteristics up to the school level are not desirable statistical approaches. Instead the correct statistical method involves the estimation of a hierarchical linear model (HLM). The major part of our paper involved illustrating the application of an HLM equation. In our brief HLM example, we only discussed the straightforward regression results dealing with the effects of the student-level and school-level characteristics on student mathematics achievement. There are many additional features of the HLM approach not considered in our brief article. For instance, we did not present information on the variances in mathematics achievement explained at the levels of the students and the schools. We did not address issues of explaining variances not in mathematics achievement but in the effects across the schools of the student level slopes. See Raudenbush and Bryk (2002) for more discussion.

We showed essentially that HLM involves performing regressions of regressions. Regressions are first estimated to predict a level-1, that is, student, outcome as a function of other level-1, i.e. student, characteristics. These equations are then estimated separately for the various level-2 units, that is, schools, and are referred to as within-unit models. When estimating an HLM equation, the researcher often allows the intercepts and slopes from these level-2 units to vary randomly, that is, to permit each level-2 unit to have its own intercept and slopes. Thus these level-1 coefficients are next used as the dependent variables in a level-2 regression equation. At this point, the level-2 units are the units of analysis, and other level-2 characteristics are the independent, that is, *X* variables. These regressions are known as between-unit models.

As just noted, this could all be done within an OLS framework, that is, one could estimate level-1 OLS equations for a series of level-2 units; and then use these level-1 coefficients as dependent variables at the higher level. But if this were done within an OLS framework, it would not be possible to take into account the variances of the parameters at one level in the estimates of the parameters and their variances at the next level. We have shown in this paper that such a strategy is a major part of HLM.

HLM has several advantages. Within the context of a 2-level HLM, there are at least four:

1. the HLM approach takes a level-1 outcome and partitions its variance among the level-1 and level-2 units;

2. the HLM equation models simultaneously the effects on the outcome at both levels, using level-1 characteristics as predictors of the outcome at level-1 and level-2 characteristics as predictors of the outcome at level-2; and it can also consider in the same overall equation the cross-level effects of a level-2 predictor on the slopes of level-1 predictors on the outcome;
3. the HLM equation as presented here produces better estimates of the predictors of the level-1 outcome by "borrowing" information about these relationships from other level-2 units; this is an empirical Bayes feature of HLM, which was not addressed above (see Raudenbush & Bryk, 2002, pp13-14); and
4. the HLM approach is a more statistically correct approach for addressing multilevel inquiries. Allow us to elaborate on this fourth point.

Recall from Equation 11 that the school variables interact with the microlevel variables, and the error structure contains both microlevel terms and macrolevel terms. Equation 11 is not the typical linear model that is estimated in standard OLS models; efficient estimation and accurate hypothesis testing based on OLS require that the random errors must be independent, normally distributed, and have constant variance. In contrast, the random error in the above equation is of a more complex form, namely "$u_{0j} + u_{1j}\,(MINORITY)_{ij} + u_{1j}\,(FEMALE)_{ij} + u_{1j}\,(SES)_{ij} + u_{2j}(MINORITY)_{ij} + u_{2j}\,(FEMALE)_{ij} + u_{2j}\,(SES)_{ij} + r_{ij}$." Such errors are dependent within each level-2 unit because the components u_{0j} , u_{1j} and u_{2j} are common to every person (or level-1 unit) within each of the j level-2 units. The errors also have unequal variances; they vary across the level-2 units; they also depend on the values of the student-level variables which vary across the level-1 units. If u_{0j} , u_{1j} and u_{2j} were zero for each j, the equation would be equivalent to an OLS regression model (Bryk & Raudenbush, 1992, p. 15).

To solve the Equation 11, standard regression analysis is inappropriate. DiPrete and Forristal (1994, p. 337) have observed that under the usual assumptions, an OLS estimation of Equation 11 would produce rather consistent estimates of the coefficients, but inconsistent estimates of their standard errors.

The kind of multilevel modeling we refer to in this paper as HLM did not emerge until the early 1970s when a statistical theory for the estimation of multilevel models was developed; computer algorithms to compute these estimates were developed in the late 1970s. Raudenbush and Bryk (2002) credit the article published by Lindley and Smith in 1972 with the formulation of Bayesian methods for the estimation of linear models with nested data and complex error structures. Two articles published by Dempster and colleagues (Dempster, Laird, & Rubin, 1977; Dempster, Rubin, & Tsutakawa) in 1977 and 1981 developed the computer algorithm to estimate the covariance components in these models. The old and statistically incorrect approaches of estimating multilevel models using OLS approaches after disaggregating and aggregating the data are no longer appropriate.

REFERENCES

de Leeuw, J. (2002). Series editor introduction to hierarchical linear models. In S. W. Raudenbush & A. S. Bryk (Eds.), *Hierarchical linear models: Applications and data analysis methods* (2nd ed., pp. xix-xxii). Thousand Oaks, CA: Sage.

Dempster, A. P., Laird, N. M., & Rubin, D. B. (1977). Maximum likelihood from incomplete data via the EM algorithm. *Journal of the Royal Statistical Society, Series B 39*, 1-8.

Dempster, A. P., Rubin, D. B., & Tsutakawa, R. K. (1981). Estimation in covariance components models. *Journal of the American Statistical Association, 76*, 341-353.

DiPrete, T. A., & Fortistal, J. D. (1994). Multilevel models: Methods and substance. *Annual Review of Sociology, 20*, 331-357.

Entwisle, D. R., Alexander, K. L., & Olson, L. S. (1994). The gender gap in math: Its possible origins in neighborhood effects. *American Sociological Review, 59*, 822-838.

Heyns, B. L., & Hilton, T. L. (1982). The cognitive tests for high school and beyond: Assessment. *Sociology of Education, 55*, 89-102.

Lee, V. E., & Bryk, A. S. (1989). A multilevel model of the social distribution of high school achievement. *Sociology of Education, 62*, 172-192.

Lindley, D. V., & Smith, A. F. M. (1972). Bayes estimates for the linear model. *Journal of the Royal Statistical Society, Series B 34*, 1-41.

Murnane, R. J. (1975). *The impact of school resources on the learning of inner city school children.* Cambridge, MA: Ballinger.

Poston, D. L., Jr. (2002). The effects of human capital and cultural capital characteristics on the economic attainment patterns of male and female Asian-born immigrants to the United States: Multi-level analyses. *Asian and Pacific Migration Journal, 11*, 197-219.

Raudenbush, S., & Bryk, A. S. (1986). A hierarchical model for studying school effects. *Sociology of Education, 59*, 1-17.

Raudenbush, S. W., & Bryk, A. S. (2002). *Hierarchical linear models: Applications and data analysis methods* (2nd ed.). Thousand Oaks, CA: Sage.

Robinson, W. S. (1950). Ecological correlations and the behavior of individuals. *American Sociological Review, 15*, 351-357.

CHAPTER 22

GRADE INFLATION

An Examination at the Institutional Level

Sharon L. Weinberg

In a recent *New York Times* article titled "Princeton Tries to Put a Cap on Giving A's" (Arenson, 2004), Nancy Weiss Malkiel, dean of Princeton's undergraduate college, was quoted as saying that grade inflation "was a national problem and that it would be terrific if a university had the courage to take it on" (p. B5). Grade inflation has been defined (Goldman, 1985; Rosovsky & Hartley, 2002) as an upward shift in the grade point average (GPA) of students over an extended period of time without a corresponding increase in student achievement. According to this article, "65 percent of the graduating seniors [at Princeton] in the class of 2002 had grade-point averages of B-plus or better, and fewer than 5 percent fell below B-minus. A student with a straight C average stood second to last" (p. B5).

Evidence that grade inflation is, in fact, a national problem, comes from the work of Stuart Rojstaczer, a professor at Duke University, who has collected data at over 80 colleges and universities, some of which include grade point average (GPA) trends of over 15 years or longer. These data confirm that, regardless of institution selectivity, grade infla-

Real Data Analysis, pp. 315–323

tion "has continued unabated at virtually every school for which data are available," (2003b). The reported rate of change is 0.146 points per decade, on average, since 1967, which "is consistent with the trends over the past 11 years." In a *Washington Post* article, Professor Rojstaczer (2003a) provides a number of particular instances of grade inflation. He notes that "at Pomona College, C's are now less than 4 percent of all grades. About half of all grades at Pomona, Duke, Harvard and Columbia are in the A range. State schools are not immune to this change. At the University of Illinois, A's constitute more than 40 percent of all grades and outnumber C's by almost three to one" (p. A 21).

While improved student quality has been offered as a possible reason for this increase, Professor Rojstaczer has argued against this as a plausible explanation. He notes that statements linking increased student quality to increased grades typically have been qualitative in nature, and that those few statements that are quantitative in nature suggest the absence of such a relationship. Using SAT or ACT as a proxy for student quality, he writes that "at both Texas and Duke, GPA increases of about 0.25 were coincident with mean SAT increases (Math and Verbal combined) in the student population of about 50 points. At Wisconsin, ACT increases of 2 points (the equivalent to an SAT increase of about 70 points) were coincident with a GPA rise of 0.21." According to Professor Rojstaczer, these data support the notion that increases in student quality do not, in large part, account for the magnitude of grade inflation observed.

Given that SAT and GPA are in different metrics, and that we cannot judge the magnitude of the GPA increase by the information provided other than that it exceeds the reported average 10-year rate of change of 0.146 points, it is not clear that these facts, by themselves, support Professor Rojstaczer's interpretation. Furthermore, different metrics aside, analyses that are based solely on aggregated mean values are not sufficiently sensitive to patterns of individual covariation in student quality and GPA to be as informative as Professor Rojstaczer suggests at the institutional level. A more appropriate approach for addressing whether increases in student quality account for increases in GPA would utilize a regression framework with the individual as the unit of analysis. Within this framework, increases in GPA could be assessed after partialling out or controlling for increases in student quality, as measured, for example, by combined verbal and math SAT. In this way, one could determine directly to what extent an increase in student quality accounts for the increase in GPA.

The following describes such an analysis using real data collected at a large private university in the northeast and shows that (1) while there is a statistically significant increase in the graduation GPA of two cohorts of undergraduate students, one entering in 1993 and the other entering in

1997, (2) after controlling for the increase in student quality of these two cohorts, the statistically significant increase in GPA becomes nonsignificant, and, (3) after including high school GPA as an additional covariate in the analysis, the observed nonstatistically significant cohort effect turns significantly negative, indicating a grade deflation effect.

DATA

The data for this analysis were obtained from the records of all undergraduate students enrolled in the college of arts and science of this private university who were from one of two cohorts. The first cohort consisted of all students who first enrolled in the college of arts and science in September, 1993 and who graduated in May, 1997; the second cohort consisted of all students who first enrolled in the college of arts and science in September, 1997 and who graduated in May, 2001. These data may be found at http://homepages.nyu.edu/~slw1/gradeinflation-data.htm. Students with missing data on any one of the three key variables (graduation college GPA, high school GPA, combined verbal and math SAT score) were excluded from the analysis. The resulting sample of data consisted of a total of 1,204 students, 526 from cohort one and 678 from cohort two. As Table 22.1 indicates, the distribution of students by discipline is similar across cohorts.

EVIDENCE OF GRADE INFLATION PRESENT IN THESE DATA

Like Princeton, 65% of the graduating seniors of the class of 2001 at this northeast university had a GPA of B+ or better and 6% fell below B-. That only 60% of the graduating seniors of the class of 1997 at this northeast

Table 22.1. Distribution of Disciplines by Cohort

		Frequency	*Percent*
1993	HUMANIT	136	25.9
	SCIENCE	248	47.1
	SOCSCIEN	142	27.0
	Total	526	100.0
1997	HUMANIT	184	27.1
	SCIENCE	318	46.9
	SOCSCIEN	176	26.0
	Total	678	100.0

university had a GPA of B+ or better and 10% fell below B–, further suggests an overall grade increase at this university, but not necessarily grade inflation per se. By factoring in student quality, using a regression framework, as shown in the next section, a different picture emerges, one which provides a more conclusive and definitive answer to the question of whether grade inflation exists at this private university in the northeast.

REGRESSION ANALYSES

Table 22.2 gives the results of a series of descriptive univariate analyses on the three key variables included in this study.

According to Table 22.2, these variables may be considered by some to be significantly skewed by virtue of their *t* ratios (skew statistic/standard error). Given the large sample size per cohort and the fact that the skew statistics themselves are within one unit of zero, normalizing transformations are contraindicated (Weinberg & Abramowitz, 2002). Subsequent residual analyses on the regression results (to be presented later in this chapter) suggest that all assumptions underlying the regression model are met and, therefore, confirm this assessment. As expected from the recent reports on grade inflation at both the college and high school levels, there is an observed average increase of .078 points in college GPA over the four years studied, from 3.333 in cohort one to 3.411 in cohort two. Extrapolating to a period of 10 years, this amounts to an increase of .195 points, which is slightly larger in magnitude than the 0.146 increase in GPA reported by Rojstaczer. Likewise, there is an observed average increase in high school GPA of .209 points over this 4-year period, from 3.427 to 3.636. This increase, over only 4 years, surpasses the 0.18 increase reported by the College Board (2001) over a 10-year period from

Table 22.2. Descriptive Statistics of Key Study Variables

		N	*Mean*	*Std.*	*Skewness*	
		Statistic	*Statistic*	*Statistic*	*Statistic*	*Std. Error*
1993	Graduation GPA	526	3.33391	.366200	–.559	.106
	High school GPA	526	3.42669	.424467	–.590	.106
	SAT total score (recentered)	526	1238.88	127.534	.076	.106
1997	Graduation GPA	678	3.41166	.337799	–.578	.094
	High school GPA	678	3.63614	.307524	–.713	.094
	SAT total score (recentered)	678	1323.14	106.693	–.298	.094

Table 22.3. Regression Model Summary and Coefficients With Cohort as the Predictor

Model Summary

Model	*R*	R^2	*Adjusted* R^2	*Std. Error of the Estimate*
1	.109[a]	.012	.011	.350487

Coefficients[b]

Model		*Unstandardized Coefficients* *B*	*Std. Error*	*Standardized Coefficients* *Beta*	*t*	*Sig.*
1	(Constant)	3.334	.015		218.160	.000
	cohort	.078	.020	.109	3.818	.000

[a]Predictors: (Constant), cohort.
[b]Dependent variable: graduation GPA.

1991 to 2001 (from 3.10 in 1991 to 3.28 in 2001) based on national data. Finally, there is, as expected with respect to this particular university, an impressive 85 point increase in student quality over these 4 years as measured by these students' combined verbal and math SAT scores.

To determine whether (1) there is a statistically significant increase in the graduation GPA of these two cohorts of undergraduate students spaced 4 years apart, a simple regression analysis was carried out with graduation GPA as the dependent variable and cohort as the single independent variable. For these analyses, the 1993 entering cohort was coded 0 and the 1997 entering cohort was coded 1. Results of this simple regression analysis appear in Table 22.3.

According to Table 22.3, the cohort effect is statistically significant (t = 3.818, p = .000) and positive, suggesting that, as expected, there is a statistically significant increase in the average graduation GPA from 1997 to 2001 and that as noted earlier, the increase, according the b-coefficient, is .078 points.

To determine whether (2) after controlling for the observed increase in student quality from cohort one to cohort two, the statistically significant increase in GPA becomes nonsignificant, an analysis was carried out with the combined verbal and math SAT score added as a covariate to the simple regression model. The correlation between the two predictors (cohort and graduation SAT) is moderately low at r = 0.339 and the assumption of homogeneity of regression (parallel slopes fitted to each cohort) was shown to be met for these data. Other results of this analysis are given in Table 22.4.

Table 22.4. Regression Model Summary and Coefficients With SAT as Covariate and Cohort as the Predictor

Model Summary

					Change Statistics				
Model	*R*	R^2	*Adjusted* R^2	*Std. Error of the Estimate*	R^2 *Change*	*F Change*	*df1*	*df2*	*Sig. F Change*
1	.418[a]	.175	.174	.320305	.175	254.656	1	1,202	.000
2	.420[b]	.176	.175	.320212	.001	1.695	1	1,201	.193

Coefficients[c]

		Unstandardized Coefficients		*Standardized Coefficients*		
Model		*B*	*Std. Error*	*Beta*	*t*	*Sig.*
1	(Constant)	1.843	.097		19.071	.000
	SAT total score (Recentered)	.001	.000	.418	15.958	.000
2	(Constant)	1.812	.099		18.230	.000
	SAT total score (Recentered)	.001	.000	.430	15.461	.000
	cohort	–.026	.020	–.036	–1.302	.193

[a]Predictors: (Constant), SAT total score (Recentered).
[b]Predictors: (Constant), SAT total score (Recentered), cohort.
[c]Dependent variable: graduation GPA.

According to Table 22.4, after controlling for student quality, as measured by combined verbal and math SAT score, the variable cohort is no longer statistically significant ($t = -1.302$, $p = .193$), suggesting that the increase in student quality at this university accounts for the increase in graduation GPA from cohort one to cohort two. The amount of graduation GPA variance explained by both combined SAT and cohort is approximately 18 percent.

Finally, to determine whether (3) the observed nonstatistically significant cohort effect in analysis (2) becomes significantly negative after controlling for high school GPA as well, a new regression analysis was carried out with high school GPA added to the equation as a second covariate. The correlation between the two covariates (combined SAT and high school GPA) is computed as $r = .369$ and the correlation between high school GPA and cohort is $r = .275$. The assumption of homogeneity of regression for these data was tested and found to be tenable. Results of the full regression with the two covariates and one predictor are given in Table 22.5.

Table 22.5. Regression Model Summary and Coefficients With Two Covariates and One Predictor

Model Summary

					Change Statistics				
Model	*R*	R^2	*Adjusted* R^2	*Std. Error of the Estimate*	R^2 *Change*	*F Change*	*df1*	*df2*	*Sig. F Change*
1	.514[a]	.264	.263	.302605	.264	215.523	2	1,201	.000
2	.521[b]	.272	.270	.301179	.008	12.401	1	1,200	.000

Coefficients[c]

		Unstandardized Coefficients		*Standardized Coefficients*		
Model		*B*	*Std. Error*	*Beta*	*t*	*Sig.*
1	(Constant)	1.214	.105		11.557	.000
	SAT total score (Recentered)	.001	.000	.300	11.251	.000
	High school GPA	.300	.025	.321	12.072	.000
2	(Constant)	1.104	.109		10.107	.000
	SAT total score (Recentered)	.001	.000	.325	11.834	.000
	High school GPA	.315	.025	.338	12.554	.000
	cohort	–.066	.019	–.094	–3.522	.000

[a]Predictors: (Constant), high school GPA, SAT total score (Recentered).
[b]Predictors: (Constant), high school GPA, SAT total score (Recentered), cohort.
[c]Dependent variable: graduation GPA.

According to Table 22.5, the addition of high school GPA as a covariate makes cohort statistically significant ($t = -3.522$, $p = .000$) with a negative sign, suggesting that after controlling for both combined SAT score and high school GPA (which are both statistically significant), there is a statistically significant deflation in graduation GPA from cohort one to cohort two. With all three variables in the equation, a reasonably large percent (approximately 27%) of graduation GPA variance is explained, suggesting that together both high school GPA and combined SAT are more effective in defining student quality than either variable alone.

When combined as a linear composite, high school GPA and SAT also can be said to form a more reliable indicator of student quality than either variable alone, and to contain, therefore, less error than either variable alone. We know that, for example, in a simple regression context, random error in the dependent variable has no effect upon a regression coefficient, but such error in the independent variable attenuates the coefficient of that variable (Johnston, 1963). We also know that if a dummy variable, like cohort, is added to the equation, then the coefficient of that variable will be positively biased as a function of the magnitude of error contained in the covariate (student quality, in this case), the strength of the relationship between the covariate and dependent variable (student quality and graduation grades), and the magnitude of difference between the 1997 and 1993 cohorts in terms of graduating grades without controlling for student quality (Director, 1979). Accordingly, given that one can argue that SAT alone is a more imperfect proxy of student quality than SAT and high school GPA combined, with SAT as the sole covariate in the equation, the non-significant b-weight for cohort may be considered to be more upwardly biased than the significant negative *b*-weight for cohort that results from having both covariates, high school GPA and SAT, in the equation. Said differently, the negative *b*-weight for cohort with the two covariates in the equation provides a better (less upwardly biased) estimate of the difference between the cohorts in terms of graduating grades, and, as such, offers stronger evidence for the conclusion of grade deflation in this case.

One may speculate that the type of behavior that gives rise to such grade deflation is grading on a curve, either explicitly or implicitly. In such instances, the instructor would give a set percentage of each grade, norm-referenced to the current class, despite the increase in student quality in that class as compared to prior years. One may also speculate that such norm-referenced grading is a general practice of instructors in higher education.

CONCLUSION

The topic of grade inflation in higher education has garnered much attention in recent years. In addition to the references cited earlier in this paper, a comprehensive report on grade inflation by Rosovsky and Hartley (2002) cites more than 50 published articles and reports on the subject, and many more such references may be found in a recently published book on grade inflation by Johnson (2003). The totality of evidence presented in these works leaves little doubt that, on a national level, grade inflation has existed from the late 1960s to the present. What the analysis in this chapter demonstrates is that the national phenomenon of grade inflation may not replicate at the institution level when, in particular, improvement in student quality at an institution outstrips grade increases at that institution over the same time period. The extraordinary improvement in the quality of students during the period studied at this private university in the northeast accounts for the increase in grades over this same period, despite the fact that as noted by Rosovsky and Hartley

(2002), most evidence for the improvement in student quality on a national level "goes in the opposite direction" (p. 11).

In sum, this chapter does not contradict the dean of Princeton's undergraduate college and others that grade inflation is "a national problem." It does suggest, however, that universities ought to take seriously the challenge to investigate whether grade inflation exists at their own institutions by conducting the type of analysis presented here as a first step.

REFERENCES

Arenson, K. (2004, April 8). Princeton tries to put a cap on giving A's. *The New York Times*, p. B1.

College Board. (2001, August 28). 2001 college bound seniors are the largest, most diverse group in history. Press Release No. 131. http://www.collegeboard.com/sat/cbsenior/yr2001/pdf/CompleteCBSReport.pdf.

Director, S. M. (1979). Underadjustment bias in the evaluation of manpower training. *Evaluation Quarterly, 3*, 190-218.

Goldman, L. (1985). The betrayal of the gatekeepers: Grade inflation. *Journal of General Education, 37*(2), 97-121.

Johnson, V. (2003). *Grade inflation: A crisis in college education.* New York: Springer-Verlag.

Johnston, J. (1963). *Econometric methods.* New York: McGraw-Hill.

Rojstaczer, S. (2003a, January 28). Where all grades are above average. *The Washington Post*, p. A21.

Rojstacaer, S. (2003b). National trends in grade inflation: American colleges and universities. Retrieved March 17, 2003, from http://www.gradeinflation.com

Rosovsky, H., & Hartley, M. (2002). *Evaluation and the academy: Are we doing the right thing? Grade inflation and letters of recommendation.* Cambridge, MA: American Academy of Arts and Sciences.

Weinberg, S. L., & Abramowitz, S. K. (2002). *Data analysis for the behavioral sciences using SPSS.* London: Cambridge University Press.

CHAPTER 23

USING DISCRETE-TIME SURVIVAL ANALYSIS TO STUDY GENDER DIFFERENCES IN LEAVING MATHEMATICS

Suzanne E. Graham and Judith D. Singer

Mathematics courses are important for numerous fields of study and occupations, yet few students, particularly women, take mathematics throughout high school and college. To design interventions increasing mathematics participation for all students, educators, and policymakers need to know when students are most likely to terminate their mathematics educations and whether women and men have different patterns of risk of leaving math. Many researchers have studied this question (e.g., Catsambis, 1994; Davenport, Davison, Kuang, Kim, & Kwak, 1998; Ma, 2001; Walker, 2001), yet few have done so using prospective, longitudinal data. Of those who have used prospective, longitudinal data, only a handful have used analytic methods sensitive to questions about timing (e.g., Downer-Assaf, 1995; Ma, 2001; Walker, 2001) and those researchers focused their analyses only on secondary school students.

Real Data Analysis, pp. 325–333

In this chapter, we describe research done by Graham (1997), who used discrete-time survival analysis (Singer & Willett, 1993, 2003) to study the mathematics course-taking history of 3,790 students (1,875 boys and 1,915 girls) from 10th grade through the fourth semester of college. The data used in Graham's research came from the National Science Foundation funded Longitudinal Study of American Youth (LSAY), a 7-year study of U.S. secondary and college students. While Graham examined the impact of several individual and contextual characteristics on the risk that students will leave mathematics during high school and college, here we focus specifically on the effect of gender, describing analyses that allow us to determine: (1) *when* during high school and the first 2 years of college students are most likely to first stop taking mathematics; (2) *whether* women are more likely to end their study of math than men; and (3) if the effect of gender varies with time.

ANALYTIC METHOD

Traditional methods of analysis, such as multiple regression and logistic regression, are ill suited for analyzing event occurrence because of a problem known as *censored observations*, individuals for whom we do not observe the event of interest (Singer & Willett, 1993, 2003). In this study, censored students are those who did not drop out of mathematics during the periods in which they were studied, those who were lost due to study attrition, and those who did not attend college. Although we do need to assume that censoring is noninformative (that is, it is independent of event occurrence and the risk of event occurrence), we do not need to resort to ad hoc fixes known to bias results (such as eliminating the censored cases from the analysis or treating the last known time period of mathematics course taking as the student's final year in mathematics).

The methods of discrete-time survival analysis are ideal for studying event occurrence because they allow us to analyze simultaneously data from noncensored and censored cases alike. We first define the "beginning of time," here 10th grade since all students in the United States are required to take mathematics until at least 10th grade. Next, we follow students prospectively to record whether and, if so, when they leave mathematics *for the first time*, with time measured as occasions of enrolling in mathematics (years in high school, semesters in college). All students who leave mathematics during the time periods in which they were observed are assigned event times equal to the year (or semester) when they actually leave mathematics. Individuals who do not leave mathematics during data collection are assigned *censored event times*, set equal to the year (or semester) when data collection ended or when the student was no longer at risk of leaving mathematics.

How can the risk of event occurrence be summarized when some students have censored event times? In discrete-time survival analysis, the fundamental quantity representing the risk of event occurrence in each time period is called the *hazard probability*, defined as the conditional probability that a student will first stop taking mathematics during a specific year (or semester), *given that he or she did not already drop out*. We estimate the hazard probabilities that answer our first research question about when students are at greatest risk of leaving mathematics for the first time by fitting an initial hazard model (Singer & Willett, 1993, 2003):

$$\text{logit } h(t_{ij}) = \alpha_1 D_{1ij} + \alpha_2 D_{2ij} + \ldots + \alpha_6 D_{6ij} \tag{1}$$

where $h(t_{ij})$ represents the hazard probability for student i during time period j. The α parameters are multiple intercept terms describing the risk of leaving mathematics during each time period, up until time period 6, in which the person either stops taking mathematics or is censored. D_{1ij}, D_{2ij}, ... are a sequence of dummy variables which take on a value of 1 during the j-th time period (i.e., D_{1ij} will take on a value of 1 when $j = 1$, and 0 otherwise). The initial hazard model can be easily expanded to include the effects of substantive predictors, as we show below.

RESULTS

Table 23.1 contains parameter estimates and goodness of fit statistics obtained by fitting the initial hazard model in Equation 1 to the mathematics dropout data. By substituting these parameter estimates into Equation 1, we can compute the estimated probability of leaving mathematics for the first time during each year of high school and semester of college. The profile of these estimated hazard probabilities over time, the fitted hazard function, is presented in Figure 23.1. Examination of the fitted hazard function allows us to determine when students are at highest risk of leaving mathematics. The estimated probability of dropping out of mathematics during 11th grade, given enrollment in 10th grade, is fairly low (13%). Of the students who enroll in mathematics in both 10th and 11th grades, nearly a third (32%) drop out at the start of 12th grade. The estimated hazard decreases to 26% at the start of freshman year of college, possibly reflecting general mathematics requirement for many college students, but it climbs to 39% during the second semester. At the start of sophomore year, the hazard declines somewhat, only to increase again during the second semester of sophomore year. Forty-three percent

Table 23.1. Results of Fitting Three Discrete-Time Hazard Models to the Mathematics Dropout Data

	Parameter Estimate (SE)		
Predictor	*Model 1*	*Model 2*	*Model 3*
Time periods			
11th grade	–1.93 (.05)	–2.13 (.06)	–2.06 (.06)
12th grade	–0.74 (.04)	–0.94 (.05)	–0.92 (.05)
Semester 1	–1.26 (.06)	–1.45 (.06)	–1.48 (.07)
Semester 2	–0.44 (.07)	–0.62 (.08)	–0.69 (.08)
Semester 3	–0.61 (.14)	–0.77 (.14)	–0.88 (.15)
Semester 4	–0.27 (.20)	–0.39 (.20)	–0.50 (.21)
Gender			
FEMALE		0.38 (.05)	.15 (.11)
FEMALE*PERIOD			.10 (.04)
–2LL	10,007 (6)	9949 (7)	9944 (8)
Comparison model		Model 1	Model 2
Change in –2LL (*df*)		57.50 (1)	4.90 (1)
p-value		< .0001	0.03

Note: $n = 3{,}790$.

of the students who take mathematics continuously through high school and the first three semesters of college are predicted to drop out during their fourth semester. This is particularly alarming given that a mere 18% of the students who took mathematics during 10th grade were still enrolled at the end of the third semester of college.

As students leave mathematics courses over time, during each successive year (or semester) there is an increasingly smaller group of students still enrolled in mathematics. The proportion of the original group of students still enrolled in mathematics during any period is called the *survival probability*. The fitted survivor function, also presented in Figure 23.1, displays the pattern of estimated survival probabilities. By examining the fitted survivor function, we see that at the start of 11th grade, 87% of the students who took mathematics in 10th grade are still enrolled in mathematics. By 12th grade, slightly over half (59%) of the students are still in mathematics and at the beginning of the first semester of college, only 46% of the original group remains. At the start of second semester of sophomore year, a mere 10% of the original group continues their study of mathematics. Of 100 students who took mathematics in 10th grade, only 10 are estimated to take mathematics continuously through their second year of college.

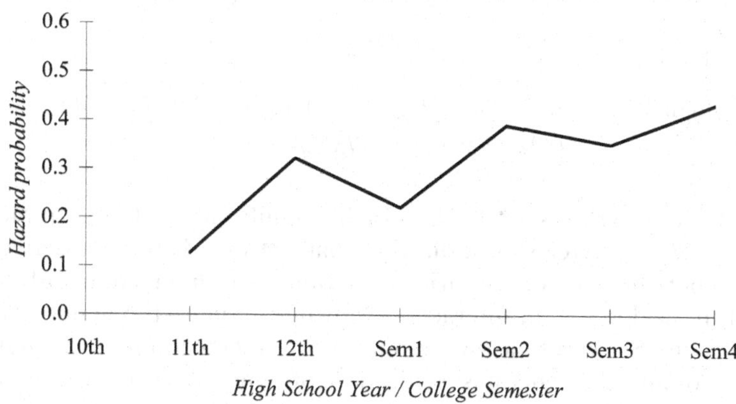

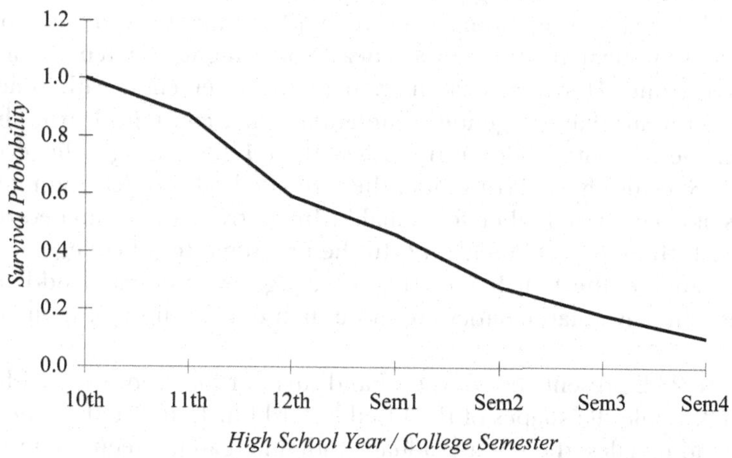

Figure 23.1. Fitted hazard and survivor functions from Model 1.

How does this pattern differ for males and females? We address this question by expanding our initial hazard model to include the effect of gender. We first investigate a time-invariant gender effect (Model 2) and then continue the analysis by determining whether the gender effect, in fact, varies over time (Model 3). The following pair of models are fit:

Model 2:

$$\text{logit}\, h(t_{ij}) = [\alpha_1 D_{1ij} + \alpha_2 D_{2ij} + \ldots + \alpha_6 D_{6ij}] + \beta_1 FEMALE_i$$

Model 3:

$$\text{logit}\, h(t_{ij}) = [\alpha_1 D_{1ij} + \alpha_2 D_{2ij} + \ldots + \alpha_6 D_{6ij}] + \beta_1 FEMALE_i + \beta_2 (FEMALE_i * TIMEj)$$

As Table 23.1 shows, while Model 2 fits significantly better than Model 1, Model 3 fits better still, indicating that not only is there an effect of gender but that this effect varies over time. The interaction with time tested in Model 3 is an interaction with linear time—the gender effect changes linearly with time. We also tested an interaction between gender and a completely general specification of time—allowing the gender effect to differ nonsystematically over time—but this specification did not improve the fit enough to warrant the decrease in model parsimony.

The gender effect estimated in Model 2 indicates a constant gender effect over time. This estimated differential can be quantified as an estimated odds ratio by antilogging the parameter estimate associated with *FEMALE*. The resulting estimate is 1.46, implying that the estimated odds of leaving mathematics courses are nearly 50% higher for females at all points in time. However, examination of the interaction with time in Model 3 reveals that the gender differential is not constant. During high school, the estimated odds ratio is less than 1.46; during college it is greater. Specifically, in 11th grade, the estimated odds of leaving mathematics are only 28% higher for females. In contrast, the estimated odds ratio in 12th grade is higher, 1.42. In the first semester of college it rises to 1.57 and by the fourth semester of college the estimated odds that women will leave mathematics are more than double those of their male peers.

Figure 23.2 presents fitted hazard and survivor functions derived from Model 3. While the shapes of the fitted hazard functions are the same for males and females, there is a gradually widening gap between the lines in both plots, showing the increasing difference in the risk of leaving mathematics over time. In 11th grade the difference in the estimated hazard rate for males compared with females is quite small—males are predicted to have a hazard probability of 11% while the hazard probability for females is 14%, a difference of only 3 percentage points. However, by 12th grade the difference has widened to 8 percentage points (28% for males versus 36% for females). By the start of second semester of sophomore year the estimated hazard probability for females is almost 20 percentage points higher than for males. At this point in time, 38% of the males and

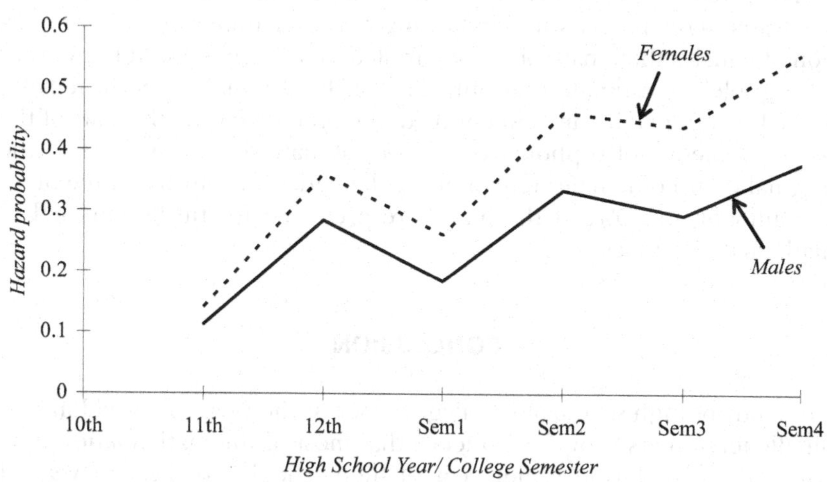

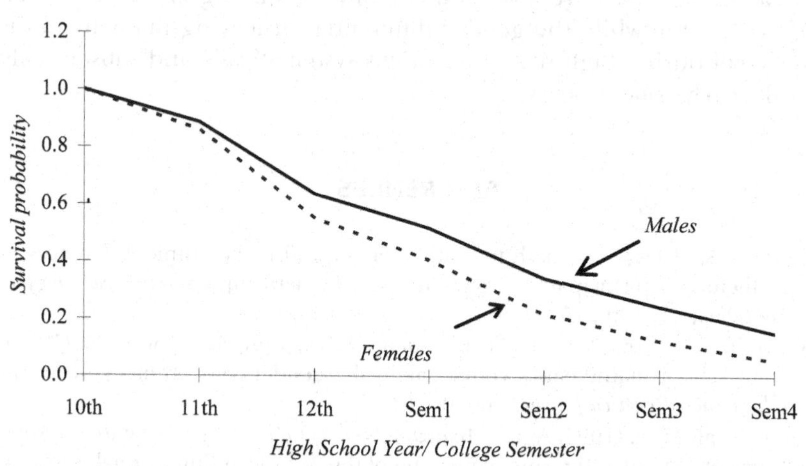

Figure 23.2. Fitted hazard and survivor functions from Model 3.

56% of the females who have taken mathematics continuously through high school and the first three semesters of college drop out.

The fitted survivor functions for males and females also show a gradually widening gap over time, indicating that over time a smaller proportion of females than males are still enrolled in mathematics. At the start of 12th grade, we estimate that only 54% of the original group of females and 64% of the males are still enrolled in mathematics. By the start of the second semester of sophomore year, we estimate that a mere 5% of the original group of females remain in mathematics; in contrast, three times this amount, or 15%, of the males are predicted to still be enrolled in mathematics courses.

CONCLUSION

Our study of high school and college students who were followed longitudinally for 7 years provides evidence that most of the mathematics pipeline is drained during senior year of high school and the first year of college. While this finding is consistent with prior research on mathematics course taking, the use of discrete-time survival analysis has allowed us to more precisely estimate the proportion of students who leave mathematics during each year or semester. Additionally, by using discrete-time survival analysis we were able to model a time-varying effect of gender, finding that the while the gender differential in leaving mathematics is quite small during high school, it widens systematically and substantially over the early college years.

REFERENCES

Catsambis, S. (1994). The path to math: Gender and racial-ethnic differences in mathematics participation from middle school to high school. *Sociology of Education, 67,* 199-215.

Davenport, E. C., Jr., Davison, M. L., Kuang, S. D., Kim, S, & Kwak, N. (1998). High school mathematics course-taking by gender and ethnicity. *American Educational Research Journal, 35,* 497-514.

Downer-Assaf, M. E. (1995, April). *Analyzing the amount of time a student studies math.* Paper presented at the annual meeting of the American Educational Research Association, San Francisco, CA.

Graham, S. E. (1997). *The exodus from mathematics: When and why?* Unpublished doctoral dissertation, Harvard University, Graduate School of Education.

Ma, X. (2001). Participation in advanced mathematics: Do expectation and influence of students, peers, teachers, and parents matter? *Contemporary Educational Psychology, 26,* 132-146.

Singer, J. D., & Willett, J. B. (1993). It's about time: Using discrete-time survival analysis to study duration and the timing of events. *Journal of Educational Statistics, 18*, 155-195.

Singer, J. D., & Willett, J. B. (2003). *Applied longitudinal data analysis*. New York: Oxford University Press.

Walker, E. N. (2001). *On time and off track? Advanced mathematics course-taking among high school students.* Unpublished doctoral dissertation, Harvard University, Graduate School of Education.

CHAPTER 24

NONPARAMETRIC PROCEDURES FOR TESTING FOR DROPOUT RATES ON UNIVERSITY COURSES WITH APPLICATION TO AN ITALIAN CASE STUDY

Rosa Arboretti Giancristofaro, Fortunato Pesarin, Luigi Salmaso, and Aldo Solari

INTRODUCTION

The analysis of university student careers has been receiving increasing attention in recent years. There are many reasons for applying this kind of analysis to Italian universities. First, many attempts have been made to introduce reforms into the Italian higher education system due to poor levels of productivity (high dropout rates and graduation rates barely reaching 40% of those enrolled) which has made the need for reform very clear. In November 1999 the Italian government began the process of

Real Data Analysis, pp. 335–353

restructuring higher education with the passing of a ministerial decree (Law 509/99) that has helped redefine the Italian higher education.

This chapter mainly looks at the problem of dropping out (by censoring all graduate students). A inferential analysis that jointly concerns time to dropout and time to graduation is presented at the end of the third section. Dropout is defined as withdrawal from the degree program for whatever reason. No distinction is made between the various reasons for withdrawal, such as course transfers, academic failures, and health problems, inter alia.

The inferential analysis is performed in analogy with survival studies, where it is of interest to determine if subjects from one group live longer than those from a second group. In the present context, the event of interest (dropout) can only be observed on a small number of students, because we fail to observe all graduate students. The problem can be formalized by considering the groups as the "agents" (i.e. universities, faculties, etc.) with different institutional policies and practices. For each student, if the dropout occurs, we observe the length of time to dropout, whereas if it does not occur, we observe the length of time to graduation.

In the next section we introduce the model and discuss some of the literature. The third section is devoted to describing our solution. In the fourth section, we analyze administrative data regarding all students who began a new first level engineering degree program at the University of Padova (Italy) in the academic year 2001-2002. In the fifth section we report some Monte Carlo results to analyze the validity and power properties of the proposed test in some situations. The sixth section summarizes the results.

MODEL AND A BRIEF OUTLINE OF LITERATURE

We shall refer to a problem in which n units are partitioned into K groups of size $n_j > 0, j = 1, \ldots, K$ with $n = \sum_{j=1}^{K} n_j$. Units belonging to the j-th group are presumed to receive a treatment at the j-th level. Let us now consider the type II censoring model (also called random censorship model); we observe the pairs of independent random variables (Z_{ji}, O_{ji}), $i = 1, \ldots, n_j, j = 1, \ldots, K$, with positive $Z_{ji} = \min(X_{ji}, C_{ji})$ and $O_{ji} = \mathbf{I}\{X_{ji} \leq C_{ji}\}$. Here $\mathbf{I}\{\cdot\}$ denotes the indicator function with value 1 if event $\{\cdot\}$ occurs and 0 otherwise.

In our dropout context, the X variables are the length of "time to dropout", the censoring variables C refer to the length of "time to graduation", the O indicators denote if the dropout occurs or not, the K groups represent the "agents" (i.e. universities, faculties, etc.) and finally the j-th treatment corresponds to the institutional policy and practice of the j-th agent. The random variables of interest are the X_{ji}, which in terms of our problem represent the time to dropout and so cannot be observed for every unit. All random variables X_{ji} and C_{ji} are assumed to be independent and defined in a suitable background space.

The inclusion indicator $\mathbf{O} = \{O_{ji}, i = 1, \ldots, n_j, j = 1, \ldots, K\}$ represents the observed configuration in the data set. Hence, the whole set of observed data is summarized by the pair of associated vectors $(\mathbf{Z}, \mathbf{O})$, where $\mathbf{Z} = \{Z_{ji}, i = 1, \ldots, n_j, j = 1, \ldots, K\}$. Moreover, we use $\nu_j = \sum_{i=1}^{n_j} O_{ji}, j = 1, \ldots, K$, to define the effective sample size of data actually observed in the j-th group, and $\nu_. = \sum_{j=1}^{K} \nu_j$ to define the total effective sample size of data actually observed.

Let F_j denote the distribution function of variable X in group j and G_j the corresponding distribution function of variable C. If we assume that the K groups are defined according to increasing levels of a treatment (i.e. in the present context, institutional policy and practice of the agents), it may be of interest to test the restricted null hypothesis (equal censoring)

$$H_0: F_1 = \ldots = F_K, G_1 = \ldots = G_K,$$

against the trend alternative

$$H_1: F_1 \leq \ldots \leq F_K, G_1 \leq \ldots \leq G_K,$$

where at least one inequality is strict, because the expected treatment effects of interest are assumed to decrease time to dropout.

In this setting a widely used method is the log-rank type test (that is an extension to the case of $K > 2$ groups of the log-rank test for $K = 2$; Heimann & Neuhaus, 1998), which is based on the statistic

$$L = \sum_{j=1}^{K} d_j \sum_t (m_{jt} - E_{jt}).$$

This statistic, when properly standardized, has asymptotic standard normal distribution under the null hypothesis. Here

$m_{jt} = \sum_{i=1}^{n_j} \mathbf{I}\{Z_{ji} = t\} \cdot O_{ji}$ are the observed cases in group j at time t. Similarly, define $m_{\cdot t}$ as the observed cases in all groups at time t and define $n_{jt} = \sum_{i=1}^{n_j} \mathbf{I}\{Z_{ji} \leq t\}$ as the number of students in group j at risk at time t. Let $n_{\cdot t}$ be the total number at risk in all groups, then we can define $E_{jt} = n_{jt} \cdot m_{\cdot t}/n_{\cdot t}$ as the expected observed cases in group j at time t. Finally, $\mathbf{d} = (d_1, \ldots, d_K)$ is a row vector with nondecreasing components (i.e. $d_1 \leq \ldots \leq d_K$), where d_j denotes the rank of j-th dose of the treatment. Note that the sum in L extends over all $t \in \Re$, where a dropout occurred in at least one of the K groups. In the present context, we may suppose that events are observed at times $t = 1, \ldots, T$, where the time unit for the event is the academic year.

As frequently occurs in such studies the event of interest (dropout) can only be observed in a relatively small number of students. Therefore, the asymptotic distribution under the null hypothesis of the abovementioned test statistics may not be appropriate. This has been observed by several authors, who then proposed so-called exact methods. Unfortunately, it was also noted (Heimann & Neuhaus, 1998) that the conditional permutational distribution for the log-rank test is only valid when there is equal censoring for the groups to be compared. In fact, the permutational distribution in the case of small event numbers under unequal censoring will usually yield worse results than the asymptotic critical value in terms of attained type I error rate, though the latter is also rather inaccurate. However, for large event numbers (over 25%), the permutational version becomes particularly insensitive to unequal censoring. Therefore, Heimann and Neuhaus (1998) suggest that the conditional test should be applied to small event numbers only if the censoring distributions are equal.

THE PROPOSED SOLUTION

Breaking Down Hypotheses and Using Information From the Missing Data Process

It is worth noting that H_0 must take into consideration the homogeneity associated to the K groups of the actually observed, collected data $\mathbf{X} = \{X_{ji}, i = 1, \ldots, n_j, j = 1, \ldots, K\}$ jointly with that associated to missing data process $\mathbf{O}$ because in this setting it is assumed that, in the alternative, the treatment may also influence missingness. Hence, the null hypothesis requires the joint distributional equality of the missing data process in the

K groups, giving rise to $\mathbf{O}$, and of response variable $\mathbf{X}$ conditional on $\mathbf{O}$, that is

$$H_0: \left\{ [O_1 \stackrel{d}{=} \ldots \stackrel{d}{=} O_K] \cap [(X_1 \stackrel{d}{=} \ldots \stackrel{d}{=} X_K) \middle| \mathbf{O}] \right\}.$$

The assumed exchangeability in the null hypothesis of the n individual data vectors in $(\mathbf{X}, \mathbf{O})$, with respect to K groups, implies that the treatment effects are null on all observed and unobserved responses. In such a context, we consider K groups which are defined according to increasing levels of a treatment, thus we may write the alternative hypothesis as

$$H_1: \left\{ [O_1 \stackrel{d}{\leq} \ldots \stackrel{d}{\leq} O_K] \cup [(X_1 \stackrel{d}{\geq} \ldots \stackrel{d}{\geq} X_K) \middle| \mathbf{O}] \right\},$$

where at least one inequality is strict because the expected treatment effects of interest are: (i) increasing probability of dropout, indicated by variable O; (ii) stochastically lower time to dropout, indicated by variable $X|O$.

Testing for Stochastic Ordering

In order to deal with this problem in a permutation context, let us imagine that for any $j \in \{1, \ldots, K-1\}$, the whole data set is split into two pooled pseudo-groups, where the first is obtained by pooling together data of the first j (ordered) groups and the second by pooling the rest. More specifically, we define the first pooled pseudo-group as $(\Delta_{1(j)}, \mathbf{Y}_{1(j)}) = (\mathbf{O}_1 \oplus \ldots \oplus \mathbf{O}_j, \mathbf{X}_1 \oplus \ldots \oplus \mathbf{X}_j)$ and the second as $(\Delta_{2(j)}, \mathbf{Y}_{2(j)}) = (\mathbf{O}_{j+1} \oplus \ldots \oplus \mathbf{O}_K, \mathbf{X}_{j+1} \oplus \ldots \oplus \mathbf{X}_K)$, where $\oplus$ is the symbol for pooling data into one pseudo-group and $(\boldsymbol{Oj}, \boldsymbol{Xj}) = \{(O_{ji}, X_{ji}), i = 1, \ldots, n_j\}$ is the data set in the j-th group. Moreover, for $j = 1, \ldots, K-1$, let $N_{1(j)} = \sum_{h=1}^{j} n_h$ and $N_{2(j)} = \sum_{h=j+1}^{K} n_h$ indicate the sample size of $\mathbf{Y}_{1(j)}$ and $\mathbf{Y}_{2(j)}$ respectively, and $\nu_{1(j)} = \sum_{h=1}^{j} \nu_h$ and $\nu_{2(j)} = \sum_{h=j+1}^{K} \nu_h$ indicate their effective sample size.

In the null hypothesis, data from every pair of pseudo-groups are exchangeable because related pooled variables satisfy the relationship

$(\Delta_{1(j)}, Y_{1(j)}) \stackrel{d}{=} (\Delta_{2(j)}, Y_{2(j)})$, $j = 1, \ldots, K-1$. In the alternative we see that $[\Delta_{1(j)} \stackrel{d}{\leq} \Delta_{2(j)}] \cup [(Y_{1(j)} \stackrel{d}{\geq} Y_{2(j)}) | \Delta]$, which, for each component variable, corresponds to monotonic stochastic ordering (dominance) between any pair of pseudo-groups. This suggests expressing the hypotheses in the equivalent form

$$\mathrm{H}_0: \left\{ \bigcap_{j=1}^{K-1} [\mathrm{H}_{0j}^{\Delta} \cap \mathrm{H}_{0j}^{Y|\Delta}] \right\} = \left\{ \bigcap_{j=1}^{K-1} [[\Delta_{1(j)} \stackrel{d}{=} \Delta_{2(j)}] \cap [(Y_{1(j)} \stackrel{d}{=} Y_{2(j)}) | \Delta]] \right\}$$

against

$$\mathrm{H}_1: \left\{ \bigcup_{j=1}^{K-1} [\mathrm{H}_{0j}^{\Delta} \cup H_{0j}^{Y|\Delta}] \right\} = \left\{ \bigcup_{j=1}^{K-1} [[\Delta_{1(j)} \stackrel{d}{\leq} \Delta_{2(j)}] \cup [(Y_{1(j)} \stackrel{d}{\geq} Y_{2(j)}) | \Delta]] \right\}$$

where H_{0j}^{Δ} indicates the equality in distribution of the inclusion indicator (missing) process, $H_{0j}^{Y|\Delta}$ indicates the equality in distribution of Y, conditional on Δ, and a breakdown into a set of subhypotheses is emphasized (for details see Pesarin 2001, p. 161).

Let us consider the j-th subhypothesis $\mathrm{H}_{0j}^{Y|\Delta}: \left\{ [(Y_{1(j)} \stackrel{d}{=} Y_{2(j)}) | \Delta] \right\}$ against $\mathrm{H}_{1j}^{Y|\Delta}: \left\{ [(Y_{1(j)} \stackrel{d}{\geq} Y_{2(j)}) | \Delta] \right\}$. We note that the related subproblem corresponds to a two-sample comparison for restricted alternatives with missing values, a problem which has an approximate solution, as described in Pesarin (2001, chapter 9). In order to deal with this problem using a permutation strategy, it is necessary to consider the role of permuted inclusion indicators $\Delta^* = \left\{ \Delta_{1(j)}^*, \Delta_{2(j)}^* \right\}$, especially with respect to numbers of missing data. The permutation effective sample sizes of valid data within each group, $\nu_{k(j)}^* = \sum_{i=1}^{N_{k(j)}} \Delta_{k(j)}^*$, $k = 1, 2$, vary according to the random attribution of units, and relative missing data, to the two pseudo-groups. This, of course, is because units with missing data participate to the permutation mechanism as well as all other units. As the effective sample sizes of valid data vary according to the permutation of units with missing data, the vector $\mathbf{\upsilon}^* = \left\{\nu^*_{1(j)}, \nu^*_{2(j)}\right\}$ of permutation effective sample sizes of valid data, is not invariant in the permutation sample space. In other words, if for some k we have $\nu_{k(j)} < N_{k(j)}$, so that the related number of missing data is positive, then the permutation probability $\Pr\left\{(\nu^*_{1(j)} = \nu_{1(j)}) \cap (\nu^*_{2(j)} = \nu_{2(j)})\right\} = \Pr\left\{\nu^*_{1(j)} = \nu_{1(j)}\right\}$ of finding the two permutation effective sample sizes of valid data all equal to those observed is strictly less than one. Thus, the key solution described in Pesarin (2001) is to use a test statistic which is at least approximately invariant with respect to the permutation effective sample sizes of valid data. This partial test statistic (which is significant for large values) takes the form

$$T^{Y|\Delta^*}_{(j)} = S^*_{1(j)} \cdot \left(\frac{\nu^*_{2(j)}}{\nu^*_{1(j)}}\right)^{\frac{1}{2}} - S^*_{2(j)} \cdot \left(\frac{\nu^*_{1(j)}}{\nu^*_{2(j)}}\right)^{\frac{1}{2}},$$

where $S^*_{k(j)} = \sum_{i=1}^{N_{k(j)}} Y^*_{k(j)i} \cdot \Delta^*_{k(j)i}$, $k = 1, 2$, is the permutation total of the k-th pseudo-group, assuming that $\Delta^*_{k(j)i} = 0$ implies $Y^*_{k(j)i} \cdot \Delta^*_{k(j)i} = 0$. Tests $T^*_{(j)}$ are consistent, approximately exact and unbiased. Finally, in order for the given solution to be well-defined, we must assume that $\nu^*_{1(j)}$ and $\nu^*_{2(j)}$ are jointly positive. This means that we must consider a sort of restricted permutation strategy which consists of discarding from the analysis all points of the permutation sample space in which even a single component of permutation matrix $\mathbf{\upsilon}^*$, of effective sample size of valid data, is zero. Of course, this kind of restriction has no effect on inferential conclusions.

For each of the $K - 1$ subhypotheses $\mathrm{H}^{\Delta}_{0j}: \left\{[\Delta_{1(j)} \overset{d}{=} \Delta_{2(j)}]\right\}$ against $\mathrm{H}^{\Delta}_{1j}: \left\{[\Delta_{1(j)} \overset{d}{\leq} \Delta_{2(j)}]\right\}$, an exact, unbiased, consistent partial test, significant for large values (permutationally equivalent to Fisher's exact probability test), is appropriate:

$$T^{\Delta *}_{(j)} = \nu^{*}_{2(j)} .$$

Nonparametric Combination of Dependent Partial Tests

Pesarin (2001) introduced in a permutation context the method of nonparametric combination of a finite number of dependent partial tests (NPC) as a general tool for multivariate testing problems. One major feature of the NPC is that the underlying dependence relation structure is nonparametrically captured by the combining procedure, so it is not necessary to specify it.

For the problem at hand, the nonparametric combination of $2 \cdot (K-1)$ partial tests $(T^{\Delta *}_{(j)}, T^{Y|\Delta *}_{(j)}, j = 1, \ldots, K-1)$ may be carried out by considering $K - 1$ second order combinations, one for each comparison of two pseudo-groups,

$$T^{''*}_{(j)} = \psi_1(\lambda^{\Delta *}_{(j)}, \lambda^{Y|\Delta *}_{(j)}),$$

followed by a third order combination

$$T^{''*} = \psi_2(\lambda^{''*}_{(1)}, \ldots, \lambda^{''*}_{(K-1)}),$$

where ψ_1 and ψ_2 are two suitable combining functions, which may not necessarily coincide, and $\lambda^{*}_{(j)}$ is the permutation p value associated with test $T^{*}_{(j)}$. Since partial tests $T^{\Delta *}_{(j)}$ on the components of Δ are exact, unbiased and consistent, whereas $T^{Y|\Delta *}_{(j)}$ on the components of $\mathbf{Y}$ are consistent but approximately exact and unbiased, the combined tests $T^{''*}_{(j)}$ and $T^{''*}$ are consistent and approximately exact and unbiased for all suitable ψ.

It should also be emphasized that componentwise testing may also be useful in a marginal sense. After p value adjustment due to multiplicity, we can identify which subset of pseudo-groups present statistically significant ordering. This analysis cannot be done with log-rank type statistics.

Finally, due to the extreme difficulty of finding general exact computing algorithms to estimate the multivariate permutation distribution, we use a Conditional Monte Carlo (CMC) procedure as in Pesarin (2001).

An Extension by Considering Time to Graduation

Imagine also that the expected treatment effects of interest are (iii) higher time to graduation, conditional on $\mathbf{O}^c$, indicated by variable $\mathbf{C}|\mathbf{O}^c$. Thus we may express the hypotheses of interest as

$$H_0: \left\{[O_1 \overset{d}{=} \dots \overset{d}{=} O_K] \cap [(X_1 \overset{d}{=} \dots \overset{d}{=} X_K)\big|\mathbf{O}] \cap [(C_1 \overset{d}{=} \dots \overset{d}{=} C_K)\big|\mathbf{O}^c]\right\}$$

against

$$H_1: \left\{[O_1 \overset{d}{\lesssim} \dots \overset{d}{\lesssim} O_K] \cup [(X_1 \overset{d}{\gtrsim} \dots \overset{d}{\gtrsim} X_K)\big|\mathbf{O}] \cup [(C_1 \overset{d}{\lesssim} \dots \overset{d}{\lesssim} C_K)\big|\mathbf{O}^c]\right\},$$

where $\mathbf{O}^c = \mathbf{1}_{[1\times n]} - \mathbf{O}$ and $\mathbf{1}_{[1\times n]}$ is a $[1 \times n]$ vector of ones. As before, in order to deal with a stochastic ordering solution, we express the hypotheses in an equivalent form

$$H_0: \left\{\cap_{j=1}^{K-1}\left[H_{0j}^{\Delta} \cap H_{0j}^{Y|\Delta} \cap H_{0j}^{W|\Delta^c}\right]\right\}$$

$$= \left\{\cap_{j=1}^{K-1}[[\Delta_{1(j)} \overset{d}{=} \Delta_{2(j)}] \cap [(Y_{1(j)} \overset{d}{=} Y_{2(j)})\big|\Delta] \cap [(W_{1(j)} \overset{d}{=} W_{2(j)})\big|\Delta^c]]\right\}$$

against

$$H_1: \left\{\cup_{j=1}^{K-1}\left[H_{0j}^{\Delta} \cup H_{0j}^{Y|\Delta} \cup H_{0j}^{W|\Delta^c}\right]\right\}$$

$$= \left\{\cup_{j=1}^{K-1}[([\Delta_{1(j)} \overset{d}{\lesssim} \Delta_{2(j)}] \cup [(Y_{1(j)} \overset{d}{\gtrsim} Y_{2(j)})\big|\Delta]) \cup [(W_{1(j)} \overset{d}{\lesssim} W_{2(j)})\big|\Delta^c]]\right\}$$

where we define the first pooled pseudo-group on $\oplus$ variable C as $\mathbf{W}_{1(j)} = \mathbf{C}_1 \oplus \dots \oplus \mathbf{C}_j$ and the second as $\mathbf{W}_{2(j)} = \mathbf{C}_{j+1} \oplus \dots \oplus \mathbf{C}_K$, where $\mathbf{C}_j = \{C_{ji}, i = 1, \dots, n_j\}$ is the vector that describes the time to graduation in the j-th group. Thus, according to the previous discussion and with clear meaning of the symbols, for each of the $K - 1$ subhypotheses $H_{0j}^{W|\Delta^c}$ against $H_{1j}^{W|\Delta^c}$ we consider the following partial test statistic

$$T_{(j)}^{W|\Delta^c *} = R_{2(j)}^{*} \cdot \left(\frac{N_{1(j)} - \nu_{1(j)}^{*}}{N_{2(j)} - \nu_{2(j)}^{*}}\right)^{\frac{1}{2}} - R_{1(j)}^{*} \cdot \left(\frac{N_{2(j)} - \nu_{2(j)}^{*}}{N_{1(j)} - \nu_{1(j)}^{*}}\right)^{\frac{1}{2}},$$

that is significant for large values, consistent and approximately exact and unbiased, where $R^*_{k(j)} = \sum_{i=1}^{N_{k(j)}} W^*_{k(j)i} \cdot (1 - \Delta^*_{k(j)i}), k = 1, 2$, is the permutation total of the k-th pseudo-group.

The combination problem may be faced in the following way: we consider the three variables (O, X, C) as having the same importance, as seems reasonable in the present problem, and so we perform $K - 1$ second order combinations, ${}^{e}T''^{*}_{(j)} = \psi_1\left(\lambda^{\Delta*}_{(j)}, \lambda^{Y|\Delta*}_{(j)}, \lambda^{W|\Delta^c*}_{(j)}\right)$, followed by a third order combination ${}^{e}T''^{*} = \psi_2(\lambda''^{*}_{(1)}, \ldots, \lambda''^{*}_{(K-1)})$. Remember that in order for the given solution to be well-defined, we must assume that $\nu^*_{1(j)}$, $\nu^*_{2(j)}$, $N_{1(j)} - \nu^*_{1(j)}$, and $N_{2(j)} - \nu^*_{2(j)}$ are jointly positive.

Note that only one variable between X and C can be observed in each unit, that is, if we observe X_{ji} in the i-th unit of j-th group, we cannot observe C_{ji}, and vice versa. As a consequence, there is not enough information for proper evaluation of dependence relations, even though these are taken into consideration in a nonparametric way. Therefore, the nonparametric analysis becomes unavoidable, unless one is able to take into consideration all underlying dependences.

APPLICATION TO AN ITALIAN CASE STUDY

Many attempts have been made to introduce reforms into the Italian higher education system, especially after the 1960s, when social demand exploded in Italy as it did all over Europe. Over the years, the lack of any institutional relationship with the labor market and with society, together with the system's poor level of productivity (high dropout rates and graduation rates barely reaching 40% of those enrolled) have made the need for reform very clear (Moscati, 2002).

In November 1999 the Italian government began the process of restructuring higher education with the passing of a ministerial decree (Law 509/99) that has helped redefine the landscape of Italian higher education. The first and most relevant change included the creation of a binary system with a university track made up of a three-level structure of courses and degrees: a first level "*laurea*", after a 3-year program; a second level "*laurea specialistica*", after a further 2-year program; and a third level, "*dottorato di ricerca*" (PhD), after another three years of studies.

The objective of this application is to better understand the features of changes going on in Italian universities, but with evaluations made for internal purposes (internal evaluations). Each university evaluates its activities to improve its performance, using an evaluation model that is considered more suitable to its objectives and culture. It is appropriate to emphasize that the nature of our approach is positive rather than normative. It may be questionable to define degrees as "more effective" with a lower dropout hazard. But dropout rates prior to the reforms of 1999 are so high (and graduation rates so low) that it is very important to try and improve the situation; moreover this provides a benchmark against which results for future cohorts can be judged when data become available.

Since the introduction of the new first-level degree programs began in the 2001/2002 academic year, as provided for by Law 509/99, our data are referred to students enrolling at that time in one of the 15 new *laurea* programs of the Faculty of Engineering at the University of Padua, Italy. The follow-up period for each freshman is 3 years, and the time unit for events (dropout and graduation) is the academic year. Although data refer to the most recent cohort for which time to dropout is currently available over an appropriate time-frame, we acknowledge that information regarding time to graduation is not complete. In fact, students who completed their engineering degree program in 2004 after 3 years of study would have enrolled in 2001. However, if we were to look only at these students, we would fail to observe students taking more than 3 years to complete the course. For this reason we prefer to restrict our analysis only to time to dropout (i.e. to variable X), so that we consider all events other than dropout as censored observations.

The analysis included $K = 3$ groups, that correspond to the three areas of Padua's Faculty of Engineering: civil ($j = 1$), industrial ($j = 2$) and information ($j = 3$), that included 3, 7, and 5 new first-level degree programs respectively (see Table 24.1). In accordance with previous studies, the ordering is based on the presumed hardness of each of the three areas. In this way we can model the problem according to the hypotheses

$$\mathrm{H}_0\colon \left\{ [O_1 \overset{d}{=} O_2 \overset{d}{=} O_3] \cap (X_1 \overset{d}{=} X_2 \overset{d}{=} X_3) \middle| \mathbf{O} \right\}$$

against

$$\mathrm{H}_1\colon \left\{ [O_1 \overset{d}{\leq} O_2 \overset{d}{\leq} O_3] \cup (X_1 \overset{d}{\geq} X_2 \overset{d}{\geq} X_3) \middle| \mathbf{O} \right\}.$$

Table 24.1 reports sample size n_j (and the corresponding effective sample size ν_j) in the j-th group (with details about the specific courses) and provides some information on dropout rates. The 2001 cohort consists of 2,205 students, and the unconditional noncompletion rate for all students is around 36%. Looking at the conditional dropout rates of engineering students we can see that, as students progress through the program, the conditional dropout rate declines rather drastically. About 65% of those who do not complete their engineering degree leave before the beginning of their second year.

For this data set, the multidimensional system of overall hypotheses can be written, and correspondingly analyzed, either within-pseudo-groups with respect to variables, as

$$H_0: \left\{ [H_{01}^{\Delta} \cap H_{01}^{Y|\Delta}] \cap [H_{02}^{\Delta} \cap H_{02}^{Y|\Delta}] \right\}$$

against

Table 24.1. Dropout Rates by Course and Area

Area (Course)	n_j	v_j	$\%X_j = 1$	$\%X_j = 2$	$\%X_j = 3$	$\%X_j$
Environmental and territorial engineering	78	16	11.54%	5.13%	3.85%	20.51%
Civil engineering	149	44	17.45%	8.72%	3.36%	29.53%
Building engineering	133	48	23.31%	10.53%	2.26%	36.09%
Civil area	*360*	*108*	*18.33%*	*8.61%*	*3.06%*	*30.00%*
Aerospace engineering	127	46	26.77%	5.51%	3.94%	36.22%
Chemistry engineering	55	12	10.91%	3.64%	7.27%	21.82%
Electrotechnic engineering	96	32	25.00%	7.29%	1.04%	33.33%
Energetic engineering	21	5	9.52%	9.52%	4.76%	23.81%
Managerial engineering	271	87	22.88%	6.64%	2.58%	32.10%
Material engineering	30	7	13.33%	3.33%	6.67%	23.33%
Mechanic engineering	327	123	22.63%	10.40%	4.59%	37.61%
Industrial area	*927*	*312*	*22.22%*	*7.66%*	*3.78%*	*33.66%*
Automation engineering	38	20	39.47%	10.53%	2.63%	52.63%
Biomedical engineering	88	37	19.32%	19.32%	3.41%	42.05%
Electronic engineering	198	77	27.27%	8.59%	3.03%	38.89%
Data processing engineering	412	170	27.18%	10.19%	3.88%	41.26%
Telecommunication engineering	182	75	24.73%	12.64%	3.85%	41.21%
Information area	*918*	*379*	*26.47%*	*11.22%*	*3.59%*	*41.29%*
Total	2,205	799	23.36%	9.30%	3.58%	36.24%

$$H_1: \left\{ [H_{11}^{\Delta} \cup H_{11}^{Y|\Delta}] \cup [H_{12}^{\Delta} \cup H_{12}^{Y|\Delta}] \right\},$$

or within-variables with respect to pseudo-groups, as

$$H_0: \left\{ [H_{01}^{\Delta} \cap H_{02}^{Y|\Delta}] \cap [H_{01}^{Y|\Delta} \cap H_{02}^{Y|\Delta}] \right\}$$

against

$$H_1: \left\{ [H_{11}^{\Delta} \cup H_{12}^{Y|\Delta}] \cap [H_{11}^{Y|\Delta} \cup H_{12}^{Y|\Delta}] \right\}.$$

The solution for the former system of hypotheses is based on the global test statistic $T''^{*} = \psi_F(\lambda''^{*}_{(1)}, \lambda''^{*}_{(2)})$ and the partial test statistics $T''^{*}_{(j)} = \psi_F(\lambda^{\Delta*}_{(j)}, \lambda^{Y|\Delta*}_{(j)})$, $j = 1, 2$, whereas the latter is based on the global test statistic $T''^{*} = \psi_F(\lambda''^{\Delta*}, \lambda''^{Y|\Delta*})$ and the partial test statistics $T''^{\Delta*} = \psi_F(\lambda^{\Delta*}_{(1)}, \lambda^{\Delta*}_{(2)})$, $T''^{\Delta*} = \psi_F(\lambda^{Y|\Delta*}_{(1)}, \lambda^{Y|\Delta*}_{(2)})$, where we consider Fisher's combining function ψ_F (Pesarin, 2001, p. 147). This is useful because, after p-value adjustment due to multiplicity, we can identify either which sub-set of pseudo-groups and which sub-set of variables are statistically significant. The proposed solution is performed along with the most frequently used conditional log-rank type test $L = \sum_{j=1}^{3} d_j \sum_{t=1}^{3} (m_{jt} - E_{jt})$, (where we consider ranks $\mathbf{d} = (1, 2, 3)$, and the results are shown in Table 24.2.

The third-order combined p value, with Fisher's combining function, for the overall hypotheses on second-order p values $(\lambda''_{(1)}, \lambda''_{(2)})$ and $(\lambda''^{\Delta}, \lambda''^{Y|\Delta})$ gives $\lambda''' = 0.0002$ both ways (the two third-order p values are approximately equal, agreeing to four decimal places). This leads us to the rejection of the overall null hypothesis at a significance level of $\alpha = 0.001$. Hence, there is a global monotonic stochastic ordering among the three areas. However, from the adjusted second-order p values, we observe that the three areas are strictly ordered (since the adjusted p values $\lambda''_{(1)}$ and $\lambda''_{(2)}$ are both significant). Furthermore, students of the three areas dropout substantially at the same time ($\lambda''^{Y|\Delta}$ is not significant) but with significantly different frequencies (adjusted λ''^{Δ} is highly significant). It is worth noting that this kind of analysis, which allow us to examine the

Table 24.2. Simulation Framework

Case		Restricted Null Hypothesis		Active Subalternatives
I	$O_1 = O_2$	$X_1 = X_2$, $[X_1 \| O_1 = 1] = [X_2 \| O_2 = 1]$	$C_1 = C_2$, $[C_1 \| O_1^c = 1] = [C_2 \| O_2^c = 1]$	H_1^O
		Alternative Hypothesis, Equal Censoring		
II	$O_1 < O_2$	$X_1 > X_2$: $[X_1 \| O_1 = 1] = [X_2 \| O_2 = 1]$	$C_1 = C_2$, $[C_1 \| O_1^c = 1] < [C_2 \| O_2^c = 1]$	$H_1^{X\|O}$
III	$O_1 = O_2$	$X_1 > X_2$: $[X_1 \| O_1 = 1] > [X_2 \| O_2 = 1]$	$C_1 = C_2$, $[C_1 \| O_1^c = 1] = [C_2 \| O_2^c = 1]$	$H_1^{X\|O}, H_1^{C\|O^c}$
IV	$O_1 < O_2$	$X_1 > X_2$: $[X_1 \| O_1 = 1] > [X_2 \| O_2 = 1]$	$C_1 = C_2$, $[C_1 \| O_1^c = 1] < [C_2 \| O_2^c = 1]$	$H_1^O, H_1^{X\|O}, H_1^{C\|O^c}$
		Alternative Hypothesis, Unequal Censoring		
V	$O_1 < O_2$	$X_1 > X_2$: $[X_1 \| O_1 = 1] = [X_2 \| O_2 = 1]$	$C_1 < C_2$, $[C_1 \| O_1^c = 1] < [C_2 \| O_2^c = 1]$	$H_1^O, H_1^{X\|O}, H_1^{C\|O^c}$

contribution of each pseudo-group or of each component variable to the possible global significance, is not possible with log-rank type tests, which focuses only on the global significance ($\lambda_L = .0001$). These results were obtained by considering $B = 1{,}000$ Conditional Monte Carlo iterations from the permutation space.

SIMULATION STUDY

The performance of the tests was studied using Monte Carlo (MC) simulations. Since the new first-level degree program lasts for a minimum of 3 years, distribution function G_j of time to graduation must be set at 0 for the periods up to the 3 years, i.e. no graduations were observed before year 3; therefore G_j takes the form

$$G_j(t) = \begin{cases} 0 & \text{for } t \in \{1, 2\} \\ \Pr\{C_j \le t\} = \sum_{h=3}^{t} \Pr\{C_j = h\} = \sum_{h=3}^{t} g_{jh} & \text{for } t \in \{3, \ldots, T\} \end{cases}$$

where $g_{j1} = g_{j2} = 0$, $0 \le g_{jh} \le 1$ and $\sum_{h=1}^{T} g_{jh} = 1$, $h = 3, \ldots, T$, and $j = 1, \ldots, K$.

We assume that distribution function F_j of time to dropout takes the form

$$F_j(t) = \Pr\{X_j \le t\} = \sum_{h=1}^{t} \Pr\{X_j = h\} = \sum_{h=1}^{t} f_{jh} \qquad \forall t \in \{1, ..., T\}$$

where $0 \le f_{jh} \le 1$ and $\sum_{h=1}^{T} f_{jh} \le 1$, $h = 1, ..., T$ and $j = 1, ..., K$. Note that F_j may be defined arbitrarily for $t > T$, since $G(T) = 1$ (i.e. all observations greater than T are censored anyway).

For the sake of simplicity we consider $K = 2$ groups of size n_j, $j = 1, 2$; it also seems realistic to have $T = 6$ (twice the length of time to graduation institutionally planned) so that by the end of the sixth year there is assumed to be a forced termination: successful completion or dropout.

When $K = 2$, the standardized log-rank statistic is based on

$$L = \sum_{t=1}^{6} (m_{2t} - E_{2t}) / \left(\sum_{t=1}^{6} V_t\right)^{1/2} \xrightarrow{n \to +\infty} N(0, 1),$$

with $V_t = n_{2t} n_{1t} m_{\cdot t}(n_{\cdot t} - m_{\cdot t}) / n_{\cdot t}^2 (n_{\cdot t} - 1)$. We know that under the restricted alternative hypothesis (H_1: $F_1 \overset{d}{\le} ... \overset{d}{\le} F_K$, $G_1 \overset{d}{=} ... \overset{d}{=} G_K$) the permutational distribution of the log-rank test is exact. But what about the case of unequal censoring? For that purpose we maintain the framework described in Table 24.3, that includes five cases, where both equal and unequal censoring situations are considered and a different number of subalternatives are active.

It is worth noting that, in the case of equal censoring (i.e., $G_1 = G_2$), if $F_1 < F_2$ such that $[X_1 | O_1 = 1] \overset{d}{=} [X_2 | O_2 = 1]$, it follows that $O_1 \overset{d}{>} O_2$ and $[C_1 | O_1 = 0] \overset{d}{>} [C_2 | \mathrm{O}_2 = 0]$, thus H_1^O is active, but $\mathrm{H}_1^{X|O^c}$ is mis-specified. Moreover, in the case of unequal censoring, if $G_1 \overset{d}{>} G_2$ and $F_1 \overset{d}{=} F_2$, it follows that $O_1 \overset{d}{>} O_2$ and $[C_1 | O_1 = 0] \overset{d}{>} [C_2 | O_2 = 0]$ and $[X_1 | O_1 = 1] \overset{d}{>} [X_2 | O_2 = 0]$, thus H_1^O is active, but $\mathrm{H}_1^{X|O}$ is mis-specified (vice versa if $G_1 < G_2$).

We have carried out a simulation study that contains the estimated size and power using a 5% significance α-level of the conditional (L^*) and unconditional (L^a) log-rank test mentioned above and the two tests discussed in the third section, namely

$$T''^{*} = \psi_F(\lambda^{O*}, \lambda^{X|O*}) = -2 \cdot \{\log(\lambda^{O*}) + (\lambda^{X|O*})\}$$

and

Table 24.3. *P* Values of Partial and Global Tests on Engineering Data

	Partial Test			
	$\lambda''_{(1)}$	$\lambda''_{(2)}$	λ''^{Δ}	$\lambda''^{Y\mid\Delta}$
Raw *p* value	.0004	.0078	.0002	.3315
Adjusted *p* value	.0004	.0078	.0003	.3315
	Global Test			
	λ''	λ_L		
p value	.0002	.0001		

$$ {}^{e}T''^{*} = \psi_F\left(\lambda^{O^*}, \lambda^{X|O^*}, \lambda^{C|O^{c*}}\right) = -2 \cdot \left\{ \log(\lambda^{O^*}) + \log(\lambda^{X|O^*}) + \log\left(\lambda^{C|O^{c*}}\right)\right\}, $$

where we consider Fisher's combining function ψ_F. The results for the global tests (L^*, L^a, T''^*, ${}^eT''^*$) and the partial tests (T^{O^*}, $T^{X|O^*}$, $T^{C|O^{c*}}$) are reported in Table 24.4.

For each student, time to dropout X and time to graduation C were independently generated. A student is classified as a dropout if $X \le C$ and as a censored observation if $X > C$; note that

$$ \Pr\{Oj = 1\} = \textstyle\sum_{t=1}^{6} F_j(t) \cdot g_j(t) $$

and $P(X_j = t|O_j = 1) = f_{jt} \sum_{k=1}^{6} g_{jk}/P(O_j = 1), t = 1, \ldots, 6, j = 1, 2.$

The values of $\mathbf{f}_j = (f_{j1}, \ldots, f_{j6})$ and $\mathbf{g}_j = (g_{j1}, \ldots, g_{j6})$ are chosen such that probability $\Pr\{O_j = 1\}$ of observing a dropout in the j-th group attains a prescribed percentage (reported in Table 24.4).

For each configuration we performed 1,000 MC simulations and for evaluating the permutation distribution 1,000 CMC iterations. Of course, when considering CMC distributional approximations, as we discharge a set of permutations, the actual number of iterations to be considered is larger than the required number. Sample sizes of $n_1 = n_2 = 100$ and $n_1 = 100$, $n_2 = 300$ were used.

The results in Table 24.4 show a very good behaviour of the proposed solution in all situations, both under the null hypothesis (achieved significance levels are close to nominal ones) and in power. The size and power of the conditional and unconditional version of the log-rank statistic behave similarly in all cases. For the power comparison, we consider the

Table 24.4. Achieved Significance Levels and Power

Case	j	n_j	$\mathbf{f}_j = (f_{j1}, \ldots, f_{j6})$	$\mathbf{g}_j = (g_{j1}, \ldots, g_{j6})$	Pr$\{O = 1\}$	L^* $[L^a]$	$T^{''*}$	${}^eT^{''*}$	*Partial Tests* T^{O*}	$T^{X\|O*}$	$T^{C\|O^c*}$
I	1	100	(.27, .09, .03, .01, .01, .01)	(.40, .30, .20, .10)	.400	.043	.038	.039	.029	.043	.041
	2	100	(.27, .09, .03, .01, .01, .01)	(.40, .30, .20, .10)	.400	[.044]					
	1	100	(.16, .08, .04, .02, .02, .02)	(.40, .30, .20, .10)	.300	.052	.051	.049	.037	.042	.052
	2	100	(.16, .08, .04, .02, .02, .02)	(.40, .30, .20, .10)	.300	[.050]					
	1	100	(.08, .04, .02, .01, .01, .01)	(.40, .30, .20, .10)	.150	.048	.058	.058	.037	.050	.054
	2	300	(.08, .04, .02, .01, .01, .01)	(.40, .30, .20, .10)	.150	[.045]					
II	1	100	(.27, .09, .06, .03, .03, .03)	(.40, .30, .20, .10)	.400	.143	.107	.103	.120	.052	.041
	2	100	1.1· (.27,.09,.06,.03,.03,.03)	(.40, .30, .20, .10)	.440	[.143]					
	1	100	(.16, .08, .04, .02, .02, .02)	(.40, .30, .20, .10)	.300	.106	.094	.078	.084	.052	.052
	2	100	1.1· (.16,.08,.04,.02,.02,.02)	(.40, .30, .20, .10)	.330	[.112]					
	1	100	(.08, .04, .02, .01, .01, .01)	(.40, .30, .20, .10)	.150	.092	.085	.074	.080	.046	.038
	2	300	1.1· (.08,.04,.02,.01,.01,.01)	(.40, .30, .20, .10)	.165	[.080]					
III	1	100	(.27, .09, .03, .01, .01, .01)	(.40, .30, .20, .10)	.400	.060	.218	.175	.035	.280	.040
	2	100	(.33, .06, .01, .01, .01, .01)	(.40, .30, .20, .10)	.400	[.057]					
	1	100	(.16, .08, .04, .02, .02, .02)	(.40, .30, .20, .10)	.300	.057	.148	.129	.043	.185	.047
	2	100	(.20, .06, .02, .02, .02, .02)	(.40, .30, .20, .10)	.300	[.055]					
	1	100	(.08, .04, .02, .01, .01, .01)	(.40, .30, .20, .10)	.150	.048	.135	.108	.028	.175	.054
	2	300	(.10, .03, .01, .01, .01, .01)	(.40, .30, .20, .10)	.150	[.040]					

(*Table continues on next page*)

Table 24.4. Continued

Case	j	n_j	$\mathbf{f}_j = (f_{j1}, \ldots, f_{j6})$	$\mathbf{g}_j = (g_{j1}, \ldots, g_{j6})$	$\Pr\{O = 1\}$	L^* $[L^a]$	T''^*	${}^eT''^*$	Partial Tests T^{O*}	Partial Tests $T^{X\|O*}$	Partial Tests $T^{C\|O^c*}$
IV	1	100	(.18, .15, .09, .03, .03, .03)	(.40, .30, .20, .10)	.450	.211	.391	.325	.120	.362	.059
	2	100	(.24, .20, .04, .02, .02, .02)	(.40, .30, .20, .10)	.500	[.213]					
	1	100	(.16, .08, .04, .02, .02, .02)	(.40, .30, .20, .10)	.300	.429	.589	.511	.331	.388	.056
	2	100	(.27, .09, .03, .01, .01, .01)	(.40, .30, .20, .10)	.400	[.431]					
	1	100	(.08, .04, .02, .01, .01, .01)	(.40, .30, .20, .10)	.150	.964	.934	.872	.950	.180	.053
	2	300	(.18, .09, .03, .01, .01, .01)	(.40, .30, .20, .10)	.310	[.963]					
V	1	100	(.18, .12, .06, .03, .03, .03)	(.70, .15, .10, .05)	.375	.190	.347	.988	.158	.271	.994
	2	100	(.24, .15, .03, .01, .01, .01)	(.25, .40, .25, .10)	.432	[.190]					
	1	100	(.16, .08, .04, .02, .02, .02)	(.70, .15, .10, .05)	.290	.486	.556	.997	.448	.234	.995
	2	100	(.27, .09, .03, .01, .01, .01)	(.25, .40, .25, .10)	.402	[.495]					
	1	100	(.08, .04, .03, .02, .02, .02)	(.70, .15, .10, .05)	.160	.256	.326	1.0	.255	.149	1.0
	2	300	(.12, .06, .02, .01, .01, .01)	(.25, .40, .25, .10)	.212	[.245]					

(conditional or unconditional) log-rank test and the combined test T''^{*}. In *cases III, IV, V* and *VI* the combined test T''^{*} is more powerful than L^{*} and L^{a}, whereas in *case II* the log-rank test performs better than T''^{*}. Note that the behavior of the partial tests are in accordance with theoretical expectations, that is, if a specific subalternative is active, then the corresponding partial test has greater power.

CONCLUSIONS

This chapter mainly looks at the problem of testing for dropping out (by censoring all graduate students) in analogy with survival analysis. The application of the proposed solution to all students who began a new first level engineering degree program at the University of Padova allows us to examine the separate contribution of the frequency of dropout and of the time to dropout to the possible global significance, whereas this kind of analysis is not possible with the log-rank type tests. Finally, a comparative simulation study show that the proposed solution presents a very good overall performance.

REFERENCES

Heimann, G., & Neuhaus, G. (1998). Permutational distribution of the log-rank statistic under random censorship with applications to carcinogenicity assays. *Biometrics*, *54*(1), 168-184.

Moscati, R. (2002). Italy: A hard implementation of a comprehensive reform. *International Higher Education*, *26*, 3-5.

Pesarin, F. (2001). *Multivariate permutation tests with applications in biostatistics.* Chichester, England: Wiley.

CHAPTER 25

NONPARAMETRIC APPROACHES FOR MULTIVARIATE TESTING WITH MIXED VARIABLES AND FOR RANKING ON ORDERED CATEGORICAL VARIABLES WITH AN APPLICATION TO THE EVALUATION OF PhD PROGRAMS

Rosa Arboretti Giancristofaro, Fortunato Pesarin, and Luigi Salmaso

INTRODUCTION

Within the evaluation of the university system and in particular of the PhD programs, complex problems of hypothesis testing arise. The complexity of the study is mainly referred to the presence of mixed variables (ordinal categorical, binary or continuous) and missing values. Surveys

Real Data Analysis, pp. 355–385

performed to evaluate the PhD programs are observational where very little is known about the multivariate distribution underlying the observed variables and their possible dependence structure. In such cases conditional nonparametric methods are a reasonable approach.

Permutation methods are considered here for multivariate testing on mixed variables. Unconditional parametric testing methods may be available, appropriate and effective when: (1) data sets are obtained by well-defined random sampling procedures on well-specified parent populations; (2) population distributions (the likelihood models) for responses are well-defined; (3) with respect to all nuisance entities, well-defined likelihood models are provided with either bounded complete estimates in H_0 or at least invariant statistics; (4) at least asymptotically, null sampling distributions of suitable test statistics do not depend on any unknown entity. Accordingly, just as there are circumstances in which unconditional parametric testing procedures may be proper from a related inferential result interpretation point of view, there are others in which they may be improper or even impossible.

In addition, it may be desirable to adopt conditional testing inferences, not only when their unconditional counterparts are not possible, but also when there is the need to give more importance to the observed data set than to the population model. Conditional inferences are also of interest when, for whatever reason, we wish to limit ourselves to conditional methods by explicitly restricting the analysis to the actual data set. Thus, both conditional and unconditional points of view are important and useful in real problems and often both may be employed to analyse the same data set.

However, in conditional testing procedures, provided that exchangeability of data in respect to groups is satisfied in the null hypothesis, permutation methods play a central role. This is because they allow for quite efficient solutions, are useful when dealing with many difficult problems, provide clear interpretations of inferential results, and allow for weak extensions of conditional to unconditional inferences.

A nonparametric approach is presented based on the combination of permutation dependent tests (NPC; Pesarin, 2001) to solve a multidimensional testing problem with mixed variables. Moreover, an extension of a nonparametric method for the assessment of satisfaction with some products or services is discussed in this paper for situations in which this satisfaction depends on values observed on $k > 1$ variables, where each variable is assumed to provide information on a partial aspect of interest for satisfaction assessment.

A difficult methodological problem arises when there is more than one informative variable to be taken into consideration. This difficulty is increased by the fact that these variables can have different degrees of importance assigned to them. In general, for each single variable it is rather easy to establish a suitable assessment criterion leading to a partial ranking of units or a partial satisfaction indicator for each unit. Obtaining a reasonable combination of the many dependent partial rankings or indicators into a combined one immediately arises. This task can be performed via principal component analysis, provided that observed variables present a rather strong linear relation structure. Moreover multidimensional scaling procedures may also be applied. However, by standard multidimensional procedures it is rather difficult, if not impossible, to take different degrees of importance into consideration for the many variables. Here, an extension of the nonparametric combination of dependent rankings (NPC ranking; Lago & Pesarin, 2000) is proposed in order to construct a synthesis of composite indicators measuring the satisfaction on peculiar aspects of PhD programs. The methodological approaches based on NPC are applied to an observational study for the evaluation of PhD programs currently present in the Italian university system.

NONPARAMETRIC COMBINATION OF PERMUTATION TESTS FOR MULTIVARIATE MIXED VARIABLES

The extension of a multivariate permutation procedure is considered for cases in which some of the responses are ordered categorical and others are quantitative. Assume that data are generated according to nondegenerate probability distributions P. No other assumptions about the distributional properties of the data are needed, except that, in the alternative, cumulative distributions of quantitative variables are pairwise stochastically ordered.

Assume that the observed responses have the form of p real variables $\mathbf{X} = (X_1, \ldots, X_p)$ and q categorical variables $\mathbf{Q} = (Q_1, \ldots, Q_q)$. Also assume that the data are partitioned into C groups or samples of size n_j, $j = 1, \ldots, C$, according to C levels of a symbolic treatment. The q categorical variables may present respectively $m_1, \ldots, m_q$ classes (note that it is not necessary for the number of classes to be invariant in respect to categorical variables). If appropriate, ordered categorical variables may be processed as quantitative, after attribution of suitable scores to ordered classes.

Due to the complete robustness in respect to multivariate dependence relations among the variables (which extends the notion of multicollinearity) in nonparametric combination procedures, no relationship between cardinality of data and dimensionality of variables is required, in the sense that for some $j = 1, \ldots, C$, the sample size n_j may be less than $p + q$ with no drawbacks in the testing procedure. Such a situation may influence power functions and computing time. Moreover, if the data are time-dependent, time invariance of covariance matrices is not needed.

The data set $(\mathbf{X}, \mathbf{Q}) = \{(\mathbf{X}_1, \mathbf{Q}_1), \ldots, (\mathbf{X}_C, \mathbf{Q}_C)\}$ may be written in accordance with a unit-by-unit representation of individual records, such as:

$$(\mathbf{X}, \mathbf{Q}) = \{[X_r(t), r = 1, \ldots, p, Q_s(t), s = 1, \ldots, q], t = 1, \ldots, n; n_1, \ldots, n_C,$$

where it is intended that first n_1 records in the list belong to the first group, next n_2 to the second, and so on. The treatment effects model is assumed to be the following:

1. with regard to the p quantitative variables, treatment effects may behave according to the ANOVA layout, relaxing the normality assumption and some forms of homoscedasticity for responses in H_1 (such as pairwise dominance relationship);
2. the q categorical distributions may vary without restriction;
3. data vectors are assumed i.i.d. within groups, and groups are independent;
4. all marginal distributions of the sets of variables $\mathbf{X}$ and $\mathbf{Q}$ are assumed to be nondegenerate.

The $(p + q)$-dimensional joint distribution of (X_j, Q_j) is indicated by P_j; moreover, $\mathbf{X}$ and $\mathbf{Q}$ are assumed to be dependent in some unspecified ways, and their dependence relations are assumed to be invariant in respect to units and treatment levels. Formally, the hypotheses are:

$$H_0\text{: } \{\mathsf{P}_1 = \ldots = \mathsf{P}_C\} = \left\{(\mathbf{X}_1, \mathbf{Q}_1) \stackrel{d}{=} \ldots \stackrel{d}{=} (\mathbf{X}_C, \mathbf{Q}_C)\right\}$$

against H_1: $\{H_0$ is not true$\}$.

Hypotheses and assumptions 1 and 3 are such that the permutation testing principle (Pesarin, 2001) can be applied properly. However, the complexity of the problem is such that one overall test statistic is very difficult to find directly, even in a full parametric setting. The problem can therefore be solved by first considering a set of $k = p + q$ partial tests, followed by their nonparametric combination, provided that all k partial tests are marginally unbiased. This procedure is appropriate because, under assumptions (1) and (2), the global hypothesis may be broken down equivalently into:

$$H_0\text{: } \left\{[\mathbf{X}_1 \stackrel{d}{=} \ldots \stackrel{d}{=} \mathbf{X}_C] \cap (\mathbf{Q}_1 \stackrel{d}{=} \ldots \stackrel{d}{=} \mathbf{Q}_C)\right\}$$

against H_1: {H_0 is not true}. This form emphasizes the equality in distribution among the C levels of p-variate real variables $\mathbf{X}_j$ jointly with q-variate categorical variables $\mathbf{Q}_j$.

Note that the global null hypothesis may be further broken down into the equivalent form:

$$H_0: \left\{\left[\bigcap_{r=1}^{p} (X_{r1} \overset{d}{=} \ldots \overset{d}{=} X_{rC})\right] \cap \left[\bigcap_{s=1}^{q} (Q_{s1} \overset{d}{=} \ldots \overset{d}{=} Q_{sC})\right]\right\}$$

which is easier to process. In particular,

$$\mathrm{H}_{0r}^{\mathbf{X}}: \left\{X_{r1} \overset{d}{=} \ldots \overset{d}{=} X_{rC}\right\}, r = 1, \ldots, p,$$

indicates the equality in distribution among the C levels of the r-th quantitative variable X_r, whereas

$$\mathrm{H}_{0s}^{\mathbf{Q}}: \left\{Q_{s1} \overset{d}{=} \ldots \overset{d}{=} Q_{sC}\right\}, s = 1, \ldots, q,$$

indicates the equality in distribution among the C levels of the s-th categorical variable Q_s. In short we have:

$$H_0: \left\{\left[\bigcap_{r=1}^{p} \mathrm{H}_{0r}^{\mathbf{X}}\right] \cap \left[\bigcap_{s=1}^{q} \mathrm{H}_{0s}^{\mathbf{Q}}\right]\right\},$$

against the alternative:

$$H_1: \left\{\left[\bigcup_{r=1}^{p} \mathrm{H}_{1r}^{\mathbf{X}}\right] \cup \left[\bigcup_{s=1}^{q} \mathrm{H}_{1s}^{\mathbf{Q}}\right]\right\}.$$

In the next section we present some appropriate permutation test statistics for partial tests.

Under assumptions 1-3, all $p + q$ partial tests are marginally unbiased because they refer to sub-hypotheses each related to a different component variable. Hence the nonparametric combination of p and q partial tests provides for an effective solution to the overall hypotheses.

The testing problem presented above is extremely difficult when approached within the likelihood ratio method. Within the nonparametric combination approach discussed in this contribution, it is possible to consider satisfactory solutions to the problem.

For ordered variables, a suitable test statistic for permutation partial tests, one for each component variable *Qs*, $s = 1, \ldots, q$, in case of unrestricted alternatives, is the Anderson-Darling test statistic given by:

$$T_{ADs}^{*2} = \sum_{j=1}^{C} \sum_{h=1}^{m_s - 1} (F_{jh}^{*} - \bar{F}_h)^2 [\bar{F}_h \times (1 - \bar{F}_h) \times (n - n_j)/n_j]^{-1},$$

where $F_{jh}^{*} = N_{jh}^{*}/n_j$, in which $N_{jh}^{*} = \Sigma_{k \le h} f_{jk}^{*}$, $h = 1, \ldots, m_i - 1, j = 1, \ldots$ C, are permutation cumulative frequencies, and $F_h = N_{\cdot h}/n$ and $N_{\cdot h} = \Sigma_j N_{jh}$.

If response variables are continuous or binary, $X_r = 0$ or 1, $r = 1, \ldots, p$, appropriate permutation partial tests are:

$$T_r^{*2} = \sum_{j=1}^{C} n_j (\bar{X}_{jr}^{*})^2,$$

where $\bar{X}_{jr}^{*} = \Sigma_j X_{jr}^{*}/n_j$ are the permutation sample means of variable X_r, $r = 1, \ldots, p$, in the jth sample, $j = 1, \ldots C$.

In the nonparametric combination framework, it is possible to find solutions for multidimensional hypothesis testing problems even if some data are missing. Dealing with missing data depends on assumptions related to the procedure that generates the missing data and on the type of inference we are interested in. Generally, it can be distinguished between data missing completely at random (MCAR) and data not missing at random (not-MAR) (Little & Rubin, 1987). The NPC allows us for solving multidimensional hypothesis testing problems with directional or nondirectional alternatives in both situations (Pesarin, 2001). Consider, for instance, an MCAR model where the inference of interest is only on observed data, where an approximated solution for the comparison of C independent samples is given by the following test for unrestricted alternative hypotheses:

$$T_r^{*} = \sum_{j=1}^{C} \left\{ S_{jr}^{*} \cdot \left(\frac{\nu_r - \nu_{jr}^{*}}{\nu_{jr}^{*}} \right)^{1/2} - (S_r - S_{jr}^{*}) \cdot \left(\frac{\nu_{jr}^{*}}{\nu_r - \nu_{jr}^{*}} \right)^{1/2} \right\}^2,$$

where S_{jr}^{*} and *Sr* represent, respectively, the sum of the data observed in a permutation of data for the continuous or binary variable X_r, $r = 1, \ldots, p$, in the j-th group, and the sum of the data observed for variable X_r, while ν^*_{jr} and ν_r are, respectively, the permutation number of observed values for X_r in the j-th group, and the total number of observed values.

From the definition of the test statistics, it is easy to apply existing theory on nonparametric combination of dependent permutation tests in order to obtain a global test (for details see Pesarin, 2001).

CONTROL FOR MULTEPLICITY IN MULTIPLE TESTING PROBLEM

Closed Testing Procedure Using Permutation minP Method (Tippett's Test)

When carrying out multiple testing there should be a guarantee against incorrect decisions. This can be obtained by controlling the maximum Familywise Error Rate (FWE), that is, the maximum probability that one or more null hypotheses are erroneously rejected. In recent years specialized literature seems to agree that the closed testing procedures (Marcus, Peritz, & Gabriel, 1976) are preferable for multiplicity control. Indeed, these procedures prove to be easily adaptable to a wide range of experimental situations, at the same time enjoying properties consistent with the logical formulation of the analysis (control of the FWE, consistency, consonance). In particular they are easily adaptable to permutation tests.

Suppose it is desired to test a set of hypotheses of primary interest, say H_1, H_2, H_3. These hypotheses might be comparisons of three treatment groups with a common control group on a single response variable (example of a multiple comparison problem), or comparisons of two groups on three distinct response variables (example of a multiple testing problem). Closed testing methods work by firstly testing each minimal hypothesis H_1, H_2, H_3 using an appropriate α-level partial test. Then, compose hypotheses as necessary to form the closure of the family of inferences, including all intersection hypotheses, in the specific example the hypotheses H_{12}, H_{13}, H_{23}, H_{123}. In this way, the closure set consists of a hierarchy of hypotheses.

Next, test each member of the closed family using a suitable α-level combined test and choosing an appropriate test for each composite hypotheses H_{12}, H_{13}, H_{23}, H_{123}. After testing the composite hypotheses, reject any hypothesis H_i, with control of the FWE, provided that its corresponding test is statistically significant at level α and that every hypothesis in the family includes it in an intersection, thus implying it is rejected at level α. The results of a closed testing procedure are expressed in terms of adjusted p values: for a given hypothesis H_i, the adjusted p value is the maximum of all p values for tests that include H_i as a special case, including the p-value for the H_i itself. Different testing methods for minimal and composite hypotheses result in different closed testing procedures, so the use of powerful tests can lead to the best closed testing methods.

A brief review follows for some tests for composite hypotheses based on the minimum p value (minP) of the individual component tests corresponding to the minimal hypotheses included in the composite hypothesis. The "Bonferroni minP method" tests a composite hypothesis by comparing the minp of the individual component tests to α/g, where g is the number of components in the composite hypothesis and α is the desired FWE level. The composite hypothesis will be rejected when minP $\leq \alpha/g$, or equivalently when $g \times$ minP $\leq \alpha$, so that $g \times$ minP is the p value for the composite test. For example, the p value of the composite hypothesis H_{12} is $p = 2 \times \min(\lambda_1, \lambda_2)$, where λ_1, λ_2 are the p values of the component hypotheses H_1, H_2. After testing all the composite hypotheses, reject any hypothesis, say H_3, with control of the FWE, if its corresponding test and all null hypotheses that include it, H_{13}, H_{23}, H_{123}, are rejected at level α. Obtain the adjusted p value of H_3 as the maximum of all p values for tests on hypotheses H_3, H_{13}, H_{23}, H_{123}. Holm demonstrated a short procedure to apply the closed testing procedure and to derive adjusted p values based on Bonferroni's minP test that avoid calculating p values for all the composite hypotheses. Closed testing using Bonferroni's minP test is known as the Bonferroni-Holm minP method (see Westfall, Tobias, Rom, Wolfinger, & Hochberg, 1999).

The Bonferroni minP test tends to be conservative particularly when the correlation structure among variables is high. Westfall and Young (1993) suggest comparing the observed minp for a given composite hypothesis to the actual α-quantile of the minP null distribution, instead of α/g, where minP represents the random variable of minp for the given composite hypothesis. Formally, this is equivalent to calculating the p value of the composite test as $p = \Pr[\text{minP} \leq \min_{1 \leq i \leq g}(\lambda_i)]$, where $\min_{1 \leq i \leq g}(\lambda_i)$ is the observed value of minp for the given composite hypothesis. Reject the composite hypothesis comparing the obtained p value to the FWE level α.

The distribution of minP, usually unknown, can be estimated via bootstrap resampling (Westfall & Young, 1993). Alternatively, estimate the distribution of minP via resampling without replacement, by a Conditional Monte Carlo Procedure (Pesarin, 2001). In this case, the comparison of the observed minp for a given composite hypothesis to the estimated α-quantile of the minP distribution, is equivalent to calculating the p value of a composite hypothesis as $p = \Pr[\min_{1 \leq i \leq g}(\lambda_i)^* \leq \min_{1 \leq i \leq g}(\lambda_i)]$, where $\min_{1 \leq i \leq g}(\lambda_i)^*$ refers to the permutation distribution of MinP, and

$\min_{1 \le i \le g}(\lambda_i)$ is the observed minimum p value from the given composite hypothesis. Note that

$$\begin{aligned} p &= \Pr[\min_{1 \le i \le g}(\lambda_i)^* \le \min_{1 \le i \le g}(\lambda_i)] \\ &= \Pr[1 - \min_{1 \le i \le g}(\lambda_i)^*] \ge 1 - \min_{1 \le i \le g}(\lambda_i)] \\ &= \Pr[\max_{1 \le i \le g}(1 - \lambda_i)^*] \ge 1 - \max_{1 \le i \le g}(1 - \lambda_i). \end{aligned}$$

Thus, testing the composite hypotheses using the permutation minP test is equivalent to testing the composite hypotheses using the nonparametric combination of permutation partial component tests with Tippett's combining function T_T.

As in the case of the Bonferroni-Holm minP method, not all composite hypotheses need to be tested using the permutation minP test. For example, the minP observed for the three minimal hypotheses on the variables of adequacy (H_1), coherence (H_2) and use (H_3)—as will be discussed below—is the p value of H_3 and its value is 0.00015, while the p value of the global hypothesis H_{123} is 0.00035 (Figure 25.4). In this way hypotheses H_{13}, H_{23} need not be tested since it is guaranteed that their p values will be smaller then that of H_{123}. For example:

$$\Pr[\min(\lambda_1, \lambda_3)^* \le 0.00015] < Pr[min(\lambda_1, \lambda_2, \lambda_3)^* \le 0.00015] = 0.00035.$$

After testing the composite hypotheses, reject any hypothesis, say H_3, with control of the FWE, if its corresponding test and all hypotheses that include it, that is, H_{13}, H_{23}, H_{123}, are statistically significant at level α, or we may refer to the adjusted p value of H_3 obtained as the maximum of all p-values for tests on hypotheses H_3, H_{13}, H_{23}, H_{123}.

The adjusted p values for the permutation minP test (Tippett's test) are smaller than those of the Bonferroni-Holm method since they incorporate the underlying correlation structure among variables. Furthermore, see simulation studies by Finos, Pesarin, and Salmaso (2003) who showed favorable properties of Tippett's test.

AN EXTENSION OF NPC RANKING FOR ORDERED CATEGORICAL VARIABLES

An appropriate synthesis indicator is now defined of a set of k informative ordered categorical variables representing judgments on a specific quality aspect under evaluation (e.g. external effectiveness of educational processes within the university system). Denote the responses as a k-dimensional variable $\mathbf{Y} = [Y_1, \ldots, Y_k]$, where each marginal variable can assume m ordered discrete scores, $h = 1, \ldots, m, m \in \mathbf{N}\backslash\{0\}, m > 1$, and large values of h correspond to higher satisfaction rates. For application reasons these variables are given different (nonnegative) degrees of importance: $(0 < w_i \leq 1, i = 1, \ldots, k)$. Such weights are thought to reflect the different role of the variables in representing indicators of the specific quality aspect under evaluation (e.g., indicators of PhD researcher's success in entering the labor market or academic field), and are provided by responsible experts or by results of surveys previously carried out in the specific context.

The methodological problem is to find a global satisfaction index or a global ranking of N statistical subjects starting from k dependent rankings on the same N subjects, each representing a specific aspect under evaluation. Two main aspects should be considered when facing the problem of finding a global index or a global ranking of satisfaction:

1. the search of suitable combining function of two or more indicators or rankings;
2. the consideration of extreme units of the global ranking. Bird, Cox, Farewell, Goldstein, Holt, and Smith (2005) pointed out that "the principle that being ranked lowest does not immediately equate with genuinely inferior performance should be recognized and reflected in the method of presentation of ranking".

The nonparametric combination (NPC) of dependent rankings (Lago & Pesarin, 2000) provides a solution for problem (1). The main purpose of the NPC ranking method is to obtain a single ranking criterion for the statistical units under study, which summarizes many partial (univariate) rankings.

Consider a multivariate phenomenon whose variables $\mathbf{Y}$ are observed on N statistical units. Starting from component variables Y_i, $i = 1, \ldots, k$, each one providing information about a partial aspect, construct a global index or combined ranking T:

$$T = \phi(Y_1, \ldots, Y_k; w_1, \ldots, w_k),\ \phi:(\mathsf{R}^{2k} \rightarrow \mathsf{R}^1),$$

where ϕ is a real function that allows us to combine the partial dependent rankings and $(w_1, \ldots, w_k)$ is a set of weights which takes the relative degrees of importance among the k aspects of $\mathbf{Y}$ into account.

A set of minimal reasonable conditions related to variables Y_i, $i = 1, \ldots, k$ is introduced:

(a) for each of the k informative variables a partial ordering criterion is well established, that is to say, large is better;
(b) regression relationships within the k informative variables are monotonic (increasing or decreasing);
(c) the marginal distribution of each informative variable is non-degenerate.

Notice it is not necessary to assume the continuity of Y_i, $i = 1, \ldots, k$, so that the probability of ex-equo can be positive. The combining real function ϕ is chosen from class Φ of combining functions satisfying the following minimal properties:

1. ϕ must be continuous in all 2k arguments, in that small variations in any subset of arguments imply small variation in the ϕ-index;
2. ϕ must be monotone nondecreasing in respect to each argument:

$$\phi(\ldots Y_i, \ldots; w_1, \ldots, w_k) \geq \phi(\ldots Y_i', \ldots; w_1, \ldots, w_k) \text{ if } Y_i > Y_1' > 0, i = 1, \ldots, k$$

3. ϕ must be symmetric with respect to permutations of the arguments, in that if for instance $u_1, \ldots, u_k$ is any permutation of $1, \ldots, k$ then:

$$\phi(Y_{u_1}, \ldots, Y_{u_k}; w_1, \ldots, w_k) = \phi(Y_1, \ldots, Y_k; w_1, \ldots, w_k).$$

Property 1 is obvious; property 2 means, for instance, two subjects have exactly the same values for all Ys, except for the i-th, then the one with $Y_i > Y_1'$ must have assigned at least the same satisfaction ϕ-index. Property 3 states that any combining function ϕ must be invariant with respect to the order in which informative variables are processed. For example, Fisher's combining function: $\phi = -\sum_{i=1}^{k} w_i \times \log(1 - Y_i)$ can be useful for quality assessment. Of course, other combining functions previously presented may be of interest for the problem of quality assessment. Fisher's combining function seems to be more sensitive when assessing the best quality than when assessing lower quality, in the sense that small differences in the lower quality region seem to be identified with greater difficulty than those in the best quality region.

For problem 2, an extension of the NPC ranking method is proposed for the case of ordered categorical variables based on extreme satisfaction profiles. Extreme satisfaction profiles are defined a priori on a hypothetical frequency distribution of variables Y_i, $i = 1, \ldots, k$. Consider data $\mathbf{Y}$, where the rule large is better holds for all variables. Observed values for the k variables are denoted as y_{ji}, $i = 1, \ldots, k$; $j = 1, \ldots N$. Examples of extreme satisfaction profiles are given below.

The strong satisfaction profile is defined as follows:

- the maximum satisfaction is obtained when all subjects have the highest value of satisfaction for all variables:

$$f_{hi} = \begin{cases} 1 & \text{for } h = m \\ 0 & \text{otherwise} \end{cases}, \forall i, i = 1, \ldots, k$$

  where f_{ih} are the relative frequencies of categories h, $h = 1, \ldots, m$, for variable Y_i, $i = 1, \ldots, k$;

- the minimum satisfaction is obtained when all subjects have the smallest value of satisfaction for all variables:

$$f_{hi} = \begin{cases} 1 & \text{for } h = 1 \\ 0 & \text{otherwise} \end{cases}, \forall i, i = 1, \ldots, k$$

The weak satisfaction profile is defined as follows:

- the maximum satisfaction is obtained when the same relative frequency (say 70%) of subjects have the highest value of satisfaction for all variables:

$$f_{hi} = \begin{cases} u & \text{for } h = m \\ u_h & \text{otherwise, where } \sum_{h=1}^{m-1} u_h = (1-u) \end{cases} \quad \forall i, i = 1, \ldots, k;$$

- the minimum satisfaction is obtained when the same relative frequency (say 70%) of subjects have the smallest value of satisfaction for all variables:

$$f_{hi} = \begin{cases} u & \text{for } h = 1 \\ l_h & \text{otherwise, where } \sum_{h=2}^{m} l_h = (1-l) \end{cases} \quad \forall i, i = 1, \ldots, k$$

Another way to define weak satisfaction profiles is obtained when:

- the maximum satisfaction is obtained when subjects have the highest value of satisfaction with relative frequencies varying across the variables:

$$f_{hi} = \begin{cases} u_i & \text{for } h = m \\ u_{hi} & \text{otherwise, where } \sum_{h=1}^{m-1} u_{hi} = (1 - u_i) \end{cases} \qquad i = 1, \ldots, k;$$

- the minimum satisfaction is obtained when subjects have the smallest value of satisfaction with relative frequencies varying across the variables:

$$f_{hi} = \begin{cases} l_i & \text{for } h = 1 \\ l_{hi} & \text{otherwise, where } \sum_{h=2}^{m} l_{hi} = (1 - l_i) \end{cases} \qquad i = 1, \ldots, k.$$

In order to include the extreme satisfaction profiles in the analysis, transform original values h, $h = 1, \ldots, m$. Separate the values of h corresponding to a judgment of satisfaction, say the last t, $1 \le t \le m$, from those values corresponding to judgments of dissatisfaction, that is $(m - t)$. For the last t values of h corresponding to a judgment of satisfaction, the transformed values of h are defined as:

$$h + f_{hi} \times 0.5 \qquad h = m - t + 1, \ldots, m; i = 1, \ldots, k.$$

For the first $(m - t)$ values of h corresponding to judgments of dissatisfaction, the transformed values of h are defined as:

$$h + (1 - f_{hi}) \times 0.5 \qquad h = 1, \ldots, m - t; i = 1, \ldots, k.$$

Such transformation is equivalent to the assignment to original values h, $h = 1, \ldots, m$ of additive degrees of importance which depend on relative frequencies f_{ih} and which increase the original values h up to $h + 0.5$. Suppose, for example, that $h = 1, 2, 3, 4$ and values 3 and 4 correspond to judgments of satisfaction. By applying the above transformation, the value of 3 tends to the upper value 4 which represents higher satisfaction, when f_{i3} increases. On the contrary the value of 1 tends to 2 (less dissatisfaction), when f_{i1} decreases. Figure 25.1 displays the example.

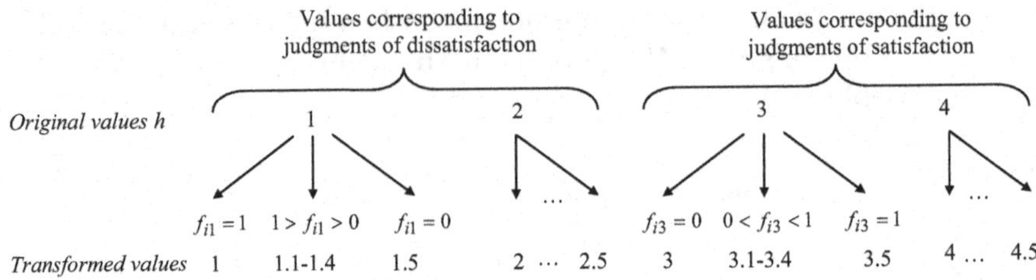

Figure 25.1. Transformation of orginal h values.

The transformation of values h, $h = 1, \ldots, m$, weighted by relative frequencies f_{ih}, is applied to observed values y_{ji}, $i = 1, \ldots, k$; $j = 1, \ldots N$. For the last t values of h corresponding to a judgment of satisfaction, the transformed values of y_{ji} are defined as:

$$z_{ji} = y_{ji} + \sum_{h = m-t+1}^{m} \mathbf{I}_h(y_{ji}) \times f_{ih} \times 0.5, \qquad i = 1, \ldots, k; j = 1, \ldots, N,$$

with:

$$\mathbf{I}_h(y_{ji}) = \begin{cases} 1 \text{ if } y_{ji} = h \\ 0 \text{ if } y_{ji} \neq h \end{cases}.$$

For the first $(m - t)$ values of h corresponding to judgments of dissatisfaction, the transformed values of y_{ji} are defined as:

$$z_{ji} = y_{ji} + \sum_{h=1}^{m-t} \mathbf{I}_h(y_{ji}) \times (1 - f_{ih}) \times 0.5, \qquad i = 1, \ldots, k; j = 1, \ldots, N.$$

In this setting, consider the following transformations (partial rankings):

$$\lambda_{ji} = \frac{(z_{ji} - z_{imin}) + 0.5}{(z_{imax} - z_{imin}) + 1}, \qquad i = 1, \ldots, k; j = 1, \ldots, N,$$

where z_{imin} and z_{imax} are obtained accordingly to an extreme satisfaction profile. Consider the strong satisfaction profile:

$$z_{imin} = y_{ji} + \sum_{h=1}^{m-t} \mathbf{I}_h(y_{ji}) \times (1 - f_{ih}) \times 0.5 = 1 \text{ where } f_{ih} = 1 \text{ and } y_{ji} = h = 1, \quad i = 1, \ldots, k$$

$$z_{imax} = y_{ji} + \sum_{h=m-t+1}^{m} \mathbf{I}_h(y_{ji}) \times f_{ih} \times 0.5 = m + 0.5 \text{ where } f_{ih} = 1$$

$$\text{and } y_{ji} = h = m, \quad i = 1, \ldots k.$$

For a weak satisfaction profile, with $u = 0.7$ and $l = 1$:

$$z_{imin} = y_{ji} + \sum_{h=1}^{m-t} \mathbf{I}_h(y_{ji}) \times (1 - f_{ih}) \times 0.5 = 1 \text{ where } f_{ih} = 1 \text{ and } y_{ji} = h = 1, \quad i = 1, \ldots, k$$

$$z_{imax} = y_{ji} + \sum_{h=m-t+1}^{m} \mathbf{I}_h(y_{ji}) \times f_{ih} \times 0.5 = m + 0.35 \text{ where } f_{ih} = 0.7$$

$$\text{and } y_{ji} = h = m, \quad i = 1, \ldots k.$$

Note that z_{imax} represents the preferred value for each variable. It is obtained when satisfaction is at its highest level accordingly to the extreme satisfaction profile; z_{imin} represents the worst value, and it is obtained when satisfaction is at its lowest level accordingly to the extreme satisfaction profile. Scores $\lambda_{ji}, i = 1, \ldots, m, j = 1, \ldots, N$ are one-to-one increasingly related with values y_{ji}, z_{ji} and are defined in the open interval (0, 1) (+0.5 and +1 are added in the numerator and denominator of λ_{ji} respectively). In order to synthesize the k partial rankings based on scores $\lambda_{ji}, i = 1, \ldots, m, j = 1, \ldots, N$, by means of the NPC ranking method, we use a combining function ϕ:

$$[T_j = \phi(\lambda_{j1}, \ldots, \lambda_{jk}; w_1, \ldots, w_k), j = 1, \ldots, N].$$

In order the global index varying in the interval [0, 1] put:

$$S_j = \frac{T_j - T_{min}}{T_{max} - T_{min}}, j = 1, \ldots, N,$$

where:

$$T_{min} = \phi(\lambda_{1min}, \ldots, \lambda_{kmin}; w_1, \ldots, w_k),$$
$$T_{max} = \phi(\lambda_{1max}, \ldots, \lambda_{kmax}; w_1, \ldots, w_k),$$

and λ_{imin} and λ_{imax} are obtained accordingly to the extreme satisfaction profiles:

$$\lambda_{i\min} = \frac{(z_{i\min} - z_{i\min}) + 0.5}{(z_{i\max} - z_{i\min}) + 1}, \qquad i = 1, \ldots, k,$$

$$\lambda_{i\max} = \frac{(z_{i\max} - z_{i\min}) + 0.5}{(z_{i\max} - z_{i\min}) + 1}, \qquad i = 1, \ldots, k.$$

Note that value $T_{\min}$ represents the unpreferred value of the satisfaction index since it is calculated from $(\lambda_{1\min}, \ldots, \lambda_{k\min})$, while $T_{\max}$ represents the preferred value since it is calculated from $(\lambda_{1\max}, \ldots, \lambda_{k\max})$. $T_{\min}$ and $T_{\max}$ are reference values in order to evaluate the distance of the observed satisfaction values from the situation of highest satisfaction defined accordingly to the extreme satisfaction profile.

POSTDOC SURVEY AT THE UNIVERSITY OF FERRARA

The Italian Context of Research Doctorate Evaluation

Set up in Italy in 1980, research doctorates (PhDs) represent the third level of university education and constitute a strategic resource in university for the provision of high standards of education and scientific research methods. In Italy the PhD has established itself predominantly as an academic qualification with the PhD researcher's career naturally continuing in the academic field or in research institutions, unlike other countries (e.g., the United States, Germany, and the United Kingdom) in which the PhD qualification also holds recognized professional value without the academic context, in the industrial field or in administration.

The Italian university and research system's growing difficulty of absorbing growing numbers of postdocs, united with growing awareness that PhDs can make an important contribution to the cultural and technological innovation of which the entire economic-production system perceives the need, have represented recent incentives for universities and central authorities to support initiatives for the appreciation, recognition and improvement of the education program represented by PhDs. Evaluating the quality of a PhD is somewhat complex and includes several dimensions of analysis (adequacy of education content, success of entry into employment, etc.) and several subjects involved in the education process at various levels: PhD researchers and postdocs; teaching staff and doctorate tutors; PhD structures both internal (departments, institutes) and external in which study and research activities take place; the university-research system and labor market (public and private sector subjects operating in the academic and research field and in the labor market) in which postdocs are placed.

By considering the PhD as a process characterized by elements of initial inputs and final outcomes, evaluation of the doctorate is based on process quality indicators and outcome indicators, taking elements of initial inputs (input characteristics of PhD researchers, resources available for the PhDs, characteristics of the territorial context, etc.) into account. In some cases, to define and calculate quality indicators reference is made to objective data (structural data, etc.) which can be obtained from existing sources (e.g. administrative sources); in other cases reference is made to subjective data (opinions, suggestions, judgments of satisfaction) perceived and declared by the various subjects involved (PhD researchers, teachers, etc.), obtained by means of ad hoc surveys and instruments (e.g. sample surveys with a questionnaire).

Research doctorate evaluation provided for by current Italian legislation refers to evaluation of the suitability requisites of doctorate courses (e.g., teaching staff with an adequate number of lecturers and researchers in the specific scientific field, availability of adequate financial resources and specific operational and scientific structures for the course and for PhD researchers' study and research, etc.). Such evaluations are carried out by the evaluation group (EG) operating inside the university. Centrally there is provision for an annual report (the first evaluation took place in 2002) on the state of teaching in doctorate courses and on the evaluation procedures adopted by universities, carried out by the National Committee for the Evaluation of the University System (NCEUS).

As of the 2003/2004 academic year, a national database containing information regarding the offer of third-level courses (PhD register) has made it possible to acquire information on doctorates and to automatically verify their suitability requisites provided for by law, both for existing and new doctorates. Almost all universities have recently ensured that evaluation procedures are activated with regard to suitability requisites and the structural and administrative data of doctorate courses. Some universities have also carried out ad hoc surveys on PhD researchers' opinions of the education and research activities that characterize doctorate courses and some organizational aspects of the education programs. Still lacking and sporadic, however, are surveys for the evaluation of PhD outcomes and employment opportunities. In this context at the University of Ferrara, a sample survey of postdocs was conducted in 2004 with the objective of acquiring knowledge on the professional placing of postdocs, on the relationship between education received during the PhD and employment, and on their satisfaction with a number of aspects of the education and research program carried out during the doctorate.

Postdoc Survey

The postdoc survey at the University of Ferrara concerned a representative sample of 120 PhD holders, selected from the 4 cohorts of 288 postdocs who gained the qualification from 2001 to 2004. The various PhDs were grouped into 4 macro areas: economic-legal (EL), medical-biological (MB), scientific-technological (ST) and the humanities (HU). A random sample of 30 postdocs was extracted for each year, stratified by doctorate area with proportional allocation.

The survey was carried out by means of computer assisted telephone interviews (CATI). The electronic questionnaire was divided into six sections: personal details and education, postdoctorate training, employment condition and characteristics, education used at work, job searching, and opinion of education received on doctorate course.

To observe postdoc satisfaction with regard to various aspects of their work, the education received and the PhD organization, a scale of scores from 1 to 4 was used (*not at all, not very, quite, very satisfied*).

Figure 25.2 illustrates a time diagram of the survey and its date of reference (October 12, 2004). This date is used to calculate the time intervals for each cohort from the moment of obtaining the qualification to the time of the survey.

Statistical Analysis

The statistical analysis of the gathered data was structured into two steps. The first aims to highlight differences among scientific-technological, medical-biological and economic-legal doctorates (Figure 25.3). The humanities area, as it is present only in the 2004 cohort, was not included in the analysis by doctorate area. The second step, not reported here, identifies diversity among the four time cohorts. On Web page http://web.unife.it/ateneo/comstat, results are available of the descriptive analysis carried out on the various sections of the questionnaire and the employment condition of postdocs, by doctorate area and by doctorate title cohort.

This chapter reports the results of the analysis by doctorate area relating to four aspects of postdoc satisfaction: education-employment relationship, teaching and the research work carried out during doctorate, doctorate structures and services, employment expectations and opportunities. The objective is to verify differences in satisfaction of postdocs belonging to different areas and to understand if observed differences are linked to their disciplines, or if they reflect differences in quality of the courses' internal and external effectiveness. Tables 25.1-25.4 show the

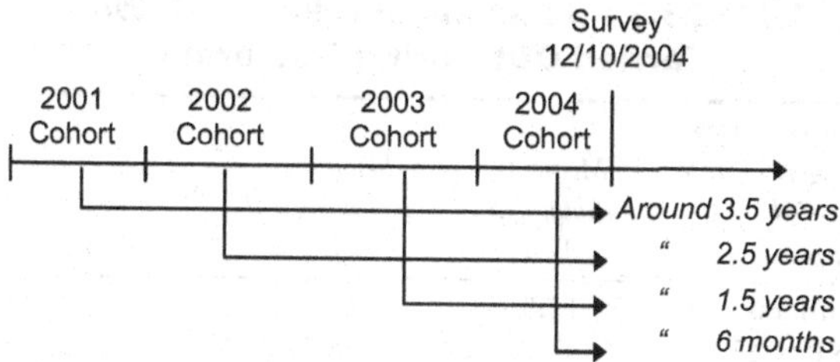

Figure 25.2. Time diagram of survey.

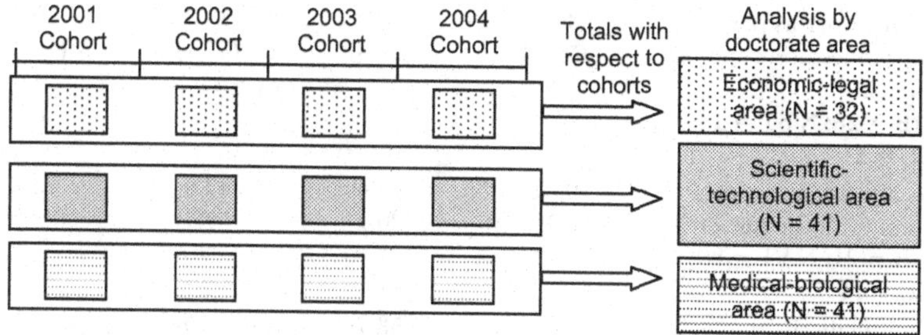

Figure 25.3. Diagram of analysis by doctorate area.

Table 25.1. Education-Employment Relationship

Education-Employment Relationship % Very Satisfied (% Quite Satisfied)*	*Medical-Biological Area N = 20*	*Scientific-Technological Area N = 23*	*Economic-Legal Area N = 23*	*Areas Total N = 66*
Education/employment coherence	30.0 (35.0)	60.9 (21.7)	91.3 (8.7)	62.1 (21.2)
Use of education at work	10.0 (45.0)	39.1 (17.4)	65.2 (30.4)	39.4 (30.3)
Adequacy of education with regard to employment	25.0 (30.0)	26.1 (30.4)	56.5 (34.8)	36.4 (31.8)

*Subjects in training, with study grants, research allowances or unpaid collaborations are excluded.

percentages of very satisfied and quite satisfied postdocs in relation to the variables regarding the four aspects under examination.

Figure 25.5 and Tables 25.5-25.8 illustrate the results of tests of hypotheses for the comparison among the three macro areas regarding the four aspects of satisfaction indicated above, following the nonparametric procedure described above. Moreover, closed testing based on the

Table 25.2. Teaching and Research Work Carried Out During Doctorate

Teaching and Research Work Carried Out During Doctorate % Very Satisfied (% Quite Satisfied)	*Medical-Biological Area*	*Scientific-Technological Area*	*Economic-Legal Area*	*Areas Total*
Courses and seminars N.MB = 26; N.ST = 27; N.EL = 27	11.5 (57.7)	14.8 (48.1)	37.0 (55.6)	21.2 (53.8)
Individual research work N.MB = 41; N.ST = 41; N.EL = 32	48.8 (34.1)	53.7 (41.5)	59.4 (37.5)	53.5 (37.7)
Research work as part of groups of lecturers and/or students N.MB = 28; N.ST = 18; N.EL = 21	39.3 (50.0)	50.0 (27.8)	33.3 (57.1)	40.3 (46.3)
Stays abroad or in structures outwith the university N.MB = 21; N.ST = 29; N.EL = 14	95.2 (0)	72.4 (20.7)	42.9 (57.1)	73.4 (21.9)
Doctorate thesis N.MB = 41; N.ST = 41; N.EL = 32	46.3 (46.3)	53.7 (39.0)	62.5 (37.5)	53.5 (41.2)

permutation minP method (Tippett's test) outlined in a previous section was applied to control for multiplicity.

With reference to the relationship between PhD education and employment, postdocs (excluding those in training, with study grants, research allowances and/or unpaid collaborations) expressed an evaluation of the coherence between education and employment, of use in employment of the abilities acquired during the PhD, and of the adequacy of the PhD training for the work carried out. Both the global test regarding the hypothesis of equality in the multivariate distribution of the three categorical variables (with the following responses: not at all, not very, quite, very satisfied) and the partial tests regarding the contribution of each variable are statistically significant results at level $\alpha = 0.05$, after controlling for multiplicity (Figure 25.4), thus highlighting a difference in satisfaction among the three analyzed macro areas. Those nodes in Figure 25.4 shown as "$p \leq$" rather than "$p =$" are calculated by implication, not directly, according to remarks above. Table 25.5 shows the adjusted p values for partial tests.

In relation to opinions expressed about teaching and research work carried out during the PhD, three variables recodified as binary with miss-

Table 25.3. Doctorate Structures and Services

Doctorate Structures and Services % Very Satisfied (% Quite Satisfied)	*Medical-Biological Area*	*Scientific-Technological Area*	*Economic-Legal Area*	*Areas Total*
Libraries N.MB = 34; N.ST = 36; N.EL =25	38.2 (52.9)	25.0 (55.6)	36.0 (48.0)	32.6 (52.6)
Lecture theaters N.MB = 30; N.ST = 33; N.EL = 24	6.7 (73.3)	6.1 (57.6)	16.7 (66.7)	9.2 (65.5)
Study areas N.MB = 33; N.ST = 32; N.EL = 24	9.1 (54.5)	34.4 (34.4)	16.7 (54.2)	20.2 (47.2)
Laboratories N.MB = 33; N.ST = 32; N.EL = 6	30.3 (45.4)	40.6 (40.6)	0 (16.7)	32.4 (40.8)
Information received on courses and teaching N.MB = 33; N.ST = 39; N.EL = 29	21.2 (36.4)	7.7 (48.7)	31.0 (44.8)	18.8 (43.6)
Help with bureaucratic matters N.MB = 41; N.ST = 41; N.EL = 32	17.5 (60.0)	19.5 (48.8)	28.1 (43.7)	21.2 (51.3)
Support of lecturers, tutors, coordinator N.MB = 40; N.ST = 41; N.EL = 32	43.9 (39.0)	53.7 (29.3)	65.6 (28.1)	53.5 (32.5)

Table 25.4. Employment Expectations and Opportunities

Employment Expectations and Opportunities % Very Satisfied (% Quite Satisfied)	*Medical-Biological Area N = 41*	*Scientific-Technological Area N = 41*	*Economic-Legal Area N = 32*	*Areas Total N = 114*
Opportunities in the academic world	4.9 (22.0)	17.1 (22.0)	31.3 (43.8)	16.7 (28.1)
Opportunities in the labor market	4.9 (22.0)	4.9 (41.5)	3.1 (50.0)	4.4 (36.8)
Opening toward the scientific community	31.7 (41.5)	31.7 (51.2)	37.5 (53.1)	33.3 (48.3)

ing values were analyzed (courses and seminars, group research and activities outside the university; with values: 0 = not at all, not very, quite satisfied, 1 = very satisfied), and two ordered categorical variables without

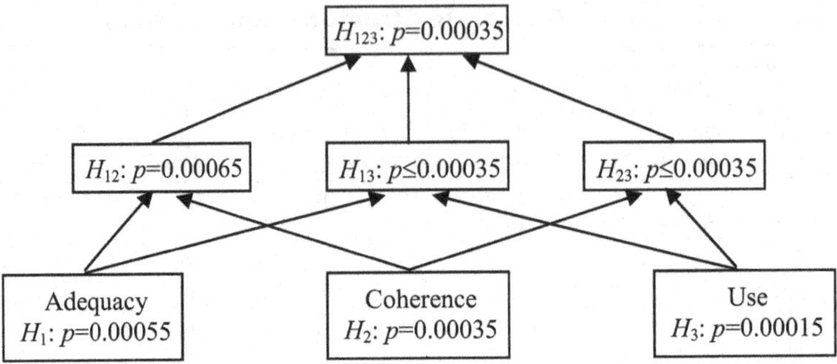

Figure 25.4. Closed testing based on Permutation minP (Tippett's test) for composite hypotheses: satisfaction with education-employment relationship.

Table 25.5. Raw and Adjusted *p* Values: Satisfaction with Education-Work Relationship

Partial Tests	*Raw p Values*	*Adjusted p Values*
Adequacy	$p = 0.00055$	$p = 0.00065$
Coherence	$p = 0.00035$	$p = 0.00035$
Use	$p = 0.00015$	$p = 0.00035$

missing data (individual research and PhD thesis; with the following responses: not at all, not very, quite, very satisfied). Table 25.6 shows the presence of a statistically significant difference at a global level among the macro areas, with a particular contribution from the satisfaction expressed in relation to study periods abroad or in institutions other than the University of Ferrara.

No statistically different evaluation among the economic-legal, scientific-technological and medical-biological PhDs emerges in relation to the courses' support services and structures. For this analysis, six variables recodified as binary with missing values were considered (libraries, lecture theatres, study areas, laboratories, information about teaching and bureaucratic support; with values: 0 = *not at all, not very, quite satisfied*, 1 = *very satisfied*), and a categorical variable without missing data (support from lecturers and tutors; with the following responses: not at all, not very, quite, very satisfied). The combination algorithm with different combining functions was iterated until the final overall p values became reasonably invariant (Table 25.7). In this way a preliminary, significant result from Liptak's combining function was no longer significant with the second iteration.

Table 25.6. Raw and Adjusted p Values: Satisfaction With Teaching and Research Work

	Raw p Values	*Adjusted p Values*
Overall test	$p = 0.01435$	
Partial tests:		
Courses and seminars	$p = 0.04495$	not significant
Individual research	not significant	not significant
Group research	not significant	not significant
Outside stay	$p = 0.00295$	$p = 0.01435$
Doctorate thesis	not significant	not significant

Table 25.7. Iterated Combination Procedure: Satisfaction With Structures and Services

	Combining Function		
p Value of Overall Test	*Tippett*	*Fisher*	*Liptak*
First iteration	0.20873	0.06864	0.03595
Second iteration	0.06764	0.06974	0.06994

Table 25.8. Raw and Adjusted *p* Values: Satisfaction With Employment Expectations and Opportunities

	Raw p Values	*Adjusted p Values*
Overall test	$p = 0.00035$	
Partial tests:		
Academic opportunity	$p = 0.00015$	$p = 0.00035$
Labor market opportunity	not significant	not significant
Scientific community opening	not significant	not significant

The final aspect regarding PhD researchers' expectations of employment after obtaining the qualification (three categorical variables: opportunities in the academic field, opportunities in the labor market and opening towards the scientific community, with the following responses: not at all, not very, quite, very satisfied) again shows a statistically significant difference at a global level among the three PhD areas, to which opinions of opportunities in the academic field contribute very significantly (Table 25.8).

In order to construct a global satisfaction indicator the NPC ranking methodology was also applied considering the strong satisfaction profile. For the three doctorate areas, Table 25.9 shows the median values and the

Table 25.9. NPC Ranking

Global Index of satisfaction *Median* *(First Quartile–Third Quartile)*	*Medical-Biological Area*	*Scientific-Technological Area*	*Economic-Legal Area*	*Areas Total*
Education-employment relationship N.MB = 20; N.ST = 23; N.EL = 23	0.34 (0.12–0.53)	0.47 (0.37–0.63)	0.66 (0.53–0.79)	0.53 (0.36–0.66)
Employment expectations and opportunities N.MB = 41; N.ST = 41; N.EL = 32	0.26 (0.20–0.41)	0.32 (0.26–0.47)	0.41 (0.30–0.50)	0.32 (0.26–0.46)

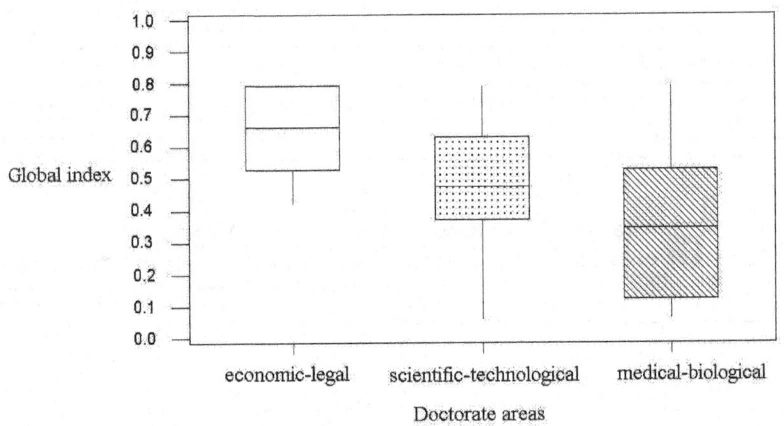

Figure 25.5. Box-plot of global index of satisfaction with education-employment relaionship.

interquartile range of the global satisfaction score expressed on a scale of 0-1 in relation to the three aspects regarding the education-employment relationship and the three aspects regarding prospects offered by the doctorate. The box-plots shown in Figure 25.5 and Figure 25.6 illustrate the distribution of the two global satisfaction indexes in the three considered groups.

With reference to participants who stated they had a stable job placement at the time of the survey (excluding therefore postdocs in training, with study grants, research allowances and/or unpaid collaborations) and for whom information regarding the education-employment relationship was available, the nonparametric correlation between the global indexes

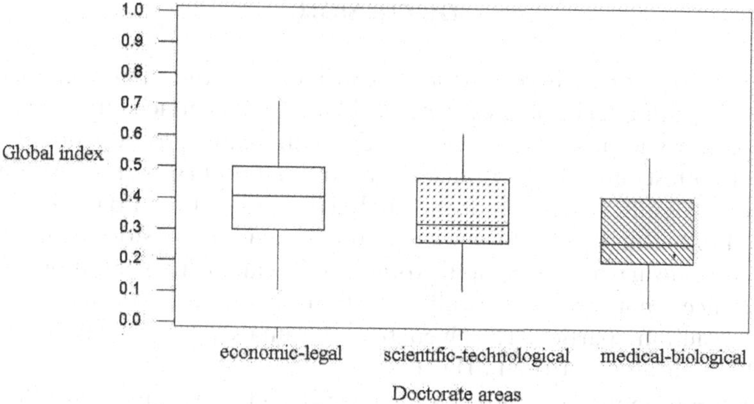

Figure 25.6. Box-plot of global index of satisfaction with employment expectations and opportunities.

Table 25.10. Nonparametric Correlation Between Global Indexes of Satisfaction

	Medical-Biological Area N = 20	*Scientific-Technological Area N = 23*	*Economic-Legal Area N = 23*	*Areas Total N = 66*
Global index of satisfaction with education—employment relationship *Median (First quartile—third quartile)*	0.34 (0.12—0.53)	0.47 (0.37—0.63)	0.66 (0.53—0.79)	0.53 (0.36—0.66)
Global index of satisfaction with employment expectations and opportunities *Median (First quartile—third quartile)*	0.21 (0.15—0.32)	0.27 (0.21—0.39)	0.43 (0.26—0.49)	0.30 (0.21—0.43)
Spearman's Correlation (Monte Carlo estimate of p value)	0.66 (0.0016)	0.11 (n.s.)	0.28 (n.s.)	0.43 (0.0002)
n.s. = not significant				

obtained using the NPC ranking methodology was calculated. The first satisfaction index concerned satisfaction with coherence, use and adequacy of education in relation to employment, the second concerned prospects offered by the doctorate. This analysis revealed a moderate, positive correlation between the two indexes and by separating data for the three doctorate areas a more substantial and statistically significant correlation is found for postdocs in the MB area (Table 25.10).

DISCUSSION

Comparison of the three PhD areas considered in the survey (economic-legal, scientific-technological, medical-biological) carried out using the nonparametric procedure based on the combination of dependent permutation tests and the permutation minP method (Tippett's test), represented a significant aspect of the analysis of the gathered data, in that it aimed to highlight any differences in the interviewed postdocs' multivariate and univariate satisfaction profiles. Subsequent interpretation of the differences that were statistically significant do in any case require adequate caution, particularly given that the analyzed variables represent quality indicators for the PhD courses.

Opinions expressed on teaching and research work carried out during PhD courses can provide information about student perception of the internal effectiveness of PhDs, intended as the suitability of course methods to the stated education objectives. In general, postdocs stated they were quite satisfied with the activities carried out (Table 25.2). Greatest appreciation is observed for the PhD thesis and for work carried out abroad or in institutions outside the university. Differences in satisfaction profiles for the three areas regarding the aspects of internal effectiveness considered in the survey are substantially due to the opinion of activities carried out externally (Table 25.6), with almost total satisfaction in the medical-biological area (95.2% very satisfied), and slightly more contained satisfaction in the economic-legal area (42.9% very satisfied) (Table 25.2).

The quality of research carried out individually, with or without the supervision of lecturers, is perceived positively (Table 25.2). Though all respondents stated that they had carried out research individually, just over half (57.3%) reported experience of research within groups of lecturers and/or students: of these 86.6% were very/quite satisfied with this type of initiative. Less positive is the opinion of the education received: a quarter of interviewees held this aspect to be not very or not at all satisfactory and little more than a fifth were highly satisfied.

The tendency to make a more critical judgment of teaching was also found in other surveys on PhDs. In a survey carried out by ADI (Association of Italian PhD Researchers and Post-Docs) in 1998 on a sample of 269 PhD students from various Italian universities (Ambrosi, Della Ratta, Saccà, & Usai, 1998), only a third of interviewees stated they were satisfied with the education received. Criticism generally concerns the poor structuring of the education programs, with characteristics at times considerably different depending on the subject taught in the PhD, and the lack of specific, high-level courses for PhD Researchers. Urged by the NCEUS, some universities have recently started initiatives to standardize PhDs and establish PhD Schools. Through common, multi-sectorial initiatives, this new organization should facilitate a more efficient and prestigious teaching program (Ministero dell'Istruzione, dell'Università e della Ricerca, 2003a).

Indications as to the external effectiveness of PhDs, understood to mean the usefulness and usability of a PhD qualification for insertion into the academic or employment field, can be derived from a combination of questions regarding coherence between employment and study, use of competencies acquired during studies, and the adequacy of education in relation to employment (Tables 25.1, 25.5, Figure 25.5). On the whole, the satisfaction area (very/quite satisfied) was high, though characterized by significant differences among the areas, with a growing trend as we move from the MB area to the ST and EL areas. More positive opinions are found in relation to coherence (62.1% very satisfied & 21.2% quite satisfied), less positive for the level of use of acquired techniques (69.7% very/quite satisfied). Room for improvement can also be identified with regard to adequacy of education (31.8% not satisfied). Differences among the areas are also highlighted by the distribution of the global satisfaction index expressed on a scale of 0-1 (Table 25.9, Figure 25.6). In the EL area, as well as a shifting of the distribution toward high values of satisfaction, less variability in scores is found, particularly compared with the MB area.

Contributing to further qualification of the data regarding certain aspects of the PhD qualification's external effectiveness are results from the evaluation of the satisfaction levels with prospects offered by the PhD in terms of opportunities for insertion into the academic field or labor market or as an opening toward the scientific community (Tables 25.4, 25.8). The low percentages of those who consider themselves very satisfied with these aspects denote a certain lack of confidence in the absorption ability of both the university (55.2% not very/not at all satisfied) and even more so the labor market in general (58.8% not very/not at all satisfied).

Contributing to the differentiation of satisfaction profiles in the three PhD areas regarding opportunities offered by PhDs are opinions on the possibility of continuing an academic career, held to be more plausible by postdocs in the economic-legal area than by colleagues in the scientific area. Distribution of the global satisfaction index expressed on a scale of 0-1 (Table 25.9, Figure 25.6) stands level with relatively low values for the three areas, which also highlights substantial homogeneity in postdoc perceptions. In the cited ADI survey, only 10% of interviewees stated they were optimistic about the possibility of obtaining an academic post within 2 years of obtaining the qualification.

As well as the perceived difficulties of entry into employment, the persistence of the PhD's strong initial characterization still stands out, perceived and structured in Italy as a pathway almost exclusively into academic circles. 71.9% of interviewees in the current survey remain in the academic field after obtaining their qualification (this percentage varies from 81.2% in the EL area to 70.7% in the ST area and 65.9% in the MB area), often only through unpaid collaborations or post PhD study grants and research allowances. Furthermore, 47.7% of those who do not yet have a structured working position state they are only interested in jobs in the academic field, and this percentage varies from 31.2% in the ST area to 47.4% in the MB area, up to 77.8% in the EL area.

CONCLUSION

The nonparametric combination of dependent permutation partial tests is a method for the combination of significance levels. Conversely, the route generally followed by most parametric tests, based for instance on likelihood ratio behavior, essentially corresponds to the combination of discrepancy measures and this is usually expressed by point distances in the sample space. In this sense, this method appears to be a substantial extension of standard parametric approaches. The nonparametric combination method is suitable and effective for many multivariate testing problems which, in a parametric framework, are very difficult or even impossible to solve.

One major feature of the nonparametric combination of dependent tests, provided that the permutation principle applies, is that one must pay attention to a set of partial tests, each appropriate for the related sub-hypothesis, because the underlying dependence relation structure is nonparametrically captured by the combining procedure. In particular, the researcher is not explicitly required to specify the dependence structure of response variables. This aspect is of great importance especially for non-normal or categorical variables, in which dependence relations are generally too difficult to define and, even when well-defined, are hard to cope with (see, e.g., Joe, 1997). The researcher is only required to make sure that all partial tests are marginally unbiased, a sufficient condition which is generally easy to check.

The nonparametric combination procedure may therefore be effective when one overall test is not directly available. In such a situation, it is usually convenient to analyze data by firstly examining a set of k partial aspects, each interesting in a marginal sense, and then combining all captured information. In principle, it is possible to apply a proper single overall permutation procedure directly, if known, and then avoid the combination step. But in most complex situations such a single test is not directly available or is not easy to justify. In addition, the direct analysis of the dependence relation structure is often very difficult because, in the general case, due to its dependence on the present data set **Y**, the permutation c.d.f. $F(z|\mathbf{Y})$ is usually expressed in numeric form and, among the partial test statistics in **T**, there may be nonlinear regression forms, monotonic functional relationships, heteroscedasticity, or other irregularities caused by categorical and/or mixed data, missing values, repeated measurements, and so forth.

In a way, the nonparametric combination procedure for dependent tests may be viewed as a two-stage testing procedure. The first stage considers a simulation from the permutation sample space by means of a CMC method based on B iterations, in order to estimate $F(z|\mathbf{Y})$. The second stage considers the combination of estimated p-values of partial tests, in order to estimate the overall p-value by using the same CMC results as the first stage. Of course, the two stages are jointly processed, so that the procedure always remains multivariate in its own right.

Furthermore, in the presence of a stratification variable, the nonparametric combination, through a multistage procedure, allows quite flexible solutions. For instance, first combine partial tests with respect to variables within each stratum, and then combine the combined tests with respect to strata. Alternatively, combine partial tests related to each variable with respect to strata, and then combine the combined tests with respect to variables. In this respect, for instance, the nonparametric component-wise analysis (POSET method) as suggested by Rosenbaum (1995) can only permit the overall solution and nothing can be said in relation to the stratified partial analyses.

As the nonparametric combination method is conditional on a set of sufficient statistics, it shows good general power behavior. Monte Carlo experiments, reported in Pesarin (2001) and Celant, Pesarin, and Salmaso (2000a,b), showed that the Fisher, Liptak, or direct combining functions often have power functions which are quite close to the best parametric counterparts, even for moderate sample sizes. Thus nonparametric combination tests are relatively efficient and much less demanding in terms of underlying assumptions compared with parametric competitors. Moreover, standard distribution-free methods based on ranks, which are generally not conditional on sufficient statistics, almost never present better unconditional power behavior.

Additionally, the Fisher, Liptak, Lancaster, Tippett and direct combining functions for nonparametric combination are not at all affected by the functional analogue of multicollinearity among partial tests. In fact, in such situations, the combination only gives rise to a kind of implicit weighting of partial tests.

Because of the versatility of permutation tests, analysis of restricted alternatives, ties, categorical and/or mixed variables, MCAR or not-MAR missing values problems, in which the number k of component variables is larger than the number n of subjects, is straightforward.

As a final remark, from a general point of view and in very mild conditions, the nonparametric combination method may be considered a way to reduce the degree of complexity of most testing problems.

Regarding extension of the nonparametric combination of dependent partial rankings for ordered variables, we can outline the flexibility of the method to construct a combined indicator starting from k dependent indicators based on ordered variables. This procedure can be used both to derive a global index of satisfaction used in comparisons among different groups or compared with an optimal desired value of satisfaction, and to construct a global ranking of units which can be useful when exploring clusters of units with a lower or upper global level of satisfaction.

REFERENCES

Ambrosi, A., Della Ratta, F., Saccà, F., & Usai M. C. (1998). *La condizione dei dottorandi di ricerca in Italia. ADI-Associazione Dottorandi e Dottori di Ricerca Italiani* [The Italian PhD student condition. ADI-Association of Italian PhDs and Post-Docs]. http://www.dottorato.it/qualità.

Bird, S. M., Cox, D., Farewell, V. T., Goldstein, H., Holt, T., & Smith, P. C. (2005). Performance indicators: Good, bad and ugly. *Journal of the Royal Statistical Society,* Series A, vol. 168, Part 1, 1-27.

Celant, G., Pesarin, F., & Salmaso, L. (2000a). Some comparisons between a parametric and a nonparametric solution for tests with repeated measures. *Metron, LVIII,* 1-2, 64-79.

Celant, G., Pesarin, F., & Salmaso, L. (2000b). Two sample permutation tests for repeated measures with missing values. *Journal of Applied Statistical Science, 9*(4), 291-304.

Finos, L., Pesarin, F., & Salmaso L. (2003). Test combinati per il controllo della molteplicità mediante procedure di Closed Testing [Combined tests for controlling multiplicity by Closed Testing procedures]. *Italian Journal of Applied Statistics, 15*(2), 301-329.

Joe, H. (1997). *Multivariate models and dependence concepts.* London: Chapman & Hall.

Lago, A., & Pesarin, F. (2000). Nonparametric combination of dependent rankings with application to the quality assessment of industrial products. *Metron, LVIII,* 1-2, 39-52.

Little, R. J. A, & Rubin, D. B. (1987). *Statistical analysis with missing data.* New York: Wiley.

Marcus, R., Peritz, E., & Gabriel, K. R. (1976). On closed testing procedures with special reference to ordered analysis of variance. *Biometrika, 63,* 655-660.

Ministero dell'Istruzione, dell'Università e della Ricerca. (2003a). *Incentivi alla ricerca e prima analisi dei corsi di dottorato* [Research grants and a first analysis on PhD programs]. In Università obiettivo valutazione, 2 Documenti, Atenei, 273-294.

Pesarin, F. (2001). *Multivariate Permutation tests (with applications in biostatistics).* Chichester, England: Wiley.

Rosenbaum, P. R. (1995). *Observational studies.* New York: Springer-Verlag.

Westfall, P. H, Tobias, R. D., Rom, D., Wolfinger, R. D., & Hochberg, Y. (1999). *Multiple comparisons and multiple test using the SAS System.* Cary, NC: SAS Insititute.

Westfall, P. H., & Young, S.S. (1993). *Resampling-based multiple testing.* New York: Wiley.

CHAPTER 26

RANDOMIZED REPLICATED SINGLE-CASE EXPERIMENTS

Treatment of Pain-Related Fear by Graded Exposure In Vivo

Patrick Onghena, Johan W. S. Vlaeyen, and Jeroen de Jong

Randomization tests are one of the most useful and straightforward statistical techniques to analyze the results collected in randomized single-case experiments (Barlow & Hersen, 1984; Edgington, 1967, 1996; Franklin, Allison, & Gorman, 1996; Kazdin, 1982; Kratochwill & Levin, 1992). Their appeal stems from the absence of any random sampling or parametric assumption, from their close connection to the actual design of the study, and from their easy and realistic "relative frequency" interpretation (Edgington, 1995; Onghena, 2005; Todman & Dugard, 2001).

However, the widespread implementation of single-case randomization tests in scientific research has yet to come. Of course, there are already some groundbreaking applications in several research domains (see e.g., de Jong, Vlaeyen, Onghena, Goossens, Geilen, & Mulder, 2005; Edgington & Bland, 1993; Holden, Bearison, Rode, Kapiloff, Rosenberg, & Onghena, 2003; McLeod, Cohen, Taylor, & Cullen, 1986; Van de Vliet et al.,

Real Data Analysis, pp. 387–396

2003; Vlaeyen, de Jong, Onghena, Kerckhoffs-Hanssen, & Kole-Snijders, 2002; Weiss et al., 1980), but these publications are much scarcer than would be expected on the basis of the unanimous advocacy in the methodological and statistical literature. As Levin and Wampold (1999) observed with respect to their generalized single-case randomization tests:

> Although the resulting methods are well-founded in logic and theory (as well as in our imagination), we are the first to admit that they are currently untested with respect to single-case interventions to be implemented with real participants, groups, or classrooms. That is, although it can be easily demonstrated how the present approaches should and could work on hypothetical examples or selected available data (as was demonstrated here), we at the same time recognize that the ultimate acceptability of the present methods is certain to depend on both how feasibly they can be applied and how effectively they will perform in actual single-case applications. (p. 85)

Taking Levin and Wampold's (1999) advice to heart, the purpose of the present contribution is to demonstrate the versatility and feasibility of the single-case randomization test approach in an applied setting. In this way, we want to provide another impetus for applied researchers to seriously consider this way of designing and analyzing empirical studies in the behavioral and educational sciences.

THE CHALLENGE: RANDOMIZED REPLICATED SINGLE-CASE EXPERIMENTS

A study was designed to examine the effectiveness of a graded exposure in vivo treatment as compared to usual graded activity in reducing fear of movement/(re)injury, fear of pain, and pain catastrophizing in four consecutive chronic low back pain patients who were referred for outpatient behavioral rehabilitation (for a detailed description of the interventions and the measurements, see Vlaeyen, de Jong, Geilen, Heuts, & van Breukelen, 2001). Three phases were included in the design: an initial no-treatment baseline phase (A), a graded activity phase (B), and a graded exposure phase (C), and the participants were randomly assigned to treatment sequence ABC or ACB. Daily measures for each of the three criteria (fear of movement/(re)injury, fear of pain, and pain catastrophizing) were taken during 63 days.

The data-analytic challenge of this design lied not in the fact that a randomization test had to be applied in a single-case three-phase design or that data had to be combined for four replicated single-case experiments (see Onghena & Edgington, 1994, for an overview of the available tools), but rather in the fact that a between-case random assignment component was an intrinsic part of the design of this study. We felt that we could gain statistical power by taking this between-case random assignment component into account.

THE SOLUTION: A CUSTOMIZED RANDOMIZATION TEST

For single-case phase designs, the commonly prescribed randomization scheme is one in which the moment of phase change is randomly determined, given a minimum number of measurement times for each phase[1] (Edgington, 1975, 1980; Onghena, 1992).

Under the null hypothesis of no differential effect of the phases/treatments, the observed responses are independent of the phase/treatment. That is, if the null hypothesis were true, the responses would have been the same even if one of the other treatments were present at that measurement time. Given this null hypothesis and the randomization scheme, a reference distribution can be constructed of test statistics that could have been observed if another randomization outcome were obtained. The proportion of test statistics in the reference distribution that are larger than or equal to the observed test statistic provides the randomization test p value.

Consider, for example, a single-case two-phase AB design with 11 measurement times, random determination of the moment of phase change, with a minimum of 1 measurement time in each phase. Suppose that the randomly selected design of the actual study consisted of 4 A measurements and 7 B measurements, and that data were obtained as given in Table 26.1 (Outcome 4). For a directional test, predicting the B phase to lead to a reduction of scores, a t statistic can be computed for the observed data and this observed statistic can be compared to the t statistics computed for each of the 9 alternative possible randomization outcomes. As shown in Table 26.1, the observed test statistic is the most extreme value in this reference distribution, leading to a randomization test p value of .10.

Notice that this is the smallest p value that can be obtained in this design, implying zero power for a conventional 5% significance level. However, consider what happens if we take the between-case random assignment component into account. The null hypothesis is still independence between treatment and response, but now there are 10 additional potential randomization outcomes, as listed in Table 26.2. This gives a total reference distribution consisting of 20 test statistics, with the observed directional test statistic being the largest. This means that if the null hypothesis were true, only one in twenty times such a large test statistic would be obtained. The randomization test p value of .05 turns out to

Table 25.1. Observed Data, Test Statistics, and Possible Randomization Outcomes

	Measurement Time											*t*
Randomization	*1*	*2*	*3*	*4*	*5*	*6*	*7*	*8*	*9*	*10*	*11*	*Statistic*
Outcome 1	A	B	B	B	B	B	B	B	B	B	B	0.36
Outcome 2	A	A	B	B	B	B	B	B	B	B	B	1.41
Outcome 3	A	A	A	B	B	B	B	B	B	B	B	1.99
Outcome 4	A	A	A	A	B	B	B	B	B	B	B	
Observed data	*10*	*12*	*11*	*13*	*7*	*8*	*9*	*8*	*8*	*9*	*8*	5.58*
Outcome 5	A	A	A	A	A	B	B	B	B	B	B	2.46
Outcome 6	A	A	A	A	A	A	B	B	B	B	B	1.79
Outcome 7	A	A	A	A	A	A	A	B	B	B	B	1.75
Outcome 8	A	A	A	A	A	A	A	A	B	B	B	1.34
Outcome 9	A	A	A	A	A	A	A	A	A	B	B	0.99
Outcome 10	A	A	A	A	A	A	A	A	A	A	B	1.22

*Observed test statistic.

Table 25.2. Additional Test Statistics and Possible Randomization Outcomes (Additional to Table 26.1)

	Measurement time											*t*
Randomization	*1*	*2*	*3*	*4*	*5*	*6*	*7*	*8*	*9*	*10*	*11*	*Statistic*
Outcome 11	B	A	A	A	A	A	A	A	A	A	A	–0.36
Outcome 12	B	B	A	A	A	A	A	A	A	A	A	–1.41
Outcome 13	B	B	B	A	A	A	A	A	A	A	A	–1.99
Outcome 14	B	B	B	B	A	A	A	A	A	A	A	–5.58
Outcome 15	B	B	B	B	B	A	A	A	A	A	A	–2.46
Outcome 16	B	B	B	B	B	B	A	A	A	A	A	–1.79
Outcome 17	B	B	B	B	B	B	B	A	A	A	A	–1.75
Outcome 18	B	B	B	B	B	B	B	B	A	A	A	–1.34
Outcome 19	B	B	B	B	B	B	B	B	B	A	A	–0.99
Outcome 20	B	B	B	B	B	B	B	B	B	B	A	–1.22

be half the p value that would be computed if we ignored the between-case random assignment.

METHOD AND RESULTS

The observed data on fear of movement/(re)injury for the four chronic back pain patients are shown in Figure 26.1. Participants 1 and 4 have been assigned to the treatment sequence ACB, and Participants 2 and 3 to

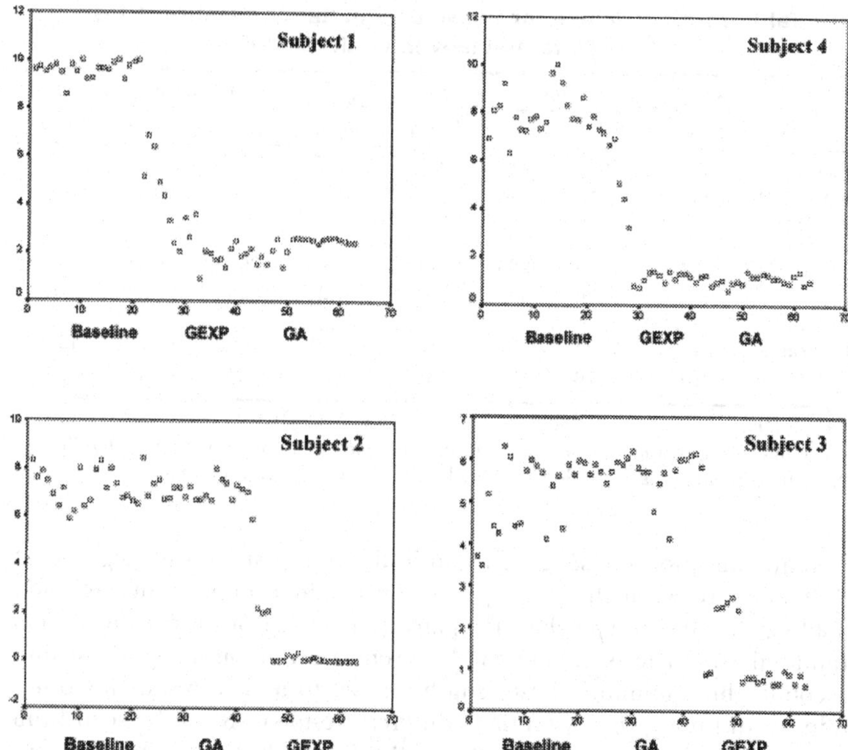

Figure 26.1. Fear of movement/(re)injury for the four chronic back pain patients during the baseline phase (day 1 to day 21), the graded activity phase (GA), and the graded exposure phase (GEXP) (day 22 to 42 or day 43 to 63).

treatment sequence ABC. Although these graphs already give an indication that there is a large effect of graded exposure, there is also strong evidence that mere visual analysis is unreliable (Borckardt, Murphy, Nash, & Shaw, 2004), and so that it is recommended to supplement visual analysis by a more formal analytical technique (Onghena & Edgington, 2005).

Therefore, we supplemented the visual analysis by randomization tests on the three dependent variables (fear of movement/(re)injury, fear of pain, and pain catastrophizing) (see Vlaeyen et al., 2001, for a parametric time series analysis on the same data). We combined the individual p values using nonparametric meta-analysis (where meaningful), tested for lagged effects, and took advantage of the between-case random assignment, as explained in the previous section. All analyses were performed using SCRT, a freeware software package for Single Case Randomization Tests (Onghena & Van Damme, 1994).

Table 25.3. *P* Values for Phase Design Randomization *T* Tests on Data by Vlaeyen et al. (2001)[a]

	Treatment Sequence[b]	*Participant* 1	*Participant* 4	*Combined P Value*	*Treatment Sequence*	*Participant* 2	*Participant* 3	*Combined P Value*
Fear of movement/ (re)injury	A-C[c]	.0606	.2727	.0556	A-B	1.000	.4848	.8673
	C-B	.2576	.2576	.1327	B-C	.0455*	.0606	.0056*
Fear of pain	A-C	.1515	.3333	.1175	A-B	.0606	.3030	.0661
	C-B	.2576	.2576	.1327	B-C	.0455*	.0606	.0056*
Pain catastrophising	A-C	.2424	.3333	.1657	A-B	.0909	.6667	.2429
	C-B	.2576	.2576	.1327	B-C	.0303*	.0455*	.0029*

[a]*$p < 0.05$.
[b]The intervention point was determined randomly with a minimum phase length of 5.
[c]A = baseline phase; B = graded activity phase; C = graded exposure phase.

Randomization *F* tests gave us an indication of statistically significant differences between the three phases on all three dependent variables. Table 26.3 shows the *p* values for pairwise comparisons using directional randomization *t* tests, taking the between-case random assignment into account (the minimum phase length was set to 5. The results for other minima did not give substantially different results). As can be seen from Table 26.3 only for Participant 2 and Participant 3 (both with treatment sequence ABC), statistically significant differences between graded activity (B) and graded exposure (C) could be detected. For Participant 1 and Participant 4 (treatment sequence ACB) the beneficial effect of graded exposure could only be detected if a randomization test was used that allowed for delayed effects (Edgington, 1975). Statistically significant effects ($p < .05$) were found if a delay of 3 to 5 days was allowed for (also multiple test corrections were applied. They raised the *p* values but did not change the general pattern of outcomes). As can be seen in Figure 26.1, this beneficial delayed effect continued during the graded activity phase. Because graded activity was only effective after a previous graded exposure phase, these results can be interpreted in favor of graded exposure. Graded activity seemed to have the potential to maintain the therapeutic effect of graded exposure, but did not have the same impact as graded exposure after a previous baseline phase.

DISCUSSION

This study and its reanalysis in terms of between-case randomized replicated single-experiments demonstrate the versatility and feasibility of the single-case randomization test approach in an applied setting. With the use of randomization tests, the analysis could be adapted to the peculiarities of the design, leading to a valid and custom-made test for the research problem at hand. Furthermore, given the availability of user-friendly software, these computer-intensive statistical procedures are now within reach of any applied researcher.

One important comment on the present reanalysis is that we analyzed the data *as if* the moment of phase change was randomly determined. In fact, in the actual study there was only random assignment to a treatment sequence (between-case random assignment) and no within-case random assignment. However, the reference distribution is still a reasonable one because both the phase structure and the sequential nature of the data are retained to construct this distribution. As Winch and Campbell (1969) argued, randomization test *p* values can be very informative even in the absence of actual randomization because its rearrangements of the data so closely matches the researcher's concepts of randomness. Furthermore, in a recent simulation study, Ferron, Foster-Johnson, and Kromrey (2003) convincingly demonstrated that randomization tests with shifting moments of phase change control the Type I error rate under a wide variety of conditions, even if systematic designs are used.

We realize that there are still several hurdles to take before the replicated single-case randomization test approach will become more popular in behavioral science applications. At least three major hurdles can be distinguished:

- *First hurdle*: It is not obvious to opt for single-case research or small-*n* research because of the dominance of group-based studies in many domains of psychology and educational sciences.
- *Second hurdle*: Even if a researcher takes the option to perform single-case studies, it is not obvious to perform statistical analyses on the resulting data. Single-case researchers frequently settle for qualitative or visual analyses and do not feel the need for a more formal statistical analysis.
- *Third hurdle*: Even researchers who want to analyze their single-case data in a statistical way could hesitate to perform a randomization test because parametric tests are more widely known (and taught!) or software might be unavailable.

However, we hope that this contribution and the availability of SCRT brought the single-case randomization test approach a bit closer to the behavioral and educational researchers. We showed how it works in an applied setting and how it can be extended.

In sum, we feel that the replicated single-case randomization test approach is much more realistic for small-*n* designs and studies that lack random sampling than any parametric statistical approach. Furthermore, the single-case randomization test approach is not only relevant for the data analysis side but also for liberating the applied researcher from the straitjacket of classical group designs and test criteria. Too often research questions, study designs, and data collection strategies get dictated by the norms of classical parametric statistics. It is time to turn this around and to look for statistical techniques that can be customized to research questions that are of intrinsic scientific interest, and to focus our attention to study designs and data collection strategies that can provide credible and useful answers.

NOTE

1. Randomization schemes for alternating treatments designs and multiple baseline designs are beyond the scope of the present contribution. Interested readers can find an overview in Onghena and Edgington (1994) and Koehler and Levin (1998).

REFERENCES

Barlow, D. H., & Hersen, M. (Eds.) (1984). *Single-case experimental designs: Strategies for studying behavior change* (2nd ed.). Oxford, United Kingdom: Pergamon Press.

Borckardt, J. J., Murphy, M. D., Nash, M. R., & Shaw, D. (2004). An empirical examination of visual analysis procedures for clinical practice evaluation. *Journal of Social Service Research, 30,* 55-73.

de Jong, J. R., Vlaeyen, J. W. S., Onghena, P., Goossens, M. E. J. B., Geilen, M., & Mulder, H. (2005). Fear of movement/(re)injury in chronic low back pain: Education or exposure in vivo as mediator to fear reduction? *Clinical Journal of Pain, 21,* 9-17.

Edgington, E. S. (1967). Statistical inference from $N = 1$ experiments. *Journal of Psychology, 65,* 195-199.

Edgington, E. S. (1975). Randomization tests for one-subject operant experiments. *Journal of Psychology, 90,* 57-68.

Edgington, E. S. (1980). Random assignment and statistical tests for one-subject experiments. *Behavioral Assessment, 2,* 19-28.

Edgington, E. S. (1995). *Randomization tests* (3rd ed.). New York: Dekker.

Edgington, E. S. (1996). Randomized single-subject experimental designs. *Behaviour Research and Therapy, 34,* 567-574.

Edgington, E. S., & Bland, B. H. (1993). Randomization tests: Application to single-cell and other single-unit neuroscience experiments. *Journal of Neuroscience Methods, 47,* 169-177.

Ferron, J., Foster-Johnson, L., & Kromrey, J. D. (2003). The functioning of single-case randomization tests with and without random assignment. *Journal of Experimental Education, 71,* 267-288.

Franklin, R. D., Allison, D. B., & Gorman, B. S. (Eds.) (1996). *Design and analysis of single-case research*. Mahwah, NJ: Erlbaum.

Holden, G., Bearison, D. J., Rode, D. C., Kapiloff, M. F., Rosenberg, G., & Onghena, P. (2003). Pediatric pain and anxiety: A meta-analysis of outcomes for a behavioral telehealth intervention. *Research on Social Work Practice, 13,* 675-692.

Kazdin, A. E. (1982). *Single-case research designs: Methods for clinical and applied settings*. New York: Oxford University Press.

Koehler, M. J., & Levin, J. R. (1998). Regulated randomization: A potentially sharper analytical tool for the multiple-baseline design. *Psychological Methods, 3,* 206-217.

Kratochwill, T. R., & Levin, J. R. (Eds.) (1992). *Single-case research design and analysis: New directions for psychology and education*. Hillsdale, NJ: Erlbaum.

Levin, J. R., & Wampold, B. E. (1999). Generalized single-case randomization tests: Flexible analyses for a variety of situations. *School Psychology Quarterly, 14,* 59-93.

McLeod, R. S., Cohen, Z., Taylor, D. W., & Cullen, J. B. (1986, March 29). Single-patient randomised clinical trial: Use in determining optimum treatment for patient with inflammation of Kock continent ileostomy reservoir. *Lancet,* 726-728.

Onghena, P. (1992). Randomization tests for extensions and variations of ABAB single-case experimental designs: A rejoinder. *Behavioral Assessment, 14,* 153-171.

Onghena, P. (2005). Single-case designs. In B. Everitt & D. Howell (Eds.), *Encyclopedia of statistics in behavioral science* (Vol. 4, pp. 1850-1854). New York: Wiley.

Onghena, P., & Edgington, E. S. (1994). Randomization tests for restricted alternating treatments designs. *Behaviour Research and Therapy, 32,* 783-786.

Onghena, P., & Edgington, E. S. (2005). Customization of pain treatments: Single-case design and analysis. *Clinical Journal of Pain, 21,* 56-68.

Onghena, P., & Van Damme, G. (1994). SCRT 1.1: Single Case Randomization Tests. *Behavior Research Methods, Instruments, & Computers, 26,* 369.

Todman, J. B., & Dugard, P. (2001). *Single-case and small-n experimental designs: A practical guide to randomization tests*. Mahwah, NJ: Erlbaum.

Van de Vliet, P., Onghena, P., Knapen, J., Fox, K. R., Probst, M., Van Coppenolle, H., et al. (2003). Assessing the additional impact of fitness training in depressed psychiatric patients receiving multifaceted treatment: A replicated single-subject design. *Disability and Rehabilitation, 25,* 1344-1353.

Vlaeyen, J. W. S., de Jong, J., Geilen, M., Heuts, P. H. T. G., & van Breukelen, G. (2001). Graded exposure in vivo in the treatment of pain-related fear: A replicated single-case experimental design in four patients with chronic low back pain. *Behaviour Research and Therapy, 39,* 151-166.

Vlaeyen, J. W. S., de Jong, J. R., Onghena, P., Kerckhoffs-Hanssen, M., & Kole-Snijders, A. M. J. (2002). Can pain-related fear be reduced? The application of cognitive-behavioural exposure in vivo. *Pain Research and Management, 7,* 144-153.

Weiss, B., Williams, J. H., Margen, S., Abrams, B., Caan, B., Citron, L. J., et al. (1980). Behavioral responses to artificial food colors. *Science, 297,* 1487-1489.

Winch, R. F., & Campbell, D. T. (1969). Proof? No. Evidence? Yes. The significance of tests of significance. *American Sociologist, 4,* 140-143.

CHAPTER 27

WHOLE BRAIN CORRELATIONS

Examining Similarity Across Conditions of Overall Patterns of Neural Activation in fMRI

Arthur Aron, Susan Whitfield-Gabrieli, and Wemara Lichty

INTRODUCTION

This chapter describes an experience in which we were forced to develop a new analytic method. We had a brain imaging data set that was remarkably well suited to bear on an important theoretical question in psychology, but there was no appropriate existing analytic method.

The data set: Functional magnetic resonance imaging (fMRI) brain activations of subjects while hearing their own name (condition S, for self), the name of a relevant other such as a same-sex friend or sibling (R, for relevant), or common names in the culture but which were not the names of anyone well known to the subject (C, for common name). Names were presented multiple times, about 3 seconds each trial, in random order (Lichty, Chyou, Aron, Anderson, Gharahremani, & Gabrieli, 2004). Thus, for each subject, for each little volume of the brain, we had a number for the average "activation" during each of the three

Real Data Analysis, pp. 397–403

name conditions. There were 23,128 little volumes of gray matter in the brain, called voxels, of the size we studied (each voxel was about 4 mm^3). "Activation" reflects blood flow to the neurons in the voxel. There were 10 subjects (all women), a typical sample size in fMRI research. Each subject also provided a rating of how close she felt to the relevant other. In sum, our focal data set was a 10 (subjects) × 3 (conditions) × 23,128 (voxels) matrix, plus a single predictor score for each subject (rated closeness to relevant other).

The research question: Does reported closeness to the relevant other predict greater similarity between response to own name and relevant other's than between own name and a common other name? Stated in terms of condition labels, does reported closeness to R predict greater S-R similarity than S-C similarity? Extensive research using various cognitive, resource allocation, and linguistic paradigms supports the general idea that "close others are included in the self" (for a review, see Aron, Mashek, & Aron, 2004). More precisely, processing in relation to close others is more similar to that of self than is processing in relation to strangers, perhaps because cognitive representations of close others share elements with cognitive representations of self that are not shared with person representations more generally (Smith, Coates, & Walling, 1999). The present analysis was intended to mine the fMRI data set using names to address this question for the first time at the level of brain activation.

The more general analysis issue: Does an individual difference variable predict greater similarity of patterns of brain activation between conditions A and B versus A and C? This kind of question is potentially of broad interest to a wide array of psychologists and other behavioral and social scientists attempting to use neuroscience methods to address theoretical issues related to cognition, affect, motivation, perception, and so forth. That is, theorizing in the behavioral and social sciences (and more generally) is primarily about principles that delineate similarities and differences among phenomena or processes. When individual differences are the focus, then the present issue is an example of the kind of question that is of great interest to researchers in these fields. The development of statistical protocols to analyze neuroimaging experiments in a way that addresses such questions may thus provide a significant opportunity for triangulating with more traditional methods in the social and behavioral sciences (Aron, 2006).

Why there are no existing methods. For the most part, fMRI data analysis methods were not developed to address theoretical issues in the behavioral and social sciences, and are not suitable for straightforward application to the issue at hand. fMRI studies have traditionally focused on within-subject differences across conditions in particular brain areas. The recent rise in studies of personality and clinical diagnoses focus on correlations of individual differences with between-subject variation in within-subject differences across conditions in brain activations, but the focus is on particular brain areas, not overall patterns over the whole brain. That is, the usual research goal is to understand brain functioning and the emphasis is on which particular brain areas show effects. Analysis of similarities or differences in the *overall* patterns of brain functioning, without regard to which particular areas are similar or different, is minimally relevant to mapping the brain. But this kind of analysis may be enormously valuable when using neuroimaging approaches to address theoretical issues in the behavioral and social sciences.

What is needed? Thus, in our case, we were left on our own to come up with a number for each subject to correlate with closeness, a number that would represent the difference in overall brain pattern similarity of S and R versus S and C.

DEVELOPMENT OF THE PROCEDURE

Our first thought was that random-coefficient multilevel modeling would be ideal. However, existing programs are not practical with ordinary computers on such large data sets. Also, the advantages of modern random-coefficient approaches are minimized in a case like this in which the number of data points per subject are equal.

Another possibility was to base our analysis on figuring a number for each subject using a standard method of comparing correlations or regressions (S-R vs. S-C) with voxel as the unit of analysis. (For example, using correlations, for each subject, this would be a test of the difference between correlated correlations.) However, the accuracy of this procedure would likely be undermined by the high level of multicolinearity among the three conditions. (Such likely multicolinearity is due to physiological variation and other differences across voxel locations arising from technical fMRI aspects that create considerable variation across voxels but are stable across conditions.)

Thus, our decision was to compute a number to correlate with closeness based on a direct difference of S-R similarity minus S-C similarity. In addition to avoiding some of the problems noted above, this method has the advantage of simplicity and transparency.

We were, however, still left with the question of how to assess similarity of each pair of conditions. One possibility was to use total activation in each condition across all voxels. For example, using total activations we could take, for each subject, the absolute (or squared) difference between total S and total R, versus the difference between total S and total C. However, we decided against this approach in the present context because total activations may reflect simple differences in attention or other relatively undifferentiated phenomena. Similarly, because our focus was directly on similarity of *patterns*, we decided against using differences in intraclass correlations (that is, taking for each subject, across voxels, the ICC for S-R minus the ICC for S-C). (ICCs take into account both overall and pattern similarity.)

This left two main possibilities, differences in correlations (for each subject, across voxels, the S-R correlation minus the S-C correlation) or differences in slopes (for each subject, across voxels, the slope from a regression predicting S from R minus the slope from a regression predicting S from C). We decided against using correlations because they are confounded with differences across conditions in variance. Our resulting decision to settle on raw score slopes (vs. correlations) is also consistent with standard practice in parallel situations in the context of multilevel modeling and with the preference for covariances versus correlations in the context of structural equation modeling. In sum, our conclusion was to correlate our measure of closeness with each subject's difference between the S-R slope minus the S-C slope.

Having made these conceptual decisions, we were faced with the practical problem of how actually to conduct the analysis. An especially thorny issue was how to compute the slopes for each subject. Existing programs for fMRI data analysis are not set up to do such computations directly. In our case, we were working with a very widely used fMRI data analysis program, SPM2, which runs under Matlab. It is menu driven, but does not have selections for computing regressions between conditions within an individual using voxel as the unit of analysis. Further, the correlations of slope differences with the predictor variable (in this case closeness ratings) was facilitated by exporting slope results to a standard statistical analysis program (we used SPSS). Thus, we conducted the analysis using the following steps:

1. We determined the effect size for each subject for each voxel for each condition (in comparison to the overall mean for all conditions for that voxel). This can be computed using SPM2 menu commands. The resultant set of effect sizes across voxels, for each subject for each condition, is called a "Beta image." (It is called an "image" because it is possible, given the location of the voxels in brain space, to display these effect sizes on two-dimensional "slices" of the brain.)
2. Using SPM2 menu commands, we computed for each subject a "gray matter mask," a delineation of which voxels are within grey matter. (That is, this "mask" sorts the grey matter voxels from the

overall set of voxels scanned that includes the entire volume of brain and surrounding areas.)

3. Using Matlab, for each subject, we intersected the Beta images with the grey matter mask to calculate slopes for the regressions predicting S from R and predicting S from C.
4. We then transferred each subject's S-R and S-C slopes to an SPSS file that included each subject's closeness ratings.
5. Using SPSS, we computed for each subject a slope difference score (S-R slope minus S-C slope).
6. Using SPSS, we computed the correlation of the closeness ratings with the slope difference score.

RESULTS

Figure 26.1 shows the scatter diagram for our data set for the linear relation between closeness score and difference in slope (predicting S from R minus predicting S from C). The correlation was .74, $t(8) = 3.09$, $p = .015$, two tailed. Thus, consistent with what has been found in cognitive and other studies, closeness to a relevant other predicts greater degree of similarity in the overall pattern of brain activation when hearing one's own name and when hearing the name of the relevant other than the degree of similarity between own name and a common name of someone not well known to the subject. This result provides triangulation from dramatically different methodological approaches using cognitive and behavioral methods. It thus has the potential to enhance substantially confidence in the theoretical model on which these predictions were based.

FUTURE DIRECTIONS

As with any global analysis, one might want to follow up with more focused comparisons. One such possibility is to compute "partial brain correlations," examining whether overall effects are largely accounted for by differences in slopes in particular brain areas, such as a particular hemisphere, lobe, structure, or more focused region of interest. Ideally, such comparisons could be based on a priori predictions from theory or previous findings.

There are many other possibilities for this general idea of analyzing similarities and differences of whole brain patterns across within-subject experimental conditions. Most simply, there might often be reason to test overall differences in slopes across conditions with a t test for paired samples. More expansively, one could conduct any kind of complex analysis

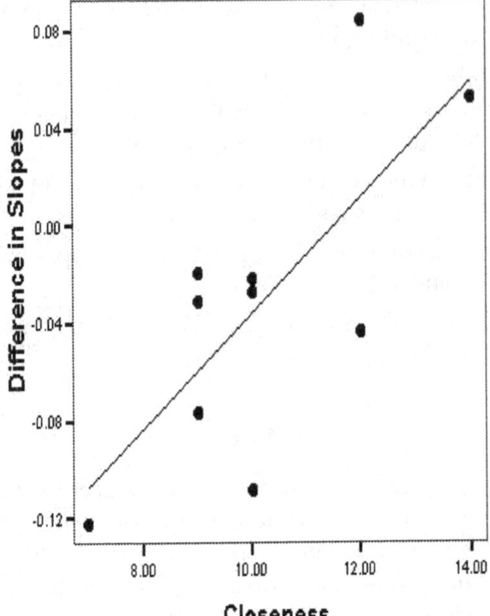

Figure 27.1. $r = .74$, $t(8) = 3.09$, $p = .015$, two-tailed.

across conditions within subjects (with voxel as the unit of analysis), such as multiple regressions, factor analysis, or cluster analysis, and then combine meta-analytically for overall effects or correlate with individual difference variables across subjects.

We hope that the whole brain correlation approach and its potential extensions may serve to advance research focusing on brain mapping as well as on psychological theory. However, a main message we hope researchers take from our experience here is the potential (and need) of going beyond existing neuroimaging analysis methods developed for brain mapping to developing new data analysis methods for such data that are geared to answering the kinds of questions that advance knowledge in the behavioral and the social sciences.

REFERENCES

Aron, A. (2006). Relationship neuroscience: Advancing the social psychology of close relationships using functional neuroimaging. In P. A. M. VanLange (Ed.), *Bridging social psychology: Benefits of transdisciplinary approaches* (pp. 267-272). Mahwah, NJ: Erlbaum.

Aron, A., Mashek, D., & Aron, E. N. (2004). Closeness, intimacy, and including other in the self. In D. Mashek & A. Aron (Eds.), *Handbook of closeness and intimacy* (pp. 27-41). Mahwah, NJ: Erlbaum.

Lichty, W., Chyou, J., Aron, A., Anderson, A. K., Gharahremani, D., & Gabrieli, J. (2004, October). *Neural correlates of subjective closeness in relation to responses to friends and own name: An fMRI study.* Paper presented at Society for Neuroscience, San Diego, CA.

Smith, E., Coats, S., & Walling, D. (1999). Overlapping mental representations of self, in-group, and partner: Further response time evidence and a connectionist model. *Personality and Social Psychology Bulletin, 25*, 873-882.

CHAPTER 28

PRINCIPAL COMPONENT ANALYSIS OF SENATE VOTING PATTERNS

Jan de Leeuw

There are various techniques available for the principal component analysis (PCA) of binary matrices. We illustrate some of them in this chapter by analyzing votes on 20 issues in the 2001 US Senate, selected by Americans for Democratic Action (Americans for Democratic Action, 2002). It must be emphasized that the techniques we discuss are general, because they apply to many different types of binary matrices. They can be used equally effectively, for example, to analyze data from choice experiments or from tests and exams.

The PCA techniques we use are chosen from two different classes (De Leeuw, 2006). First, there is *homogeneity analysis* (Gifi, 1990), also known as *multiple correspondence analysis* (Greenacre & Blasius, 2006). In this technique we make a joint two-dimensional plot of both senators and issues. In order to do this, we first have to choose a *dimensionality*. In this chapter we make all our plots in two-dimensional scape. Each issue is represented by two points, an "aye" point and a "nay" point. In homogeneity analysis the objects (in this example the senators) are stan-

Real Data Analysis, pp. 405–409

dardized, in the sense that coordinates on both dimensions are centered, have unit sum of squares, and are uncorrelated with one another. Moreover the "aye" point for each issue is the centroid (average) of all senator points voting "aye" on the issue, and the same is true for all "nay" points.

If we have a representation in the plane, then for each issue we can make a *star plot* (Michailidis & De Leeuw, 1998). This is a joint plot of senator and issue points, which contains 100 line segments, one for each senator. Each senator that votes "aye" is connected to the "aye" point for the issue, while the senators that vote "nay" are connected to the "nay" point. Since the "aye" point and the "nay" points are centroids, this will create two stars for each issue, in which senators are connected with lines to the centroid of the group of senators that voted the same as they did on the issue. Homogeneity analysis moves the senators around iteratively to find the solution in which the squared length of all the lines, over all the issues, is as small as possible. Thus we are aiming for a solution in which each issue divides the cloud of 100 senator points into two clumps, which have a small within-clump variance and a large between-clump variance. We leave it to the reader to translate this same rational into the context of preference, choice, or testing data.

If we apply homogeneity analysis to the senate data, we find the solution (for senators) in Figure 28.1. In a more complete analysis we would make the star plots for the 20 issues and discuss the solution in terms of these plots. Here we merely look at the grouping of senators, with republicans on the left, democrats on the right, and moderates like McCain and Chafee in the middle.

As an alternative to the "clumping" aimed for by homogeneity ananlysis, we can try to place the senators in the plane in such a way that the "aye" groups and "nay" groups can be separated by straight lines, with the "aye's" on one side and the "nay's" on the other. Or, equivalently, that the convex hulls of the two groups are disjoint. Or that the "aye" and the "nay" groups are in complementary half-spaces. This is a *separation technique*, because groups can be very large and still be separable by a straight line.

There are two techniques that have been proposed to quantify and optimize goodness-of-fit in these types of separation models. The first is Nonlinear PCA, a special case of the nonmetric multidimensional scaling approach of Kruskal (1964a, 1964b). It uses a least squares loss function. We find directions in the space, one corresponding with each issue, such that the one-dimensional projections of the senators on the issue direction have all "nay's" to the left of all "aye's." This means that there is a perpendicular to the direction that separates the two groups.

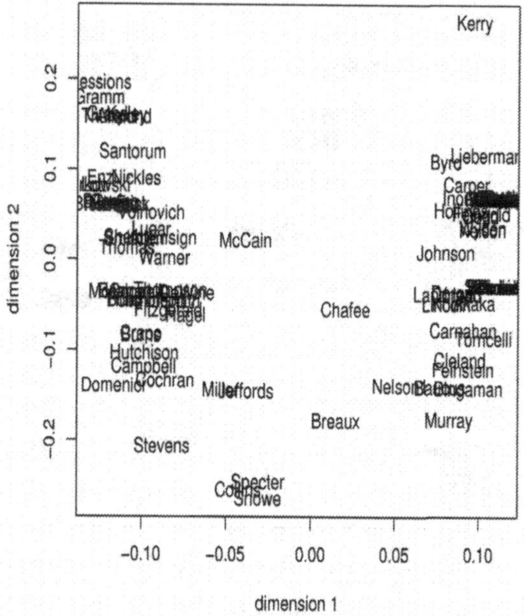

Figure 28.1. Senate homogeneity analysis solution.

The algorithm amounts to iteratively alternating PCA and transforming the binary data by monotone regression with Kruskal's *primary approach* to ties. Code in R is available from the author. Homogeneity can be shown to be Nonlinear PCA with the primary approach to ties, which is much more restrictive. If we apply the algorithm, starting from the homogeneity analysis solution, we need 209 alternating least squares iterations to find the solution in Figure 28.2. It has zero stress, which means that we can find directions for all issues weakly separating the "aye's" from the "nay's." Again, in a more complete analysis, we would look at the issue directions. Here we merely observe that imposing weaker restrictions on the representation comes at a price, because the solution, perfect as it may be in terms of the loss function, shows less detail and is more difficult to interpret. Because the algorithm only aims for weak separation, many senators are actually placed on the separating lines.

The second approach to separation uses a logistic likelihood function, and computes the maximum likelihood solution. This solution has long been popular in item response theory (Reckase, 1997) and in political science (Clinton Jackman, & Rivers, 2004). We use the majorization algorithm discussed in De Leeuw (in press), and after 975 iterations we find the solution in Figure 28.3. Again, code in R is available from the author.

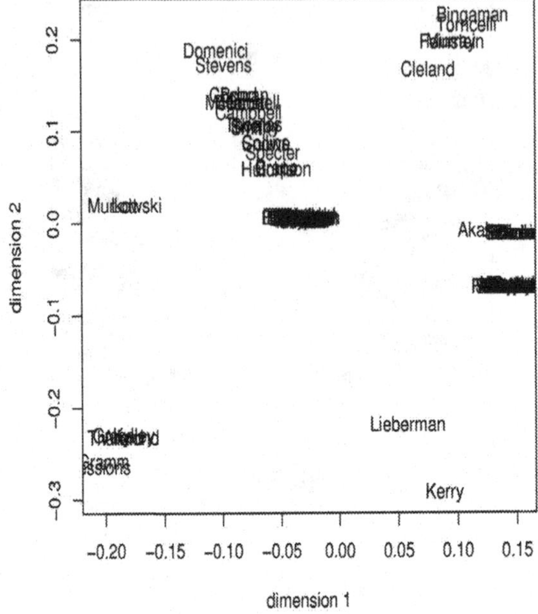

Figure 28.2. Senate nonmetric PCA solution.

For more detail we would have to look at the separating lines again, but at first sight it seems to solution is even harder to handle than the Nonlinear PCA solution.

What we find from these analyses is, in the first place a grouping and classification of the senators in the U.S. Senate. But in the second place we learn that the powerful nonmetric and likeliihood iterative methods for binary data are not necessarily an improvement from the substantive and interpretative point of view.

REFERENCES

Americans for Democratic Action. (2002) Voting record: Shattered promise of liberal progress. *ADA Today, 57*(1), 1–17.

Clinton, J., Jackman, S., & Rivers, D. (2004). The Statistical Analysis of Roll Call Data. *American Political Science Review, 98*, 355-370.

De Leeuw, J. (2006). Nonlinear principal component analysis and related techniques. In M. Greenacre & J. Blasius, (Ed.), *Multiple correspondence analysis and related methods*. New York: Chapman and Hall.

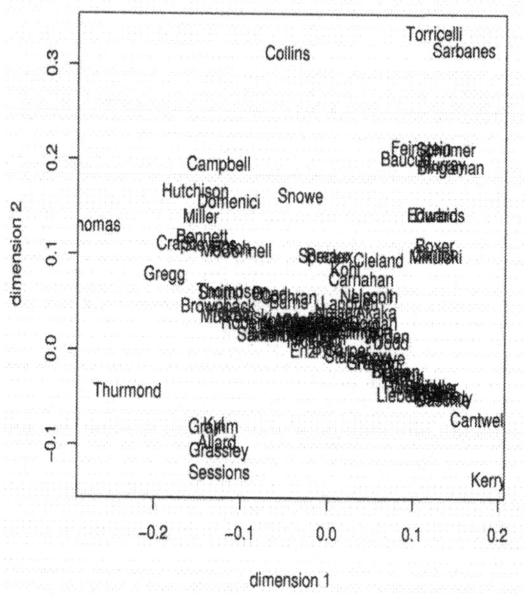

Figure 28.3. Senate logistic PCA solution.

De Leeuw, J. (in press). Principal component analysis of binary data by iterated singular value decomposition. *Computational Statistics and Data Analysis*.

Gifi, A. (1990). *Nonlinear multivariate analysis*. Chichester, England: Wiley.

Greenacre, M., & Blasius, J. (Eds.). (2006). *Multiple correspondence analysis and related methods*. New York: Chapman and Hall.

Kruskal, J. B. (1964a). Multidimensional scaling by optimizing goodness of fit to a nonmetric hypothesis. *Psychometrika, 29*, 1-27.

Kruskal, J. B. (1964b). Nonmetric multidimensional scaling: A numerical method. *Psychometrika, 29*, 115–129.

Michailidis, G., & De Leeuw, J. (1998). The Gifi system for descriptive multivariate analysis. *Statistical Science, 13*, 307–336.

Reckase, M. D. (1997). A linear logistic multidimensional model. In W. J. Van Der Linden & R. K. Hambleton (Eds.), *Handbook of item response theory* (pp. 271-286). New York: Springer.

ABOUT THE AUTHORS

Arthur Aron is a professor of psychology, State University of New York, Stony Brook. His textbook *Statistics in Psychology* (Prentice-Hall, 2005) is in its fourth edition. His research interests are in close relationships.

Charles Bernstein, is a professor of medicine, head, section of gastroenterology, director, Gastroenterology Fellowship Training Program and director of the University of Manitoba Inflammatory Bowel Disease Clinical and Research Centre.

C. Mitchell Dayton is chair and professor in the Department of Measurement, Statistics and Evaluation at the University of Maryland. For nearly 30 years, he has pursued a research interest in latent class analysis. In 1999 he published a Sage book dealing with latent class scaling models. Recently, he has focused on model comparison procedures with a special interest in approaches based on information theory and Bayes factors. He is currently working on an innovative alternative to pairwise comparison procedures.

Jeroen R. de Jong is a behavioral therapist/pain practitioner, and is active on behavioral medicine research. His main interests are studies focusing on the role of pain-related fear in the development of chronic pain disability, and the development and evaluation of a graded exposure in vivo treatment for these fears.

Jan de Leeuw is distinguished professor and chair at the Department of Statistics, University of California at Los Angeles. He has a PhD in social

Sciences from the University of Leiden, Netherlands (1973). His research is in psychometrics, multivariate analysis, multilevel analysis, and computational statistics. He has published several books and hundreds of research papers. He is an elected fellow of the American Statistical Association, the Institute of Mathematical Statistics, and the Royal Statistical Society.

Lee H. Ehman taught from 1969 through 2003 on the Bloomington campus at Indiana University in curriculum and instruction, and in counseling and educational psychology. After a stint as full-time administrator, he returned to teacher education as part of the computer education program. He is retired and lives in Bloomington, Indiana.

Ian Clara, is a doctoral student, Department of Psychology, University of Manitoba. His research interests are in the area of longitudinal designs with hierarchical and clustered data.

Du Feng is an associate professor in the Department of Human Development and Family Studies at Texas Tech University. She specializes in applications of longitudinal and multivariate data analytical techniques, ordinal statistics, and intergenerational issues.

Susan Whitfield-Gabrieli is a research scientist at Massachusetts Institute of Technology. She develops brain imaging analysis techniques to study the neural correlates of normal and abnormal cognition.

Rosa Arboretti Giancristofaro is an assistant professor of statistics at the Faculty of Economics of the University of Ferrara. Her main research interest is in applied statistics for technology and social sciences.

Suzanne E. Graham is an assistant professor of education at the University of New Hampshire. Her research interests are both substantive and methodological. Substantively, she is interested in equity issues in mathematics education, specifically related to gender differences in mathematics achievement and course-taking. Methodologically, Graham is interested in the application of statistical methods such as discrete-time survival analysis, individual growth modeling, and propensity score analysis to educational research.

Ronald K. Hambleton is distinguished university professor and chair of the Research and Evaluation Methods Program and codirector of the Center for Educational Assessment at the University of Massachusetts. He has been teaching graduate-level courses in educational and psychological testing, item response theory and applications, classical test theory models and methods, and offers seminar courses on applied measurement topics at UMass since 1969. His research interests are in the areas of large scale assessment and item response theory.

Ning Han is an associate measurement statistician in the Research & Development Division at Educational Testing Service in Princeton, New Jersey. He completed his doctoral studies at the University of Massachusetts at Amherst in 2006. His research interests are in the areas of equating methods, IRT model fit, and detection of exposed test items in computer-based testing environments.

Michael Harwell is a professor, Quantitative Methods in Education Program in the Department of Educational Psychology at the University of Minnesota. His areas of expertise include research design, statistical modeling, and nonparametric statistics.

Todd Headrick is an associate professor at Southern Illinois University-Carbondale. His primary research interests are in the areas of statistical computing methodology and nonparametric statistics. In the former area, he has several publications dealing with methods for simulating observations from a variety of statistical distributions to examine the properties of statistical procedures for data analysis. The latter includes comparing and contrasting various parametric or nonparametric statistical procedures using Monte Carlo techniques. His work has appeared in *Computational Statistics and Data Analysis*, *Communications in Statistics*, *Journal of Educational and Behavioral Statistics*, *Psychometrika*, and the *Australian and New Zealand Journal of Statistics*.

Joel D. Hetzer received his bachelor's degree from the United States Air Force Academy. He served in the military for 5 years where he was the chief of production analysis section, Headquarters Air Force Recruiting Service at Randolph Air Force Base and deputy flight commander for information systems flight at Fairchild Air Force Base. He is a PhD student in the Department of Statistical Sciences at Baylor University.

Joseph M. Hilbe is professor emeritus at the University of Hawaii and adjunct professor of statistics and sociology at Arizona State University. Since 1997 he has been software reviews editor for *The American Statistician* and is currently on the editorial board of three academic journals. Dr. Hilbe is the author of the forthcoming book, *Negative Binomial Regression* (Cambridge University Press), and with James Hardin is coauthor of two widely read texts, *Generalized Linear Models and Extensions* (Stata Press 2001) and *Generalized Estimating Equations* (Chapman & Hall/CRC Press 2003). Hilbe has written some 50 statistical programs and procedures that have been made part of Stata, SAS, and XploRe commercial software. He has lectured on the topic of generalized linear models and correlated data worldwide.

Aynslie Hinds is a master's student in the Department of Community Health Sciences, University of Manitoba. Her research interests include research methodolgy, psychiatric epidemiology, and health geograpy.

Schuyler Huck is distinguished professor and chancellor's teaching scholar at the University of Tennessee, Knoxville. Sky's expertise is in applied statistics, research design, and measurement. His concern for improving statistical instruction shows through in his books, his journal articles, and his convention presentations. A former chair of AERA's Educational Statistician's Special Interest Group, Sky is interested in the power of puzzles to help students learn statistics.

H. J. Keselman is a professor and head of psychology at The University of Manitoba, Winnipeg, Manitoba, Canada. He is a fellow of the American Psychological Association and the American Psychological Society. He has published over 135 journal articles and book chapters on the analysis of repeated measurements, multiple comparison procedures, and robust estimation and testing. His publications have appeared in journals such as *British Journal of Mathematical and Statistical Psychology, Journal of Educational and Behavioral Statistics, Journal of Modern Applied Statistical Methods, Psychological Methods, Psychometrika, Psychophysiology,* and *Statistics in Medicine.*

Roger E. Kirk is a distinguished professor of psychology and statistics at Baylor University. He has published extensively in the area of statistics and is the author of five books on statistics. He is a fellow of the American Psychological Association (Divisions 1, 2, 5, and 13), the American Psychological Society, and the American Association of Applied and Preventive Psychology. He is a past president of the Society for Applied Multivariate Research, Division 5 of the American Psychological Association, and the Southwestern Psychological Association.

Thomas R. Knapp is professor emeritus of education and nursing, University of Rochester and The Ohio State University. His specialty is the reliability of measuring instruments, and he has recently written a book with that title, which is available on the Internet free of charge at http://www.tomswebpage.net/images/reliability.doc

Xiaojing Kong is a doctoral student in the PhD program in assessment and measurement at James Madison University. Her research interests include response-time information as indicators of examinee behavior, human-computer interaction, adaptive testing, and multilevel item response theory.

Huy Ahn Le received his PhD in human resources management at the University of Iowa in 2003. He is research scientist, HumRRO (Human Resources Research Organization). His research interest is in the areas of research methods (meta-analysis, structural equation modeling, Monte-Carlo simulations), psychometrics, educational testing, and personnel selection.

Joel R. Levin is a professor of educational psychology at the University of Arizona. His research specialties include students' learning strategies and study skills, as well as educational research methodology and statistical analysis. He has received numerous recognitions for his research and teaching. He previously served as president of AERA's Educational Statisticians SIG, associate editor of the *American Educational Research Journal*, and editor of the *Journal of Educational Psychology*; and he is currently the American Psychological Association's Chief Editorial Advisor.

Wemara Lichty is a research associate, Psychology Department, Stanford University. She uses fMRI to investigate self-esteem, self-relevance, and closeness.

Show-Mann Liou is an associate professor in the Department of Civic Education and Leadership at National Taiwan Normal University. She teaches and writes about citizenship education, teacher education, and quantitative research methodology.

Lisa Lix is an assistant professor in the Department of Community Health Sciences, University of Manitoba. Her areas of specialization include multivariate analysis, robust estimation techniques, and longitudinal data analysis

Richard G. Lomax is a professor of education and applied statistics at the University of Alabama, where he teaches courses in quantitative research methodology. His research primarily focuses on multivariate analysis and models of literacy acquisition, resulting in numerous articles and three statistics textbooks.

Theodore Micceri obtained the PhD in measurement and research from the University of South Florida in 1997. He is a researcher in the USF Office of Institutional Effectiveness. He has 20 refereed publications and over 375 technical reports on real data distributions, robustness of statistics, instrument validation, evaluation of teacher practices, courseware design, and data base design. He is a church deacon and a wood badge trained Boy Scout leader. He received the Best Paper Award at the 2005 9th World Multi-conference on Systemics, Cybernetics and Informatics.

Patrick Onghena is a professor at the K. U. Leuven, where he teaches methodology and statistics to majors in educational sciences, and to majors in speech and hearing sciences. He authored several books on methodology and statistics and some 100 papers in the scientific literature. He is the associate editor of *Behavior Research Methods* and the *Journal of Statistics Education*.

Kathrin A. Parks is a PhD candidate in sociology at Texas A&M University. Her master's thesis was a multilevel analysis of the academic achievements of school children. In her doctoral work she is specializing in qualitative analysis of race and ethnicity, specifically focusing on inequality and education. Her minor area of study is demography.

Chao-Ying Joanne Peng is a professor of educational inquiry methodology at Indiana University–Bloomington. Her teaching and research interests are in research methods pertinent to social science research.

Fortunato Pesarin is professor of statistics at the Faculy of Statistics of the University of Padova. His main research interest is in nonparametric statistics with particular reference to multivariate permutation tests.

Dudley L. Poston, Jr. is a professor of sociology, and the George T. and Gladys H. Abell Endowed Professor of Liberal Arts, at Texas A&M University. He has coauthored/edited 12 books and over 220 refereed journal articles, chapters and reports on various sociological, statistical, and demographic topics.

Luigi Salmaso is an associate professor of statistics at the Faculy of Engineering of the University of Padova. His main research interest is in nonparametric statistics and experimental design.

Shlomo S. Sawilowsky is professor and program coordinator of Educational Evaluation and Research in the College of Education, and Wayne State University Distinguished Faculty Fellow. He is the editor of the *Jour-*

nal of Modern Applied Statistical Methods. He has published more than 100 articles in applied statistics, research, and measurement journals, and *Statistics via Monte Carlo Simulation with Fortran* (2003).

Frank L. Schmidt is Ralph Sheets Professor in the Department of Management and Organization in the Tippie College of Business at the University of Iowa. He has served on the faculties of Michigan State University and George Washington University. He has authored or coauthored several books and over 150 articles and book chapters on measurement, statistics, research methods, individual differences, and personnel selection. He is a fellow of the American Psychological Association, the American Psychological Society, and SIOP, and is past president of Division 5 (Measurement, Statistics, & Evaluation) of APA.

Judith D. Singer is James Bryant Conant Professor of Education and former academic dean at the Harvard Graduate School of Education. One of the nation's leading applied statisticians, her professional life focuses on improving the quantitative methods used in social, educational and behavioral research. Singer is primarily known for her contributions to the practice of multilevel modeling, survival analysis, and individual growth modeling, and to making these and other statistical methods accessible to empirical researchers. Her most recent book with John Willett is *Applied Longitudinal Data Analysis: Modeling Change and Event Occurrence* (Oxford, 2003).

Patric R. Spence is an assistant professor of communication at Western Kentucky University. His research interests are in the area of crisis communication and communication research methods.

Aldo Solari is a PhD student in statistics at the University of Padova. His main research interest is in survival analysis and nonparametric methods for categorical data analysis.

Stacy Hughey Surman is a PhD student in educational research methodology at the University of Alabama. She holds MA and BS degrees in elementary/early childhood education.

Johan W.S. Vlaeyen is a professor of behavioral medicine at the Maastricht University, and leader of the chronic pain research program of the Research Institute for Experimental Psychopathology. His main interests are the cognitive and behavioral mechanisms of chronic pain disability, and the development and evaluation of customized cognitive-behavioral management strategies for chronic pain.

Sharon Lawner Weinberg is a professor of quantitative methods and psychology and former vice provost for faculty affairs at New York University. She is a past president of AERA SIG/ES. She has authored more than 50 articles, books, and reports on statistical methodology, statistical education, evaluation, and on such applied areas as clinical and school psychology, special education, and higher education, including completing the second edition of *Data Analysis for the Behavioral Sciences Using SPSS*, coauthored with Sarah Knapp Abramowitz (Cambridge University Press, 2002).

Rand R. Wilcox is a professor of psychology at the University of Southern California. He has published six books (one is in its second edition) and 242 journal articles. He is an APS fellow, and received the T. L. Saaty Award (Best Paper of the Year, *American Journal of Mathematical and Management Sciences*). He is an associate editor of *Computational Statistics and Data Analysis* and *Psychometrika*.

Steven Wise coordinates the Institute for Computer-Based Assessment at James Madison University. He is a professor of psychology and has published extensively in educational measurement, with particular emphasis in computer-based testing and the psychology of test taking. He has published over 50 articles in refereed research journals, 3 books edited or coedited, and over 20 nonrefereed publications.

Amery D. Wu is completing her PhD in measurement, evaluation, and research methodology at the University of British Columbia. She is interested in psychometrics, test theory, and statistical methods. She has published in international journals and presented research at the American Educational Research Association meetings.

Bruno D. Zumbo is a professor of measurement, evaluation, and research methodology, as well as member of the Department of Statistics and the Institute of Applied Mathematics at the University of British Columbia. His professional interests center on developing statistical theory and quantitative methods for conducting research, testing, and evaluation. He is the 2005 recipient of the Samuel J. Messick Memorial Award in recognition of his contributions to psychometrics and validity theory.